THE GOVERNORS
OF NEW JERSEY

1664–1974

Woodrow Wilson, the thirty-fourth governor of New Jersey. Portrait by Seymour Thomas, ca. 1913. Collection of the State of New Jersey. Originally published in volume 25 of *The Papers of Woodrow Wilson*. Photo: Princeton University Press.

THE GOVERNORS
OF NEW JERSEY
1664–1974

Biographical Essays

Edited by
Paul A. Stellhorn
Michael J. Birkner

Trenton   New Jersey Historical Commission   *1982*

Printed in the United States of America
by Book-Mart Press, Inc.

Typography by Trentypo

New Jersey Historical Commission
113 West State Street, CN 520
Trenton, New Jersey 08625

Designed by Lee R. Parks

Illustration 3, courtesy Brinton Coxe

Illustration 48, courtesy Peggy Lewis

Illustrations 1, 7, 8, 15, 24, 26, 29, 32, 34, 40, 41, 42, 43, 45, 50, courtesy The
New Jersey Historical Society

Illustrations 13, 44, 46, 49, 53, 54, 55, courtesy Bureau of Archives and History,
New Jersey State Library

Illustrations 11, 14, 18, courtesy New Jersey State Museum

Illustrations 4 and 5, courtesy The New-York Historical Society

Illustrations 2, 25, 47, 51, 52, courtesy New Jersey Reference Division, Newark
Public Library

Illustration 20, courtesy Princeton University

Illustrations 6, 9, 10, 12, 16, 17, 19, 21, 22, 23, 27, 28, 30, 31, 33, 35, 36, 37,
38, 39, courtesy Special Collections Department, Alexander Library, Rutgers
University

PUBLISHED WITH GRANTS FROM

THE NEW JERSEY AMERICAN REVOLUTION BICENTENNIAL
CELEBRATION COMMISSION

AND

THE CHARLES EDISON FUND

Library of Congress Cataloging in Publication Data
Main entry under title:
The Governors of New Jersey, 1664–1974

Bibliography: p.
Includes index.

1. New Jersey—Governors—Biography. 2. New Jersey—Politics and govern-
ment. I. Stellhorn, Paul A., 1946–   II. Birkner, Michael J., 1950–
F133.G68   974.9'009'92 [B]   81-16795
ISBN 0-89743-053-0   AACR2

For Donald A. Sinclair

CONTENTS

THE CONSTITUTION OF 1947

ALPHABETICAL LIST OF ESSAYS

LIST OF ILLUSTRATIONS

Frontispiece:

Woodrow Wilson

Following Page 144:

FOREWORD

Many of the vast changes that have occurred in New Jersey since the Revolution are reflected in the state's selection of its governors. This is what makes *The Governors of New Jersey* a particularly unique and instructive way to view New Jersey's history. A sense of history is personalized when the events are seen through the eyes of the individuals who have been chosen to be at the helm, guiding the state's course over the three centuries since Philip Carteret became the first proprietary governor in 1664.

The methods used to elect governors in New Jersey give just one interesting example of how times have changed. Before the Revolution governors were not elected but appointed. Under the constitution of 1776 the first fifteen governors were elected annually in joint meetings of the council (forerunner of the present senate) and the assembly, without any limit to the number of terms they might serve.

This was changed in 1844 so that the governors were elected by the people to three-year terms but could not directly succeed themselves. Under the constitution of 1947 the rules were refined into our present electoral system, whereby governors are elected by the people, serving four-year terms and able to succeed themselves so long as they do not hold more than two consecutive terms.

This volume is the product of contributors who have given considerably of their time and talents. The devoted and scholarly services of the editors, Paul A. Stellhorn and Michael J. Birkner, are deserving of special attention.

Historians, students and interested citizens are sure to find many hours of interesting reading in this volume. I welcome this important contribution to an understanding of our state.

October, 1981   BRENDAN BYRNE
Governor

PREFACE

This volume is intended to fill a gap in the literature of New Jersey politics and government. Although there have been many studies of the state's political leaders and several monographs on prominent governors, there is no ready reference book that offers reliable assessments of the lives and political careers of all the governors.

The planners of this book faced two problems. Information about many of New Jersey's early governors is scanty, scattered, and often simply inaccurate; on the other hand material about several of the twentieth-century chief executives is almost too plentiful, a mass of data that is difficult to absorb and sort. To surmount these problems, specialists in New Jersey history were commissioned to write brief interpretive essays, shaping them as they wished. The only condition was that they should pay special attention to the gubernatorial careers of their subjects.

A book of this scope has intrinsic limitations. Most notably, it is difficult to provide fully balanced assessments of the more recent governors. The editors hope that the essays define the main problems of each administration and offer starting points for those interested in pursuing particular matters further. Above all, we trust that through these essays readers will come to know something of the men who have held New Jersey's chief executive office since 1664.

We have had the assistance and counsel of more people than we can properly acknowledge here. Several, however, deserve special mention. William C. Wright, head of the Bureau of Archives and History in the New Jersey State Library, helped to conceive the book and choose the contributors when he was associate director of the Historical Commission. He also deserves thanks for his frequent good offices since he left the project.

Joseph F. Mahoney, Carl E. Prince and Donald A. Sinclair read the original manuscripts and offered many helpful suggestions. Bernard Bush, who read the book in galleys, and Don C. Skemer, who prepared the index, pointed out many flaws in time to correct them. Maja M. P. Basioli, Nancy H. Dallaire, Howard L. Green, Ronald J. Grele, Peggy Lewis and Richard Waldron of the Historical Commission staff contributed immensely to the editorial process. We cannot thank them enough for diligently reading and rereading each essay and for their many suggestions and their constant good humor. Above all, we are deeply indebted to Lee R. Parks, editor at the commission, for his patient and thoughtful assistance at every stage in the production of this book. He did not simply make the book better; he made it possible. Diane E. Kauffman, Judith A. Raider, Frances Smith and Carol D. Wacker deserve thanks for typing the manuscript. We must also express our appreciation to the New Jersey American Revolution Bicentennial Celebration Commission and to the Charles Edison Fund for grants that helped meet the costs of publication.

Finally, we are grateful to the members of the New Jersey Historical Commission, whose judgment led to the undertaking of this project. We hope the result is worthy of their goals.

Left: The original New Jersey state seal, used from 1776 to 1928. The supporters are Liberty (left) and Ceres. The date and the helmet beneath the horse's head were inserted by the engraver without authorization.

Right: The modern seal, adopted in 1928. It officially incorporated the date and helmet. The words "Liberty and Prosperity," which had already "largely been adopted as a motto in sundry representations," were also added.

Although the seal itself can be used only in the official form, its inner elements have often been redrawn for ornamental use. This book is decorated with variations from *Historical Collections of New Jersey*, by John W. Barber and Henry Howe (New York, 1844), and *Specimens of Printing Types: Cuts, Borders, Etc.*, published by the State Gazette Printing Establishment (Trenton, 1886). Both works are in the collection of the Bureau of Archives and History, New Jersey State Library.

THE GOVERNORS
OF NEW JERSEY
1664–1974

Introduction

The role of the governor of New Jersey has shrunk, then grown as the men of successive eras have applied new ideas about what good government is and how to provide it. Under different systems men with different abilities and motives have been chosen for the office, and different kinds of leadership have been expected of them. In the long run, however, the variations are relatively unimportant.

The history of the office divides into four periods. In colonial times the governor was the agent of autocratic, external power. Under the constitution of 1776 he was a figurehead with little official responsibility. His scope increased under the constitution of 1844, but the legislative branch remained stronger than the executive. Under the constitution of 1947 he is generally supposed to be quite powerful.

From the beginning, however, the governors have performed fairly consistently whether their legal boundaries were narrow or wide. Most of them lacked force and significance, and many were controlled by interests outside the government. But in each period a few influenced their own times and the future as well. The careers of New Jersey's governors show that both good government and the executive's importance depend less on the structural relations among the branches of government than on the qualities of the men elected governor.

In 1664 the English took control of the Dutch colony of New Netherland, which comprised the middle Atlantic region of the eastern seaboard. James, duke of York, gained title to the tract and divided it into colonies, defining New Jersey for the first time. He granted New Jersey to two aristocrats, John, Lord Berkeley, and Sir George Carteret—the original proprietors.

Except for several hundred Dutchmen in the northeast and a small enclave of Swedes in the south, no Europeans had moved into the region. To promote immigration Berkeley and Carteret promised a good measure of economic opportunity, political participation and religious freedom. For the next century settlers of diverse ethnic and religious groups came in growing numbers from other colonies, the British Isles, and even the continent.

There were two New Jerseys until 1702. West New Jersey was established when Berkeley sold his interest to a group of

5

Quaker proprietors. East New Jersey remained under Carteret's authority until his death in 1681, when his interest was sold to twenty-four proprietors. The two proprieties differed in social composition —for example, East New Jersey had a large Scottish population and many New England Puritans, whereas West New Jersey had a predominance of Quakers— but they were politically similar. In both, local and county jurisdictions held much of the real power. Both were relatively open and democratic—especially West New Jersey, where the remarkably liberal "Concessions and Agreements of the Proprietors, Freeholders and Inhabitants of the Province of West New Jersey in America" were made the basis of government in 1677. Both were weakened by factional disputation, political opportunism, and shifting arrangements of power.

During this early period the governors were appointed by the proprietors. Those who held the office, whether competent and conscientious or not, had trouble governing effectively for several reasons. Most of the proprietors remained in England, and the instructions they sent, aimed mainly at fostering their own interests from afar, gave too little thought to the good of the colony and its inhabitants. In addition, certain questions about land titles were never clarified. For example, Edmund Andros, a governor appointed by James, made two attempts to rule the Jerseys in spite of the proprietors. Meantime the East Jersey proprietors persisted in claiming certain quitrent rights that the inhabitants disputed.

More important, the governors had to deal with a large number of factions that grouped and regrouped ceaselessly to aggrandize themselves, thwart each other, and, sometimes, flout the proprietary authority. And furthermore, provincial government was never very important during the period; local and county power was so strong that many conflicts were beyond the governor's control.

In the 1690s discord reached the point where no one, including the governor, was effectively in charge of either of the Jerseys; the major accomplishment of government was to survive. Even so tactful a governor as Andrew Hamilton, who served both colonies for much of the decade, could not stabilize affairs. By 1701 most proprietors were willing to transfer their governmental authority to the king provided they could insure their own economic and political standing. In 1702 Edward Hyde, Lord Cornbury, was appointed by the crown to be New Jersey's first royal governor.

Although the colony grew and prospered under royal government, it remained politically unstable for many years. The governorship was usually given to court favorites or men the king was obliged to, who had little or no experience as executives and cared more about making money than governing well. Until 1738 New Jersey had to share its royal governors with New York, which, being larger, received more attention. Furthermore, the old economic, social and religious divisions continued to afflict the colony. Groups the governor failed to satisfy often worked with allied interests in New York or appealed to English patrons to have the crown intervene.

Moreover, the governmental system itself hampered all but the most adroit. Officially the crown-appointed governor was a figure of nearly final authority. He had the power to convene and adjourn the legislature at his pleasure, to veto legislation, and to prorogue or dissolve recalcitrant assemblies. He controlled the appointment and dismissal of most nonelected public officials. He also had the authority to call elections, though the political advantage of this was small. In spite of this official power, however, his real authority depended heavily on political skill.

Even though all the citizens from the meanest farmer to the richest proprietor were loyal to it, the English system of mixed government did not work as well in the colonies as it did at home. The executive in England had the means to make it work, but the royal governor did not. He lacked the leverage engendered by broad patronage. He was forced to adhere to crown instructions that often restricted the flexibility necessary where various institutions shared power. He could not easily compromise or play loose with instructions to mollify one or another interest group. And he could be dismissed at any time, either for disregarding royal instructions or for displeasing some faction that had influence at court.

The royal governor also faced increasing pressure from the assembly, which initiated all legislation and controlled the government's purse strings. The governor could argue, threaten, cajole, or even veto, but he could not spend public money or even establish his own pay without the consent of the people's representatives. To get that he often had to give special privileges. The assemblymen never formed permanent coalitions because their interests were too local, but frequent single-issue confrontations with the governor gradually increased their ability to resist royal policies. The rising power of democratically elected assemblies was an important condition for a revolution in the 1770s.

The lot of the royal governors, then, was unenviable. To serve the crown's interests and the colony's at the same time required special abilities that few governors had. Some, like the notorious Lord Cornbury, were virtually helpless in the face of deep-seated and persistent local antagonisms. Men like John Lovelace, John Montgomerie and William Cosby, who gained the office without previous executive experience and saw it primarily as a personal financial resource, were outright failures. More able men, like Robert Hunter, Jonathan Belcher and William Franklin, achieved modest success in overseeing a growing rural economy, stabilizing finances, and exercising crown authority throughout the colony so long as no local issues exploded or upsetting imperial directives arrived. But even their position was precarious.

Frustrating though the system was for the governors, it worked well enough through the first half of the eighteenth century. Local government took care of most colonial needs and affected individuals more directly than provincial affairs. But in 1763 the imperial policies changed. Parliament and the agents of George III began trying to subordinate a population that believed itself virtuous and intelligent enough to handle its own affairs. As the British line grew harsher, not even an able administrator like Franklin could carry out the governor's ideal dual function. To continue as the crown's representative he had to oppose the people he was charged to govern.

Colonial politics, however open and turbulent, always operated within the context of the needs and ambitions of a distinct elite. The people could express opinions, but policy was always decided by a group of acknowledged leaders. After the Revolution the elite did not disappear, but the populace at large had more influence because political initiative came from their direct representatives in the legislative branch of the government.

Revolutionary leaders throughout the country were convinced by their experience with monarchy that one of the chief threats to liberty was "executive influence." Legislatures, they believed, were the proper institutions of authority. In New Jersey the state constitution adopted in July 1776 stripped the governor of virtually all significant authority and made him thoroughly dependent on the legislature.

He was elected annually by the two legislative houses in joint meeting. He had no specific executive responsibilities and few patronage powers. He had no vote, no formal influence in the making of legislation, and no powers of fiscal control.

He did have a few substantive functions: he attended council meetings with the right to cast tie-breaking votes; he commanded the state militia; he served as chancellor of the state and presiding judge of its highest appeals court. But he was not responsible for carrying out the legislature's programs and policies or enforcing its laws. These activities were performed by officials elected by the voters or appointed by the legislature.

The office was so unimportant that the framers of the constitution neglected to establish any limits of age, residence, property, or even citizenship as qualifications for it. To perform his judicial duties the governor had to be a lawyer, but even this requirement was not officially stated.

New Jerseyans had carried the idea of checks on the executive as far as it could go. Many of the problems of the governorship between 1776 and 1844 resulted from extreme fear of the executive and unrealistic optimism about legislatures.

But the governor was not always the weak reed he was meant to be. A few exercised significant influence from the office. Men like William Livingston, William Paterson and Joseph Bloomfield were formidable leaders who commanded respect and deference from the legislature. Livingston was particularly influential because of his lineage, his talents and his stature in the revolutionary movement. Organization and leadership were essential to success in the war, and Livingston offered both. Even so, his influence over the legislature diminished enough during the last years of his tenure to make him doubt at times whether he would be reelected.

Other governors under the constitution of 1776 enhanced the office by working actively as party leaders. Aaron Ogden, a Federalist, Peter D. Vroom, a Jacksonian Democrat, and the younger William Pennington, a Whig, exercised influence by distributing patronage, espousing party platforms, and informally helping to shape legislative programs.

By and large the office was sought without enthusiasm and held without tenacity. Mahlon Dickerson and Samuel L. Southard quickly abandoned it for the United States Senate, and one prominent politician, Garret D. Wall, actually declined to serve after his party elected him governor in 1829. Wall wanted the more

lucrative position of federal attorney for the District of New Jersey, to which President Jackson soon appointed him.

In its worst times, the governorship from 1776 to 1844 was an insignificant position held by second-rate men such as Richard Howell, a Federalist, and Elias P. Seeley, a Whig. At other times it was held by men of personal ability but little political skill. Isaac Williamson, a prominent Essex County attorney who served twelve notably uneventful terms (1817–29), took the most literal view of his job. He delivered no annual State of the State messages, kept out of legislative policy making, and generally stood aloof from the factions of the nearly formless polity of the day. In the late 1820s, when new political alignments began to form, Williamson sided with the adherents of President John Quincy Adams. This new activism proved his undoing, for when the Jacksonians gained control of the legislature in 1829 they replaced him with Peter D. Vroom.

Vroom's record may give the best example of the opportunities and limitations of the office. Next to Livingston Vroom was probably the strongest governor during the period. He certainly was one of the most vigorous and admirable. During his terms (1829–32, 1833–36) Vroom brought the office new repute and influence by supporting such projects as a new state prison and the Delaware and Raritan Canal and leading in struggles over such issues as paper money. He was an effective and respected party leader and a skillful and prudent chancellor.

He had no illusions that as governor he wielded much power. Indeed, he criticized the constitutional definition of the office on several grounds. It made the governor too dependent, denied him adequate executive authority, and neglected the evolving doctrine of the separation of powers. Convinced that the governor had no business participating in purely legislative activities, Vroom declined to preside over the legislative council. He also suggested that the judicial responsibilities of the office unfairly restricted it to lawyers, disqualifying the mass of the population.

These convictions led him to call for an overhaul of the constitution of 1776. In the late 1830s politicians from both major parties who shared his attitude formed a revision movement that reached fruition in the bipartisan constitutional convention of 1844.

The constitution of 1844 strengthened but did not radically transform the executive role of New Jersey's governor. It abolished the legislature's authority to grant divorces, establish lotteries, or enact bills of attainder or *ex post facto* laws, and strongly limited its ability to lend or borrow or to enact bank-charter laws. It removed the governor's judicial duties and augmented his administrative responsibilities and authority. It increased his term of office from one year to three (though it prohibited consecutive terms), and provided for his election by direct popular vote rather than by the legislature. It gave him a limited veto, which could be overridden by simple majorities in both houses. In addition it empowered him to make many appointments that the legislature had formerly controlled.

These provisions were meant to redistribute the unbalanced powers of the system. In reality the new constitution restricted the legislature very little and undercut many of the new powers it gave the governor. The majority-override provision limited what little leverage he had. The impossibility of succeeding himself made him a lame duck from the moment he was sworn in. Officers largely independent of him had most of the responsibility for spending public funds. And because the governorship and the legislature could now be controlled by opposite parties, his chances of contributing to the legislative process were often no better than under the old constitution, when the office belonged to the majority party but lacked all formal authority.

The governor's new patronage power was weak as well. All his appointments were subject to the senate's approval, and he lacked the authority to create new agencies as new needs arose. As the government grew during the century of rapid change after 1844, the legislature set up more and more boards and commissions outside his supervision, drastically shrinking his share of administrative responsibility.

In the main it was still true that the importance of the office depended on the man who occupied it. Only in extraordinary circumstances did gubernatorial leadership prove decisive under the new system. In time, to be sure, the governorship acquired increasing influence because government action was growing more important in the lives of the citizens. The state spent $31,000 in 1804, $89,000 in 1838, and $114,000 in 1854. As the population grew and the economy diversified, the government took increasing responsibility for education, criminal justice, corporate aid and regulation, mental health, internal improvement and other affairs.

Governors joined in controversies over these issues and often took the lead. Even a relatively bland executive like William A. Newell, who "considered the executive function of government secondary to the legislative," promoted a raft of legislative proposals. And Newell and his successors, Joel Parker, Charles S. Olden, and Marcus L. Ward, strongly identified themselves with controversial positions on important national issues—notably, North-South relations, slavery in the territories, the conduct of the Civil War, and, after 1865, the reconstruction of the South.

The expanded power of the governor's office was weakened by more than the residual strength of the legislature. Now that the executive was officially more than a ceremonial figure he was an attractive target for influence seekers. And new interests were arising quickly. Not only was the expanding industrial economy putting new demands on the state, but the business community was acquiring enormous political power. Early in the century certain corporations that had grown out of the new technology—notably the Joint Companies, a transportation monopoly—had begun to advance their ambitions through the government. During the second half of the century all forms of business sought to increase their influence. After the Civil War businessmen dominated high elective offices, and a few interests, such as the public utilities, held much power in local and state governmental affairs. The strongest of all were the railroads.

From the inauguration of Theodore F. Randolph in 1868 to the retirement of Robert S. Green in 1890, every chief executive had strong, direct ties with the railroad industry at some point in his career. Randolph and George B. McClellan served railroad companies as officers, Green and George C. Ludlow as lawyers, before becoming governor. Joseph D. Bedle became counsel to a railroad after his term ended. Even Leon Abbett, who made his reputation by breaking the industry's influence in Trenton, began his political career as a spokesman for the Camden and Amboy.

Between 1868 and 1895 the Democrats won eight consecutive gubernatorial contests. But the political power of the railroad industry did not depend on the fortunes of one party. More often than not, the Republican opposition was as partial to the railroad interests as the Democrats in power were. For example, Frederic A. Potts, the Republican whom Ludlow defeated for governor in 1880, was a major stockholder in the Jersey Central. Although control of the legislature shifted back and forth between the parties, nothing much threatened the political hegemony of the railroads. Nevertheless, support for them had become virtually institutionalized in the Democratic party by 1870. A group of Democratic legislators and officeholders known as the State House Ring protected the privileged position of the railroads and received substan-

tial support from them in return.

The Democratic governors of this era were caught in a dilemma. On one hand they wanted to hold taxes down and limit public expenditures to maintain what they believed was the best climate for business. On the other hand the government needed more revenues so that it could increase its activities in response to the needs created by industrialization. Taxing the railroads and public utilities as much as other property would have provided considerable fiscal relief, but the governors of the period generally lacked the courage or inclination to try it.

Leon Abbett (1884–87, 1890–93) was the outstanding exception. Abbett, who had no binding ties to the state's business interests, is most noted for destroying the tax-exempt status of the railroads and enabling future administrations to tax them—and the public utilities—more fairly.

Abbett rose above not only the business powers but also the constitutional weaknesses of his office. A master politician, he understood the full potential of the office and used its existing powers more fully than any of his predecessors had. He also added to its power in another way: he perceived himself as a statewide leader whose election gave him the right to interpret the needs of the people and to work for the policies he believed were important. Opportunistic and a bit demogogic, he aroused much stronger feelings of love and hate than most governors do. He was more than the state's chief executive; he also assumed political leadership. Abbett added immeasurably to the importance of the office. But he was succeeded by men who saw the role less boldly, and the state did not have such a forceful governor again until Woodrow Wilson.

More important than Abbett's distinction in office is his significance as a transitional figure, for his rise signaled the initial political stirrings of the state's urban working class. He was the first governor to come from that class. He was also the first New Jersey politician to use ethnic politics successfully and the first to earn the name of "machine boss." His gubernatorial career opened a period that lasted far into the twentieth century. After 1890 business leaders had to make room for two new political forces: reformism and machines.

The reform impulse in New Jersey is often dated 1900–1913, but to confine it so narrowly to the "Progressive Era" is to overlook its origins and precursors. After the Civil War the predominantly agrarian state began turning into an industrial center. Urban areas grew quickly; immigrants poured in, especially from Catholic and non-English speaking countries; the labor movement gathered strength. Economic depression, rapid advancements in technology, radically new business practices, widespread government corruption, and debates over such issues as taxation, gambling and drinking all worked to outmode traditional customs and laws. Calls for reform came from many segments of society.

Governor Abbett responded to the desire of his urban constituents for significant reform of the labor laws, working especially to protect children and convicts and to improve working conditions. Reform activities were not exclusive to his Democratic party, however. Indeed, Democratic machines generally ignored calls for reform and neglected progressive politicians, driving young crusaders such as George L. Record to the Republicans. The upswing in the reform impulse, in fact, coincided with the Democrats' fall from power during the term of George T. Werts (1893–96).

Antagonized by the corruption, mismanagement, and partisanship of the Democratic administration, and hurt by the depression of 1893, the voters elected a Republican legislature in 1894 and the first of five consecutive Republican governors in 1895. The first organized reform gathering took place in Newark in the same year. Progressivism grew into a significant political force in New Jersey during the fifteen years of Republican domination that followed.

The Republican governors, conservatives whose ties to the business world were even stronger than those of their Democratic predecessors, neither supported nor sanctioned the reform movement. But in a sense they assisted its growth. They freed the state GOP from the South Jersey machine of General William J. Sewell and made it a statewide organization. Giving new vitality to Republican groups throughout the state, particularly in the northeast, the party served reform politicians.

To all appearances the Republican party was more business-oriented than ever. Franklin Murphy, elected governor in 1901, was a manufacturer—the first non-lawyer in the office since General McClellan a quarter of a century before. But a reform element known as the "New Idea" movement challenged the party's conservative leadership, pressing for an extensive list of reforms that ranged from local taxation of utilities to primary elections for United States senators. The New Idea faction was most active and had most of its modest success during the terms of the conservative Murphy and his successor Edward C. Stokes, a bank president.

Meantime a new machine in Essex County, run by former United States Senator James Smith, Jr., unified the Democratic party and backed the president of Princeton University, Woodrow Wilson, for governor in 1910. To Smith's dismay Wilson gave his campaign a strong progressive tone. The Democrats, winning the office for the first time in fifteen years, assumed the progressive mantle.

Like Abbett, Wilson exploited the office to the fullest. He vigorously played the roles of chief executive, legislative leader and politician. Quickly breaking with Smith, he undertook the most ambitious and successful reform program in the state's history.

When Wilson resigned in 1913 to become president of the United States he left the state's progressive movement in the far less capable hands of James F. Fielder, who had progressive credentials and inclinations but lacked Wilson's power to lead. The progressive movement faltered during his administration.

The influence of machine politics began to grow after World War I. Machines of both parties had operated in various localities since the 1880s, and the larger of these, such as Smith's Essex County Democratic organization, had made their strength felt widely. But until Mayor Frank Hague of Jersey City built his Hudson County machine none of them truly dominated a state party.

Under Hague, Hudson County was known as the "Gibraltar of the Democracy." The machine provided the votes to keep Hague in control of the party for thirty years and the party in the governor's office for six of the eight terms between 1920 and 1943. No other political figure in the state's history wielded so much power for so long. Besides controlling the selection of Democratic gubernatorial candidates, Hague often influenced the Republican choices as well.

Hague established his power in the 1919 gubernatorial primary. He promoted Edward I. Edwards for the Democratic nomination in a clear challenge to James R. Nugent, Smith's successor as state party leader. Giving Edwards a huge plurality in Hudson County, Hague destroyed Nugent's political standing. He solidified his control of the state party when Edwards went on to become governor.

Edward I. Edwards was more than just the first of Hague's sycophantic governors. A master of ethnic politics, he realigned the parties in the state. His opponent in the 1919 election was Newton A. K. Bugbee, a prohibitionist. Edwards appealed to the urban ethnic voters, who saw prohibitionism as an assault on their way of life, by promising to make New Jersey as "wet as the Atlantic Ocean." He also opposed the blue laws and took other stands that gathered the urban ethnics into a powerful new constituency. The Republicans—despite warnings from many of their own leaders—refused to relax their conservative stance on these issues. They nominated another prohibitionist for the governorship in 1922 and lost again.

For the next two decades Hague dominated gubernatorial selection by providing enormous Hudson County pluralities and strongly supporting the interests of the ethnic communities. With his partisans serving as governor, Hague controlled a broad range of patronage. He made judicious use of it to increase the influence of his machine throughout the state. His pervasive influence even enabled him to work comfortably with the two Republican governors elected during the twenties and thirties, Morgan F. Larson and Harold G. Hoffman.

Hague did not control the governors or dictate state policies. He expected the governors to cooperate with him whenever his interests were involved. Their dependence on Hague and the hostility of Republican legislatures made them largely ineffectual. Even during the Great Depression the Hague governors rarely tried to rise to the challenge of their responsibility.

The only countervailing force to Hague during the 1920s and 1930s was a remnant of Republican progressivism. It was less dramatic than Hagueism and slower to develop power, but far more lasting in its legacy. A group led by a young progressive lawyer, Arthur T. Vanderbilt, kept the New Idea spirit alive in Essex County. This group dominated the government of the county through the 1920s but regular Republicans in Newark kept them from taking control of the entire county party until the spring of 1934. Then Vanderbilt formed the Essex County Clean Government Movement, a tight organization with a nonpartisan appearance. The movement identified itself with the liberalism of President Franklin D. Roosevelt by expressing partial support for the New Deal. Since the state Democratic organization was only lukewarm for the policies of the enormously popular president, even a superficial connection was enough to bring the movement great strength. Vanderbilt solidified his county power and went on to seek allies in the state party.

Soon the Clean Government group was dominant in the Republican-controlled legislature. Vanderbilt was building one of the most powerful liberal Republican organizations in the country. In 1937 he challenged the Hague Democrats. The Republicans nominated the Clean Government candidate, Lester H. Clee, to run for governor against A. Harry Moore, a popular Hague man. Although Moore won, Clee ran well against him. Furthermore, allegations of voting fraud gave the Republicans ammunition for several damaging investigations of the Hague machine.

In 1940 the Republicans ran another Clean Government candidate. He also lost, but the Democrat who beat him, former Secretary of the Navy Charles Edison, broke with Hague. Hague's era was ending, for more reasons than Vanderbilt's opposition and Edison's rebellion. Social and economic changes were weakening machines throughout the country.

After 1940 the Clean Government Movement and other groups from both parties worked persistently for constitutional revision. Although Hague frustrated their efforts during Edison's term and the voters turned down a new constitution submitted in 1944 by a Republican governor, Walter E. Edge, the revision movement continued to grow.

In 1946 the Clean Government Republicans won a clear-cut victory. Their candidate, Alfred E. Driscoll, easily defeated Hague's favorites in the Republican primary and the general election and then gathered support for a bipartisan constitutional convention. He guided it through several serious disputes, and in November 1947 a large majority of the electorate approved the new constitution.

The constitution of 1947 accomplished the Vanderbilt group's main goal of restructuring the judiciary. It also significantly strengthened the governor. Many of the changes merely formalized developments in the executive that had already taken place, but others were more substantive. The constitution increased the governor's term from three years to four, made an incumbent eligible to succeed himself once, and raised the vote needed to override a veto from a simple majority of both houses to two-thirds. Administratively, it empowered the governor to consolidate the numerous boards and commissions into a manageable number of departments under his authority, putting him in a stronger position to influence policy and spending.

It is unclear how much leadership the governors after 1947 exercised over the legislature. The general impression is that the governor became a primary policy maker who initiated most legislation or approved it before it was passed. If so, the altered constitution had little to do with it. The strong veto increased the governor's negative control over policy, but the constitution gave him no positive leverage with the lawmakers. Beyond transferring administrative functions to the governor it hardly affected the legislature; generally, county organizations still had more influence over individual legislators than the governor did.

The governors between 1947 and 1970 sometimes tried to exercise the powers implicit in their heightened status by championing broad legislative programs. Their efforts had mixed results. They increased the activities of state government in many ways, but they failed repeatedly to reform the tax structure.

Perhaps the office since 1947 seems stronger than it really is. The governor undoubtedly has greater administrative control, but when historians judge the modern period the executive qualities they reveal will depend only partly on the structure of the government. The constitution of 1947 does not assure New Jersey that its governors will be efficient and dynamic leaders inspired by vision and tempered by wisdom. That always was and always will be determined largely by the governors themselves.

The Colony

PHILIP CARTERET (1639–83), a native of the Isle of Jersey and a distant cousin of the proprietor Sir George Carteret, was appointed New Jersey's first governor in August 1665, at the age of twenty-five. His father was attorney general of the island. Until then Richard Nicolls, under the proprietor James, duke of York, had governed New Jersey as a part of New York. In June 1665 the duke presented New Jersey to two Stuart followers, Sir George Carteret and John, Lord Berkeley. Having no interest in colonization, in March 1674 Berkeley sold his portion to two Quakers, John Fenwick and Edward Byllynge.

Sir George, however, sent Philip out at the head of an expedition of thirty colonists from the Isle of Jersey who spoke English and French. In August 1665 they arrived at Elizabethtown, in the northeast corner of New Jersey, where several hundred Puritans from Long Island and New England had settled at the invitation of Governor Nicolls. From 1664 to 1669 they founded six towns, the largest of which were Elizabethtown and Newark. The Dutch town of Bergen, incorporated in 1661, antedated all of them. In addition to incorporating several of these settlements, Governor Carteret granted large patents to a half-dozen wealthy men, several of them Quaker exiles from Barbados.

Hoping to attract additional settlers from New England, in February 1665 the proprietor, Sir George, issued the Concessions and Agreement, which set forth a frame of government and a land system. Its terms were liberal. All taking the oath of allegiance would be freemen, and the guarantee of religious liberty was so generous that no New England Puritan could take offense. The Concessions provided for an elected lower house with law-making powers and a council appointed by the governor. The assembly would constitute the courts, incorporate towns, impose taxes except on unimproved proprietary lands, and provide for the collection of quitrents due the proprietors. The stipulated quitrent was 1/2d. per acre for individuals and a fixed sum, usually £15 per annum, on public township lands. Under the prevailing headright system, the Concessions also provided for grants of land to families and their indentured servants. Quitrents were not due until March 25, 1670. Since the settlers resented paying them, collecting them

15

turned out to be a bane for Governor Carteret and his successors. By 1673 about four hundred seventy males had taken the oath of allegiance, indicating a population of twenty-five hundred. The migration from New England and Long Island gradually diminished, while few settlers emigrated from Great Britain.

Carteret's troubles began at Elizabethtown in May 1668. The first assembly met, but broke up when the governor refused to permit the council to sit with the representatives. By creating additional associates through skillful repurchase, Carteret took over the control of hostile Elizabethtown. The associates were first purchasers, who alone voted in town meeting. When Carteret insisted on the payment of quitrents there, the unrest spread to other towns. Middletown and Shrewsbury had actually refused to send deputies to the assembly, fearing that they would jeopardize their rights under their Nicolls patents. They insisted that participation in the assembly would constitute the recognition of absolute authority in the proprietor. Newark adopted the specious argument that it would not pay quitrents because it had purchased its lands from the Indians.

In the summer of 1671, the chance arrival of Captain James Carteret, son of the proprietor, afforded the settlers an opportunity to stage a rebellion. A "rump" assembly proceeded to elect this naive young man "president of the country" in May 1672. Governor Carteret, alarmed, left for England to consult Sir George. The "Rebellion of 1672" was crushed. Several "Declarations" supported by the crown repudiated the settlers' claims under the old Nicolls patents and required all settlers to take out proprietary patents and pay up their quitrents. The "Declarations" also stripped the assembly of its principal powers: land distribution, charter incorporation, and appointive powers. It gave the governor and council veto power and ordered the assembly to finance the cost of government. When Carteret returned from England in March 1674 he

reigned supreme in East New Jersey. For years the lower house strove bitterly for the restoration of its powers, and despite a period of tranquility from 1674 to 1679 old wounds festered. Alienation from proprietary government was complete.

During Carteret's absence several external events changed the complexion of the province. In July 1673, the Dutch reconquered New York and New Jersey, and they remained until Britain regained the two colonies in November 1674. With the sale of Lord Berkeley's interest to Fenwick and Byllynge, in March 1674 Sir George agreed to a partition of the province into East and West New Jersey. The diagonal boundary gave Sir George all the inhabited lands. The two "divisions" remained separate until 1702, when New Jersey became a royal province.

From 1668 to 1681 the East Jersey assembly held seven meetings. Indian trade and relations became stable. The Concessions gave the inhabitants certain guarantees: no freeholder could be arrested for debt; no man could be deprived of the benefits of the common law, and no one could interfere with the course of justice. But the proprietor's prohibitions of 1672 remained. The governor's power to appoint justices, a violation of the Concessions, flawed the judicial system. The "prerogative courts," appointed by the governor and dominated by a clique of rich land holders, were hated by the people.

In July 1674 the duke of York commissioned Edmund Andros governor of New York. Andros assumed that he had jurisdiction over the Jerseys; however disturbed by the opposition there, he returned to England in 1678 for clarifying instructions. He returned with the duke's mandate to impose his authority on both divisions. When he insisted that all vessels bound for East Jersey put in at New York to pay the duke's customs, Governor Carteret rejected his claim. Andros then ordered all in East Jersey "to desist distinct governance" within the duke's jurisdictions "to their utmost peril." In March 1679 Carteret wrote to An dros that "it was by His Majesty's command that this government was established" and that he would not surrender East Jersey. Carteret was taken into custody in spring 1680, and tried by a special court of assize. He argued courageously that "his imprisoner and accuser" was also his judge, and in May the jury, to Andros's chagrin, brought in a verdict of not guilty. The court, however, under pressure from Andros, ruled that should Carteret return to East Jersey he could not assume any jurisdiction. Andros journeyed to Elizabethtown and guaranteed the inhabitants their rights as "free-born Englishmen." The assembly demanded that he recognize the privileges granted them under their Concessions, but Andros, then and later, rejected their claims.

Unfortunately for Governor Carteret, Sir George, the influential and "testy" proprietor, died in January 1680. The governor expected little assistance from the duke of York, whose advisers steadily admonished him about his error in giving away the Jerseys. Indeed, Carteret's appeals were ignored. In August, however, through William Penn's efforts in behalf of Quaker West Jersey, James accepted Sir William Jones's dictum that he had no right to withhold the right of government bestowed on Berkeley and Carteret in 1664. James, at that time an exile in Scotland, had no desire to add the Quakers to his list of enemies on the sensitive succession question. A new indenture, signed in October 1680, recognized young Sir George, a minor, as proprietor. Governor Andros was recalled, and in March 1681 Governor Carteret issued a proclamation that he was resuming his post. He ordered the inhabitants not to heed the authority of any officers appointed by Andros.

Philip Carteret's last days as governor were inconsequential. He had learned little since 1665. In October 1681 the assembly demanded that he recognize the rights of the people under the Concessions and especially repudiate the noxious "Declarations" of 1672. A prolonged wrangle ensued, growing more bitter day by day, with Carteret refusing to yield one iota. Finally, on November 2, Carteret dissolved the assembly, and government came to a standstill. Meanwhile Sir George's widow resolved to sell East Jersey at a figure of £5,000. Since no bidders appeared she put it up for auction and sold it for £3,400 in February 1682 to a group of twelve men, principally Quakers, headed by William Penn. In August the group added twelve more partners, thus inaugurating the regime of the twenty-four proprietors. Carteret died scarcely a year after quitting his post. His widow was the thrice-married daughter of Richard Smith of Long Island.

New Jersey's first governor held office longer than any of his successors—for more than sixteen years. Though he lacked neither courage nor industry, he had not been able to cope with the all-but-insoluble problems that confronted him. He was caught between an arbitrary proprietor and an equally uncompromising populace. Most of his successors, proprietary and royal governors and their deputies, shared his dilemma.

Latschar, John A. "East New Jersey, 1665–1682: Perils of a Proprietary Government." Ph.D. dissertation, Rutgers University, 1978.

Leaming, Aaron, and Spicer, Jacob, eds. *The Grants, Concessions, and Original Constitutions of the Province of New Jersey.* Philadelphia: William Bradford, 1758.

Pomfret, John E. *The Province of East New Jersey, 1609–1702: The Rebellious Proprietary.* Princeton: Princeton University Press, 1962.

Tanner, Edwin P. *The Province of New Jersey, 1664–1738.* New York: Columbia University Press, 1908.

John E. Pomfret

EDMUND ANDROS (December 6, 1637–February 1714) played a central role in implementing England's colonial policy during the last quarter of the seventeenth century. From 1674 to 1681 he managed the duke of York's proprietary interests in New York. In 1686, James II commissioned him to consolidate and administer the northern colonies as the Dominion of New England. This attempt to tighten imperial control was defeated in 1689. Between 1692 and 1697 Andros reached the summit of his career as governor of Virginia, England's most valuable North American colony.

During his tenure at New York and for his final year as governor of the Dominion, Andros was vested with nominal control over New Jersey's affairs. He exercised his authority actively for ten months in 1680–81 and never extended his rule beyond East Jersey. His impact on the development of New Jersey was short but significant, for the policies he was ordered to enforce there and in New England showed that the mother country viewed her colonies as exploitable dependencies rather than as potential equals with rights of their own. When Andros acted on his instructions, he inevitably aroused bitter colonial opposition and earned himself a reputation as an implacable foe of colonial liberties and self-government. To his American antagonists he was a tyrant bent on reducing them to the will of a distant and arbitrary power. But to his employers he was a trusted public servant charged with ensuring proper submission to duly constituted authority. Andros never questioned the right of his masters in England to govern the North American colonies; it was his misfortune to rule people who did.

Edmund Andros was born into a family which had for generations ranked among the wealthiest and most aristocratic inhabitants of the Isle of Guernsey. His ancestors had spelled the name "Andrewes," and, though the French-speaking islanders had corrupted the spelling, the name apparently retained its original pronunciation. Though Andros never said so, it is evident that his family's position on Guernsey influenced his character profoundly. His father Amias was a staunch Anglican who strongly supported Charles I's claims to supremacy over Parliament. Unfortunately for Amias and his family, the predominantly Puritan inhabitants of Guernsey favored the parliamentary cause. The sense of religious and political isolation which the young man shared with his father undoubtedly contributed to his reserved, austere demeanor and left him with a cold insensitivity to popular opinions. With no desire for employment in Puritan England, in 1656 Edmund turned to the continent and a career as a professional soldier. He served for three years under Prince Henry of Nassau and apparently distinguished himself in a campaign against Sweden.

The restoration of Charles II in 1660 retrieved the fortunes of the Andros family and opened the door to preferment for Edmund. The king rewarded his loyalty with a place at court and two years later, on June 4, 1662, commissioned him an ensign in the Regiment of Guards. England's bitter trade rivalry with Holland soon afforded Andros the opportunity to serve his king in a more responsible position. Early in 1667, he was appointed major of the Barbados Regiment, and he went with his men to garrison that tiny but fertile Caribbean outpost. After serving two tours of duty on Barbados, from February 1667 to February 1669 and again from September 1672 to May 1674, he came home with a reputation for expertise in the management of a colony far removed from the center of power and authority.

Andros's experience eventually came to the attention of James, duke of York and brother of Charles II, a man in need of someone with ability in colonial affairs. In 1664, the king had given James a vast tract of land centered around the Dutch settlements on Manhattan Island. Charles had drawn the boundary of the patent generously, east to the Connecticut River and west to the Delaware River, including half of Connecticut and all of New Jersey in his gift to his brother. Once the Dutch were conquered, James was free to rule in a manner "not contrary to the laws of England" and to do so without the consent of any representative assembly. But the duke had insufficient resources to develop his entire patent, and he sold the land between the Hudson and the Delaware to Sir George Carteret and John, Lord Berkeley. Since James had no legal right to sell or share the powers of government conferred by his charter, the New Jersey proprietors purchased the right to the profits of the land with no authority to collect taxes, levy customs duties, or establish a separate government. James, however, raised no objection when Berkeley and Carteret proceeded to rule their proprietary as though they possessed a valid royal charter.

The Dutch recapture of Manhattan Island for a few months in 1673–74 voided the duke's original patent. When the king issued him a duplicate in 1674, James did not reconfirm the sale of New Jersey. He regarded his colony as a commercial venture and took this opportunity to introduce a new scheme for raising enough money to pay the costs of government and provide him a profit. New Jersey and Connecticut were the key elements in his plans to impose a customs duty in addition to the rate already levied by the Navigation Acts. He had to bring both areas under his control to prevent New York merchants from evading the tax simply by moving across the Hudson River or into Connecticut.

On July 1, 1674, James commissioned Edmund Andros governor of New York and issued him a set of instructions certain to displease the settlers he had to rule. The Dutch Calvinists on Manhattan Island and in the Hudson Valley, already fearful that an English Anglican governor might alter their forms of worship, disliked paying increased taxes on their trade. The English Puritans on Long Island bitterly resented the ban on representative assemblies and sought to annex themselves to the neighboring, self-governing colony of Connecticut. Connecticut, for her part, had no intention of relinquishing her western half and stood ready to defend her charter rights. Oddly enough the inhabitants of New Jersey had the least to fear from the new governor. Though New Jersey was vital to the duke's commercial schemes, for the moment friends in high places protected her government. Andros had to step carefully because Sir George Carteret was a favorite of Charles II. For five and a half years, Andros soft-pedaled James's claims in the Jerseys and found himself powerless to realize the revenues his master expected.

Despite this failure, Andros showed commendable ability in reconciling the Dutch to English rule and in keeping the Indians of New York at peace while their brothers ravaged New England in King Philip's War (1675–76). Both situations encouraged the aristocratic governor to act with a paternalistic concern for his inferiors, a style of government he found quite congenial. At the same time, he was shrewd enough to realize that a representative assembly with limited powers was a small price to pay for making the English settlers more amenable to the duke's government. Andros communicated this suggestion to James, but nothing came of it during Andros's tenure at New York. Andros was intelligent, though insensitive; nevertheless, at no point in his career did he have any say in formulating the policies he was charged with enforcing.

Andros's principal shortcoming as a colonial governor was his lack of tact and imagination in dealing with people who resented his rule. Ordered to annex half of Connecticut, he pressed the issue to the point of armed confrontation at the very time southern New England was fighting for its life against King Philip. When the death of Sir George Carteret in January 1680 freed Andros to move against East

Jersey, he acted with a studied ruthlessness which did him little credit. In March he placed Governor Philip Carteret under arrest and then brought him to trial for infringing on the duke's rights. When the jury persisted in finding Carteret innocent, Andros browbeat the jurors, and though they declined to change the verdict they encouraged Carteret to retire. Andros consistently ignored the need to work subtly and flexibly to attain his ends and preferred to stick as closely as possible to the letter of his instructions.

Having ousted Carteret, Andros for the first time exercised his authority over East Jersey. But he had little time to enjoy his triumph or to implement the duke's system. He was recalled in January 1681, ostensibly to answer charges of financial corruption laid against his administration but actually because he had become a liability to James. His heavy-handed tactics in East Jersey had antagonized the Carteret family, and the threat of similar treatment had alienated the Quaker proprietors of West Jersey. Since James could not afford to lose the support of either group, he removed the offending governor and finally, after seven years, released his claims to the Jerseys.

Though temporarily unemployed, Andros was not out of favor. Knighted in about 1681, he received a post at court in 1683 and became lieutenant colonel of the Princess of Denmark's Regiment of Horse in 1685. During these years Charles II laid plans to combine the colonies from Maine to Connecticut into a single royal province. When the duke of York came to the throne as James II in February 1685, he knew at first hand the wisdom of his brother's plans. The multiplicity of colonies had thwarted his commercial schemes in New York, and now, with the rise of French power in Canada, James believed that both the prosperity and the survival of England's colonies were at stake. He realized that Andros was his ablest and most conscientious colonial official and, on August 1, 1686, appointed him royal governor of the Dominion of New England.

Immediately on his arrival at Boston on December 20, 1686, Andros offended the Massachusetts Puritans by demanding a place to conduct Anglican services. The following spring he once more demonstrated his lack of diplomatic skill by raucously celebrating the king's coronation on a sabbath and by sanctioning the erection of a maypole in Charlestown, Massachusetts. His actions convinced the suspicious Puritans that James II, a covert Roman Catholic, was planning to suppress their forms of worship. The governor's needlessly antagonistic behavior hurt his mission, but he quickly proved himself an able administrator by introducing new taxes to put the government on its feet. Though the land tax distributed a lighter burden more equitably across the society, it provoked the most heated opposition, particularly in Essex County north of Boston. Andros moved rapidly to put down this unrest, acting with the severity of a professional soldier accustomed to seeing authority obeyed. He so rigorously enforced the Navigation Acts that in a short time New England's flourishing commerce was brought to a standstill. He reorganized both the judiciary and the system of land tenure to conform to English practice. He gave the justices of the peace added responsibilities which he had stripped from town control and made them administer justice in the king's name. He regularized ownership by regranting land to its occupants and by instituting quitrents. Ironically, his greatest service did little to win over the New Englanders. He shored up the defenses against French aggression by overseeing the construction of frontier forts, by overhauling the militia, and by dealing fairly with the Indians. But his concern for the Indians annoyed the colonists, who were bent on exterminating the savage menace.

Andros had undertaken an impossible task, for James demanded nothing short of a radical restructuring of New England society. Andros managed to impose the maximum degree of centralized government which that recalcitrant region would endure before 1775 and, given time, he might even have made the idea of imperial regulation more acceptable. But his time ran out in April 1689. Immediately on receipt of the news that William of Orange had replaced James II, the people of Boston arrested and imprisoned the governor and other Dominion officials. Recalled in disgrace for the second time, Andros appeared to have reached the end of his career. But William III, a good judge of men, recognized Andros as the most experienced colonial servant available, and a man who stood ready to serve the king of England rather than the House of Stuart. Andros made his final journey to North America in 1692. He came as governor of Virginia, an honorable and on the whole easy appointment after the tumult of New York and New England.

In Virginia, Andros's conduct seemed to belie the reputation for tyranny he had earned in New England. He encountered little overt hostility from the House of Burgesses and dealt with it in a spirit of compromise. While pressing for measures he thought he must have, he was ready to relent when the house stubbornly opposed him. The fact that his instructions—to promote the Virginia tobacco economy—harmonized with the interests of the people he governed aided him. But Andros was unhappy in Virginia, and he resigned in 1697 amid a bitter dispute with the Anglican commissary, James Blair. Scheming to increase his power and influence, Blair had unjustly charged the governor with failing to support the Anglican Church and being indifferent to the fate of the College of William and Mary. The commissary was the kind of man Edmund Andros neither understood nor knew how to combat. An aristocrat trying to do the best job he could, Andros would not stoop to refute absurd charges, confident that the people who mattered would assess the situation correctly without his help. Defenseless against this unscrupulous liar, he left office a frustrated man.

Andros became lieutenant governor of Guernsey in 1704. He had inherited the office of bailiff from his father thirty years before, and he now joined in his person the entire civil and military authority of the island. Needless to say, the inhabitants thought that this put too much power in the hands of one man, and they made life difficult for him until 1706, when he resigned both offices. He retired to London, where he died in February 1714.

Andros married three times but had no children. He married Mary Craven in Febrary 1671; she died at Boston on January 22, 1688. He married Elizabeth Cripse in August 1692; she died in August 1703. Andros's third wife was Elizabeth Fitz Herbert, whom he married April 21, 1707. She survived him.

Andrews, Charles M. *The Colonial Period of American History.* Vol. 3. New Haven: Yale University Press, 1934.

Barnes, Viola F. *The Dominion of New England: A Study in British Colonial Policy.* New Haven: Yale University Press, 1923.

Bloom, Jeanne Gould. "Sir Edmund Andros." Ph.D. dissertation, Yale University, 1962.

Breen, Timothy. *The Character of the Good Ruler: A Study of Puritan Political Ideas, 1630–1730.* New Haven: Yale University Press, 1970.

Hall, Michael G. *Edward Randolph and the American Colonies, 1676–1703.* Chapel Hill: University of North Carolina Press, 1960.

Hawke, David F. *The Colonial Experience.* Indianapolis: Bobbs-Merrill, 1966.

Harold E. Selesky

EDWARD BYLLYNGE (d. 1687), born of an old small-gentry family of Hengar, was a Cornishman. While serving as a cornet of cavalry with General Christopher Monk in Scotland, he was converted to Quakerism by George Fox. In 1661, after the civil war had ended, he worked as a brewer in London. As a Foxian Friend he constantly courted trouble with the authorities. On one occasion he was "roughly used by soldiers." On another, he refused to remove his hat in court until ordered to do so; he lifted his hat, and a pile of ashes he had concealed under it covered the floor. But more than a radical demonstrator, Byllynge was an idealist seeking relief for the persecuted Friends. He wrote several well-known tracts espousing the political and social liberties that Parliament should guarantee to free-born Englishmen.

By 1675 Byllynge had gone bankrupt and had been charged with making off with Friends' funds and bringing the Society into disrepute. Fearing to involve the Friends, Byllynge apologized publicly for his misdeeds. In later years his reputation became still more tarnished, but Fox and the other Quaker leaders, despite the doubts of William Penn, never lost confidence in him.

John, Lord Berkeley, coproprietor with Sir George Carteret of all New Jersey since 1664, lacked interest in the province and suggested that Byllynge might reinstate his shattered fortune by purchasing Berkeley's portion of the property. Berkeley and Byllynge completed the sale in March 1674, and Major John Fenwick, also a Friend, as assignee for the legally bankrupt Byllynge, put up part of the purchase price. Then Fenwick and Byllynge quarreled about the portion to which each was entitled, and they had to call on William Penn, a leading Quaker, to arbitrate the dispute. This was Penn's initial venture in the New World, and during the negotiations, he found the stubbornness of both men highly irritating. Finally he persuaded Byllynge to agree to a trusteeship of three Quakers— Penn and two of Byllynge's creditors—to straighten out his finances. The trusteeship continued from February 1675 to September 1683, when Byllynge became solvent, and it divided the province into one hundred shares or proprieties, giving Fenwick ten and Byllynge's credi-

tors twenty-odd. The remaining shares were put up for sale among interested Friends, many of them prospective settlers. Dissatisfied with his share, Fenwick took off on his own to found Salem County in November 1675.

The trustees, with Byllynge's consent, proceeded to found a Quaker colony on the east bank of the Delaware. They effected a division of New Jersey with the proprietor George Carteret; issued the famous Concessions and Agreements of West New Jersey, which spelled out a frame of governance and land purchase for prospective settlers; and undertook negotiations to obtain a recognition of the right of government. The boundary of Byllynge's proprietorship, named West New Jersey, ran from Little Egg Harbor diagonally to 41° 40′ on the upper Delaware. The Concessions and Agreements, prepared in 1676 by Byllynge with the knowledge and assent of William Penn, bore the date March 3, 1677. Finally, through Penn's influence, an acknowledgement of the right of government was obtained from the duke of York, the original proprietor, in August 1680. Since the duke turned out to have no authority to assign the right of government to a third party, the crown later repudiated it.

The chief proprietor, Byllynge, the trustees, and eventually over one hundred purchasers of shares or fractions of shares, including many prospective settlers, signed the Concessions and Agreements. Burlington, the first of several Quaker settlements, was founded in August 1677. The Concessions provided for an elected assembly of council and lower house, thus promising self-government. The document spelled out other privileges in keeping with the convictions of the Society of Friends: trial by jury, religious liberty, and freedom from imprisonment for debt. The Concessions is famous for its guarantees of individual liberty; however, its system of land ownership and land distribution, with its fractioned shares and sporadic land dividends, proved cumbersome.

During the years 1677–83 four of the

projected tenths or districts were settled, mainly by Quakers from England and Ireland. Fenwick, the self-styled lord proprietor of Salem Tenth, at first stood aloof. As chief proprietor and governor, Byllynge appointed a recent settler, Samuel Jennings, deputy-governor, in violation of the Concessions. Penn, believing Jennings a worthy man, advised the inhabitants to accept him. But in May 1683, when Byllynge intimated that he was coming out as governor, the assembly adopted strong resolves: the governor, council and representatives would meet together as the general assembly; the governor would read and explain his proposed laws; and the assembly would either adopt or reject them. The assembly then elected Jennings—who had agreed to accept the Concessions—governor, thus repudiating Byllynge. On the last day Fenwick and Penn joined in the deliberations. The legislature was unanimously resolved that since the land and government together had been purchased from the trustees, the Concessions alone constituted the fundamentals of government. In a special session of March 1684 the assembly voted to send Jennings and Thomas Budd, a councilor, to England to deal directly with Byllynge.

The emissaries arrived in London in the early summer and first interviewed Byllynge. But when he threatened them with imprisonment for usurpation, they informed him that they would seek a remedy from Whitehall or Westminster (the crown or the courts). At this juncture the Society of Friends, disapproving actions in court, persuaded Jennings to submit the dispute to the arbitration of leading Quakers. The arbitration, with George Fox present, lasted from July 31 to October 11. Though six of the fourteen arbiters refused to sign the award, the complainants lost. The decision went in Byllynge's favor because the Concessions could not grant the right of government, which had not been obtained from the duke until 1680. Byllynge, therefore, could not be divested of it without his own consent. Moreover, the award stated that the government should be vested in one person or one corporation; patently, it could not be divided into one hundred parts or shares. The decision also pointed out that since the assembly had accepted Jennings as deputy-governor it could not legally elect him governor. The award concluded that Byllynge, insofar as possible, should fulfill his commitments to the resident shareholders and settlers and made a strong plea for peace "in the name of Jesus Christ."

By virtue of the award Byllynge was undisputed chief proprietor and governor. Though Jennings and Budd remained in London for ten months appealing to the crown for a remedy, their efforts were ignored. Jennings never recovered from the repudiation and, for the rest of his long life, he remained an unyielding foe of arbitrary authority. In November 1685 Byllynge appointed John Skene, a supporter, his deputy. Skene's first act was to clear the court bench of Byllynge's opponents. The assembly met in November 1685 with representatives from the five settled tenths. "Reserving their just rights and privileges," though recognizing Skene, they appointed a committee to examine the new charter and laws proposed by Byllynge. One of these laws would enable the English shareholders to vote by proxy, thus assuring Byllynge of control of the assembly.

In May 1686 the assembly voted to reject Byllynge's charter and his proposed laws on the ground that an absentee governor was incapable of making laws for the province. They also objected that Byllynge's appointments of officials in the government and in the courts violated the Concessions. The session of 1686 was the last during Byllynge's regime. His health had been deteriorating since 1684; consequently he designated his son-in-law, Benjamin Bartlet, as his successor. He died of tuberculosis in January 1687, and in the fall Bartlet and the two Byllynge daughters sold the twenty-odd Byllynge shares, with the right of government, to Dr. Daniel Coxe, one of early America's great land speculators.

Holdsworth, L. V. "The Problem of Edward Byllynge. . . His Connection with Cornwall." In *The Children of Light,* edited by H. H. Brinton. New York: Macmillan, 1938.

Jennings, Samuel. *Truth Rescued from Forgery and Falsehood. . . .* Philadelphia: Reynier Janson, 1699.

Leaming, Aaron, and Spicer, Jacob, eds. *The Grants, Concessions, and Original Constitutions of the Province of New Jersey.* Philadelphia: William Bradford, 1758.

[Leeds, Daniel.] *The Case Put and Decided. . . .* New York: W. Bradford, 1699.

Nickalls, J. L. "The Problem of Edward Byllynge: His Writings. . . and Influence on the First Constitution of West Jersey." In *The Children of Light,* edited by H. H. Brinton. New York: Macmillan, 1938.

Pomfret, John E. "Edward Byllynge's Proposed Gift of Land to Indigent Friends." *Pennsylvania Magazine of History and Biography* 61 (1937): 88–92.

_____. "The Problem of the West Jersey Concessions of 1676/77." *William and Mary Quarterly* 5 (1948): 95–105.

_____. *The Province of West New Jersey, 1609–1702: A History of the Origins of an American Colony.* Princeton: Princeton University Press, 1956.

_____. "Thomas Budd's 'True and Perfect Account' of Byllynge's Proprieties in West New Jersey." *William and Mary Quarterly* 5 (1948): 325–31.

John E. Pomfret

ROBERT BARCLAY (December 23, 1648–October 3, 1690), a man of uncommon versatility, was one of the principal leaders of seventeenth-century Quakerism. By the age of thirty he was considered the greatest Quaker apologist of his day, and by the time of his death, eleven years later, he had excelled in four disparate occupations—scholarship, the ministry, court politics, and colonial government.

Barclay was born at Gordonstown, Murrayshire, Scotland, on December 23, 1648, the first son of David Barclay (1610–86) and Katharine Gordon. His father was a professional soldier who supported the royalist cause during the Civil War, his mother the daughter of Sir Robert Gordon, second cousin to England's King James I. In 1659 young Barclay was sent to Paris to study with his uncle, rector of the Scot's College, an institution for training missionary priests to reconvert Scotland to Roman Catholicism. He returned to Scotland on his mother's death in 1663 and pursued the study of Greek, Hebrew and ecclesiastical history. Shortly after, a set of confusing political circumstances led to his father's imprisonment, during which he met the persuasive Quaker John Swinton. Profoundly moved by Swinton's sincerity and enthusiasm, the elder Barclay publicly acknowledged himself a Friend in 1666, and Robert followed suit a year later. Robert's marriage in 1670 to Christian Molleson, daughter of a pioneer Scottish Quaker family, cemented the Barclay commitment. The couple had nine children, seven of whom lived to become vigorous and influential Friends.

During the succeeding decade, Barclay devoted his intellect and energy to the propagation of his new faith. Between 1670 and 1678 he published more than a dozen religious treatises, including *An Apology for the True Christian Divinity* (1676), a seventeenth-century religious classic. So great was the impact of these works that D. Elton Trueblood, Barclay's biographer, credits him with saving Quakerism from extinction. Between treatises Barclay spent considerable time traveling, speaking, and corresponding in the Friends' behalf, and these activities assumed even greater importance during the last dozen years of his life.

As his literary production waned, Barclay concentrated his energies on politics. Familial and social connections most profoundly affected his career. Like many Scottish Quakers, he suffered persecution and imprisonment. His relentless efforts to win over the king's brother and heir,

James, duke of York, to a policy of religious toleration—a task for which Barclay was particularly well suited—dominated his later life. James remembered the financial assistance the elder Barclay had given his father, the ill-fated Charles I, and moreover he appreciated the political power of Robert's cousin, the earl of Perth. Furthermore, as a Catholic, the future king tended to sympathize with religious nonconformity. James was so fond of Barclay that in 1680 George Fox, a leading spokesman for the Friends, pleaded with his young colleague to use his influence to obtain the right of self-government for the Quaker colony of West Jersey.

Barclay's association with the English heir set the stage for his final, and perhaps most ambitious, undertaking—the proprietary governorship of East New Jersey. After Sir George Carteret died in 1680, his heirs made several efforts to sell his East Jersey holdings. Early in 1682 the province was put up at auction and purchased by twelve men—all Quakers but one—headed by William Penn. Within a few months the group increased to twenty-four, including twenty Quakers, Barclay among them. In September 1682, when the proprietors elected him governor, Barclay recorded the event in his diary with characteristic modesty: "The proprietors of East Jersey would have me a partner with them and did choose me their governor." Under the terms of the agreement, Barclay was given a full proprietary share plus 5,000 acres, and he received the right of government for life from King Charles II, without the requirement of residence in the province. To be made an influential partner in the enterprise with no personal investment testifies to Barclay's reputation. The proceedings became official in 1683, when the duke of York granted a patent to the proprietors, and Barclay was appointed governor on July 17.

The governorship of East Jersey presented Barclay the opportunity to realize a persistent vision—the establishment of a colony for persecuted Scottish Quakers.

William Penn had recently begun the great Quaker experiment in Pennsylvania, and, for a number of years, the province of West Jersey had provided a climate of religious toleration. Now it was Barclay's turn to apply his principles to the reality of colonial administration. No doubt, another colony devoted to religious liberty bounding his province of New York satisfied James's concern for the Catholic minority in England. Barclay, therefore, had good reason to expect powerful backing from his royal friend. His association with James and the influence of his powerful cousins the earls of Perth and Melfort had been instrumental in his selection as governor. The relationship between Barclay and the other proprietors was meant to be complementary. While James, Perth and Melfort provided the solidity of political power, Barclay gave the venture the stamp of moral respectability.

Having insured the initial success of their venture with Barclay's election to the governorship, the proprietors sent a letter to the inhabitants of East Jersey expressing the hope that they would be pleased with their new governor. In it they pledged to strive for prosperity, adding that success was contingent upon the settlers' cooperation: "We are resolved to advance, knowing that your interest is now so bound up with ours, that we cannot suffer if you prosper, nor prosper when you are injured." The proprietors next drew up several articles of government, the Fundamental Constitutions. While the elaborate system of laws was never put into effect, it is interesting as a revelation of what they considered a model form of government. The system's principal drawbacks lay in its undue complexity and its concentration of power in the hands of the absentee proprietors. After a cautious delay, the proprietors presented the articles to the resident legislators for approval, only to have them rejected by the assembly, the council and the deputy governor. The historian John E. Pomfret attributes the rejection to the liberal concessions issued by Sir George

Carteret and a workable system of town government, both of which had enjoyed two decades of precedence in East Jersey.

To attract Scottish settlement, the proprietors sponsored two promotional tracts during the development years. The first, published by John Reid in 1683, maintained that the time was ripe for Scottish colonization in America. It minimized the advantages of remaining in the old country and expounded at length on the financial and political benefits of emigration. A more ambitious effort, George Scot's *Model of the Government of the Province of East New Jersey . . . ,* provided an interesting account of the province after twenty years of settlement. To counter the natural Scottish predisposition against colonization, it rhapsodized about the climate, soil, fish, game, waterways, forests and available land and enthusiastically described the successful settlements at Woodbridge, Piscataway, Newark, Elizabethtown, Shrewsbury, and Middletown (Middletown Township, Monmouth County), and of the liberal system of government. The tract concluded with a discussion of the terms of settlement in the province and included more than thirty favorable letters from Scottish residents.

But the vision of a Scottish colony, Quaker or otherwise, was never realized. The first ship embarked in August 1683, and two more sailed the following summer. Others followed, but always fewer than Barclay and his associates had hoped. As for Quaker migration, the extraordinary success of Pennsylvania meant that few Friends would choose to settle in East Jersey. As this became apparent, the governor gradually altered his vision to include all persecuted Scots. After some initial setbacks, he secured permission to bring twenty-four prisoners to America. They sailed aboard the *Henry* and *Francis* in September 1685, with about seventy-five others described by a critical contemporary as a mixture of debtors, paupers, "whoores or prodigal wasters," and some of "phaniticall principles." But the voyage ended in disaster when an epidemic of malignant fever killed more than two-thirds of the passengers en route. Barclay suffered a more personal loss when his younger brother, David, died aboard a ship that had embarked the previous month. By this time, the duke of York had acceded to the English throne, and as James II he drastically curtailed religious persecution in Scotland, removing a primary motive for emigration.

A steady decline in Scottish settlement marked Barclay's closing years as governor. The general antipathy of the Scots toward emigration, the economic failure of Perth Amboy, the increased religious toleration in Britain after the death of Charles II, and the virtual commercial monopoly of the port of New York all contributed to dissolve Barclay's dream. To aggravate matters, the other proprietors were losing interest because of poor land sales. Though Barclay should have realized the experiment had failed, his continuing efforts betrayed no sense of defeat. These efforts, however, were of brief duration. On October 3, 1690, the governor died prematurely at his home estate of Ury, at the age of forty-one.

Though an absentee governor, Barclay appears to have been popular in the province. In 1687 the resident proprietors praised him for his services, which included his appointment of George Keith as surveyor of the colony's western boundary. His disinterested commitment to proprietary duties nearly cost him the friendship of his noted associate, William Penn. As the pressure from New York for the annexation of the Jerseys intensified, Penn moved toward some kind of appeasement. He may have felt that a concession in East Jersey would save West Jersey (he held interests in both colonies), but Barclay saw this as a sign of weakness which would fail. Obviously he was unwilling to sacrifice the interests of his other partners for any one of them, even if that one was William Penn. Ultimately, Penn must have respected Barclay's courage, for his tribute was the most eloquent of those following the governor's untimely death.

The governorship of Robert Barclay is generally recognized as a positive influence on the development of New Jersey. In intellect he rivaled his most accomplished contemporaries, and his compassion offset the selfish interests of many of his associates. He left a legacy of altruism conspicuous in the colonial history of New Jersey.

Pomfret, John E. *The Province of East New Jersey, 1609–1702: The Rebellious Proprietary.* Princeton: Princeton University Press, 1962.

Trueblood, D. Elton. *Robert Barclay.* New York: Macmillan, 1968.

Clark L. Beck, Jr.

DANIEL COXE (ca. 1640–January 19, 1730), evinced little concern for the welfare of the inhabitants of his dominion when he governed West New Jersey in absentia from 1687 to 1692. He became involved in colonial land speculation for profit only, and West Jersey was just part of his empire, which at various times extended from Maine to the Gulf of Mexico. He enjoyed some degree of support from fellow proprietor William Penn, but he emulated little of the latter's pragmatism. He spent most of his governing tenure working against the express wishes of his constituents and was apparently unconcerned that his policies were unadaptable to the political climate of the province. Historians have regarded Coxe's governorship as a negative influence on the development of West New Jersey.

Coxe devoted his early years to the study of science and maintained a chemical laboratory. One of the first men to conduct scientific experiments on the effects of nicotine on animals, he read a paper on that subject before the Royal Society at Gresham College in 1665, the year he was admitted to the Society. Five years later he received his doctorate of medicine at Cambridge University. In 1674 he published papers on the crystallization of salt in *Philosophical Transactions,* and in 1680 he was elected an honorary fellow at the College of Physicians. Meanwhile he rose rapidly in the medical profession, serving as court physician to King Charles II and Queen Catherine, and later to Queen Anne.

While at court he became interested in the Americas and purchased several properties, including three proprietary shares in West Jersey. In February 1687 he purchased the right of government and five additional shares from the heirs of Edward Byllynge, late chief proprietor. The sale made him the largest proprietor in the province, and he continued to accumulate shares until in 1692 he possessed twenty-two out of one hundred.

In a long letter written in September 1687 Coxe informed the resident proprietors of the change in governorship and the reasons for it. He stated that the London proprietors had been alarmed at the proposed sale of Byllynge's interests to an unidentified party whose ownership of the right of government would have caused "great uneasiness" among both absentee and resident shareholders. The absentee proprietors had decided "for the good of our country and our own security" that Coxe, as the largest shareholder among them, should gain control. Coxe accepted the responsibility but stipulated that he would gladly relinquish the right of government for 1,000 guineas. His associates, including William Penn, assured him that he was well suited for the governorship and that his authority would be respected. Coxe was unaware that as an Anglican he might be resented in the Quaker-dominated colony, and Penn apparently failed to raise the issue with him.

Coxe immediately alienated the residents by denying that the Concessions of 1677—the colony's liberal articles of government—were binding on him. The West Jersey proprietors had proclaimed them before the duke of York granted sole governing rights to Byllynge, and Coxe therefore considered them superseded. He did, however, promise to adhere to such fundamental concepts as religious liberty and the right of trial by jury. He swore to invest the assembly with "all powers and priviledges consistent with the ends of good government." He would retain all elected and appointed officials, including resident Deputy Governor John Skene, a Byllynge appointee recommended by William Penn and greatly respected by the colonists. He did not join the residents, however; he had originally planned to emigrate to the province once his home affairs were settled, but he changed his mind, presumably in response to the wishes of friends and relatives and to the confusion wrought by Edmund Andros's attempt to absorb a number of proprietary colonies into the "Dominion of New England." He was formally announced as absentee governor at the February 1688 meeting of the Burlington court.

As a land speculator, Dr. Coxe was vitally concerned with the boundary dispute between East and West Jersey. East Jersey Governor Robert Barclay (1682–90) had commissioned George Keith to survey the boundary, and the result favored the eastern province. In his September letter, Coxe instructed the proprietors that for their own protection he had rejected Keith's line. But one year later he surprisingly accepted the line as the legitimate division between the provinces. The resident West Jersey proprietors ratified this action. Though they were quick to note that they had been swindled out of some of their finest land, they issued a proclamation of thanks to Coxe for bringing to an end "those differences and debates . . . [which] have so long disquieted us." At the same time they urged the governor to secure the disputed area for himself either under his

West Jersey or his East Jersey rights (he was an East Jersey proprietor as well). The dispute was to have repercussions for almost another century.

Meanwhile the colony's inhabitants acted to counter what they considered the possibility of encroachment on their land interests by the new governor. In the fall of 1688, the resident proprietors organized themselves as the Council of Proprietors of the Western Division of New Jersey. The council was to record proprietary rights to the soil, supervise the distribution of dividends, issue survey warrants, and administer unappropriated lands. The proprietors understandably wanted to protect themselves against the favoritism an absentee governor was bound to show himself and his associates, especially when he had Coxe's reputation as a speculator. Their fears were intensified when Coxe appointed John Tatham, an unpopular Anglican and suspected Jacobite, as his resident agent.

The attempts of the British imperial administration to include West Jersey in its proposed Dominion of New England spelled further trouble for Coxe. In 1685 the Lords of Trade had convinced the new king, James II, that proprietary governments should no longer exist without a clearer dependence on the crown. Within a year writs of quo warranto (judicial writs demanding proof of governing authority) had been issued against the Jerseys, Delaware, Maryland, Connecticut and Rhode Island. It was evident that James II, so instrumental in creating some of the proprietary colonies, was now attempting to abolish them. The appointment of Sir Edmund Andros as governor of the Dominion—which included the Jerseys from the spring of 1688 to April 1689—angered virtually all inhabitants from Maine to Maryland and further eroded James's already minimal support in the colonies. When the news of James's overthrow reached Boston in April 1689, Andros and his aides were seized and the Dominion was dissolved.

At that time the Council of Proprietors of the Western Division of New Jersey, apprehensive over the future of the province, temporarily overlooked their differences with Coxe and offered to proclaim him governor if he would furnish irrefutable evidence of his right to govern. As evidence of their good faith they pointed to their judicious conduct during the turbulent Andros interlude, especially to the voluntary restraint exercised in increasing their landholdings. Although the resident proprietors stressed the urgency of the situation, Coxe, uncertain of the status of the province under the new rulers, William and Mary, delayed his answer for several months.

Although the resident proprietors refrained from acquiring additional lands for themselves during the Andros regime, Coxe systematically and covertly increased his own holdings in West Jersey. His ambitious plans for exploiting this empire included whaling, establishing sturgeon fisheries in Delaware Bay, and importing French artisans skilled at panning salt for use in the export of salted fish. Late in 1689, at Town Bank, just above Cape May, he built Coxe's Hall, which he intended as a neofeudal manor. Plans there called for winemaking, shipbuilding and lumber manufacture. He invested in a pottery at Burlington. He suspected that his holdings to the north contained sizeable deposits of lead and copper, and he had even more spectacular expectations for the fur trade. The culmination of his grandiose plans was to control a "circular trade," whereby he could exchange the raw products of the domain for the finished goods of Europe and the sugar, cotton, indigo and ginger of the West Indies. Such predictions did not seem out of line to someone of Coxe's commercial vision, and some of his ventures took hold. But he tended to exaggerate the value of his possessions, as his "Account of New Jersey," an inventory of his real property in New Jersey drawn up about 1688, demonstrates. Moreover, competition from Pennsylvania for settlers was intense, and prospective emigrants were unlikely to choose what seemed to them a poorer and less dynamic province.

Coxe's tenure as governor came to a close in March 1692, when he sold the bulk of his holdings and the right of government to the West Jersey Society, a large land and trading company consisting of London businessmen whose sole interest lay in speculation. It is not known whether his decision was prompted by continued friction with the resident proprietors, the outbreak of war with France, or the unfriendly attitude of the British government toward proprietary colonies. Unfortunately, Coxe's withdrawal did not arrest the political deterioration in the province. On the contrary, it was hastened by the appointment of Jeremiah Basse, a notorious anti-Quaker, as agent for both Coxe and the society. Basse proceeded to purchase lands from the Indians and to relocate the Indians without consulting the Council of Proprietors. Daniel Coxe's exit did not put an end to the legacy of absentee interference.

Coxe lived another forty years after pulling out of West Jersey. His disappointments in the province did not dampen his spirit, and between 1692 and 1698 he purchased the tract of Carolana, which included most of present-day Georgia, Alabama, Mississippi, Louisiana, Tennessee, Arkansas and Oklahoma. He remained a land speculator until his death on January 19, 1730, in his ninetieth year. To him West Jersey had been little more than an investment, and not one of his more lucrative ones. He had no higher motive for encouraging colonization; therefore he felt no compunction about withdrawing in the face of an adverse economic and political climate. This disregard for the welfare of the West Jersey inhabitants had been a constant source of conflict between him and his constituents. As a scientist Coxe was brilliant; as a businessman he was shrewd; but as a governor he lacked the compassion necessary to good administration. His governorship must be considered an unfortunate failure.

Pomfret, John E. *The New Jersey Proprietors and Their Lands.* Princeton: Van Nostrand, 1964.

———. *The Province of West New Jersey, 1609–1702: A History of the Origins of an American Colony.* Princeton: Princeton University Press, 1956.

Scull, G. D. "Biographical Notice of Doctor Daniel Coxe, of London." *Pennsylvania Magazine of History and Biography* 7 (1883): 317–37.

Clark L. Beck, Jr.

ANDREW HAMILTON (d. April 26, 1703) served as deputy governor of East Jersey from March 1687 to August 1688. He held the position of governor of both East and West Jersey from April 1692 to April 1698 and again from December 1699 to April 1703. He also briefly filled the office of deputy governor of Pennsylvania.

A talented and effective administrator, Hamilton ranks as one of the most attractive governors of proprietary New Jersey and the foremost figure in New Jersey politics of the 1690s. His career proved highly uneven, the successful administrations of his middle term contrasting sharply with those of the last years, during which New Jersey's proprietary era came to an inglorious end amidst disorder and chaos.

In the 1680s, supervision of East Jersey colonization shifted from English Quakers to Scottish businessmen. Hamilton, an Edinburgh merchant, aided in the recruitment of settlers. He acquired a financial stake in East Jersey, procuring one-twentieth of a proprietary share and investing in ten servants, who came to the province in 1683. The future governor made his move to the colony in the summer of 1686 as a confidential proprietary agent. Immediately a man of influence, he held seats on the governor's council

and on the resident Board of Proprietors. He began his long career as chief executive in New Jersey in March 1687 when he was named deputy governor.

Throughout that career Hamilton labored under serious problems. Royal authorities challenged the right of East and West Jersey proprietors to govern and sought to bring all private colonies under the control of the monarch. New York claimed jurisdiction over Raritan Bay and required ships trading at Perth Amboy to clear customs at the port of New York. During the war with France, authorities in London regarded the defense of New York as vital and expected New Jersey, itself in no danger, to aid in that defense. New Jersey had internal troubles as well. At best, inhabitants tolerated proprietary rule. Governors appointed by the proprietors appeared as the representatives of unpopular absentee landowners whose interests clashed with the people's well-being. Groups in East Jersey contested the proprietors' land title and resisted efforts to collect quitrents.

These problems existed when Hamilton first took office. In 1686, quo warranto proceedings had been instituted calling on the proprietors to show "by what authority" they pretended to govern. New York officials seized vessels at Perth Amboy for failure to pay customs at New York. In addition, the Stuarts' consolidated province, the Dominion of New England, had been organized; initially it consisted only of New England colonies, but both Jerseys were included from the spring of 1688 to April 1689.

This term was brief and only mildly productive. Several governmental activities concerned New York. A council of November 1687 issued proclamations to implement a recent decision of the Lords of Trade that ships bound for Perth Amboy might legally enter that port so long as they paid the same customs as were collected in New York. When war threatened, New York called on East Jersey for military assistance that would require a grant of tax revenues by the legislature.

Hamilton convened the general assembly in May 1688, and it passed seven acts, including a tax to raise money for the defense of New York. The lower house showed no enthusiasm for the tax bill, but Hamilton secured its passage and even warded off an attempt to include as taxable the proprietors' unimproved lands. Meantime, in April 1688, the East Jersey proprietors had surrendered their government to the crown in apparent despair of maintaining their authority, and four months later, Sir Edmund Andros, the governor of the Dominion of New England, arrived to annex New Jersey, and Hamilton's term as deputy governor ended.

The Glorious Revolution caused the Dominion of New England to collapse and its component provinces to resume their former status. That development paved the way for Hamilton's return, this time as governor of both East and West Jersey. Robert Barclay, the nonresident governor of East Jersey, died in 1690. Subsequently, Dr. Daniel Coxe, governor and largest proprietor of West Jersey, sold his holdings and the right of government to a London company known as the West Jersey Society. In the spring of 1692, the society and the East Jersey proprietors in England chose Hamilton to govern both of their provinces.

Although the Stuart monarchs and Governor Andros had been removed, old problems persisted for the New Jersey proprietors and their governor. In 1692 the Lords of Trade ordered a writ of scire facias impeaching the proprietors' right of government. Nothing immediately resulted from this action, but it demonstrated that crown authorities retained their design to transform private colonies into royal provinces. Any wrong moves by Hamilton would further that design. During this administration, from 1692 to 1698, Hamilton avoided providing grounds for serious new complaints by officials. He also muted antiproprietary sentiments within the two provinces and provided both with orderly governments.

Evidence of East Jersey's political har-mony can be found in the regular functioning of the courts, the governor's council, and the general assembly. From 1692 to 1696, the assembly met annually and usually had worthwhile sittings. Four tax measures supplied monies for the support of government and for the defense of New York. Although the military taxes were smaller than Hamilton desired, they removed a possible criticism by authorities against the proprietors. At times the assembly proved obstreperous, as in 1695 when it successfully resisted Hamilton's recommendations, which included a plan for the collection of quitrents. (The quitrents issue also came before the courts, where juries, reflecting popular feelings, ruled against the proprietors.) East Jerseymen seemed to appreciate the worth of their governor, but they remained hostile to the proprietors who had appointed him.

West Jersey presented Hamilton with a unique problem. The governor had to secure approval of war taxes, despite the pacifism of the Quaker majority in the lower house. Conflict with Quaker scruples was avoided by omitting mention in tax acts of the specific purposes for which funds were raised. This left expenditures to the discretion of Hamilton and his non-Quaker councilmen, who appropriated money to aid New York in the war. For his part, Hamilton accepted the Quaker political hegemony and defended Friends against their critics. The cooperation between Hamilton and the Quakers resulted in annual legislative sessions which passed numerous useful bills. In November 1697, when Hamilton received notice that he would be dismissed as governor, the usually tightfisted assembly voted him £200 as a token of the people's "Gratitude and Affection."

The termination of Hamilton's administrations in both provinces proved unnecessary and unfortunate. Anxious lest their deeds be grounds to end their political jurisdiction, the proprietors in London decided that an act of Parliament of 1696 made Scots ineligible for positions in colonial governments, and in 1697 they named Jeremiah Basse governor; there followed a year of turmoil, confusion and intense factionalism in both provinces. Responding to that sorry condition, the East Jersey proprietors late in 1698 petitioned the king on behalf of Hamilton's eligibility, and subsequently the crown's attorney general ruled that Scots were not disqualified. In March 1699, Hamilton was reappointed to office in both colonies.

During Hamilton's absence from New Jersey, conditions had changed drastically and irreversibly. The turmoil of the Basse interim persisted and, indeed, intensified because of the news that the proprietors were once again negotiating to surrender their right of government. Hamilton's caretaker position was most precarious, since like Basse before him he had not obtained the required royal approval of his appointment. His final years as governor witnessed popular disturbances and factional feuds. Division appeared among the proprietors in England; a majority sought the designation of Hamilton as the first royal governor, and a minority actively opposed it. A deluge of angry petitions and counterpetitions from both sides of the Atlantic persuaded the Board of Trade (which had replaced the Lords of Trade under the Navigation Act of 1696) to recommend as the first royal governor someone unconnected with the bitter factionalism.

During Hamilton's last term in West Jersey, Quakers prevailed in both the council and the assembly. Despite their support, the governor could not maintain an effective administration. The assembly met three times and approved some beneficial legislation, but it became preoccupied with partisan maneuvers. The Hamilton-Quaker regime moved against its enemies on several fronts. The assembly reduced the number of its seats to ensure continued Quaker control. Opponents of a tax act of 1700 were imprisoned. These measures provoked resistance, and in a riot in March 1701 a large number of men descended on the Burlington jail and set free several persons confined by the administration.

In East Jersey, a half dozen riots occurred. Most resulted from efforts to disrupt provincial courts on the grounds that the government lacked legitimacy. That charge was also asserted at the only general assembly to meet, and it caused the governor quickly to dissolve the legislature. Hamilton's authority met challenges even within his council, most dramatically when a councillor displayed a commission as governor he had received from anti-Hamilton proprietors in England. Beginning in the summer of 1701, with the courts disrupted, the assembly dissolved and the council divided, no government prevailed in East Jersey. Only slightly better conditions existed in West Jersey. Not until August 1703 and the arrival of the first royal governor did provincial government again function.

In April 1703, when Hamilton died, he had not yet been officially relieved of his Jersey positions. He was also wearing a third hat, having begun his duties as deputy governor of Pennsylvania in November 1701. His attendance at numerous meetings of the Pennsylvania council during the next year accounts in part for his frequent absences from New Jersey; more significant, however, New Jersey had become hostile territory for its last proprietary governor.

Hamilton married three times. When he died, he was survived by his third wife and by John, the son of his first marriage. His second wife had been the daughter of a former deputy governor of East Jersey, Thomas Rudyard. John Hamilton followed in his father's path, and during the first half of the eighteenth century he held important offices in the provincial government of New Jersey and on the East Jersey Board of Proprietors.

In addition to his political career, Andrew Hamilton merits attention as the architect of an early postal system in colonial America. In 1691, the English government granted Thomas Neale, a minor courtier, a private monopoly for carrying mail in the colonies. Neale never went to America, but authorized Hamilton to establish and operate a postal system.

The New Jersey governor persuaded the assemblies of five colonies to enact the necessary legislation, although neither of his own governments joined the system. Commencing operations in 1693, the service consisted of weekly mail deliveries carried over routes between major towns in New England and the Middle Colonies. The system worked as well as could be expected until 1699, when it declined. In 1707 the English government purchased the private monopoly, established a royal post office, and appointed John Hamilton as postmaster general.

Leaming, Aaron, and Spicer, Jacob, eds. *The Grants, Concessions, and Original Constitutions of the Province of New Jersey.* Philadelphia: William Bradford, 1758.

Pomfret, John E. *The Province of East New Jersey, 1609–1702: The Rebellious Proprietary.* Princeton: Princeton University Press, 1962.

——. *The Province of West New Jersey, 1609–1702: A History of the Origins of an American Colony.* Princeton: Princeton University Press, 1956.

Frederick R. Black

JEREMIAH BASSE (d. 1725) served concurrently as proprietary governor of East New Jersey and West New Jersey from April 1698 (when he presented his commission to the council) to November 1699, filling a hiatus in the gubernatorial career of Andrew Hamilton. Conspicuous because of the rapid descent of both colonies into fierce factionalism and confusion, Basse's administration began the final disintegration of proprietary government in New Jersey that culminated in 1702 in the creation of a new royal province. The difficulties in East and West Jersey were inherent in the proprietary system of government as practiced in the Jerseys. Basse probably merits a more favorable place in New Jersey history than he generally receives: though his conduct as governor added fuel to the fire, he was more victim than perpetrator of the strife and disorder.

In 1696 the newly formed Board of Trade intensified an intermittent campaign to extend royal authority over charter and proprietary colonies. Several conditions made the Jersey proprietorships especially vulnerable to that campaign. The challenge by officials in England to proprietary authority encouraged critics in the provinces, such as the East Jersey townsmen who contested proprietary land titles. The tactful Andrew Hamilton had avoided overt antagonism between proprietors and townsmen, and in West Jersey, where dissatisfaction existed among non-Quakers resentful of the hegemony of the Friends, he had formed an effective partnership with the Quakers so that anti-Quakerism could only mark time. His removal as governor unleashed the dissident elements. The resulting turmoil would have severely tested even a resourceful and seasoned executive; Jeremiah Basse, having limited talents and virtually no experience in public affairs, was particularly ill equipped to deal with the situation.

Little is known of Basse's early life. In 1676 a half brother, Joshua Barkstead, migrated to West Jersey; Basse himself first appears in New Jersey records as a resident of Cohansey in 1686, when he was designated Barkstead's agent to sell land. After that he served as agent or attorney for numerous landowners, including Dr. Daniel Coxe, William Penn and the West Jersey Society. The society, a company of Londoners claiming extensive proprietary landholdings and the right of government in West Jersey, was organized in 1692, when Basse was in England. Recruited by the company, he returned to New Jersey and during Governor Andrew Hamilton's first term performed various services as agent. A non-

Quaker and the spokesman for a company that was both absentee landlord and largest proprietor, Basse aroused the hostility of West Jersey Friends. In spite of his unpopularity and his failure to produce any profits, the West Jersey Society decided to retain him as its agent when he returned to England in 1696.

While in England, Basse—always alert for the main chance—found bigger fish to fry. Both the society and the East Jersey proprietors in London believed, erroneously, that a recent act of Parliament disqualified Andrew Hamilton from service as governor because he was a Scotsman. Basse made the most of the opportunity; he sought to persuade the proprietors, the society and the colonial authorities to substitute him for Hamilton, which they did in the spring of 1697. A leading West Jersey Quaker labelled the act a "miserable . . . exchange."

Winning the proprietors' appointment proved the easiest step in Basse's bid for office. The Navigation Act of 1696 required royal approval for proprietary governors, and the Board of Trade refused to recommend Basse for approval unless the proprietors posted a bond of £3,000 as security for his performance. The proprietors would not provide that guarantee. In numerous appeals to the board, Basse presented himself as a champion of the king's prerogative and implied that unless his commission received royal approval, New Jersey would be beset by pirates, Scottish traders, smugglers, Quakers, and others prejudicial to good order. When his entreaties failed, Basse decided to act as royal governor without approbation. The society acquiesced, and the East Jersey proprietors went so far as to inform Hamilton and his council that Basse had been "presented to the king and is owned by him and approved of."

Basse began his term with several liabilities. As a replacement for the popular Hamilton, he had to contend with the enmity of resident proprietors, East Jersey Scotsmen, West Jersey Quakers, and other groups favored by the former governor. They had legitimate grounds for opposing Basse because of his failure to secure royal approval, and his arrival in East Jersey in April 1698 occasioned some protest. However, he succeeded in getting his administration under way. He removed some councillors who might cause trouble, such as Lewis Morris; others voluntarily chose not to attend meetings. A general assembly met from February 21 to March 13, 1699, and passed seven acts. Although provincial courts sat, they functioned mainly to repress opposition.

During his term, Basse's most positive endeavor was his defense of the proprietors' claim to a legal port at Perth Amboy. New York regarded East Jersey as a commercial appendage and required vessels trading at Perth Amboy to clear customs at the port of New York. Authorities in England differed about the legality of this practice, but in November 1697 the crown ordered ships bound to and from Perth Amboy to pay customs at New York. Following the instructions of the East Jersey proprietors, Basse proclaimed Perth Amboy a free port. New York's governor, Richard, Lord Bellomont, challenged the proclamation, and Basse engineered a test case involving the *Hester*, a ship he and his brother-in-law owned. While unloading a cargo at Perth Amboy in November 1698, the *Hester* was seized. The episode had its comic aspects, with an allegedly terrified Jeremiah Basse presenting a bottle of brandy to the New York force commander making the seizure. In spite of such idiosyncratic behavior, Basse persevered, and in 1700, though no longer governor, he won a suit against Bellomont in Westminster. Basse's conduct during the *Hester* seizure earned him ridicule in East Jersey, and his efforts to finance prosecution of the suit in England by having the assembly vote a tax of £675 generated protest and contributed to the disruption of the lower house. These were not Basse's only conflicts with the assembly.

During the assembly's first session, Basse had hoped to gain the legislature's cooperation by signing bills that appealed to the delegates. One such act defined the

"Rights and Privileges" of the inhabitants. Several others contained provisions contrary to the interests of the proprietors; the controversial tax imposed a rate on their unimproved lands, and another act reduced their influence in the lower house. Despite these antiproprietary enactments, opposition to Basse mounted. Young Lewis Morris, who had dramatically denied the governor's claim to authority at a May 1698 meeting of the Court of Common Right, headed that opposition. Several days later at Perth Amboy, he organized and led a disorderly demonstration against the government. Under his encouragement, the town meetings of Newark and other communities resisted the tax act and complained to England about the governor. Morris was twice fined and imprisoned; in May 1699, a large group of men from Elizabethtown broke into the Woodbridge jail and released him.

The Basse administration also failed to establish itself completely in West Jersey. The council was fully compliant and antiQuaker; and, since council members were ex officio justices, the governor also controlled the courts. However, the Quakerdominated assembly refused to accept him as legal governor.

The rejection of Basse's authority took many forms. The governor's summons of a general assembly went unheeded. The former provincial treasurer refused to provide the new administration with his accounts. Samuel Jennings, speaker of the assembly, concealed the "Book of the Laws" and other important papers. Mobs obstructed courts at Salem and Burlington.

By the summer of 1699, provincial government in both colonies had ceased to function. The news of Hamilton's reappointment contributed to the disarray. As early as December 1698 the East Jersey proprietors, who had come to regret their selection of Basse, had sought to restore the former governor. Furthermore, the possiblity of their erecting an acceptable government appeared so hopeless that several months later they agreed to surrender their political pretensions to the crown. The West Jersey Society removed Basse not only as governor but also as agent, and the actual exchange of governors took place at the end of 1699. Basse left the governmental machinery of both provinces in a condition beyond repair, and in 1702 the crown took over the administration of both colonies.

After his return to England, Basse intervened in the surrender proceedings, opposed the nomination of Hamilton as first royal governor, and sought a place for himself in the new government. Though he failed to secure a seat on the governor's council, he won an appointment as provincial secretary. He returned to New Jersey in 1703, and until his death in 1725 he was a persistent if minor political figure. In 1715 he lost his post as provincial secretary, but afterwards he filled other offices, serving for five years as attorney general and for brief terms as representative from Cape May, collector of provincial taxes in Burlington County, and provincial treasurer. His later career shows his effectiveness and occasional distinction in executing lesser political positions. But Jeremiah Basse's tenure in 1698–99 as governor of East and West Jersey magnified the flaws in New Jersey government under the proprietors.

Leaming, Aaron, and Spicer, Jacob, eds. *The Grants, Concessions, and Original Constitutions of the Province of New Jersey.* Philadelphia: William Bradford, 1758.

Pomfret, John E. *The Province of East New Jersey, 1609–1702: The Rebellious Proprietary.* Princeton: Princeton University Press, 1962.

———. *The Province of West New Jersey, 1609–1702: A History of the Origins of an American Colony.* Princeton: Princeton University Press, 1956.

Frederick R. Black

EDWARD HYDE, VISCOUNT CORNBURY (1661–
April 1, 1723) was the son of Henry Hyde,
second earl of Clarendon, who was lord
privy seal under James II. In his youth
Cornbury hardly appeared likely to go
down in history as "a spendthrift, a
grafter, a bigoted oppressor and a
drunken vain fool." His grandfather, after
whom he was named, had served as lord
chancellor under Charles II, and his
father's sister was the wife of James II.
With such a distinguished background—
an important father, a king as uncle, a
good education in Geneva, a seat in Parliament (1685) and a profitable marriage
(1688) to Katherine, daughter of Lord
O'Brien—Cornbury's prospects sparkled.

Fate seemed to be on his side. From
youth he had been taught to regard his
first cousin, Princess Anne, as "the
ground work of his fortunes." This bias
proved highly fortunate in 1689, when
Cornbury had to choose between supporting his Catholic uncle and siding with the
Protestant rebels under William of Orange and Anne's sister Mary. An
Anglican like Anne, Cornbury became
one of the first army officers to desert
James II, thus ingratiating himself with
the victorious William and Mary, as well
as with Anne. Since the Bill of Rights
named Anne as the successor to William
and Mary unless, as was unlikely, that
long-childless couple produced an heir,
Cornbury's fortunes appeared assured.

Despite all these advantages, Cornbury
embarked on a course of conduct that
earned him an odious reputation in history. In a quest to satiate his lavish tastes,
he overspent his considerable income and
found himself pursued by numerous creditors. Impatient to escape their grasp and
recoup his fortunes, he sought a post in
the colonies. William obliged in 1701 by
naming him the governor of New York,
and Anne, who became queen in 1702,
added the governorship of New Jersey.

Cornbury attached particular importance to his royal relationship. He
convinced himself that he acted with the
sovereign authority of his cousin,
stretching this identification to the extreme in emulation by "dressing publicly
in women's clothes every day." Evidently, Cornbury assumed that he resembled
his cousin in appearance as well as authority.

When Cornbury first came to New Jersey in the summer of 1703, he found the
colony consumed, as usual, with factional
political strife. In what had been the
proprietorships of East and West Jersey,
a variety of parties sought the first royal
governor's favor as they fought with each
other over land, money, power and religion. Cornbury cared little about the
issues, but he immediately sensed the
possibility of personal gain.

Instead of allying himself with an existing faction, he began to build his own, the
"Cornbury Ring." Using his broad appointive power, he placed a group of
avaricious men on the provincial council
and in other high offices. With their connivance, he designed an overall strategy
for grabbing land and looting public
funds. The first step was to try to dis-
franchise the Quakers, who dominated
West Jersey politics, and seize control of
the assembly. Then, the Ring planned to
stack the East Jersey Board of Proprietors
and the West Jersey Council of Proprietors with accomplices who would
grant them huge tracts of land. Cornbury
also expected the assembly to vote him
substantial personal revenues. Finally, he
and his cohorts considered themselves not
accountable for the expenditure of various public funds.

Cornbury began almost immediately to
pursue these designs. In his first report to
the Lords of Trade, he suggested that
Quakers be excluded from holding public
office. When the first assembly met in
November 1703, he asked for a revenue.
The assembly, however, engaged in factional bickering, and he prorogued it. In
May 1704, when the house convened once

nore and passed a bill granting him a housand pounds for a year, Cornbury leclared "the sum was not suitable," again prorogued the assembly, and again asked the Lords of Trade to bar Quakers from public office. He could afford to be patient, since his political machinations n neighboring New York had brought him a gift of two thousand pounds beyond revenue for seven years.

Furthermore, he soon lined his pockets with New Jersey money. Dr. John Johnstone, representing the East Jersey proprietors, twice gave him sums of two hundred pounds in the hope of buying support for his faction. Richard Slater, a reputed felon whom Cornbury had commissioned as a justice of the peace, traveled throughout East Jersey soliciting money from the opponents of the proprietors. He promised that Cornbury would dissolve the assembly, which had reconvened in June 1704, and also hold new elections, seek to abolish the quitrents, and reduce the property qualifications for voting and office holding. Cornbury received between £500 and £1,500 and dissolved the assembly, even though it had offered him a revenue of £1,500 for three years. He had more ambitious plans.

Cornbury's designs quickly unfolded. He called for new elections, and the Cornbury Ring resorted to unlawful tactics. As their opponents noted, "many of the towns had not any (much less due) notice of the day of election." In Burlington, Sheriff William Fisher, a Cornbury appointee, "refused to allow any person to vote unless for such men as he named and the Quakers in particular were wholey excluded." In spite of such tactics, the Cornbury Ring failed to control the new assembly.

Two of Cornbury's henchmen on the council quickly remedied the situation. Daniel Leeds and Thomas Revell objected to the qualifications of three newly elected Quaker assemblymen, Thomas Lambert, Thomas Hardner and Joshue Wright. Cornbury, ignoring the law that made the assembly the judge of its members' qualifications, refused to confirm the three Quakers in their seats, thereby winning his party a majority of one.

The Cornbury Ring then passed a number of bills designed to enhance his fortunes financially and politically. Cornbury accepted a revenue bill providing him £2,000 a year for two years—a victory over the Quakers, who had "bragged that there should be no revenue settled." The Ring also pushed through a militia bill that included a £1 fine on all who refused to serve and allowed militia officers to levy taxes for the support of their forces. This severely hurt the pacifist Quakers when the militia confiscated their property for refusing to pay, but it earned the Ring an estimated £1,000 a year. The Ring also passed a tax of £10 per 100 acres on all land, including unimproved acreage. This proved particularly burdensome to the proprietors, who protested to London and succeeded in having the law disallowed. In the interim, however, Cornbury spent the receipts, pocketing £830 and distributing the rest among his party. The assembly also enriched the Ring by authorizing a 6-shilling tax on every freeman. Finally, in a bid for increased political support and in return for bribes already paid, the Ring lowered the property qualification for voting from ownership of 100 acres to ownership of as little as a freehold.

The succession of legislative victories ended in May 1705, when the Board of Trade ordered Cornbury to seat the three Quakers in the assembly. Having lost his majority, Cornbury prorogued the assembly and for the next two years governed without it. During this time he and his cohorts found additional ways to enrich themselves. They seized the records of the East Jersey proprietors, and Cornbury certified the appointment of Peter Sonmans, a member of the Ring, as receiver general of the East Jersey Board of Proprietors. Sonmans then engineered the sale of hundreds of thousands of acres of land to speculators, many of them members of the Ring. Cornbury also insisted that the Quaker members of the

West Jersey Council of Proprietors swear an oath of allegiance. The illegal demand violated their convictions. Cornbury used their refusal as an excuse to prevent the West Jersey council from functioning, and the Ring helped itself to as much as one-half million acres of land.

In neighboring New York, Cornbury administered his office in an equally corrupt and arbitrary manner. He allied himself with the so-called Anti-Leislerian party to secure gifts and a revenue. He twice dismissed uncooperative assemblies, and during Queen Anne's War he embezzled a large part of the money raised for the defense of the colony. He also illegally seized the Presbyterian parsonage and church in Jamaica and unjustly prosecuted the Presbyterian minister, Francis Makemie, for preaching without a license. Even when Makemie was found innocent, the court insisted that he pay all the costs of his trial. Cornbury's role in the affair hastened his recall as governor.

Cornbury's record of political tyranny, religious oppression, graft and theft—as well as transvestitism—angered the populace of both colonies. The New Jersey assembly acted first. Cornbury called the house back into session in April 1707 to ask it to grant him a revenue bill of twenty-one years' duration, but the house instead opened an investigation of his conduct and drew up a list of grievances. The speaker of the house, Quaker Samuel Jennings, read the long list in Cornbury's presence, and the assembly sent a copy with supporting affidavits to the Board of Trade asking the body "to relieve them from the oppressions they groan under by the arbitrary and illegal practices of his excellency." In September 1708, the New York assembly followed suit by unanimously adopting resolutions condemning Cornbury's illegal activities in the colony. This brought action from London. In December the queen concluded that "his near relation to her . . . should not protect him in oppressing her subjects," and she dismissed him from office.

As soon as the word of this development

reached America, Cornbury's numerous creditors had the sheriff of New York arrest him for debt. He languished in a New York jail until the death of his father, when his inheritance enabled him to pay his debts and return to England. Cornbury then took his seat in the House of Lords as the third earl of Clarendon. He was raised to the Privy Council in 1711, and in 1714 served as envoy extraordinary to Hanover. He died in London on April 1, 1723, unmourned in America, where he had become a symbol of despotism. Most Jerseyans probably agreed with Lewis Morris's assessment of Cornbury as "a wretch who by the whole conduct of his life has evidenced he has no regard for honor or virtue."

Cody, Edward J. "The Growth of Toleration and Church-State Relations in New Jersey, 1689–1763: From Holy Men to Holy War." In *Economic and Social History of Colonial New Jersey,* edited by William C. Wright. Trenton: New Jersey Historical Commission, 1974.

McCreary, John R. "Ambition, Interest and Faction: Politics in New Jersey, 1702–1738." Ph.D. dissertation, University of Nebraska, 1971.

Pierce, Arthur D. "A Governor in Skirts." *Proceedings of the New Jersey Historical Society* 83 (1965):1–9.

Pomfret, John E. *Colonial New Jersey: A History.* New York: Scribner's, 1973.

Rubincam, Milton. "The Formative Years of Lord Cornbury, The First Royal Governor of New York and New Jersey." *New York Genealogical and Biographical Record* 81 (1904): 106–16.

Smith, William, Jr. *The History of the Province of New-York.* Vol. 1. *From the First Discovery to the Year 1732.* Edited by Michael Kammen. Cambridge, Mass.: Harvard University Press, Belknap Press, 1972.

Spencer, Charles Worthen. "The Cornbury Legend." *New York State Historical Association Proceedings* 13 (1914): 309–20.

Wilson, James Grant, ed. *The Memorial History of the City of New-York . . . .* 4 vols. New York: New York History Co., 1892–93.

Edward J. Cody

JOHN LOVELACE, BARON OF HURLEY (d. May 5, 1709) was a grandson of Francis Lovelace, the governor of New York from 1668 to 1673. Residence in America proved unkind to both. Francis returned to England in disgrace after New York City surrendered to the Dutch in 1673; in 1674 his estate was seized for debt; he was eventually imprisoned, and he died in 1675. John, even more unlucky, died in New York less than five months after his arrival there.

Though a member of an aristocratic family and a great-grandson of the first baron of Hurley, John Lovelace spent his youth in relative poverty, while the title and family estate went to his cousin, also named John. When his cousin died in 1693 without a male heir, Lovelace succeeded to the peerage only to find that the previous baron had dissipated the family fortunes through gambling and debauchery. A decree of the high court of chancery ordered the estate sold to pay the accumulated debts, leaving Lovelace with a title and a pile of unpaid bills.

During the following years Lovelace served in a number of military posts, including those of guidon of the horse guards, military attaché to the earl of Westmoreland, and colonel of the New Regiment. In 1702 he married Charlotte Clayton, but neither her dowry nor his military career significantly improved his financial position. Consequently, he must have seen his March 1708 appointment to the governorship of New York and New Jersey as a golden opportunity.

In September Lovelace sailed from South Hampton, accompanied by fifty-two families from the Palatinate who had fled their homeland in the face of French armies to seek a better life in America. Queen Anne had allowed them to be transported to England, and they were sailing for New York. Though not the first German immigrants to America, these families were the vanguard of thousands of German refugees who in the next few years would make their way through England and Amsterdam to the new world. When the ship arrived in New York on December 18, 1708, the Germans went north to settle Newburg, and Lovelace assumed his office as governor of New York and New Jersey.

Lovelace faced a delicate situation, both as a representative of the crown and as a man seeking his fortune. He was replacing Edward Hyde, Lord Cornbury, who had been recalled for gross corruption and maladministration. Lovelace's instructions took this into account. They specifically forbade him to accept any "gift or present"; they instructed him to see that the assemblies specified the disposition of all appropriated funds; they required him to provide for his own living by requesting revenues from the New York and New Jersey assemblies. Since both bodies were keenly aware of his predecessor's corruption—and were highly independent as well—Lovelace faced the difficult task of protecting royal prerogatives while getting money from the groups most likely to ignore the crown's rights. When forced to choose, Lovelace bent prerogative in favor of his pocketbook.

In New Jersey Lovelace began his career on December 20 by calling a meeting of the council in Bergen. Because this group included former members of the "Cornbury Ring," as well as their archenemy Lewis Morris, Lovelace probably received a quick introduction to the bitter factionalism which pervaded New Jersey politics. Since becoming a royal colony in 1702, New Jersey had been bitterly divided between two political groups—the "Scotch faction" and the "Cornbury Ring"—whose members sought to obtain huge tracts of land for themselves without concern for the public good. If the Cornbury supporters harbored any hopes of continuing their maneuvers with the new governor's connivance, they were disappointed when

Lovelace summoned the assembly into session in March 1709.

No doubt realizing that his personal fortunes depended on cooperation with the lower house, Lovelace adopted a conciliatory tone. "I persuade myself," he told the assemblymen, "I shall not give you any just cause to be uneasy under my administration . . . . Let past differences, and animosities be buried in oblivion," he continued, "and let us seek the peace and welfare of our country." With these blandishments completed, Lovelace got to the heart of the matter and asked for a revenue, but tactfully added, "You know best what the province can conveniently raise for its support, and the easiest methods of raising it."

The assembly responded in terms designed to persuade the governor to follow its lead, promising to "contribute to the support of Her Majesty's government to the utmost of our abilities and most willingly so at a time when we are freed from bondage and arbitrary encroachment." This promise, it turned out, had a few strings attached. The assembly did not simply provide Lovelace with a revenue; it also sought to oversee that revenue, first by demanding to examine the books of receiver general Peter Fauconnier, and then by insisting that Lovelace submit his nominee for treasurer, Miles Forster, for assembly approval. Lovelace complied, and the house had won a new right.

Meanwhile, the assembly pressed its attack against the Cornbury faction. It secured indictments against former governor Jeremiah Basse, who had been province secretary under Cornbury, for perjury, and against Peter Sonmans, the corrupt East Jersey receiver general and Cornbury lieutenant, for perjury and adultery.

With these successes against the Cornbury Ring and the now evident cooperation of the governor, the assembly turned its attention to the question of revenue. In early April, it passed a one-year measure that specified the salary of each colonial official. The assembly was so specific, it informed Lovelace, not because it dis-

trusted him but because it lacked co[n]fidence "in these gentlemen that are n[ow] of her majesties council." Lovelace h[ad] no choice but to accept this new meth[od] of allocating money.

With one revenue now secure, Lovel[ace] quickly returned to New York to m[eet] with its assembly, and a similar situat[ion] ensued. He made a conciliatory addr[ess] that included an unfavorable reference [to] Cornbury. The assembly respond[ed] positively but complained of past [in]justices. The house then spent a mo[nth] debating a revenue bill. On May 5[,] finally agreed to grant Lovelace £1,[...] for one year and specified further how [the] additional revenue would be spent, est[ab]lishing a precedent in New York.

Lovelace was now financially secu[re.] Unfortunately, he never received the b[en]efits, for he suffered a fatal stroke on M[ay] 6, 1709, before he could enjoy his [new] wealth.

McCreary, John R. "Ambition, Interest[, and] Faction: Politics in New Jersey, 1702–17[..]. Ph.D. dissertation, University of Nebra[ska,] 1971.

Pomfret, John E. *Colonial New Jersey[: A] History.* New York: Scribner's, 1973.

Smith, William, Jr. *The History of the P[rov]ince of New-York.* Vol. 1. *From the [First] Discovery to the Year 1732.* Edited by Mic[hael] Kammen. Cambridge, Mass.: Harvard [Uni]versity Press, Belknap Press, 1972.

Edward J. C[...]

RICHARD INGOLDESBY (d. March 1, 17[..]), British army officer and lieutenant g[ov]ernor of New York and New Jers[ey,] 1702–9, was acting governor of both [col]onies from May 1709 to about April 17[10.]

Richard Ingoldesby's early life is la[rge]ly obscure. He was born into "a wor[...]

amily" and may have been the son of Thomas Ingoldesby, a captain in a parliamentary army during the English Civil War. Before the Glorious Revolution, Richard served the Prince of Orange as a field officer in Colonel Thomas Tollemache's English regiment of foot. In 1688, borne along by the celebrated "Protestant Wind," Ingoldesby accompanied his regiment back to England in support of William and Mary, and in the Irish campaign the year following he took part in the successful siege of the Jacobite stronghold of Carrickfergus. As a reward for his services to the new monarchs, in September 1690 Ingoldesby was commissioned captain and major of one of the independent companies of English regulars that were being sent to New York with Governor Henry Sloughter to help restore royal authority in the wake of Leisler's Rebellion. The duke of Bolton, an eccentric Whig nobleman and military officer who sometimes acted as Ingoldesby's patron, also influenced the appointment.

Ingoldesby arrived in New York at the head of two independent companies in January 1691, two months before Sloughter, and promptly set about the task of reestablishing royal authority with a vengeance. He refused to recognize the authority of Jacob Leisler, the rebel leader who had assumed the office of lieutenant governor of New York after the collapse of the Dominion of New England in 1689, and demanded the surrender of a fort in New York City held by Leisler and his adherents. Leisler denied Ingoldesby's authority and refused to hand over the fort. In March 1691, a skirmish resulting in the deaths of two English soldiers brought the conflict between Ingoldesby and Leisler to a head. Sloughter appointed Ingoldesby, among others, to a special commission of oyer and terminer to try Leisler and several of his supporters on charges of murder and treason. The tribunal found Leisler and Jacob Milborne, his chief lieutenant, guilty of treason and sentenced them to be hanged, which was done in May 1691. Ingoldesby's role in the suppression and execution of Leisler earned him the undying hatred of the fallen leader's followers. One of them, hearing a rumor that Ingoldesby might be appointed governor of New York, angrily exclaimed: "No, that Murtherers dogg will never have ye place."

After Sloughter's death in August 1691, the New York Council, dominated by anti-Leislerians, selected Ingoldesby to serve as commander in chief of the colony until the imperial administration chose a successor for Sloughter. Ingoldesby, ever ambitious for preferment, besought the duke of Bolton to obtain the office of governor of New York for him, but in vain. Benjamin Fletcher received the post instead and superseded Ingoldesby in August 1692. In the meantime Ingoldesby governed in the interests of the anti-Leislerians, although even they eventually tired of his arbitrary ways and complained that he "carried things with a high hand, [and] received Severall Sums of Money without a Concurrance in the Councill."

Under Fletcher's administration Ingoldesby was stationed with his company at Albany and put in charge of military security for New York's northern frontier. Inadequate supplies for his men and irregular pay for himself led him to return to England in 1696 on a one-year furlough. He remained in England for seven years, however, soliciting payment of his accounts and engaging in intrigue for promotion to a higher office. He gained the patronage of the duke of Ormonde, a Tory peer who commanded a unit of the king's Life Troops, and he formed an acquaintance with William Dockwra, the leader of a faction of East Jersey proprietors living in England. During the negotiations in 1701 leading to the establishment of New Jersey as a royal colony, Dockwra, backed by Ormonde, advanced Ingoldesby as a candidate for the post of first royal governor of New Jersey. But the imperial administration, anxious to combine in one man the governorships of New Jersey and New York, passed over Ingoldesby in favor of Edward

Hyde, Lord Cornbury, who had already been appointed governor of New York. Ingoldesby's claims were not ignored entirely, however, for in November 1702 he was commissioned lieutenant governor of New Jersey and New York.

Ingoldesby finally returned to America in March 1704 and soon found himself in a peculiarly frustrating situation. Although the imperial administration expected him to administer New Jersey or New York when Cornbury was absent, its expectation was never realized. Cornbury refused to allow Ingoldesby to exercise authority in either colony, reducing him to the status of a cipher. Since Cornbury spent the greater part of his time in New York, the New Jersey Assembly was especially distressed that the lieutenant governor "declined doing any act of government at all" in the province. Ingoldesby brought this anomaly to the attention of the imperial administration, and in April 1706 the Privy Council approved an order revoking his commission as lieutenant governor of New York, continuing his commission as lieutenant governor of New Jersey, and making him a member of the New Jersey Council. The Board of Trade informed Cornbury of this order, but since Queen Anne neglected to sign a warrant putting it into effect, Ingoldesby's status and authority remained uncertain for several more years. Despite his differences with Cornbury, however, Ingoldesby loyally defended the governor when the New Jersey Assembly brought serious charges of misgovernment against him.

On the death of John Lovelace in May 1709, Ingoldesby became acting governor of New Jersey and New York. He assumed office in New Jersey when the reaction against Cornbury's misrule there was in full swing and when the struggle between the proprietary and antiproprietary parties was approaching a climax. Not surprisingly, in view of his previous association with William Dockwra and his defense of Cornbury, Ingoldesby aligned himself with the Anglican wing of the antiproprietary party, which then controlled the New Jersey Council and had support in England from Dockwra's faction of proprietors. Consequently, Ingoldesby temporarily dashed proprietary party hopes of purging certain leading Anglican leaders from the council and bestowed on his supporters a lush bounty of public offices and splendid land grants. Ingoldesby's alliance with the Anglicans elicited a challenge to his authority from Lewis Morris, the foremost proprietary party leader. Morris charged that Ingoldesby's commission was invalid and claimed that by virtue of his position as New Jersey's senior councillor, he himself was entitled to succeed Lovelace. Although Ingoldesby suspended Morris from the council and convinced a majority of assemblymen that his commission was valid, an undercurrent of suspicion about the legitimacy of his authority plagued him throughout his administration.

During his first meeting with the assembly in May 1709, the most pressing issue facing Ingoldesby was New Jersey's role in the "Glorious Enterprise," a projected land and sea invasion of Canada by a joint expedition of American and British forces. Ingoldesby urged the assembly to raise New Jersey's quota of 200 men for the expedition, but the assembly, with a large minority of Quaker members, was initially less enthusiastic about the project than he. Eventually the assembly decided not to raise the men but to emit £3,000 in bills of credit to pay and equip 200 volunteers. The Quaker minority voted against a bill for this purpose on all three readings, serenely confident the non-Quaker majority would pass the measure and spare Friends the embarrassment of thwarting a measure deemed vital to local and imperial interests. But Ingoldesby and his allies decided to use the situation to bring the Quakers into disrepute, and on the third reading of the bill, two erstwhile supporters from the antiproprietary party changed their vote and thus defeated it. Ingoldesby thereupon declared an adjournment until the end of July, when it probably would hav een too late in the season for New Jersey o fulfill its quota, and joined the council n urging the home authorities to exclude Quakers from all public offices in the rovince. However, Samuel Vetch and rancis Nicholson, the chief promoters of he expedition, persuaded Ingoldesby to ecall the assembly only ten days after its djournment, and it finally approved an mission of £3,000 in bills of credit for he 200 volunteers—the first emission of aper money in the colony's history. Unortunately, the British government, beause of untoward military developments n Europe, sent no British regulars to nvade Canada, and the "Glorious Enerprise" came to an inglorious end.

Ingoldesby recognized that the imperial dministration would not grant his reuest to be appointed governor of New ersey, and thus the remainder of his dministration was almost anticlimactic. n November 1709 Ingoldesby opened a ewly elected assembly with a curt adionition to act with dispatch "that I may e Speedily enabled to Attend her Majess Service in . . . New Yorke," which as exactly the sort of sentiment that ade many New Jerseyans long for a overnor of their own. At this time his ain concern was to persuade the asembly to alter the support act passed arlier in the year for Lovelace and to ivert to himself most of the salary anted to his prematurely deceased redecessor. He secured the passage of a vised support act for this purpose at the ost of allowing the assembly to strength its control over the salaries of royal ficials, a practice that ran counter to e British government's policy of keepng such officials independent of local presentative bodies.

In September and October 1709 the nperial administration revoked Inoldesby's commission as lieutenant govrnor of New York and New Jersey. News this apparently did not reach America ntil around the following April, when he eased to be acting governor in both colies. Thereafter he returned to New ork to command an independent com-

pany, and after living for a time in "necessitous circumstances" he died there on March 1, 1719.

A man with ability incommensurate to his ambition, Ingoldesby sought several times in his career to become royal governor of New Jersey or New York, but, as contemporaries noted, he was "a rash hot-headed man" unsuited to the tasks of civil government. His record in New Jersey—where he placed a higher value on discrediting his Quaker adversaries than on securing the colony's participation in an important military venture and where, for personal gain, he acquiesced in a serious encroachment by the assembly on royal authority—fully justifies this assessment.

East Jersey Papers, The New Jersey Historical Society, Newark, N.J.

Livingston-Redmond Papers, Franklin D. Roosevelt Library, Hyde Park, N.Y.

Morris Family Papers, Rutgers University Special Collections, New Brunswick, N.J.

Records of the Society for the Propagation of the Gospel in Foreign Parts, Series A, vols. 3 and 4, Library of Congress microfilm.

Calendar of State Papers, Colonial Series, America and West Indies, 1689-1720; Documents Relative to the Colonial History of the State of New York. Vols. 3-5.

Dalton, Charles, ed. English Army Lists and Commission Registers, 1661-1714. Vol. 2. London: Eyre & Spottiswode, 1894.

———. George the First's Army, 1714-1725. Vol. 1. London: Eyre & Spottiswode, 1910.

Ingalsbe, Frederick W., comp. Ingoldesby Genealogy. Grand Rapids, Mich.: Press of U. G. Clarke, 1904.

Kemmerer, Donald L. Path to Freedom: The Struggle for Self-Government in Colonial New Jersey, 1703-1776. Princeton: Princeton University Press, 1940.

McCreary, John R. "Ambition, Interest and Faction: Politics in New Jersey, 1702-1738." Ph.D. dissertation, University of Nebraska, 1971.

Webb, Stephen Saunders. "Officers and Governors: The Role of the British Army in Imperial Politics and the Administration of the

American Colonies, 1689–1722." Ph.D. dissertation, University of Wisconsin, 1965.

Eugene R. Sheridan

ROBERT HUNTER (1666–1734), born in Edinburgh, Scotland, was the son of a lawyer and the grandson of the laird of Hunterston. He seems to have been well educated, for his correspondence shows a familiarity with Latin, Spanish and French as well as an unusual felicity in English. He received his first commission in the army in 1689 and for nearly twenty years pursued a military career, serving under the first duke of Marlborough in the War of the Spanish Succession (in America called Queen Anne's War). Though he fought at Blenheim and Ramillies and reached the rank of colonel, he had neither a regiment of his own nor the large patronage which that position often gave.

Having quarreled with Marlborough, Hunter successfully moved into the nascent colonial service by wangling the lieutenant governorship of Virginia. His means of access to the source of political appointments is obscure, but it is likely that the initial link was through his literary friends, who often doubled as courtiers and civil servants. Among them were Jonathan Swift, Joseph Addison, Richard Steele and Dr. John Arbuthnot, the Queen's physician. En route to Virginia in 1707, Hunter was captured by the French, and he spent nearly two years in France in what was reportedly a socially dazzling captivity. Exchanged in 1709 (though not for the bishop of Quebec, as is customarily reported), Hunter was appointed governor of New York and New Jersey. He arrived in New York in June 1710.

Each of the two provinces offered grave dangers to a royal governor. New York, a frontier outpost in the long wars between Great Britain and France, lived in constant dread of Indian attack. (Only twenty years before, the town of Schenectady had been destroyed.) As though that were not enough, a long series of corrupt governors had driven the colonists to the point of refusing to raise taxes unless the elective assembly controlled the returns which meant, in effect, controlling the local government. New Jersey had internal rather than external problems, but they were much more virulent: the province, only recently taken over by the crown, was disrupted by disputing proprietors.

In 1664 James, duke of York, had given New Jersey to two cronies, John, Lord Berkeley, and Sir George Carteret. Ten years later, Berkeley had sold his interest (the western) to the Quakers John Fenwick and Edward Byllynge, beginning a pattern of fragmentation that after thirty years had left each half with dozens of proprietors—a "muddle of perplexity." At Hunter's arrival, there were two sets of contending proprietors. Colonel Daniel Coxe, the son of Governor Daniel Coxe, Jeremiah Basse, who had been governor of the colony between 1697 and 1699, Peter Sonmans; Hugh Huddy; Richard Townley, and William Hall formed one group. They were outspoken in their high church Anglicanism, though in an age when religion and politics were almost interchangeable they probably had no religious motives per se but used religion as a stalking horse. They had been protected and rewarded by the egregious Lord Cornbury, the first royal governor of New Jersey. The other group was led by Lewis Morris, Thomas Gordon, George Willocks, John Johnstone, Thomas Farmer and Thomas Gardiner. Some of them, Quakers, owned shares bought from the older Coxe's receivers. The younger Coxe made a claim to the property, which if successful would ruin many of these men, for bankruptcy could easily mean life in prison. To add to the confusion, each side had support from proprietors who lived in England: Edward Richier and Paul Doeminique supported the Morris faction (called by Hunter the "country party"), and William Dockwra supported the Coxe group.

When Hunter arrived in New Jersey, he found members of the Coxe party happily ensconced in the provincial council, the upper house of the legislature, where they could refuse to pass laws unfavorable to themselves (for example, a law that would permit Quakers to affirm rather than take oaths to serve on juries) and where they could act as the colony's supreme court. Queen Anne's reign was politically unstable, and when a new faction came into power in London it displaced its rivals' appointees in the colonial service. Consequently, new governors came prepared to believe the worst about their predecessors and to discover evidence of it to disgrace them and embarrass their political supporters in England. In 1711 Hunter, whether to pursue such a plan, or to retaliate for Peter Sonmans's attack on him in an election poll of 1710, or, as he himself said, to stop the obstructionism that plagued the government, began calling for the ouster of the Coxe group from the council. His Whig patrons had fallen from power in London in 1710, however, and their Tory successors were not especially inclined to please him. Not until 1713, after Doeminique and Richier pressured the Board of Trade, did the London administration remove Coxe, Sonmans and their cohorts from the council and replace them with members of the country party. In the interim, Hunter dealt with the Coxe party by moving to eliminate it from local judgeships and by failing to call any meetings of the legislature. When the legislature met in 1713, it passed a spate of bills. Some of these were designed to relieve the Quakers by permitting them to serve on juries and to hold local offices such as tax assessor and collector. Other bills made reforms in the court system, and one established a new county named in honor of the governor: Hunterdon.

Coxe and his men tried to regain power in 1715 and 1716 through the assembly elections; Coxe was named speaker, but Hunter, in no mood to be conciliatory or patient, repeatedly dissolved the assembly and called for new elections until the Quaker or country party had 50 percent of the seats. Coxe and his party boycotted the meeting of the legislature, but Hunter informed the remainder that they had a quorum, and the Quakers gleefully expelled the Coxe faction for nonattendance. Coxe fled to Pennsylvania and then to England, returning after Hunter's departure to play a prominent though less controversial role in the colony.

Hunter did not limit his interests to politics in New Jersey. He owned extensive property: more than one house in Perth Amboy, 500 acres along the Raritan River and on Burlington Island. He urged the establishment of an Anglican episcopate in America, with the cathedral church at Burlington and his old friend Jonathan Swift as the first bishop. In 1715 he recommended that the home government permit minting of copper coins from local mines to relieve the currency shortage that hurt the small farmers. The crown accepted neither of these suggestions, though both were consistent with Hunter's philosophy that "the true Interests of the People and the Government are the same, I mean A Government of Laws. No other deserves the Name, and are never Separated or Separable but in Imagination by Men of Craft."

Sick, and worried about political enemies who were traveling to London to try to replace him, Hunter left New York and New Jersey in 1719. The following year he exchanged positions with William Burnet, the comptroller of the customs. In 1727 he was appointed governor of Jamaica, where he died in 1734.

A tall, vigorous and personable man who was literary as well as literate, Hunter wrote the first published play in America, an astonishingly ribald political satire on New York entitled *Androboros*.

Logan Family Papers, Historical Society of Pennsylvania, Philadelphia, Pa.

Morris Family Papers, Rutgers University Special Collections, New Brunswick, N.J.

Rutherfurd Collection, The New-York Historical Society, New York, N.Y.

Pomfret, John E. *Colonial New Jersey: A History.* New York: Scribner's, 1973.

Scanlon, James E. "A Life of Robert Hunter, 1666–1734." Ph.D. dissertation, University of Virginia, 1969.

———. "English Intrigue and the Governorship of Robert Hunter." *New-York Historical Society Quarterly* 57 (1973): 199–211.

James Edward Scanlon

WILLIAM BURNET (1687–September 7, 1729), who governed New York and New Jersey from 1720 until 1728, was born in the Netherlands, at the Hague. His father, Gilbert Burnet, who became the bishop of Salisbury, had been a chaplain to Charles II, but he was one of the first English subjects to transfer his allegiance from James II to William and Mary. Gilbert Burnet had gone to the Netherlands to pay court to William, and, while there, had married his second wife, Mary Scott, a wealthy Dutchwoman of Scottish extraction. Young William Burnet was named for his godfather, the man who became king of England in 1689. After the Glorious Revolution, Gilbert's fortunes waxed and waned with the rise and ebb of the Whigs, but in general the family held a privileged position because of its leading role in the events of 1688–89. William developed into a personable but hot-headed young man. Though he entered Trinity College, Cambridge, at the age of thirteen, he was expelled for laziness and disobedience. He was, however, privileged in having Sir Isaac Newton tutor him for a time.

As an adult he reportedly continued to be personable and hot-tempered, but he also desplayed an active intellectual curiosity. His younger brother, Gilbert, concluded that William's curiosity was undisciplined and essentially frivolous. When informed that William was writing a book, Gilbert told him that he feared the book would make him a subject of derision. Nonetheless, William wrote the book, *An Essay on Scripture Prophecy, Wherein it is Endeavoured to Explain the three periods Contain'd in the Xii Chapter of the Prophet Daniel With some Arguments to make it Probable that the FIRST of the PERIODS did Expire in the Year 1715.* It was published anonymously in New York in 1724, and one of William's brothers-in-law suggested that he might have done better to spend his time at backgammon.

Burnet obtained the dual governorship of New York and New Jersey in 1720 by trading his post as comptroller of the customs with his friend Robert Hunter, who in 1719 had returned to England. Since Hunter and Burnet both had strong Whig connections the trade was easy to arrange. Burnet, whose first wife had died in 1717 and left him with a two-year-old son, willingly accepted the inconvenience of living in the colonies because he hoped the governorship would prove more lucrative than his post at the customs. He needed money because his heavy investment in the South Sea Company was rapidly depreciated after 1720. Through most of his term as governor, until the death of George I in 1727, he had few worries about opposition at home. Whatever problems he encountered originated in the colonies.

In both New York and New Jersey Burnet relied heavily on the advice of Lewis Morris and James Alexander, who had been principal advisors to Governor Hunter. In New Jersey both men were closely allied with the main proprietary interests, and Burnet, throughout his term, tended to favor legislation designed to protect or enhance proprietary claims. This meant that the landholders who claimed titles which had not originated in patents from proprietors, primarily the so-called Nicolls patentees, were predisposed against Burnet.

These antiproprietary forces dominated Burnet's first assembly in 1721. The assembly had been elected in 1716, and on Hunter's advice Burnet continued it. However, Lewis Morris, while he was acting governor after Hunter's departure, had alienated many of its members with policies favoring the proprietors. After Burnet's arrival the assemblymen's own reluctance restrained them from engaging in open opposstion to the governor. But they criticized Burnet's reliance on Morris, and they tried to use their control of finances, unsuccessfully, to effect a change in Burnet's attitude.

Throughout his early stay in the colonies Burnet reflected his family's history by tending to brand his opponents as Jacobites and high churchmen. In 1721 he harried George Willocks, one of his East Jersey critics, out of the province by calling him a Jacobite and fomenter of opposition. By harassing Willocks, shrewdly electioneering among an electorate as lacking in deference as any in America, and using patronage after the election, Burnet contrived in 1722 to have a second assembly that was more amenable to his wishes. This assembly sat in three sessions before new elections were occasioned in 1727 by the death of George I. In 1722 the assembly passed an act for the financial support of the government for the years 1720–25; it also agreed to a stringent anti-Jacobite law. In 1723 it passed its famous Loan Act. In its last session, in 1725, it renewed the 1722 support act through 1730.

The Loan Act was the most significant piece of legislation during Burnet's tenure. In spite of the enthusiasm for copper mines that developed in the 1720s, New Jersey was still almost entirely dependent on agriculture. Its trade was largely in the hands of New York and Philadelphia merchants. Since New Jersey had no medium of exchange, its economy fluctuated with the currencies of New York and Pennsylvania. In 1709 New Jersey had begun to issue bills of credit, but after 1716 it had begun to retire them, producing a deflation that in 1720 caused, or at least aggravated, a depression.

James Alexander, a lawyer, land speculator, and New York merchant, strongly favored a new paper issue. So did most of the assemblymen. They made it clear that they would reward Burnet handsomely for his cooperation. Because Burnet insisted that any new currency had to have proper backing, they created a loan office authorized to lend £40,000. Loans to landowners secured by mortgages on their New Jersey farms put the money into circulation. The act provided an extremely stable medium of exchange. Burnet defended the act against the mounting criticisms of London merchants and officials. He even gathered testimonials to the soundness of New Jersey money from New York City merchants. For his troubles Burnet received sizable "incidental" appropriations in addition to his regular salary from 1723 on.

Burnet governed a rapidly growing New Jersey. At the request of the Board of Trade he took a census in 1726. It indicated that the population, which in 1702 may have totaled 12,500, had more than doubled to 32,442, including 2,581 slaves. The growth brought about increasing problems over land titles as more and more of the disputed areas became populated, but the storm did not break until after Burnet's departure.

Burnet's last Jersey assembly, elected in 1727, was led by a vocal anti-prerogative Quaker, John Kinsey, Jr. It proved almost as troublesome as his first. Burnet spent hardly any time in the colony between 1725 and 1727. The assembly that gathered at Perth Amboy in December 1727 knew when it convened that Burnet was due to be replaced. It began by requesting that New Jersey be given a governor of its own. The assembly engaged in a continual struggle with Burnet and his council over a bill that amended the procedures for registering deeds. The council sought to protect proprietors, the assembly to circumvent the council's authority over land. Eventually the assembly gained Burnet's assent for a triennial act which was later disallowed. The assembly also continued a practice of using the interest collected on the loan-office notes to support the government, which met strong disapproval from the Board of Trade. Burnet was more than willing to accede to this practice.

Governor Burnet drew an annual salary of £600 in New Jersey, and he also received fees. In addition, the assembly approved "incidentals," which varied from a first grant of £1,000 in 1723 to the £600 his last assembly voted him early in 1728. In return Burnet presided over a growing colony and approved legislation favorable to its growth, but he spent little time in the colony. Between 1720 and 1728 he was absent twice for more than a year. In 1722 Burnet married Mary Van Horne, the oldest daughter of a prominent New York Dutch merchant; together they enjoyed the social life of Manhattan. The elder Van Horne, who had been a staunch supporter of Hunter's, continued to support Burnet, and Mary's brother Cornelius was added to the New Jersey council in 1727. Burnet's wife bore him three children in New York, but both she and her lastborn died in the autumn of 1727. Soon after, Burnet was notified that John Montgomerie, special favorite of the new monarch, George II, would replace him as governor of New York and New Jersey. Burnet's friends protested the change to no avail. Burnet, however, was not forgotten, and he was transferred to Massachusetts. On April 24, 1728, he turned over the government of New Jersey to Montgomerie and headed for Boston where he encountered a disagreeable assembly and received no salary. As the result of a carriage accident he died there on September 7, 1729.

Ellertsen, E. Peter. "Prosperity and Paper Money: The Loan Office Act of 1723." *New Jersey History* 85 (1967): 47-57.

McCreary, John R. "Ambition, Interest and Faction: Politics in New Jersey, 1702-1738." Ph.D. dissertation, University of Nebraska, 1971.

Nelson, William. "The Administration of William Burnet, 1720-28." In *The Memorial History of the City of New-York . . .*, edited by James Grant Wilson. Vol. 2. New York: New York History Co., 1892.

_____, ed. *Original Documents Relating to the Life and Administrations of William Burnet, Governor of New York and New Jersey, 1720-28*. Paterson: Press Printing and Publishing Co., 1897.

Whitehead, William A. *Contributions to the Early History of Perth Amboy and the Adjoining Country. . . .* New York: D. Appleton & Co., 1856.

John Strassburger

JOHN MONTGOMERIE (d. July 1, 1731) was born in Dumfriesshire, Scotland. Trained as a soldier, Montgomerie served in Parliament and then turned courtier, becoming groom of the bedchamber to the Prince of Wales. In 1716, when the prince quarreled with his father, King George I, Montgomerie chose to give up his office rather than risk his friendship with the heir apparent. This act of loyalty probably led the prince, after his accession as George II, to offer Montgomerie the lucrative governorship of New York and New Jersey.

Historians have described Montgomerie as a man of little natural ability, limited education and intelligence, and no real ambition, who was mainly concerned with leading a life of leisure and material comfort. Reputed also to have considerable wealth, he was noted chiefly, according to historian William Smith, for the number of household possessions he brought to New York. Cadwallader Colden, however, an important New York leader at the time, understood the governor and his situation somewhat differently. Colden insisted that Montgomerie lacked neither intellignce nor natural ability but that he had "given himself up to his pleasures especially to his bottle and had an aversion to business." If he had once been wealthy, according to Colden, he had left England deeply in debt, and he wanted to use his new office to recover his fortune as easily as possible. Colden's observation that Montgomerie was "as diffident of himself as any man I ever knew" may help explain some of his difficulties as governor.

During his brief term as governor (April 15, 1728–July 1, 1731), Montgomerie faced two issues in New Jersey. Either, if improperly handled, could have deprived him of part of his salary. The first was the Board of Trade's insistence that he persuade the assembly to repeal the act passed under Governor Burnet which empowered it to use the surplus money that had accumulated in the New Jersey Treasury for the support of government. This surplus represented interest paid by New Jersey citizens on money they had borrowed from the government-operated land bank set up in 1723. The original intention had been to put this money into a sinking fund. Both Burnet and Montgomerie strongly supported the assembly's position, knowing that the only alternative was to raise taxes and that the assembly would not do that. Since the governors' salaries depended on this money, they had to side with the assembly.

Burnet and Montgomerie were probably correct in contending that the assembly's position was sound. New Jersey's currency, in relation to that of the neighboring provinces, was rising steadily, and its loans were regularly paid off. Nevertheless, the board adamantly refused to accept the arrangement. The disagreement became a source of uneasiness to Montgomerie; he wanted to please both the board and the assembly but seemed, initially at least, unable to please either.

The second issue that jeopardized Montgomerie's position was the assembly's firm decision that New Jersey should have its own governor. Although Governor Burnet, in the last assembly session over which he presided, had persuaded the assembly's leaders to table their request for a separate governor, he had only postponed the issue; in the next session the assemblymen placed it first on the agenda.

As Montgomerie had no real plans of his own to initiate and no particular design to pursue apart from retaining his salaries, his governorship can be most clearly understood in the light of his determination to persuade the assembly to give him adequate financial support and to prevent it from obtaining a separate governor. The desire to exert power over men or to distinguish himself as governor appeared to be totally alien to Montgomerie's nature. Essentially, he wanted to please those he had to deal with and to offend as few as possible as long as they posed no threat to his pursuit of wealth and security.

On September 3, 1727, while still in England before officially receiving his commission as governor, Montgomerie wrote to the Board of Trade begging it to let the New Jersey Assembly apply the accumulated interest money in New Jersey's Loan Office "to the publick Services of the Government." It would be an "ungrateful proceeding," he insisted, to force him as soon as he arrived in the colony "to propose a new tax and burthen to the Province to bear the necessary Support of the Government when there lyes so much useless mony in their coffers already."

From the beginning, Montgomerie gave little indication that he had enough character or leadership to defend the royal prerogative against the more powerful assembly even if he wanted to. A few days before Montgomerie departed for New York in November 1727, New Jersey's ex-governor Hunter wrote a letter to James Alexander, an influential political figure in both New York and New Jersey, that revealed doubts about the new governor's competence. Hunter said Montgomerie "is a very honest Gentleman but will want good advice." In Barbados, where

Montgomerie's ship took refuge during the winter storms, he reportedly said that he was bringing no dependents from England because he was sure he could fill all posts of honor with qualified Jerseymen. The statement reflected his desire to please the New Jersey community rather than to lead it.

The problems facing Montgomerie, however, would not go away. He had to both prevent the assembly from applying for a separate governor and persuade it to vote him an ample salary. His problems were compounded when the Board of Trade demanded that he ask for the repeal of the act providing support of the government from the interest money. In this difficult position, Montgomerie decided for the first and only time in his short career to use his influence to retain some power over the ambitious assembly. The most urgent issue was the demand for a separate governor. On November 30, 1728, sensing the assembly's supreme confidence after a series of triumphs in its last session under Governor Burnet, Montgomerie wrote asking the Board of Trade to delay royal consent to two of the assembly's acts. The Triennial Act required elections for a new assembly every three years, and the Quakers' Oath Act excused Friends from taking oaths, a practice that was against their convictions. By asking for postponement of royal approval until the board could judge the behavior of the coming assembly, Montgomerie was trying to gain leverage for the coming dispute about a separate governor.

"To ese the Province of the expense," Montgomerie chose not to call for a new election, and the same assembly that had acquired unequaled power under Burnet met in December 1728. Its main preoccupation, as Montgomerie had expected, was the separate governor, and assemblymen were divided only over the choice of strategy. Nearly half the house, according to James Alexander, wanted to cooperate with the governor, offering him a handsome appropriation in exchange for his consent to their resolutions for a separate governor. The rest, following John Kinsey, the assembly's powerful Quaker leader, wanted to pass the resolutions without consulting Montgomerie.

Since the Kinsey group formed the majority, these resolutions would have carried had not Montgomerie, horrified at the prospect of losing his office, dissolved the assembly. The reason he publicly gave for this hasty action was that the assembly's resolutions ignored the king, showing disrespect to the crown, but his real motivation lay in the fear of being replaced by another governor. Montgomerie believed that with the prospect of another governor on the way "the people would worship the rising sun and slight him."

On April 20, 1729, Montgomerie wrote to the Board of Trade to report the "unadvisable and ungovernable" conduct of the assembly, elated with past favors and "having their heads full with impracticable Schemes calculated to weaken if not quite set aside his Majesties prerogative." Obviously he was referring to the assembly's resolutions in favor of a separate governor. He told the board that although the assembly had offered him five years' support as bait, the resolutions that followed made its dissolution absolutely necessary. Then, probably hoping that the board's opposition would undermine the power of the assembly leaders, he strongly recommended the disallowance of both the Triennial Act and the Quakers' Oath Act, implying that because of their insolent request for a separate governor, the Quakers deserved no special favors. This was Montgomerie's last firm stand, in part because the board failed to support his dissolution of the assembly but largely because he realized that the power to govern New Jersey rested in the assembly, not the crown. His best chance to retain the governorship and his salary, he now knew, lay in establishing good relations with assembly leaders.

Although Montgomerie had promised the board in his letter of April 20, 1729, that he would call on the assembly to repeal the act allocating the interest money to the support of the government, it is unlikely that he planned to follow through. Instead, on August 2 that year, in a long and somewhat agitated letter, he tried again to convince the board that this use of the interest money was safe, legitimate and necessary, warning that if the interest money was not used to support the government, New Jersey would be unsupported after the most recent appropriation ran out in September 1730. He expressed confidence that his arguments would persuade the board to reverse its position. This was an ill-founded hope in view of the board's past record.

When the new assembly convened in May 1730, Montgomerie had not yet received an answer to this letter; eighteenth-century transportation was extremely slow and Montgomerie's administration suffered from unusually long delays in mail delivery. Since mailing it, he had received only one letter relating to New Jersey affairs, a reply to the letter of April 20, 1729, in which he had denounced the assembly's resolutions for a separate governor and requested the disallowance of the Triennial Act and the Quakers' Oath Act. The reply had destroyed whatever hope Montgomerie may have had for the board's support against the assembly on the issue of a separate governor. It refused not only to censure the assembly's resolutions, calling them quite legitimate, but also to recommend that the crown disallow the Quakers' Oath Act, stating that Quakers had similar privileges in England. In the most critical part of the message, the board once more asked to hear as soon as possible that the act allowing the use of interest money for governmental support had been repealed. Otherwise, it warned the crown would disallow the act.

In his May 22, 1730, answer to the board, Montgomerie professed to feel "very uneasie" at the rebuff and claimed that he would have been glad to transmit the assembly's request for a separate governor had it been phrased dutifully and addressed "to his Majesty." The statement, in view of his strong desire to retain the governorship, seems improbable. His real concern was to prepare the board for a new assembly victory. In conversing with all the members of the house, he wrote, he had received no encouragement whatsoever that they would reverse their position on the use of the interest money.

During this session Montgomerie gave in to all the assembly's demands. Not only did he allow its leaders to petition for their own governor in exchange for five years' support, but he also accepted an act defraying that year's incidental charges of government from the interest money, a clear violation of the board's instructions. In a letter of November 20, 1730, he apologized for allowing this defiant action by explaining to the board that he had not received its letter of April 24, which explicitly rejected his arguments for this use of the interest money, until late in September after the assembly had adjourned. Having received no response to his letter, he said, he had flattered himself that the board had altered its opinion.

But even if the board's letter had arrived on time, Montgomerie could not possibly have changed the assembly's policy. According to his letter, all his attempts to convince the assemblymen that the Board of Trade was serious in threatening disallowance had brought only taunts for his inability to convince the board that the assembly's position was sound. If he had asked for a repeal, which he never had, he would, he insisted, have received nothing but "a public, or perhaps a rude refusal."

Montgomerie's cooperation in passing on to the board the assembly leaders' petition for a separate governor in the summer of 1730 resolved that issue. His willingness to give way to all the assembly's wishes may have softened the petition's wording. Its signers disclaimed any dissatisfaction with their present governor and insisted that "wee are very well pleased with his Government and desire it may continue during your Royall pleasure."

In spite of this assurance, Montgomerie continued to worry about the appointment of another New Jersey governor. He had, however, only a short time to fret. On July 1, 1731, after months of poor health, he died of a stroke in New York. According to historians, the people much mourned him, probably because of his good nature, modesty and eagerness to please.

Under Montgomerie's governorship, the power of the assembly continued to grow because the colonial authorities in England were ineffective and Montgomerie lacked the will and desire to check it. The crown did not disallow the hotly contested support act as the board had threatened it would. The petition for a separate governor was legitimately delivered to the crown at Montgomerie's own request. His only victory lay in the crown's disallowance of the Triennial Act, a veto he had recommended. Montgomerie must be characterized as one of the weakest of New Jersey's colonial governors.

Cadwallader Colden Papers, The New-York Historical Society, New York, N.Y.

Kemmerer, Donald L. *Path to Freedom: The Struggle for Self-Government in Colonial New Jersey, 1703–1776.* Princeton: Princeton University Press, 1940.

McCreary, John R. "Ambition, Interest and Faction: Politics in New Jersey, 1702–1738." Ph.D. dissertation, University of Nebraska, 1971.

Pomfret, John E. *Colonial New Jersey: A History.* New York: Scribner's, 1973.

Sheridan, Eugene R. "Politics in Colonial America: The Career of Lewis Morris, 1671–1740." Ph.D. dissertation, University of Wisconsin, 1972.

Smith, William, Jr. *The History of the Province of New-York.* Vol. 1. *From the First Discovery to the Year 1732.* Edited by Michael Kammen. Cambridge, Mass.: Harvard University Press, Belknap Press, 1972.

Tanner, Edwin P. *The Province of New Jersey, 1664–1738.* New York: Columbia University Press, 1908.

Frances D. Pingeon

WILLIAM COSBY (1690–1736) was surely New Jersey's least active governor and perhaps its most inept. The last of the colonial royal governors to hold the joint governorship of New York and New Jersey, he, like his predecessors, concentrated his efforts north of the Hudson River. He deserves mention, however, if only because he was indirectly responsible for the British government's decision in 1736 to establish a separate governorship for New Jersey.

Governor Cosby was the sixth of seven sons in an Anglo-Irish family, and the sixth to become a soldier. He entered the army in 1704, served in Flanders and Spain, and achieved a colonelcy of the Eighteenth Royal Irish in 1717. His marriage into the Montague family no doubt was hastened by the promotion. His regiment was transferred to Minorca in 1718, and for the next decade he exercised the additional responsibilities of the civil and military governorship of that little British outpost in the Mediterranean.

Cosby remains an obscure figure in the official records of Minorca, but stories of his misdeeds there became current in New York and New Jersey. The most vicious tale—about Cosby's dealings with a Portuguese merchant, Bonaventura Capedevilla—originated with Cadwallader Colden, an opponent. Cosby condemned as contraband a £9,000 cargo of snuff Capedevilla had consigned to Minorca in 1718. He cowed the local judiciary into confirming his action while refusing to allow them to investigate many of the relevant documents. He also tried to falsify some records he sent to the

Privy Council in 1722 when it investigated the affair. Colden states that the Privy Council found for Capedevilla and forced Cosby to pay £10,000 damages. "The Government of New York by the death of Coll Montgomerie came seasonably in his way to repair his broken fortune."

Colden may well have exaggerated the Capedevilla story, but later Cosby's hunger for land and his apparent ruthless intent to increase his estate were to lead many colonists to believe it. William Smith would accuse him of illicitly acquiring lands on Long Island and in the Mohawk Valley but reflect that public protestations were pointless: "No representation, repugnant to his avarice, had any influence upon Mr. Cosby. The weakness of his understanding rendered him insensible even to fear." Like almost all of the seventeenth-century and eighteenth-century British military and naval officers appointed to govern American colonies, Cosby saw the new world as a place to build a personal fortune. Further, the imperial authorities in London viewed governorships as sinecures for their friends and relatives. William Cosby was singularly well situated to be the recipient of such favoritism; neither his lack of character nor his deficiency of ability forestalled his 1732 appointment as successor to Governor Montgomerie.

The British Empire's principal administrator was the secretary of state for the Southern Department, a position held from 1724 to 1728 by the era's most accomplished manipulator of patronage, Thomas Pelham-Holles, duke of Newcastle. Colonel Cosby had direct access to Newcastle through his wife, Grace Montague, Newcastle's first cousin and the sister of the first earl of Halifax, and he flaunted his influence in America by boasting the protection of "the great interest of the Dukes of New Castle, Montague and Lord Halifax." So powerful were Cosby's connections that he, like Montgomerie, was given a choice of colonial governorships. When he was about to set sail to take the governorship of the Leeward Islands, he learned of Montgomerie's death and returned to London so that Newcastle could secure him the more lucrative governorship on the mainland. According to one of his enemies, Cosby bluntly asserted his confidence in the strength of his patrons by rejecting an accusation that he had violated the law: "How, gentlemen, do you think I mind that: alas! I have a great interest in England." Even after his death, Newcastle and his brother Henry Pelham continued to provide for Cosby's widow and family.

Little can be said about the Cosby "administration" in New Jersey. The governor spent virtually all of this time in New York, where a combination of clumsiness on his part and emerging political maturity among the colonists created years of dangerous political factionalism.

Governor Cosby arrived at Sandy Hook in early August 1732 and held office until he died of tuberculosis in New York in March 1736. He lived in New York City, seldom traveling to New Jersey. His first trip occurred shortly after his arrival in America, when he went to Perth Amboy to request the seals of government from Lewis Morris, who, as senior New Jersey councillor, had been the acting governor since the death of Montgomerie. For some time Morris had been agitating for the establishment of a separate New Jersey governorship, a position he hoped to fill. Perhaps for this reason he delayed meeting with Cosby for an hour or more while (as he claimed) he completed a chancery decree. Cosby, incensed by the delay, subsequently identified the incident as the origin of his conflict with Morris, but in fact Cosby's New Jersey governorship began quite happily.

During his tenure Cosby met the New Jersey Assembly only once and he never called an election. In his opening speech in April 1733 he promised to spend at least half of his time in the colony (thus responding to the lively separatism issue), and the representatives responded by voting him a continuation of support until 1738, although the existing support act still had two years to run. This may have been a response to Cosby's acquiescence when the assembly voted to issue an additional £40,000 in paper money contrary to royal policy. The governor also permitted the legislature to ratify his ordinance to fix legal fees in the colony although, strictly speaking, imperial theory considered such legislative authorization unnecessary. Cosby's only disagreement with the assembly was over an act establishing triennial elections, which the legislators periodically tried to sneak through; Cosby vetoed it.

Despite Cosby's promises, this was more or less the sum of his public record in New Jersey. He met eight times with the council but transacted little business during its sessions because he was occupied with defending his position in New York. The most famous episode of Cosby's governorship was the trial of John Peter Zenger, which in fact was related to Cosby's feud with Lewis Morris and James Alexander. Morris and his allies, who were active both in New York and New Jersey, established a paper in New York City, the *New-York Weekly Journal,* that was hostile to Cosby. Furious over the paper's sniping, Cosby suppressed it and arrested its editor, Zenger, for libel. Zenger was acquitted in what some have called a landmark case for freedom of the press; Cosby had failed to stifle criticism of his regime in New York or to remove Morris and Alexander from the council in New Jersey (which they had ceased to attend after the first meeting). Indeed, when Morris traveled to London in 1735–36 to organize a campaign for Cosby's removal, it became apparent that New Jersey had little importance except as a pawn in the politics involving New York. Morris tried to persuade the Privy Council to remove Cosby from the New York government; he failed, but to placate him the council separated the colonies and, two years after Cosby's death, made Morris governor of New Jersey.

Lewis Morris thought William Cosby a "weak madman"; Morris was doubtless too vehement, but, alas, little good can be said about Governor Cosby of New Jersey.

Rutherfurd Collection, The New-York Historical Society, New York, N.Y.

[Colden, Cadwallader.] "Cadwallader Colden's History of Governor William Cosby's Administration and of Lieutenant Governor George Clarke's Administration Through 1737." The New-York Historical Society, *Collections* 68 (1935): 280–355.

Katz, Stanley. *Newcastle's New York: Anglo-American Politics, 1732–1753.* Cambridge, Mass.: Harvard University Press, 1968.

Kemmerer, Donald L. *Path to Freedom: The Struggle for Self Government in Colonial New Jersey, 1703–1776.* Princeton: Princeton University Press, 1940.

McCreary, John R. "Ambition, Interest and Faction: Politics in New Jersey, 1702–1738." Ph.D. dissertation, University of Nebraska, 1971.

Sheridan, Eugene R. *Lewis Morris, 1671–1746: A Study in Early American Politics.* Syracuse: Syracuse University Press, 1981.

Smith, William, Jr. *The History of the Province of New-York.* Vol. 2. *A Continuation, 1732–1762.* Edited by Michael Kammen. Cambridge, Mass.: Harvard University Press, Belknap Press, 1972.

Stanley Nider Katz

LEWIS MORRIS (October 15, 1671–May 21, 1746), colonial American political leader and jurist, served as governor of New Jersey, 1738–46.

Morris was born in New York City, the only child of Richard and Sarah (Pole) Morris, who had come to the province from Barbados the year before. After the sudden death of his parents in the summer of 1672, Morris was brought up by an elderly Quaker uncle also named Lewis

Morris. When his uncle died in 1691, Morris inherited large estates in New Jersey and New York and became a member of the landed aristocracy in both colonies. In that year he also married Isabelle Graham, the daughter of James Graham, a highly influential New York merchant and political leader. They had fifteen children, eleven of whom—three boys and eight girls—reached adulthood. Although Morris received little formal education, he transformed himself into a highly cultured country gentleman who mastered several ancient languages, amassed a library of 3,000 books, wrote poetry, and dabbled in natural science. Yet Morris's main preoccupation was politics, and his long and complex political career in New Jersey and New York was among the more remarkable in colonial American history.

Morris's appointment as the first separate royal governor of New Jersey in January 1738 was the high point of his career. At the same time it seemed a fitting climax to New Jersey's long-standing opposition to the British government's practice of having the same official govern New Jersey and New York. For at the time of his appointment Morris had been deeply involved in New Jersey political, economic, and religious affairs for almost half a century. Morris had played a key role in negotiating the 1702 settlement between the Jersey proprietors and the imperial administration whereby the crown assumed the government of the province in return for the confirmation of proprietary rights to the soil. For the next thirty-five years he continued to be one of New Jersey's most influential political leaders while serving as a provincial councillor (1702–5; 1708–37), assemblyman (1707–8), and acting governor (1719–20; 1731–32; 1736–38, though in this last period his authority was disputed). In addition, from 1703 to 1736, Morris acted as American agent for an organization of British land speculators known as the West Jersey Society, and from 1725 to 1730 he also served as president of the Board of Proprietors of East Jersey. Finally, as the first American member of the Society for the Propagation of the Gospel, an Anglican missionary organization based in London, Morris supported the society's efforts to convert Protestant dissenters in New Jersey to the Church of England. Even between 1710 and 1737, when Morris devoted most of his time to politics in New York—managing the provincial assembly for Governors Robert Hunter and William Burnet, serving as chief justice of the supreme court (1715–33), and leading the opposition to the arbitrary rule of Governor William Cosby—he never lost interest in New Jersey affairs.

In addition to his intimate familiarity with New Jersey, Morris enjoyed another important advantage as he assumed the governorship—the support he received from some influential British connections. His daughter, Euphemia, was the widow of Matthew Norris, a captain of the Royal Navy. Her father-in-law, Sir John Norris, a British admiral who commanded the Royal Navy and held a seat in Parliament, kept a watchful eye on Morris's interests in Great Britain. A shrewd woman who had elected to remain in England after her husband's death, Euphemia Norris was familiar with some of the leaders of the opposition to the Walpole ministry, and she regularly kept her father abreast of political developments in the home country. But Morris's most important British connection was Sir Charles Wager, another admiral. In addition to being first lord of the admiralty, a privy councillor, and a member of Parliament, Wager was a close political ally of Sir Robert Walpole, then the most powerful statesman in the realm. The combined influence of Wager and Walpole did much to put Morris in the office of governor of New Jersey; and initially, the knowledge that Morris enjoyed the patronage of such highly placed British officials greatly enhanced his influence with the provincial assembly. By the same token, Walpole's fall from power in February 1742, and Wager's removal from office soon thereafter, perceptibly weakened Morris's standing in New Jersey, making it more difficult for him to rally support in the assembly.

Unfortunately Morris failed to satisfy the expectations his appointment had aroused among the people of New Jersey; instead his administration quickly degenerated into a series of bitter conflicts with the assembly. The disputes largely stemmed from his forthright defense of royal authority in New Jersey. From the outset of his administration Morris maintained that although the assembly was duty bound to provide his government with financial support, he had no reciprocal obligation to consent to the laws it passed unless they stood for the common good without infringing on the royal prerogative. Thus in 1739 he dissolved one assembly after approving only a small number of the popular bills it had passed, and in 1742 he dissolved another after withholding assent from every bill passed except one for the support of government. Even when Morris did not resort to the drastic step of dissolution, he frequently refused to approve assembly bills that the representatives considered sound pieces of legislation but he regarded as ill conceived or unconstitutional. As a result, he was often criticized for keeping the assembly in session to little purpose for inordinately long periods of time.

Morris's adherence to royal instructions also antagonized the assembly. In obedience to such instructions he badgered the assembly into supporting a British expedition against the Spanish West Indies in 1740, an effort which offended New Jersey's politically influential Quaker community. For the same reason in 1744 he carried on a fruitless campaign to persuade the assembly to pass a more stringent militia law to bolster the province's defenses against a possible French attack. In this instance Morris offended large numbers of Quakers and non-Quakers alike, who refused to believe that a French assault on New Jersey was likely. Morris himself shared their skepticism but felt his instructions obliged him to suppress his doubts and push for the passage of an unpopular law. Yet Morris was not always consistent in following his instructions from the crown. Although they clearly stated he was to exercise the power with the advice and consent of the council alone, he allowed the assembly to determine how the money it raised for the support of government should be expended. Still, he remained sufficiently inflexible in his defense of royal authority to alienate the assembly, as the shift in its attitudes about the issue of support indicated. Whereas in 1739 the assembly provided him a three-year grant of funds for the support of government, in 1741 it approved only a one-year grant and in 1744 it passed a support bill that so reduced Morris's salary and the salaries of other royal officials that the council felt obliged to reject it, leaving the government with no money from the assembly for the rest of the administration.

Morris's defense of parliamentary authority further sapped his popularity in New Jersey. Partly because colonial paper money was then under attack in Parliament and partly to avoid incurring the displeasure of the home authorities by allowing a new emission in New Jersey, he refused throughout his administration to approve a highly popular bill for the emission of £40,000 in bills of credit. And when, in 1744, the assembly denounced as subversive of American liberties a proposal by Parliament to give royal instructions the force of law, Morris admonished it for criticizing Parliament, declaring, "a British Parliament can abolish any Constitution in the Plantations that they deem inconvenient or disadvantageous to the Trade of the Nation, or otherwise." The implications of parliamentary supremacy in the empire could not have been stated more nakedly, nor can one imagine a sentiment less congenial to the people of New Jersey.

As his relations with the assembly deteriorated Morris attempted to retrieve his position by appealing over its head to the New Jersey electorate. More than any other governor before him, Morris carried his case directly to the freeholders and freemen of the province through printed speeches and pamphlets. These inevitably called forth replies from his opponents and brought about an unprecedented outburst of polemics in New Jersey during his administration. Between 1739 and 1746 at least ten political broadsides and pamphlets appeared in the province—approximately twice the number produced during the entire thirty-six years of the royal period preceding Morris's governorship. Morris himself wrote at least one pamphlet, *Extracts from the Minutes and Votes of the House of Assembly* (1743). He also had several of his speeches to the assembly printed separately, particularly those occasioned by dissolutions of this body. Unfortunately Morris's pamphlet and speeches suffered from certain shortcomings, not the least of which were their dreary prolixity and dry appeals to precedent. Even if he had written more trenchantly, however, it is unlikely that these works would have affected politically aware New Jerseyans more positively. They generally defended unpopular bills or attacked acts of the assembly that Morris interpreted as encroachments on the royal prerogative but others regarded as legitimate expressions of parliamentary privilege or popular rights. In contrast, Morris's polemical adversaries more effectively assailed his refusal to approve popular legislation, his advocacy of unpopular causes such as militia reform, his propensity for long and often unproductive assembly sessions, his explosive temper and his support of the royal prerogative.

Morris coupled his appeals to the electorate with equally unsuccessful pleas to the imperial administration for drastic British intervention in the colony's political system. Outraged by Quaker opposition to his efforts to win support in New Jersey for the British expedition against the Spanish West Indies in 1740, Morris suggested that the Board of Trade deprive Friends of their right to sit in the assembly—a suggestion the board wisely ignored. Frustrated by his failure to obtain what he regarded as adequate financial support from the assembly and convinced that its powers had grown too great, Morris advanced proposals to make himself and other royal officials fiscally independent of the assembly. Some of these proposals, when the British implemented them after 1763, helped to bring on the American Revolution. As early as 1739 he advised the Board of Trade to consider the feasibility of an act of Parliament requiring provincial assemblies to pay royal officials fixed salaries. Two years later he returned to this theme, this time urging the board to support a proposal that Parliament issue paper money in America and apply part of it to pay the salaries of the king's officers there. Finally, in 1745, he asked the board to persuade Parliament to authorize the king to determine the expenditure of the funds the provincial assemblies raised for the support of government. The board acted on none of these proposals, which had the potential for revolutionizing the relations between royal governors and colonial assemblies, and took no notice of them in its correspondence with Morris. It is difficult to determine whether this was because New Jersey did not bulk large in the board's scheme of things or because the board was too distracted by the instability resulting from the fall of Walpole's ministry and the problems arising from Great Britain's wars with France and Spain to consider Morris's proposals for radical imperial reform. In any case, it was well for the peace of the empire that the board ignored Morris's plans.

Unable to win support from the people of New Jersey or to convince the imperial administration of the need for parliamentary intervention, Morris spent the last two years of his administration in a bitter deadlock with the assembly. Between June 1744 and May 1746 he met with four different assemblies. An unvarying pattern marked the first three, with Morris insisting that the assembly provide his government with financial support before he consented to the bills it favored and the assembly refusing to pass a support bill until Morris had approved the bills it wanted passed. During the stalemate the assembly granted the government no money, and Morris withheld assent from every act it passed save one granting supplies for the New England expedition against Louisburg in 1745. Only in Morris's last assembly, which first met in February 1746, did it seem that this deadlock might be broken. Both sides appeared ready to retreat from their extreme positions and to reconcile their differences, but not for long. In the midst of its proceedings, the assembly learned that the Board of Trade, acting on Morris's advice, intended to recommend royal disallowance of a Fee Act approved in 1743 by both the governor and the assembly. Enraged at what it interpreted as an act of treachery by Morris, the assembly renewed its demand for his assent to certain popular legislation before passage of a support bill. Morris agreed, but only if the assembly promised to increase the appropriations it was planning to make to the government. This the assembly refused to do. Suddenly the prospect of stalemate once more confronted the province. In the midst of this crisis, however, Morris, who had been ill for several years, died on May 21, 1746. Yet not even death could dispel the bitterness his administration had engendered. Three years later, when his widow petitioned the assembly for payment of his salary arrears, the assembly turned down the request by an overwhelming majority, remarking that hers was "a Subject so universally disliked in this Colony, that there is none, except those who are immediately concerned in point of Interest, or particularly influenced by those who are, will say one Word in its Favour."

Morris Family Papers, Rutgers University Special Collections, New Brunswick, N.J.

Cook, Richard. "Lewis Morris—New Jersey's Colonial Poet-Governor." *Journal of the Rutgers University Library* 24 (1961): 100–113.

McGuire, Maureen. "Struggle over the Purse: Gov. Morris v. N.J. Assembly." *Proceedings of The New Jersey Historical Society* 82 (1964): 200–207.

Sheridan, Eugene R. *Lewis Morris, 1671–1746: A Study in Early American Politics.* Syracuse: Syracuse University Press, 1981.

Turner, Gordon B. "Lewis Morris and the Colonial Government Problem." *Proceedings of The New Jersey Historical Society* 67 (1949): 260–304.

Whitehead, William A., ed. *The Papers of Lewis Morris.* In *Collections of the New Jersey Historical Society.* Vol. 4. New York: G. P. Putnam, 1852.

Eugene R. Sheridan

JONATHAN BELCHER (January 8, 1681/2–August 31, 1757), Massachusetts merchant and politician, was born in Cambridge, the second son of seven children, to Andrew and Sarah (Gilbert) Belcher. The family was rooted in New England society: Jonathan's grandfather had arrived in the 1630s; his father had steadily accumulated property and become one of Boston's wealthiest merchants and a member of the provincial council. After he was graduated from Harvard in 1699, Jonathan entered his father's business. In 1705 he married Mary Partridge, the daughter of New Hampshire's lieutenant governor, and entered Boston's Second Church. On his father's death in 1717, he embarked on a public career.

In a political world rent by constitutional conflict between executive authority and the legislature, this moderate and unreflective political practitioner shunned permanent identification with either ideological position: first, as a member of the council, he defended Governor William Shute; then, as agent of the house of representatives in London, he opposed Governor William Burnet; and, finally, he returned in 1730 as governor of Massachusetts and New Hampshire with instructions to defend the principles he had left to contest. His success—eleven years' tenure as governor—rested on a careful cultivation of the Anglo-American patronage system. After four trips to London, he had important friends and allies who defended his interest with the Walpole government. For example, in return for supporting toleration for Massachusetts Quakers, his brother-in-law Richard Partridge, a prominent London Quaker, who was New Jersey's agent, recruited the English Friends to exert influence in the governor's behalf.

However, although conflict between the representatives and the executive abated during his administration, the years of politics earned him enemies whose London allies campaigned to unseat him. In 1741, the governor's uncompromising opposition to the popular Land Bank antagonized the legislature and discredited his ability to rule, and with the simultaneous demise of the Walpole government his opponents argued for his replacement by William Shirley.

In August of 1741, Belcher retired to his estate at Milton. Alone—his wife, who had borne him five children, had died in 1736—he brooded over life's mishaps. In 1744 inactivity roused him to book passage for London, where he hoped to retrieve his fortune through a pension or another appointment. He found none of his familiar patrons at Whitehall, and he could curry the favor only of Lord Hardwicke. Though officialdom received him kindly, it was unresponsive to his pleas. Humiliated and embittered by months of waiting in the anterooms of power, Belcher withdrew to the congenial community of London's dissenters, the Congregationalists and Quakers. He met Mrs. Louise Teale, a widow with some fortune, and decided to "commit matrimony" on condition that he find a suitable appointment. In 1746, he learned that Lewis Morris, the governor of New Jersey, lay dying; although the office was of little consequence and small reward, he pursued the opportunity. Rival New Jersey factions contested the post: Morris's

allies sought to maintain control of the executive, and their agent Ferdinand John Paris nominated the governor's son Robert Hunter Morris; in turn the rival Quaker leaders of Burlington hoped to name their own and, through Partridge, discovered their candidate in Jonathan Belcher. The London Friends persuaded the duke of Newcastle to appoint Belcher, collected the requisite fees, and prepared for his residence at Burlington. Before his departure they advised him on the situation in New Jersey.

In August of 1747, the new governor arrived by way of New York, a self-styled exile to an "obscure corner of the world." On his progress south to Burlington, discussions with local politicians and clergymen confirmed his initial prejudices. With its religious and ethnic diversity, this "Wilderness of Nova Caesarea" compared poorly with his native Massachusetts. An enthusiastic friend of the Great Awakening, Belcher discovered a few scattered churches to his liking in the north, but none in Burlington. On conference with the local evangelicals he concluded that "vital religion" was a tender plant in the Jerseys. The people were a crude lot: the province needed "a Nursery of religion and Learning." And most pressing, the province was aflame with riot: long-standing litigation between the East Jersey proprietors, principally James Alexander and Lewis Morris, and the farming communities in the Elizabethtown-Newark area had erupted into violence. While Jerseymen welcomed the governor with promises of support, and the Burlington Quakers admitted him to their society, the aging governor felt estranged and disappointed. Taking up residence a mile from Burlington, he put the problems of office from his mind and resolved to devote his declining years to religion. Soon, he summoned his "Queen of Nova Caesarea" and on September 9, 1748, he and Mrs. Teale were married.

Belcher entered an uneasy political calm. During the previous decade the irascible Governor Morris and the council, composed of his friends and relatives (principally James Alexander and Morris's son Robert Hunter Morris), had angered assemblymen from East Jersey by defending proprietary claims. Governor Morris had also offended prominent Quaker legislators from the west by denying them patronage, and the entire legislature by insulting its privileges. Government was at an impasse. The self-styled "ploughmen" legislators demanded regulation of the courts and legal fees and regular elections; the council pressed for strict measures against the rioters. Neither prevailed. If Belcher's appointment gratified the assemblymen, the councillors greeted the news with reservations. Agent Paris and Robert Hunter Morris warned of the governor's alliance with the "ploughmen," but Alexander convinced the majority, weary of contention, to suspend judgment. In turn, Belcher translated his predisposition to avoid the burdens of office into a principle of statesmanlike aloofness; while recognizing his debt to the Quakers, he was unwilling to antagonize the Morris faction.

In the first meeting with the legislature the governor recommended action on the riots while deftly resisting the council's pressures for vigorous action and at the same time avoiding association with the rioters. Soon the two houses, left to themselves, reached a compromise, with the assembly introducing a bill for the "preventing of Riots" and the council an amnesty bill. The tactic seemed successful: Belcher signed nineteen bills, including a treasury supply and regulations of sheriff's appointments and court fees. He also promised to recommend to the crown a bill for issuing paper money in excess of his instructions. In Burlington, surrounded by allies, he heard his praises sung and believed that he had been successful. Yet that comfort proved illusory: the rioters rejected amnesty and continued to harass the sheriffs of Morris and Essex counties. With Robert Hunter Morris seizing the initiative, the council pressed for vigorous measures. For example, when it presented Belcher with a

petition to the crown for aid against the rioters, he declined to give his support. The council was soon convinced by Morris's warnings. Belcher's open and regular consultation with the "ploughmen" and his infrequent correspondence with the Morrisites awakened fears that their interest was in jeopardy. Finally, Alexander was persuaded to join the opposition. In 1749, Morris joined Paris in London and Belcher warned Partridge to beware of their activities.

The weakness of the governor's position became apparent. Political lobbying in London severely undermined his authority: Morris outmaneuvered Partridge and persuaded the Board of Trade that the governor was consorting with the rioters. Belcher was reprimanded, and Whitehall rejected his nominations to the council in favor of Robert Morris's recommendations. Even friends proved unreliable allies. At times Belcher scolded and prodded the assembly, but to no avail: no riot or tax legislation was passed. In 1751, he grew desperate. On dissolving the assembly, he appealed to the electorate for better representatives and cajoled friends to stand for the legislature. But the results only underscored his impotence: his candidates were not elected. Though the assembly came to agreement with the council on a tax bill, Belcher's influence was negligible. And the next year he helplessly watched the two houses deadlock over taxes. Frustration drove Belcher to desperate measures. He purged the council of offensive members only to earn further reprimands from the Board of Trade. In such a mood he received a suggestion from the assembly leaders that he could sign a tax bill without the council's assent. Only Alexander's firm correction prevented him from pursuing the tactic.

Essentially, Belcher believed that religious and educational decay had brought in the province's ills. A champion of the New Lights and a friend of Jonathan Edwards and George Whitefield, he made religious awakening an integral part of his public life. He invited Gilbert Tennent to preach before the legislature on the principles of godly government. He listened with enthusiasm to Tennent's program to build a college; as New England's colleges had brought pious leadership and learning for the happiness of the community, this "infant college" could reform this "unpolisht ignorant Part of the World" and instruct the "Rising Generation" according to the standards of "vital religion." The college, "My little Daughter," captured his imagination. Quickly he lent his support, first by rewriting the charter to include himself on the Board of Trustees and then by seeking funds for its construction. After Quakers and Anglicans effectively prevented the assembly from lending aid, he persuaded the government of Connecticut to sponsor a lottery. He wrote throughout the colonies and Great Britain seeking subscriptions. His will provided that his library be given to the college. In 1748, the trustees of the College of New Jersey (later Princeton University) conferred on him the M.A. degree, and in 1756 they offered to name the first building Belcher Hall, an offer he declined, suggesting instead Nassau Hall.

By 1751, Belcher's government stood at precarious equipoise. While friendly with legislative leaders, Belcher found the assembly oblivious to his recommendations and immune to his influence. It would pass no more riot legislation, and if it passed any treasury supply Belcher could not take credit. Morris had effectively checked the governor's interest in London, but the Quakers well protected his commission. In the fall, Belcher moved his family to Elizabethtown, where he hoped to find a more healthful climate, and within the year he joined the congregation of Elihu Spencer, a friend of Jonathan Edwards. In the following years he progressively withdrew from government. Weary of politics, he called fewer assemblies and corresponded infrequently with the legislative leaders. The style of his administration reminded the "ploughmen" of Lewis Morris: his appointments violated residency requirements, and he called the legislature to locations other than the regular sites of Perth Amboy or Burlington. Yet the governor, isolated and preoccuped with the college, was oblivious to this gradual estrangement. Meanwhile, relations with the council improved. Robert Morris, appointed governor of Pennsylvania in 1754, no longer threatened Belcher. At the same time, the border dispute with New York challenged the proprietary interests of Morris and Alexander, and they joined the governor to protect the New Jersey claims. In 1756, Belcher nominated Alexander's son William to the council.

Renewed hostilities with the French forced Belcher to confront distasteful assembly politics. In 1754, Virginia Governor Robert Dinwiddie requested a contingent of New Jersey troops to join his defense of the western frontier, and the Board of Trade recommended an intercolonial conference to meet with the Six Nations. Sick in bed, Belcher summoned the assembly to Elizabethtown instead of the regular site at Perth Amboy. To his recommendations the "ploughmen" replied with a list of grievances, including the extraordinary place of meeting. The assembly disposed of the military question by declaring the peril less obvious and the province too poor. Belcher scolded, dissolved the assembly, and called new elections, but he learned once more the ineffectiveness of the tactic. His patriotic appeals brought meager contributions to the war effort. News of General Braddock's defeat in the summer of 1755 and rumors of Indians approaching the Jersey borders spurred Belcher to call for the destruction of French Canada. Instead, the assembly pressed for redress of grievances. Only after a personal address by Lord Loudon, commander of the British forces in North America, did it vote 500 men. Before the campaign concluded, Belcher was stricken with palsy, and he died on August 31, 1757.

Since his death Belcher has fared poorly in the hands of historians. They have dismissed him as a sycophant and narrow-minded puritan, epitomizing the most distasteful elements of his age. Doubtless he was a commonplace citizen of his times, but with a changing appreciation of the eighteenth century, his life requires serious reconsideration. Reevaluation need not exaggerate his importance: his accomplishments in New Jersey, with the exception of the College of New Jersey, were minor. But his career is illuminating, if only because he managed to survive in a political world where the average governor could expect to last a mere five years. In sum, his political life illustrates the dynamics of provincial politics—the limitations on the governor and the importance of both the structure of the imperial patronage system and the homegrown legislative process. His career also reflects religion's importance in politics in colonial America, in terms of alliances and in the definition of public policy.

Jonathan Belcher Letterbooks, Massachusetts Historical Society, Boston, Mass.

Jonathan Belcher Papers, The New Jersey Historical Society, Newark, N.J.

Ferdinand John Paris Papers, The New Jersey Historical Society, Newark, N.J.

Smith Family Papers, Historical Society of Pennsylvania, Philadelphia, Pa.

Pomfret, John E. *Colonial New Jersey: A History.* New York: Scribner's, 1973.

Shipton, Clifford K. "Jonathan Belcher." In Shipton, Clifford K. *Sibley's Harvard Graduates.* Vol. 4. Cambridge, Mass.: Harvard University Press, 1933.

Michael C. Batinski

FRANCIS BERNARD (July? 1712–June 16, 1779) was royal governor of New Jersey for two years, actively directing the prov-

ince's war effort from mid-1758 to mid-1760. The son of the Reverend Francis Bernard and Margery (Winlowe) Bernard, of Brightwell, Oxfordshire, he was baptized on July 12, 1712. He attended St. Peter's College, Westminster, and in 1729 he became a student at Christ Church, Oxford, from which he was graduated in 1736 with a master of arts degree. He then turned his energy and scholarship to the practice of law. In 1741 he married Amelia Offley, whose cousin, the second Lord Barrington, became his sponsor. Besides gaining sufficient legal notice to be elected to offices in Lincoln and Boston, he edited the *Latin Odes* of Anthony Alsop, published in 1752.

This capable and ambitious man, approved as royal governor of New Jersey on January 27, 1758, arrived in Perth Amboy with his wife and four of his children on June 14. The *Pennsylvania Gazette* reported that four other children had remained in England and four had died. In the autumn of 1759 another child was born to the Bernards in New Jersey. John Adams later described Bernard as "avaricious to a most infamous degree; needy, at the same time, and having a numerous family to provide for."

As the governor himself expressed it to his patron, Lord Barrington, almost a year after he arrived in New Jersey, " 'till Nature sets bounds to the Number of my children, (which is not done yet) I know not how to limit my wants or desires." Various reports state that eight or ten children survived him, and it is clear that the large family contributed to his restless wish for a more rewarding position.

In two years of service, Francis Bernard proved an efficient, politic, and considerate administrator. Certainly he was put to the test immediately. He arrived to find a colony with its government in semi-suspension, under pressures from the royal government and the other colonies to contribute increasingly to the war against the French. The colony also suffered from an atmosphere of crisis that had spread from a rash of Indian raids on the Minisink frontier. The previous governor, Jonathan Belcher, had died at the end of August 1757. With great reluctance John Reading, president of the council, though he was 73 years old and somewhat lame, had been persuaded to assume his duties as interim executive. Meanwhile the royal commanders pressed the colonial governments for substantial contributions of men and money for the next campaign against the French in Canada, and in May and June 1758, Indians raiding the region of the Minisink and upper Delaware rivers killed two dozen colonists. Shortly before this, the patrol force had been reduced from 250 to a mere 50 men, an "untimely piece of frugality" that Bernard believed had encouraged the Indians to make their first major attack on New Jersey soil.

Promptly on his arrival the forty-five-year-old governor ordered the council to meet him two days later, on Friday, June 16. At that time Justice Peter Decker and another Sussex County man arrived in Perth Amboy with the scalp of an Indian. Francis Bernard reported to the Board of Trade that "the scalp which was brought to me" was much "adorned with beads & other finery." It seems almost certain that Bernard, who is remembered for giving more conscientious attention to Indian affairs than any other colonial New Jersey governor, saw the scalp before he had seen a living New Jersey Indian. The council proposed a plan for increasing the frontier force with detachments of militia drawn on a rotating basis from different counties. Bernard adopted it immediately so that no group would have to serve long during the harvest.

After writing a lengthy report to London, the governor, accompanied by prominent residents, left Perth Amboy on Wednesday, June 21. The following day he was greeted with congratulatory statements in New Brunswick; at the College of New Jersey (later Princeton University), where he extemporaneously replied in kind to a Latin oration one of the students presented in his honor; and in Trenton, where he inquired further about the frontier situation and sent a message to William Denny, lieutenant governor of Pennsylvania. That evening the procession arrived at Burlington, New Jersey's alternate capital, amid bonfires and bell ringing. Bernard spent Friday, June 23, receiving ceremonious greetings in Burlington. Early the following morning, when he was about to return to Perth Amboy, an urgent response from Denny took him to Philadelphia. He stayed overnight consulting about rumors of Delaware Indian depredations with Denny and General John Forbes, who was preparing his march on Fort Duquesne. On Sunday, June 25, Bernard returned to Bristol and sent messages to the Munsi and Pompton Indians and to Teedyuscung as spokesman of other Delawares, inviting them with proper protocol to a conference in Burlington. On that occasion Bernard would "kindle a Council fire, and bury all the blood, that has stained our ground, deep in the earth, and make a new chain of peace." After spending the night in Trenton, Bernard, complaining about the hot weather, returned to Perth Amboy, where he was met with more rumors of Indian troubles.

The governor maintained an active pace for the rest of the summer of 1758, arranging the first phase of the Indian peace he sought and obtaining from the assembly half the augmentation he had proposed for the frontier defenses. Throughout most of October he was at Easton, attending the general treaty conference, where most Indian and British interests of the central Atlantic region were represented. This, with a purchase of claims from the Munsi and the Pomptons in the north and the establishment of a community for the Unami of central and southern New Jersey in lieu of any outstanding claims, completed his settlement of Indian troubles.

Bernard's effort was successful, and peace was established on the frontier. In February 1759, the Board of Trade responded to the news of the governor's "vigorous Measures" during the summer and fall of 1758 with "Approbation" and "the greatest Satisfaction." A month later, on March 14, the general assembly addressed "the thanks of the Public" to Bernard for his settlement of Indian claims, "tho' almost one of the first Acts of your Government, and against very popular prejudices."

Bernard's other major achievement during his first year in New Jersey was to satisfy the imperial requirement for provincial contribution to the war effort without a confrontation with the popular general assembly. This he managed by persuading the Board of Trade to recommend certain alterations in his instructions concerning bills of credit; on February 10, 1759, the Privy Council approved the revisions. During the spring of 1759 Bernard described his house as "a War-office" and boasted of the excellence of the "Jersey blues," a regiment finally dispatched up the Hudson on May 21— earlier than the previous year, better equipped than ever, all volunteer and "full to a man." The governor complimented himself to Lord Barrington, writing, "I can truly say that I have not lost a day."

Bernard then traveled to inspect the houses being constructed under the Burlington and Easton Treaty agreements for the Lenape of central and south New Jersey. He took great interest in the experimental community and named it "Brotherton." Following up the Indian dealings of 1758 with another meeting at Brotherton, he advanced a proposal (never fulfilled) to establish a provincially controlled trading post in northwest New Jersey, like the post Benjamin Franklin planned for Pennsylvania.

At this time, the governor felt he had accomplished as much as the small stage of New Jersey permitted, and he wrote his sponsor about his desire to resolve the conflicts in Pennsylvania, or in some other, larger, more remunerative governorship. While he enjoyed the "Health & Beauty" of New Jersey and its inhabitants' "favorable Opinion" of him, he wanted larger problems to solve, and larger rewards. As part of a general rearrangement of colonial governors, Bernard was

transferred to Massachusetts in the autumn of 1759, resolving his boredom and satisfying his desire for promotion. He did not move at once, however. The packet ship was delayed three months, and therefore he did not receive the November 14, 1759, letter informing him of the changes until mid-February 1760, and following that he awaited his replacement, Thomas Boone. In April he made a trip to New England to assess the prospects of making and saving money as the governor of Massachusetts. Though he assured his patron that he would leave New Jersey "with regret" and praised "the pleasantness" of Perth Amboy, he complained that it was "wholly secluded from refined conversation & the amusements that arise from letters arts & sciences," and so looked forward to Boston.

Comments after Thomas Boone's arrival and proclamation as governor continued to indicate warm feelings toward Francis Bernard. The officials of Middlesex County, while greeting his successor, referred to Bernard as one "whose inclinations as well as Abilities seemed to be studiously employed in promoting every plausible Scheme for the Welfare and Prosperity of the Province," and Boone replied that he was "too well appriz'd of the disadvantageous Light I must appear in, to aim at a Competition with my deservedly esteemed Predecessor in any Thing but Zeal for his Majesty's Service, and Ardour for the Prosperity of his People."

Bernard's commission as governor of Massachusetts arrived at the beginning of July 1760, but he delayed several more weeks, deciding to "tarry at Perth Amboy" until a warship came to take him. He finally arrived in Boston in appropriate style on August 2.

Though his nine years there began well, they ended on a different note: a mob in New York burned him in effigy in November 1768, and the public in Boston rejoiced when he finally left on August 1, 1769, officially for consultation with the British government. A Massachusetts writer said that Bernard had "a peculiar

knack for making mountains out of mole
hills, and idle chitchat, treason." It is
almost as though the Francis Bernard
who governed Massachusetts shortly
before the Revolution and the well-liked
Bernard who led New Jersey during the
French and Indian War were different
men. Bernard had arrived in New Jersey
at the age of forty-five and had waged
vigorous war on the French and made
peace with the Delawares. At the age of
fifty-seven he returned to England, where
he was knighted for his troubles. During
the remaining ten years of his life he held
some pensions but no positions of authority. He was honored in 1772 with the
degree of doctor of civil law from Oxford
University, and he seems to have lived
mostly in retirement in the country. He
died at Aylesbury on June 16, 1779.

In American history, Francis Bernard is
usually described as the unpopular royal
governor of prerevolutionary Massachusetts, but in New Jersey he should be
remembered as a skillful, energetic, successful and well-liked executive who managed the colony's part in prosecuting the
war with the French. He also maintained
a happy relationship with the legislature
despite potential conflict over money issues, and he avoided partisanship and
entanglement in local politics. Perhaps
most important of all, he was the only
governor of New Jersey in nearly three
centuries to show much concern for the
relationship between native North Americans and Euro-Americans. Bernard took
decisive military measures to improve the
Minisink defenses, but he understood
that the best defense against frontier
raids was a peace founded on an informed
Indian policy that sought to resolve disputes. Other, larger forces made his program more successful than it might have
been in isolation, but it is worth noting
that after his departure the Indians of
New Jersey were again forgotten.

Bernard, Francis. *Select Letters on the Trade
and Government of America*. . . . London: W.
Bowyer and J. Nichols, 1774.

Channing, Edward, and Coolidge, Archibald
Cary, eds. *The Barrington-Bernard Cor-
respondence*. . . . Cambridge, Mass.: Harvard
University Press, 1912.

Higgins, Sophia. *The Bernards of Abington
and Nether Winchendon: A Family History*.
London: Longmans, Green, & Co., 1903.

*The Letters to the Right Honourable the Earl
of Hillsborough from Governor Bernard, General Gage, and the Honourable His Majesty's
Council for the Province of Massachusetts-
Bay*. Boston: Edes and Gill, 1769.

Edward McM. Larrabee

THOMAS BOONE (c. 1730–1812) was one of
many colonial governors who suddenly
burst into the public arena only to fade
quickly into historical oblivion. Like most
men appointed to governorships solely
through patronage, Boone was virtually
assured by administrative inexperience
and political naivete of a brief—and
stormy—gubernatorial career.

He was born to Charles and Elizabeth
(Garth) Boone at Lee Place in Kent,
England, in either 1730 or 1731 (he graduated from college in March 1746 at age
fifteen). His was a prominent family—the
Boones of Devonshire—which not only
enjoyed great wealth and social position
but also exercised considerable political
influence. There had almost always been
a Boone in Westminster since his great-
grandfather, Thomas Boone, sat as a
member of Parliament from 1646 to 1656.
His father was the M.P. for Ludgershall
(1727–34) and a director of both the East
India Company and the Bank of England.
His half-brother Daniel served in Parliament for twenty years (1741–61), and
his brother Charles, Jr., for almost forty
(1757–96). Other members of the family
accumulated fortunes as merchants and
shippers.

Boone received a traditional gentleman's education at Eton and at Trinity

College, Cambridge. At some un-
determined time he inherited from his
cousin, Margaret Colleton, a 2,000-acre
rice and livestock plantation in South
Carolina known as Mepshoo. In 1751,
soon after his twenty-first birthday, he
journeyed to South Carolina to take over
another inheritance, "Boone's Barony," a
6,815-acre estate of three rice plantations
on the Pon-Pon River, bequeathed to him
and his brother Charles by the widow of
their uncle Joseph Boone. He returned to
England two years later, but in 1758 again
sailed for Carolina to establish permanent
residence.

Thomas Boone's life as a country gentleman abruptly ended late in 1759. On
November 14 the Board of Trade recommended his appointment to succeed
Francis Bernard as governor of New Jersey, and George III approved thirteen
days later. The announcement surprised
politicians on either side of the Atlantic—
and perhaps Boone himself—because he
had previously neither held any government post nor been active in politics.

The appointment undoubtedly
stemmed from family connections in British political circles. In addition to having
two brothers in Parliament, Boone was
closely related to the influential Garth and
Colleton clans. His uncle, John Garth
(M.P. from Devizes, 1740–64), and his
cousin, James Edward Colleton (M.P. for
Lostwithiel, 1747–68), were staunch allies
of the powerful prime minister, the duke
of Newcastle. (In part because of an obligation to John Garth, Boone in 1762
appointed Garth's son, Charles, to the
post of colonial agent for South Carolina.)

Such an unusual elevation of a political
novice, coupled with the interests of the
parties involved, suggests that the New
Jersey assignment was intended as a prelude to advancement to the more prestigious and lucrative South Carolina governorship. Boone had no association with
New Jersey, but was well placed in Carolina society. His uncle Joseph, who had
established the American branch of the
family in South Carolina in 1694 at the
age of seventeen, had become a wealthy

planter and a prominent member of the
antiproprietary faction, providing his
nephew with important social and political connections. Through his mother he
was related to Sir John Colleton, one of
the original founders of the colony, whose
numerous descendants were also prominent. With his pedigree, his education,
and his ties in London and Charleston, he
was an ideal candidate for the position.
Although there is no evidence that Boone
actively sought the Carolina governorship, his transfer at the first opportunity, after less than a year in New
Jersey, was probably both anticipated
and welcomed.

Whatever the circumstances of his appointment, Thomas Boone took over the
New Jersey government amid frustrating
delays, which foreshadowed the course of
his administration. Though he received
offical notification of his appointment in
mid-February 1760, he remained in
Charleston until the end of March awaiting his instructions (dated January 14)
and commission (dated February 13). On
arriving in New York City in early April,
he learned that his credentials were still
in transit, and he did not receive them
until early July. He hastened to Perth
Amboy and took the oath of the chief
executive on July 4, some eight months
after his appointment. Then, at the request of some assemblymen, he postponed calling the legislature; he therefore
did not meet with the general assembly
until October 30, almost a year after
being named governor. On April 14, 1761,
less than six months after first meeting
with the assembly, he was named governor of South Carolina.

New to both government service and
the province of New Jersey, Boone made
"caution" and "prudence" the watch-
words of his administration. He consistently declined to take positions on
controversial issues such as the border
dispute between New York and New Jersey and the struggle between Robert
Hunter Morris and Nathaniel Jones for
the chief justiceship. And, while firm in
support of royal prerogatives and imperial

regulations, he refused to challenge provincial political leaders and interests directly. Consequently, his meetings with the assembly were amicable as well as productive, and no serious partisan contentions troubled New Jersey politics during his tenure. Although his term was generally uneventful, several personal achievements serve as standards with which to evaluate his administration.

His first meeting with the assembly, the twenty-first session of the nineteenth assembly, was especially noteworthy. Between October 29 and December 5—the longest legislative session in nine years— the assembly enacted largely routine legislation. But mainly through Boone's efforts, the session produced two long-sought-after laws, one providing for the preservation of public records and one regulating the maintenance of roads and bridges. These were no mean accomplishments for a novice governor, but Boone did more: he secured the first two-year government appropriations bill since 1749 and the allocation of a salary for the chief justice without the traditional prior naming of the recipient, which was being delayed by the Morris-Jones controversy. And at the close of the session Boone agreed to the legislators' request for a general election, the first opportunity for Jerseymen to elect representatives in seven years.

The twentieth assembly, which convened on March 27, 1761, proved more troublesome for Boone. The problem was money. The assembly resisted the governor's request for additional tax revenue; it also balked at filling the quota of 666 soldiers requisitioned by General Jeffrey Amherst, commander in chief of the British army in North America, for the final campaign of the Seven Years' War against the French and Indians. After considerable lobbying, Boone increased the assembly's contribution on both scores—a fact he boastfully reported to the Board of Trade.

Just as Boone was beginning to become settled in the New Jersey government, his superiors in London decided to transfer him. Acting on a March 17 recommendation from the Board of Trade, the king on April 14 named Boone governor of South Carolina and Josiah Hardy his replacement in New Jersey.

From April through October Boone served as a lame-duck governor, transacting no major public business, content to preside perfunctorily while awaiting Hardy's arrival. Those long months demonstrated Boone's devotion to duty. Although authorized to return to England to take care of private business before assuming the South Carolina government, he remained in New Jersey "to deliver this Government to my Successor in its Present State of Harmony." Hardy arrived on October 29; after seeing him properly installed in office, Boone settled his personal affairs and sailed for Charleston on December 3.

Too brief to have a measurable impact on New Jersey political affairs, Boone's tenure was long enough to reveal his essential qualities as governor. As chief magistrate he exhibited a reserved manner and an accommodating style of politics. But he could be forceful if necessary, as when he suspended Edward Antill from the legislative council for nonattendance or insisted that the assembly increase its troop levy. A genuine concern about the public welfare is evident in his legislative proposals, his relinquishing a share of a forfeiture to facilitate the condemnation of a smuggling vessel, and his declining leave to remain at the head of government until the transfer of governors.

Above all he was a dedicated civil servant who placed the strict performance of duty above personal and partisan interest. The farewell address delivered to him by the Corporation of Perth Amboy succinctly explains the wide popularity and esteem he enjoyed among Jerseymen: "No selfish or lucrative schemes have appeared in your conduct, or sullied your administration; on the contrary, all your measures have been dictated by generous and benevolent principles, and your Excellency in public life has maintained that good character you so justly and universally acquired in private." In short, Boone was a popular and relatively successful governor in New Jersey because of his genial disposition and reputation for honesty rather than his political acumen and administrative ability.

Ironically, Boone's unflagging adherence to principle and his political impartiality eventually destroyed his gubernatorial career. Upon taking the New Jersey governorship, he pledged that he would "glory in exercising the utmost Impartiality." Many New Jersey politicos, however, considered "impartiality" naive instead of virtuous. That certainly was the opinion of Charles Read, leader of the council and longtime power behind governors, who was unable to deal with Boone on "intimate and friendly terms." In March 1761 a government officer scrawled in Latin on a wall in Perth Amboy, "Long live & flourish the celebrated Boone, who hath neither Generosity, Liberality nor Equity." Aaron Leaming, veteran assemblyman from Cape May, thought the doggerel gave Boone "a very wrong Character." To Leaming, Boone was "a wise knowing Just Governor who had no prime minister & that was the reason the Jersey Courtiers did not Love him."

Boone's political epitaph had been prophesied by the Legislative Council of New Jersey when, in welcoming him as governor, it had noted that he was a novice in politics—"a Stranger to the low Views and little Arts." Even had Boone remained in New Jersey, where politics were diffuse and local, his zealousness, inflexibility, and determination to reside as "a governor without a prime minister" would eventually have transformed the political skirmishes that appeared in the spring of 1761 into full-scale partisan conflicts. That Thomas Boone simply was not a politician would be quickly demonstrated by his stormy tenure in South Carolina.

Despite family ties and a salary nearly double what he had received in New Jersey, Boone took the South Carolina

governorship with some trepidation. In addition to persistent warfare with the Cherokee on the frontier, there was an increasingly bitter conflict between the popularly elected Commons House of Assembly and the royally appointed council. Partly because of the political climate, Thomas Pownall, who in 1760 had been named to succeed William Henry Lyttleton as governor, had refused to take the office; for two years Lieutenant Governor William Bull II had served as acting governor.

Boone's apprehensions proved correct, for he became embroiled in controversy almost immediately after his arrival in South Carolina on December 22, 1761. He was less a victim of partisan machinations than of his own political ineptness. In sharp contrast to his behavior in New Jersey, Boone quickly asserted his authority in Carolina. Because he was a "clumsy tactician," his zealous defense of crown prerogatives and his inflexibility on major issues compounded routine problems and created unnecessary political strife.

He antagonized many of the interested parties in several matters connected with the French and Indian War, and he became embroiled in a territorial controversy with the governor of Georgia and the Board of Trade. More damaging were his efforts to reduce the authority of the Commons House of Assembly by refusing the house certain traditional prerogatives. Though technically correct, he was flying in the face of established practice, and therefore he appeared to be infringing on the rights and privileges of the assembly. When in September 176 he voided the election of Assemblyman Christopher Gadsden on a minor technicality, challenging the constitutional right of the assembly to determine the validity of legislative elections, the dispute came to a head. The controversy brought public business to a halt for eighteen months, because the assembly refused to heed the governor's summonse to hold sessions. Boone sailed for England on May 11, 1764, to present the case to the Board of Trade. On July 16 the board announced its verdict: while criticizing the commons house for refusing to conduct business, it condemned Boone for handling the matter "with more Zeal than prudence" and with "a degree of Passion and Resentment inconsistent with good Policy, and unsuitable to the dignity of his Situation"; he was guilty of "Conduct highly deserving his Majestys Royal displeasure."

Realizing that this formal censure would prevent him from serving effectively as governor, Thomas Boone never returned to South Carolina. William Bull once again became acting governor, and in 1766 Lord Charles Greville Montagu was named to replace Boone. Within the brief span of four years a gubernatorial career which had begun with promise in New Jersey ended in ignominy in South Carolina.

Little is known about Thomas Boone after his return to England. He married a wealthy widow, Sarah Ann Tattnall Peronneau, but the date of the marriage is unknown; the evidence suggests that he began courting her shortly after becoming governor of South Carolina, that she accompanied him to England in 1764, and that they were finally married in 1771. He lobbied for repeal of the Stamp Act and successfully petitioned for the payment of £1,250 in salary the commons house had withheld. On December 5, 1769, he again entered government service, this time as a customs commissioner with an annual salary of £1,000. Because of his American ties, he served with William Bull as corepresentative for South Carolina on the Board of Loyalist Agents, which sought compensation for refugees in England after the Revolution. His South Carolina property was confiscated in 1782; he claimed £41,207.4.4 in compensation from the British government, but was granted only £22,533.8.0. In September 1805 he retired from the customs service and removed to the seclusion of his ancestral home, Lee Place in Kent. His wife died in April 1812; he died five months later, on September 25, 1812.

Namier, Lewis. "Charles Garth and His Connexions." *English Historical Review* 54 (July 1939): 443–70.

Larry R. Gerlach

JOSIAH HARDY (1715?–90) is one of New Jersey's most obscure governors. No information survives about his early life, his education, or his primary means of livelihood. He was born into a distinguished English family, which became even more prominent as Josiah reached adulthood. His father, Sir Charles Hardy (1680?–1744), worked his way through the highest ranks in the royal navy, earning peerage status and eventually becoming a vice-admiral as well as a lord commissioner of the admiralty. Sir Charles and his wife, Elizabeth Burchett, had six children, among them Josiah, the eldest son, and Sir Charles (1716?–80), who for a brief time in the 1750s, during an interlude in a distinguished naval career, served as royal governor of New York.

Family connections may have been a factor in Hardy's appointment to the New Jersey governorship. Whatever the source of influence, the Privy Council approved the Board of Trade's March 1761 recommendation that Hardy "be appointed Captain General and Governor in Chief of His Majesty's Province of New Jersey in the room of Thomas Boone Esq." Crossing the Atlantic Ocean on a ship that also carried William Alexander, better known as the aspirant to the title of earl of Stirling, Hardy and his family arrived in New York during late October 1761. The family then traveled to Perth Amboy, where Hardy published his commission. The New Jersey citizenry, although it had been spun around on a whirligig of changing governors of late, seemed pleased with the Hardys. The governor gained a reputation for promptness, attentiveness, and openness.

Knowing very little about New Jersey, Hardy willingly listened to ideas and suggestions about proper provincial administration. The only problem was that he too willingly took the advice of a small, powerful group of men who were both gubernatorial councilors and East Jersey proprietors. These men, including William Alexander and Robert Hunter Morris, wanted a pliable head of state who would support their personal interests, which involved their high provincial offices and their proprietary land claims (less well-placed citizens were still challenging East Jersey proprietary rights, sometimes through rioting). Indeed, Hardy's Atlantic crossing with Alexander may have been fatal in terms of his governorship.

Throughout his term, Hardy listened attentively to the East Jersey proprietary group, especially when making appointments to important offices. As the new governor stated in July 1762, he could not find "Persons from the Western division" who were "properly qualify'd for so important a trust" as serving on the council. Even though his instructions called for balanced council representation between eastern and western leaders, all of his nominees were men with close ties to the East Jersey group. In listening to the Morris-Alexander coterie, indeed favoring them, the new governor made one unredeemable mistake. In December 1761, he accepted "the unanimous advice of His Majesty's Council" and "renew'd the Chief Justice Robert Hunter Morris and the second and third Judges Commission" with tenure during good behavior. The East Jersey proprietary group controlled attendance at that meeting.

Hardy's instructions specifically forbade any "good-behavior" appointments. Office-holding tenure was to be limited to the "King's pleasure," even though a number of high-level provincial judges in various provinces had been appointed with good-behavior terms in previous years. The latter type of commission had become standard in England after the Glorious Revolution of 1688–89, during which time parliamentary leaders constrained crown prerogatives in general and guaranteed in particular that judges would be independent of willful monarchs. Englishmen considered good-behavior commissions to be one hallmark of the preservation of political rights and liberties because judges dependent on the crown for continuation in office could always be corrupted in judicial decision making. Despite what had become well-established English practice, home government leaders were not content with the de facto extension of the same prerogative to the colonies, particularly because some good-behavior judges had been contentious and obstinate with royal officials in America, yet virtually unremovable from office.

In this context Hardy compounded his blunder by reappointing Robert Hunter Morris, who had become an extremely obnoxious figure to Board of Trade officials during a protracted controversy over who was the legitimate New Jersey chief justice. In violating his written instructions and offering Morris a good-behavior commission, Hardy convinced the Board of Trade that he was too weak to control special provincial interests while upholding crown prerogatives and imperial policies.

Equally significant, the perceived willfulness of men like Morris was symptomatic and symbolic to crown officials; home government leaders more and more were becoming persuaded that there must be a new assertion, a tightening, of imperial authority over the American colonies. The Seven Years' War (called the French and Indian War in the provinces) so consumed leaders in England that it delayed the thrust, but it further primed British officials for the clamping-down process. During the Seven Years' War, for instance, home ministers were particularly appalled by the extensive amount of illegal provincial trade being conducted with the French enemy. In late 1761 the war was nearing its end; if there were to be effective steps toward greater imperial control, then men like Hardy (those who would countenance, even succumb to local pressures) had to be taught that crown prerogatives could not be compromised, even if they had been compromised in the past. The decision to remove Hardy was an early indicator of the move toward tighter imperial administration, part of a pattern that would become much clearer after hostilities ended in 1763.

Hardy sent letters to England in January 1762 explaining why he had violated his instructions. He thought a delay in reappointing the judges would "occasion great inconveniences and be attended with consequences that might prove very prejudicial in carrying on his Majesty's Service, and likewise much disturb the publick peace." He asked for further advice. At the same time the Privy Council was sending out a new general instruction reminding all governors that they were "to take particular care in all Commissions . . . granted to the said Chief Judges or other Justices . . . that the said Commissions are granted during Pleasure only, agreeable to what has been the Ancient Practice and Usage in our said Colonies."

The Privy Council's rationale was both bold and specious. Rather than just admit that Americans, as subordinate members of the empire, were not to have the same rights and privileges as home citizens, the council justified itself by arguing that there were not enough qualified provincial citizens who could hold high judicial office. The low quality of American judges, they claimed, proved that. Thus removal at the crown's pleasure would be necessary until more suitable, well-educated citizens became available as the colonies continued to grow and develop. In reality an independent American judiciary was a threat to royal prerogatives; it could seriously hinder programs for bringing provincials more in line with imperial goals.

Governor Hardy could find no way to placate his superiors. As soon as he received the general instruction, he persuaded Morris and the other judges to take "during-pleasure" commissions. But the Board of Trade was already acting; it recommended in March 1762 that Hardy be removed from office for "so premeditated and unprecedented an Act of disobedience" and "as a necessary example to deter others in the same situation from like Acts of Disobedience to your Majesty's . . . just Rights and Authority in the Colonies." Following through, the Privy Council, in August 1762, moved to appoint William Franklin in Hardy's stead. A month later a formal letter went to Hardy advising him of his dismissal.

Josiah Hardy was an early victim of what developed into a major new assertion of imperial authority. That assertion eventually would become a primary factor in precipitating the American Revolution. For Hardy in 1762 it meant that he would never have the opportunity to prove his capabilities, although the sources reveal good working relations with the assembly and consistent efforts to deal with such vexing issues as persuading New Jerseyans to fill their manpower quotas during the war.

Once he had learned his fate, Hardy wrote futilely that he could not comprehend "what the objections to my conduct are . . . as I never had the honour to see the Boards representation so could have no opportunity of offering any thing in my own justification; however I humbly submit to His Majesty's Commands, but I can with the greatest truth affirm that every step I have taken in the administration of this Government . . . has been to promote His Majesty's Service and the welfare of the people committed to my care." He graciously turned the government over to William Franklin when the two met in New Brunswick late in February 1763. Accepting official provincial statements of praise for his "just and mild administration," Hardy sailed with his family for England in September 1763. His controlled acquiescence in dismissal no doubt helped him gain another office, that of consul to Cadiz. Beyond that nothing is known about Josiah Hardy, a man caught for a moment in countervailing forces that were setting the stage for the American Revolution.

Fisher, Edgar Jacob. *New Jersey as a Royal Province, 1738 to 1776*. New York: Columbia University, 1911.

Kemmerer, Donald L. *Path to Freedom: The Struggle for Self-Government in Colonial New Jersey, 1703-1776*. Princeton: Princeton University Press, 1940.

Nadelhaft, J. R. "Politics and the Judicial Tenure Fight in Colonial New Jersey." *William and Mary Quarterly* 28 (January 1971): 46-63.

James Kirby Martin

WILLIAM FRANKLIN (1730?–November 16, 1813) was the last royal governor of New Jersey. An able servant of both the colony and the crown during the tumultuous years 1763–76, he ranks as the best of New Jersey's colonial governors and one of the finest chief executives in the history of the state.

William was born in Philadelphia in late 1730 or early 1731 to Benjamin Franklin and an unidentified Pennsylvania woman; it is unlikely that Deborah Read Rogers, whom Benjamin took as a common-law wife on September 1, 1730, was his natural mother. The cloud of an illegitimate birth and the shadow of a father who was a living legend threatened to eclipse William throughout his life.

William spent the years of his childhood and youth in considerable pain as well as great joy. He was constantly confronted by his bastard status and the hostility of Deborah Franklin, who openly favored her own children, Francis Folger (1732–36) and Sarah (1742–1808). But America's largest city held countless fascinations for a young boy, and there was never a dull moment in the print shop and retail store that occupied the ground floor of the Franklin home. Father and son were especially close. Young "Billy," as he was called by the family, grew up helping Benjamin operate the printing presses, and stock and sell merchandise. He also listened to conversations between his father and the parade of callers at the house, and assisted Benjamin with a variety of scientific experiments.

William advanced toward adulthood under the careful supervision of "Poor Richard." After a brief stint during King George's War (1740–48) as an ensign in a Pennsylvania company sent to Albany in 1746 to fight the French, and a trip to the Ohio country in 1748 as an assistant to the Indian trader Conrad Weiser, he settled down in Philadelphia with no higher interests than parties and women. But the elder Franklin was determined to pass on to his firstborn more than an interest in science and land speculation. Through Benjamin's influence William became clerk of the Pennsylvania assembly (1751), postmaster of Philadelphia (1753), and comptroller of the postal system in the northern colonies (1754). Both men joined the Masonic order and later shared involvement in several unsuccessful land speculation schemes in western New York and the Ohio country, particularly the Vandalia Company, which claimed over one million acres in "Indiana." In the early stages of the French and Indian War (1754–63) William assisted Benjamin in outfitting General Edward Braddock's abortive campaign against the French (1755) and organizing the colony's military defenses (1756). He also began to study law with his father's associate, Joseph Galloway. And he accompanied Benjamin to England in 1757 as representative of the Pennsylvania assembly in its dispute with the Penn family over the taxation of proprietary lands.

William stayed in England for six years, where he not only participated in the negotiations with the Penns and the crown but also received further legal training at the Middle Temple (1757). Admitted to the bar as a practicing attorney in 1758, he also became acquainted with Benjamin's circle of prominent scientists and politicians, toured Britain and Western Europe, and received an honorary master of arts degree from Oxford (1762). There, too, occurred three of the most important events in his life. Some time in 1760 he sired an illegitimate son, William Temple, whose mother's identity is unknown. On September 4, 1762, he married Elizabeth Downes, a London socialite with important West Indian family connections. Five days later he was sworn in as the new governor of New Jersey.

The unexpected selection of William Franklin to succeed Josiah Hardy as the head of the New Jersey government created a stir in both Britain and America. Some doubted his fitness for the post since he had had no previous executive experience; others were disturbed by his reputation as a playboy and by his illegitimacy; and all, including William himself, knew that he owed the position solely to Benjamin's influence with the ministry in London. On the other hand the appointment was not unreasonable. William had acquired some legislative experience in Pennsylvania and had witnessed firsthand the operations of provincial and imperial government. Moreover he was knowledgeable about military affairs and partisan politics; had influential friends on both sides of the Atlantic; and was familiar with the conditions and problems of the middle colonies. On balance, he was better qualified for the office than most men named to colonial governorships.

Upon arriving in New Jersey in February 1763 William proved his detractors wrong. From his initial introductory tour of the province until the outbreak of the Revolution in 1775, he was a strong, effective, and enormously popular chief executive. He moved easily and comfortably in New Jersey social circles, promoted economic programs designed to increase the prosperity of the province, served as an advocate for provincial interests with superiors in London, and defended the colony and its legislature against what he considered to be unwise policies and unwarranted criticisms from imperial authorities. A determined spokesman for the people of New Jersey, he was also a dedicated representative of the crown who sought to carry out the instructions of the king and Parliament as well as the duties of his office with diligence, dignity and dispatch. Commanding a nearly universal respect for his administrative abilities and possessing a keen political sense, he was able to exercise firm control of the provincial government; he was, perhaps, the single most influential political figure to emerge in colonial New Jersey. Although at times his arrogance, fiery temper, and stubborness needlessly complicated relations with the assembly, Franklin enjoyed a degree of popularity and success during his long term matched by few, if any, of the other royal governors in North America.

Like his counterparts in the other seven crown colonies, Franklin faced the difficult task of attempting to reconcile the sometimes conflicting expectations and demands of the mother country and the province. In general he performed to the satisfaction of both constituencies, primarily because of the unstructured nature of New Jersey politics and his adept avoidance of the taint of corruption and partisanship that undermined the credibility of many governors. However, the new administrative programs for America instituted by Parliament after the conclusion of the French and Indian War in 1763 ultimately destroyed the First British Empire as well as the political career of William Franklin.

The Stamp Act crisis of 1765–66 taught Franklin the political lessons that would guide his conduct during the remainder of the prerevolutionary decade. While doubting the wisdom of Britain's attempt to raise American revenue by imposing taxes on a variety of colonial publications and legal documents, he granted Parliament's authority to do so and thus strove to implement the statute. Since Jerseymen had not actively opposed earlier attempts to tighten imperial control, such as the Currency and Sugar acts of 1764 and various revisions in the customs service, the fury of the protest against the Stamp Act caught Franklin by surprise. Protests by legal and extralegal organizations, economic sanctions, civil disobedience, and threats of popular violence thwarted his efforts to enforce the measure. Realizing the impossibility of the task, he was content to ignore the statute and await its eventual repeal. Never again would the governor underestimate the determination of Jerseymen to oppose what they deemed unconstitutional actions and unwarranted encroachments into provincial affairs by imperial authorities, the impact of events occurring in other colonies (especially New York and Pennsylvania) on events in New Jersey, or the difficulty of upholding unpopular imperial policies without firm support from London or adequate military power in the province.

As Anglo-American relations deteriorated, Franklin's political influence in New Jersey diminished. He remained a firm defender of royal authority, but increasingly found himself in sympathy with the colonial position and dubious of the ability of politicians in England to devise effective programs for America. Thus he championed the much-needed currency legislation the legislature enacted despite its repeated disallowance by the British Privy Council, criticized the enactment of the import taxes known as the Townshend duties, and refrained from taking public steps to counter the popular protest against the Townshend Acts (1767), the Tea Act (1773), or the Coercive Acts (1774). Consequently, some imperial officials began to question his performance as governor, and there were periodic rumors of his dismissal. At the same time he came under increased attack from the New Jersey Assembly, aimed not so much at the man as at his position as chief representative of the crown. From 1766 to 1770 annual battles over appropriations to supply royal troops stationed in the colony, periodic disagreements over the prerogatives of the executive and legislative branches of government, and a bitter dispute over the appointment of the provincial treasurers greatly diminished his once pervasive power.

When Britons and Americans took to the battlefield to resolve their disagreements in the aftermath of Lexington and Concord, William Franklin, like all Americans, faced a crucial decision. Yet the allegiance of the native-born American was never in doubt. His years in the governor's mansion had convinced him that under no circumstances could a civil society tolerate disrespect for government and disregard of laws. By temperament and inclination he found himself committed to the established order and the social elite; to his mind the protest-independence movement was the work of a willful minority of malcontents and radicals who did not enjoy the support of the populace at large. Perhaps, too, he rejected the rebellion in a subconscious attempt to establish personal independence from his father, who dreamed of a sovereign American empire. The relationship between the two men had cooled considerably after Benjamin Franklin left in 1764 for an eleven-year stay in England; the growing rebellion drove them further apart; and after a heated argument in November 1775 they went their separate political ways, not to meet again until after the revolutionary war. Whatever his motivation, William Franklin would not betray the trust given him by his king and country.

Where other royal governors had gone into exile or had ceased to discharge their duties by the fall of 1775, William Franklin worked actively to stem the tide of revolution. He convened the general assembly in November and, capitalizing on the moderation of New Jersey and his still potent power of persuasion, obtained assembly resolutions disavowing independence and calling for reconciliation with Great Britain. Knowing that the rebels were inspecting the mails, he nonetheless sent a steady stream of intelligence to London concerning the development of the rebellion. On January 8, 1776, after one such dispatch fell into the hands of the rebel colonel William Alexander (Lord Stirling), the governor found his Perth Amboy home surrounded by an armed detachment of militia. On the tenth he was taken into custody, but he was released the same day when cooler heads prevailed. Thereafter he remained in seclusion, but maintained correspondence with superiors in England. He boldly issued a call on May 30 for the legislature to convene the following month, and on June 15 the Provincial Congress ordered his arrest. Refusing to accept an offer of parole, he was haled before the rebel conclave on June 21, and, at the direction of the Continental Congress, was sent under guard to Connecticut on June 26.

The former royal governor of New Jersey, now a prisoner of the independent United States, arrived in Lebanon, Connecticut, on July 4. After signing a parole tendered by the rebel governor Jonathan Trumbull, he was sent first to Wallingford, then to East Windsor, and finally in October to Middletown. He was permitted freedom of movement and correspondence so long as he did not leave town or do anything to hamper the American cause. In April he was imprisoned in the Litchfield town jail for issuing pardons to Connecticut and New Jersey Loyalists in violation of his parole. There he chafed at the close confinement and grew bitter as he tallied the price of his loyalty. He became despondent on learning of his wife's death on July 28, and deeply resented the fact that his father (who had been more of a father than grandfather to Temple) had taken his son to France. His depression eased and his health improved measurably when in December, Governor Trumbull permitted his transfer to a private residence in East Windsor; his spirits soared when, in October 1778, he was exchanged for John McKinley, the former president of Delaware.

William Franklin entered British-occupied New York City on October 31, bent upon seeking revenge. For the next four years he devoted his time and energy to suppressing the rebellion. He enlisted propagandists to write on behalf of the crown, aided Captain John André in the intelligence operations of the Secret Service, organized in December 1778 the "Refugee Club" (which conducted unofficial military raids and intelligence operations in Connecticut and New Jersey), devised a plan for the military defense of the city (1780), was a member of the civilian advisory council created by the military in 1779, and served on the Council to the Commissioners for Restoring Peace, established in 1780. In January 1781, when he was named president of the board of directors of the Associated Loyalists, he became responsible for directing destructive raids against the state of New Jersey. He once again became disconsolate as the war wound to an end after the American victory over Cornwallis at Yorktown in September 1781; on September 18, 1782, twenty years to the month after his appointment as the governor of New Jersey, William Franklin sailed for England.

Franklin spent the remainder of his life a lonely exile in a foreign land. During the first seven years he testified on behalf of numerous Loyalist refugees in their efforts to receive compensation from the British government for losses sustained because of the Revolution; he himself received in March 1788 an annual pension of £800 and a meager award of £1,800 for the £48,245.4.4 he claimed in lost property and income. But he never received a position in government or attained the place in society that he had known before the Revolution.

Although his public career had ended, the personal tragedies that marred his private life continued. He initiated contact with his father in 1784, hoping to heal old wounds, but when the two men met a year later for the last time, Benjamin was interested only in arranging for Temple to acquire William's lands in America for a paltry sum. In 1790, having vindictively written William out of his will, Benjamin carried his bitterness toward his son to the grave. William finally got the chance to come to know his own son when Temple came to England in 1792, but relations between them were so strained that Temple left angrily for Paris in 1798. They never saw each other again. Even William's blissful marriage to Mary D'Evelin in 1788 ended in sorrow; she became ill in 1808, was bedridden in 1810, and then lapsed into insanity before her death in 1811. The only lasting bright spot in William's life in exile was Temple's daughter Ellen Franklin, born out of wedlock in 1798 to Mary's sister-in-law, Ellen. William raised the child as if she were his own daughter, and she in turn loved and cared for him until his death on November 13, 1813.

Fennelly, Catherine. "William Franklin of New Jersey." *William and Mary Quarterly* 6 (1949): 361–82.

Gerlach, Larry R. *Prologue to Independence: New Jersey in the Coming of the American Revolution.* New Brunswick: Rutgers University Press, 1975.

———. *William Franklin: New Jersey's Last Royal Governor.* Trenton: New Jersey Historical Commission, 1975.

Mariboe, William H. "The Life of William Franklin, 1730(31)–1813: *Pro Rege et Patria.*" Ph.D. dissertation, University of Pennsylvania, 1962.

Whitehead, William A. "Biographical Sketch of William Franklin, Governor of New Jersey from 1763 to 1776." *Proceedings of the New Jersey Historical Society* 3 (1848): 137–59.

Larry R. Gerlach

The Constitution of 1776

WILLIAM LIVINGSTON (November 1723–July 25, 1790) was a son of Philip Livingston, second lord of Livingston Manor in the colony of New York, and Catrina Van Brugh. William spent his childhood in Albany. He graduated from Yale College in 1741 and began to study law under the supervision of James Alexander and William Smith, Sr. Although he was a Presbyterian, in 1747 William married Susannah French of New Brunswick at the Dutch church in Acquackanonk. Their marriage produced thirteen children, several of whom died young.

A man of broad intellectual interests, William Livingston not only learned the intricacies of the law but also grounded himself thoroughly in the arts, philosophy, and American education. As a member of the powerful Livingston family he was able to use his natural talent and his kinship with New York's elite to assume a major role in the cultural and social life of the colony.

By 1770 William Livingston had made an imprint on the politics of New York, partly because of his writings in the political and religious controversy over the role of the Anglican church in America. Livingston was a polemicist best known for his pungent prose in the *Independent Reflector* and in such essays as "Primitive Whig" and "Watch Tower." In politics he usually functioned as a manager; he became titular leader of a trio that also included John Morin Scott and William Smith, Jr., in protracted battles with the De Lancey family and its lieutenants. From 1758 to 1768 the "New York Triumvirate" controlled the New York Assembly.

On April 13, 1772, Livingston severed his ties with the province of New York and moved to Elizabethtown, New Jersey. His reasons for removing to New Jersey and withdrawing from the New York political scene are not fully known, but he had often stated his desire to enjoy a "solitary and philosophic retreat" eventually. The growing competition among New York lawyers and the economic dislocations caused by Anglo-American frictions cut into Livingston's legal practice. Whatever the reason, he decided to devote himself to the quiet enjoyment of his family, friends, and books at Elizabethtown.

The relocation of the Livingston family proceeded gradually. Formerly he had spent a good deal of time in Elizabethtown attending court, inspecting his crops, and dealing with local merchants and craftsmen. His home, Liberty Hall, modeled after the mansions of several of his former New York City associates, was completed by April 1774.

Livingston's reputation for articulate leadership and his connection with many powerful and wealthy New Jersey families assured that he would not fall into obscurity. Livingston may have gained a temporary life of rural contentment, but he did not retreat to obscurity when he moved to New Jersey. His interest in Presbyterianism was recognized when he was appointed a trustee of the College of New Jersey in 1768 and when the student newspaper, the *American Whig,* was named in his honor.

The dumping of tea in Boston harbor and the passage of the Intolerable Acts provided the impetus to launch Livingston into a position of political leadership in New Jersey. The sympathy for the liberties of American colonials that he had expressed over the previous decade makes it reasonable to assume that he gave passive, rather than reluctant support to American resistance. In June 1774 the people of Elizabethtown called on Livingston to articulate their grievances at county and provincial committee meetings. He was selected as a delegate to the First Continental Congress in Philadelphia, where he was involved chiefly in committee work, and he expressed few personal views in the debate over the appropriate response to British oppression. However, he cemented working relationships and political bonds with fellow delegates and with New Jersey's key revolutionary figures in the Provincial Congress and the new Continental army. Reelected to the Second Continental Congress, Livingston took his seat in May 1775, but early in June 1776 he left the Congress to assume his responsibilities as brigadier general of the New Jersey militia—before he could sign the Declaration of Independence.

With his headquarters at Elizabethtown, Livingston commanded all militia stationed in North Jersey, from Bergen south to Amboy. When ten thousand British and Hessian soldiers landed on Staten Island on July 2, confusion and chaos set in. Inadequate field supplies, a shortage of arms and ammunition, and insufficient cash to meet these needs increased the problem of New Jersey's defense and sorely tested Livingston's leadership. Although he professed discomfort in the field and lack of military experience, his unending activity to maintain a degree of military effectiveness indicated that he was beginning to master his complex responsibilities. He was also beginning to grasp the need for the kinds of coordination and communication he would use with skill in the future.

Livingston's appointment as governor on August 31 by the joint meeting of the two houses of the legislature opened a new and radically different phase in his career. Accorded little power by the state constitution of July 2, 1776, the governorship might well have deteriorated to the status of a benign figurehead handling routine matters. Despite his efforts to seize the initiative and to achieve limited, attainable goals, such as enabling legislation to improve the militia's pay and provisioning, his pleas were heard only politely and acted on rarely.

In the midst of the military crisis when the state was invaded in the fall of 1776, Livingston first grasped the latent power of his designation as commander in chief of the state militia. He began to move on his own to coordinate the defense of New Jersey. Thus he filled both an executive and military void, but his efforts could not halt the British and Hessian advance through Newark, Elizabethtown, New Brunswick, and Princeton. Confusion, panic, destruction, military atrocities and anarchy accompanied the assault. Livingston himself disappeared from the scene from mid-December 1776 to mid-January 1777. Despite the military successes at Trenton and Princeton, the civil establishment was so badly disrupted in December 1776 that New Jersey's state and local governments had to be totally reconstructed only months after their initial establishment. When Livingston met with the New Jersey Legislature in late January 1777, the most urgent items on the agenda included a revival of the courts and the regeneration of New Jersey Continental and militia forces.

Livingston's efforts to persuade the legislature and citizenry of the urgent issues of civil reconstruction and support for the war effort went beyond legislative messages. For the first time he appealed directly to the people. With "The Impartial Chronicle," written in February 1777, he entered his satiric talent into the Whig cause. Mixing wry and bawdy humor with lofty republican rhetoric and employing vivid characterizations of British atrocities, he attempted to galvanize the people for war and rid the state of every "sculking Neutral."

Despite his energy in supporting the militia, Livingston cautiously remained within the limits of his statutory and constitutional powers. His unremitting efforts to exercise leadership in correcting the inequities of militia legislation were finally rewarded with the passage of a crucial revised statute in March 1777. Although the act was no more than a qualified response to Livingston's pleas for increased executive powers to call out the militia and enact harsher penalties for military delinquents, it became the first instance in which the legislative branch delegated powers to the executive, a transfer of authority based on clear military necessity.

Livingston pressed the legislature on March 11, 1777, for an act creating a mixed executive body empowered to contend with military or civil emergencies, a breakdown in local justice, and threats from the Loyalists. The legislature responded with uncharacteristic dispatch, and on March 15 it created the New Jersey Council of Safety. With Livingston as its president, the council moved quickly to fill the void of civil order produced by local justices who had been unwilling to take or administer oaths of allegiance. The Council of Safety thus began the interminable process of issuing arrest orders, interrogating witnesses on the activities of suspected Loyalists, remanding many disaffected in jail and, in general, using the situation to demonstrate that the state government was functioning once again. Livingston, vitriolic in his hatred of Loyalism, grasped the opportunity that widespread disaffection provided to reassert his executive power as head of the council.

Loyalism remained Livingston's biggest problem, and he continued to confront it successfully when, in June 1777, he encouraged legislation that offered clemency to Loyalists who took oaths of allegiance but threatened the confiscation of the personal property of those who did not. Armed with a legislative act to capture Loyalists in order to compel the British to release American political prisoners, Livingston directed the raid of Bergen County that resulted in the capture of numerous Tories.

With the establishment of the *New-Jersey Gazette* in December 1777, Livingston initiated a year-long effort to provide a valuable patriotic commentary on the events of the day. Through numerous pseudonymous essays under such names as "Cato," "De Lisle," "Hortentius," and others, Livingston supported the American army's efforts to fight effectively and addressed the need for responsible legislators. He poked fun at the blustering British generals who could capture cities but could not suppress the rebellion and defeat the American army permanently. The people of New Jersey and the Continental army in Pennsylvania came to rely on the wit, moralizing, and patriotism of the poetry and prose of the governor of New Jersey in his various disguises.

The British reaction to Livingston's barbs was a tribute to their success. His severe treatment of the Loyalists and the barrage of pro-American propaganda he launched in the *New-Jersey Gazette* helped make him infamous among the British generals and the Loyalists. As early as 1778, plots to kidnap or assassinate him were undertaken, but all failed. In the fall of 1779, when the British raided New Brunswick, he barely escaped capture. These numerous plots and more frequent rumors of British retaliation compelled Livingston to continue his peregrinations through the state. He was rarely able to visit his wife and family, and his letters are filled with a yearning for a return of peace and security. Lack of clothing, constant travel, and the necessity of scattering his official papers to insure their safety were only some of his problems as an executive on horseback.

By 1780 the unremitting demands for men to serve in the Continental army and militia units, the taxes to pay the state debts to fight the war, the lack of normal trade with the city of New York, the flight of both debtors and creditors to enemy lines, and the depreciation of currency were all major problems. Livingston attempted to stem the flow of illicit trade to New York and halt the communication and traffic of suspected Loyalists to and from the New Jersey coastline and New York City. He examined the petitions of numerous widows or wives of Tories, anxious creditors, and British citizens seeking to return to their homeland. He granted few passes, exhibiting singular adherence to principle and law above sympathy, expediency and privilege. Several times he denied passports to his sisters and other relatives lest he seem to honor kinship over merit.

The fatigue of seven years of warfare finally ended in March 1783 with the news of the signing of a preliminary peace treaty on January 20, 1783. Livingston issued a proclamation on April 16 and read it before a large gathering in Trenton. On April 23, before he set out for his farm at Elizabethtown, the committee for the inhabitants of Trenton formally thanked the governor for his service to the state. They remarked: "We recollect, with pleasure and veneration, that when the helm of state was committed to your hands, at an early period of the revolution, you accepted, with firmness, the perilous station; and when the storm en-

creased and raged with the greatest vi[olence], we have seen you persevering in t[he] face of every danger and discouragemen[t] till we happily arrived at the haven [of] Peace, Liberty, and Independence."

The return to his farm was, at most, [a] part-time respite from the ongoing bu[si]ness of state. Livingston's personal esta[te] had been depleted by the war. He st[ill] had two unmarried daughters who wou[ld] require support. The farm had fallen in[to] disuse, and the gardens and fields need[ed] work.

In 1785 Livingston was recognized [for] his long relationship with the Unit[ed] Provinces (the Netherlands) when t[he] New Jersey delegation at the Continen[tal] Congress pressed for his nomination [as] ambassador to that country. On March [?] Livingston unofficially declined the po[st] citing old age. He succinctly summariz[ed] his deeply felt commitment to his role [as] chief executive: "The great Confiden[ce] they reposed in me at their first appoin[t]ment of a Governor, when I was o[nly] known to them by general Report . . . [and] from another Province," he wrote, "th[eir] long continuing me in that office, witho[ut] any Interest . . . and that often una[ni]mously, and always in the use of co[m]petitors, by a very great majority, a[nd] that notwithstanding the many d[is]agreeable Truths I have told them [re]specting their Conduct, as to public fa[ith] and integrity." He formally declined t[he] appointment on June 25, 1785. Althou[gh] he accepted a position as a New Jers[ey] delegate to the Constitutional Conve[n]tion of 1787, age and ill health sever[ely] circumscribed his contributions.

The last two years of Livingston's [life] were difficult. The first federal electi[on] that he supervised resulted in a disp[ute] over the closing of the polls. The rise [of] factions and parties in the state e[m]broiled him in controversy, and in 1789 [he] had to testify before a congressional co[m]mittee. That year, his wife died, and [his] letters reflect his depression over the l[oss] of a partner of over forty years. A fall fr[om] a carriage rendered him inactive [for] months, and in May 1790 his daugh[ter] reported him failing. On July 25, 1790, in his fourteenth term as governor of the state of New Jersey, he died in Elizabethtown. He had been the chief executive through war and peace. His standards of personal conduct and his ability to realize the power of his office have since been rarely matched.

Bernstein, David A. "William Livingston: The Role of the Executive in New Jersey's Revolutionary War." In *New Jersey in the American Revolution II,* edited by William C. Wright. Trenton: New Jersey Historical Commission, 1973.

Klein, Milton M. "The American Whig: William Livingston of New York." Ph.D. dissertation, Columbia University, 1954.

Prince, Carl E. *William Livingston: New Jersey's First Governor.* Trenton: New Jersey Historical Commission, 1975.

Prince, Carl E., et al., eds. *The Papers of William Livingston.* 2 vols. to date. Trenton: New Jersey Historical Commission, 1979–.

Sedgwick, Theodore, Jr. *A Memoir of the Life of William Livingston.* New York: Harper, 1833.

Dennis P. Ryan

WILLIAM PATERSON (December 24, 1745–September 9, 1806) was born in Ireland. His family emigrated to America in 1747 and soon settled in Princeton. William, his two younger brothers, and a sister spent their childhood doing chores around their father's store, across from the College of New Jersey (later Princeton University). Because the family's business and real-estate investments were profitable, William could attend the college and, after his graduation in 1763, study law under Richard Stockton. He was admitted to the bar in 1769, and he spent the next years trying to establish a practice in Hunterdon and Somerset counties.

In his college studies and the influential friends he made as founder of the Cliosophic Society at Princeton, Paterson saw possible avenues to higher social status. But he enjoyed his first real recognition in 1775, when he was chosen to represent Somerset County in the first Provincial Congress. He was reelected to the second Provincial Congress, and he attended all but one session of this revolutionary legislature, serving as its official secretary. During the Revolution he was a member of the legislative council (1776–77) and the Council of Safety (1777–78). He served as attorney general (1776–83), prosecuting the Loyalists and maintaining law and order during a time of political and social chaos. By the time he retired to private life at the end of the war, Paterson had established a secure niche in the leadership elite, and his estate overlooking the Raritan River—the confiscated property of Loyalist attorney Bernardus La Grange, bought from the state—reflected his new social status. Cornelia Bell, whom he married in 1779, bore him three children, but in 1783 she and a daughter died. Two years later Paterson married Euphemia White, a close friend of Cornelia's, who helped him raise his son, William Bell Paterson, and his daughter, Cornelia, later the wife of New York Congressman Stephen Van Rennselaer.

Paterson moved his family from the Raritan farm to New Brunswick and for the next few years lived comfortably on his legal business. In 1787 he was chosen to lead New Jersey's delegation to the Constitutional Convention. Paterson played a significant role at the convention, where he is best remembered for the New Jersey Plan, which he proposed as an alternative to the Virginia Plan favored by the larger states. Because of his unshakable arguments in defense of equal representation for all the states and his adroit procedural strategy as the debate over the Great Compromise reached its climax, Paterson deserves the title, "Father of the Senate." Appropriately,

New Jersey chose him as its representative to the first meeting of the United States Senate in New York, where he took part in framing the Judiciary Act of 1789 and supported the funding and assumption phases of Hamilton's financial plan. When William Livingston's death in August 1790 ended fourteen years of stability in the governor's office, many New Jersey leaders immediately turned to Paterson.

Paterson held many of the same conservative political and social ideas as Livingston, and his extensive experience was obvious; however, his really indispensable assets were a widespread reputation for public service and a practically universal popularity. The mild counterrevolution in New Jersey politics that followed the adoption of the Constitution had begun to waver. For example, some of the popular debtor relief measures, instituted in the Confederation period only to be repealed in 1787 and 1788, were already being reintroduced. Unless a candidate could be found whose bipartisan popularity would guarantee his election, the choice of a new governor might easily become a distressing contest among the state's various factions. This is why New Jersey's conservative leaders prevailed so strenuously on Paterson. Since college days, he had believed it to be the responsibility of the educated and capable to serve the society in offices of public trust. Now his friends —including John Chetwood, Nicholas Bayard, and Jonathan Dayton—played on these feelings to persuade Paterson to accept the post. At least one observer, in a newspaper piece signed "Captain Triumph," disapproved of the tone of condescension that he detected in Paterson's eventual decision to accept the nomination, but, true to the predictions of his supporters, when the legislators met the vote was unanimous.

During Paterson's tenure as governor, Trenton was chosen as the regular site for meetings of the legislature, and the building of the first state house there was begun. Paterson was active in advising New Jersey's representatives in Congress on questions relating to the federal assumption of state debts and to the reapportionment of seats in the House of Representatives. But Governor Paterson made his most significant accomplishments in the areas of economic development and legal reform.

Paterson had come to know Alexander Hamilton and some of the other leading economic thinkers of the day while he was sitting in the Senate. Tench Coxe had written to him early in 1790, explaining that because New Jersey's fertile agricultural land was filling up while her population continued to grow, some sort of commercial development would be necessary to provide jobs for future generations. A year later Coxe, Hamilton, and others, who were framing the prospectus of the Society for Establishing Useful Manufactures (S.U.M.) with a maximum capitalization of $4 million, planned their application for a charter from the New Jersey Assembly. Controversy was anticipated with the company's requests for some extraordinary privileges: to dig canals wherever it saw fit, to run lotteries for its own profit, and to be specially exempt from taxes. But in the judgment of at least one observer, Paterson's attendance at a planning meeting the promoters held in August 1791 was a sure sign that the legislature would grant the desired favors. To dramatize Paterson's approval, the company announced that it would name the industrial town it planned to build in his honor. When the legislature met in November it quickly approved the charter.

Whether Paterson lobbied actively for the passage of the charter is unclear, but his support of it as a step toward New Jersey's economic independence from neighboring New York and Pennsylvania is certain. Although the governor purchased no stock, John Bayard, his brother-in-law and one of the local promoters, bought $1,000 worth of shares in the name of Paterson's wife. Actually, the legislators probably needed little convincing. Once it became known that Paterson supported the project and that he had allowed his name to be so prominently associated with it, his reputation did the rest. The lawmakers' subsequent decision to invest $10,000 of the state's money amounted to a personal testimonial to their favorite son.

The S.U.M. had a disappointing history. The company's leadership was placed in the hands of William Duer and a group of his friends from New York. Within a few months they had become embroiled in a speculative scheme that backfired, forcing three S.U.M. directors into bankruptcy and Duer into debtors' prison. The realization that speculators threatened the entire project appalled Paterson, and he wrote in defense of those who, unlike financial schemers, were "plodding along in the common road of industry." But neither his encouragement nor Hamilton's managerial skill sufficed to repair the damage. Public opinion about the S.U.M. became tangled with the other elements of the Federalists' financial plan, and the manufacturing enterprise never got off the ground. It would take a half century for the future city of Paterson to begin to fulfill the dreams for industrial greatness its founders shared in the 1790s.

Although William Paterson's *Laws of New Jersey* was not published until 1800, it deserves discussion in connection with his governorship. In 1792 the assembly passed the legislation authorizing Paterson to digest and revise the laws so that outmoded colonial statutes could be updated and British laws, retained in force temporarily in 1776, could be finally set aside. The following year, at Paterson's suggestion, the authorization was widened to include a complete reform of the British criminal code, which still applied in New Jersey. As the governor put it, the prevailing system was "written in blood and cannot be read without horror." Because of his revision the first state prison was built, at Trenton. Besides humanizing the penal system, Paterson saw the revision as the opportunity for political, social, and moral reform. But the most enduring changes related to the practice of law and the courts. According to one legal scholar, "Paterson's Practice" did away with many of the "complications and technicalities with which the courts in England were embarrassed for several years to come."

As Paterson prepared to resign his office in March 1793 to accept President Washington's appointment to the federal bench, he expressed some of his thoughts about the governorship in an essay published over the pseudonym Aurelius in the *Guardian; or, New-Brunswick Advertiser.* According to Governor Paterson, who had been there in 1776 when the state constitution was written, the framers had considered the document "a temporary thing resulting from the exigency of the moment." To illustrate he pointed to the combination of the chancellorship with the governor's office, a peculiarity carried over from the colonial experience. Though this had not presented much of a problem in colonial days, the business of the chancery court had "wondrously increased" since the end of the war. Now, he argued, the constitution should be "thoroughly revised," and the office of chancellor should be separated from that of governor, which had more political responsibilities.

For the last thirteen years of his life Paterson served as an associate justice of the United States Supreme Court. The job was strenuous, requiring him to attend regular sessions of federal circuit courts as far away as Savannah, Georgia. While he sat on the court, Paterson took part in decisions on several significant cases that helped to define the federal government's authority over the states and provided precedents for the later establishment of judicial review over federal as well as state legislation. Paterson never completely succeeded in divorcing his political point of view from his judicial decisions, as became obvious in cases involving Matthew Lyon and others accused of breaking the 1798 Sedition Act. Although he was considered for appointments as secretary of state and as chief justice, in each case he was passed over, and he remained on the court until his death in 1806.

William Paterson Papers, William Paterson College Special Collections, Wayne, N.J.

O'Connor, John E. "Legal Reform in the Early Republic: The New Jersey Experience." *American Journal of Legal History* 22 (April 1978): 95–117.

––––––. *William Paterson: Lawyer and Statesman, 1745–1806.* New Brunswick: Rutgers University Press, 1979.

John E. O'Connor

RICHARD HOWELL (October 25, 1754–April 28, 1802), revolutionary officer, lawyer and third governor of New Jersey, was born in Newark, Delaware. He was a twin, and one of the eleven children of Ebenezer Howell, a farmer, and Sarah (Bond) Howell, Quakers who had emigrated from Wales to Delaware in about 1724. Educated at an academy and then privately, Howell became an Episcopalian during the American Revolution. He married Keziah, the daughter of Joseph Burr, who owned extensive property in Burlington County. The Howells had nine children.

Between the ages of twenty and thirty-nine, from the time he moved with his family to Shiloh, in Cumberland County, New Jersey, to his inauguration as governor, Howell played an active part in the movement for American independence. He participated in the Greenwich Tea Party and, months before the Declaration of Independence, wrote newspaper essays for the *Plain Dealer* calling for armed resistance to the British.

During the revolutionary war, Howell rose to the rank of brigade major and participated in the Canadian campaign and the battles of Brandywine, Germantown and Monmouth. He spent the winter of 1777–78 at Valley Forge with Washington, for whom he resigned his commission to perform intelligence work.

Howell first practiced law near his home, then in Trenton. While traveling to the first inauguration in New York, he participated in Trenton's reception for President Washington. After being appointed clerk of the New Jersey Supreme Court, he joined the nucleus of the New Jersey Federalist party, which was made up of members closely connected to Washington and Alexander Hamilton.

Howell became the third governor of New Jersey in 1793 and served until 1801. During most of this period he was the only candidate nominated. In 1798 the Republicans nominated several candidates, but Howell was elected by a very large majority. His victory margin was considerably smaller in 1799, when Republicans united on moderate Federalist Andrew Kirkpatrick as their alternative to Howell's reelection.

While governor, Howell carried out the varied and exacting judicial duties that constituted the major functions of the office. He performed the duties of surrogate general, of chancellor—hearing appeals from cases tried in equity—and of presiding judge of the state court of errors and appeals, the highest appellate court in New Jersey. He also was president of the council, where he possessed a tie-breaking vote. By virtue of the New Jersey constitution he also had the executive power of captain-general and commander of the militia.

In September 1794, to comply with President Washington's orders, Howell led the New Jersey militia into Pennsylvania to help crush the Whiskey Rebellion. President Washington met the troops in Pennsylvania and named Howell commander of the right wing of the army. After cowing the insurgents, the president dismissed the troops, and Howell and his men returned to New Jersey in mid-November.

In August 1798, Howell was involved in the sedition charges brought against the most ardent Republican organ in New Jersey, the Newark *Centinel of Freedom*. In May, Republican militia officers had refused to add their names to the state militia's expression of support for the Federalist president, John Adams. As head of the militia, Howell lashed out at them publicly for this. In reply, the Republicans forwarded an address to Howell, charging that the president was at fault, not they. Adams had violated the constitution they said, and therefore they had no confidence in the government. Governor Howell then attacked his addressers as "the shreds of a French faction [that operated as a] dagger in the hands of . . . [a French] assassin." In the *Centinel,* the Republicans now called him "the Prince of Blackguards." This epithet formed the basis for the governor's charges of seditious libel against the newspaper.

Considering his background, it is not surprising that when a Federalist party split occurred in the late 1790s, the militant Howell sided with war and the army. Under orders from Major General Alexander Hamilton, Howell gladly raised an infantry regiment in case of a French invasion.

Finally, in February 1799, when Fries's Rebellion broke out in Pennsylvania protesting the taxes levied to support the provisional army and other elements of the Federalist defense program, Howell responded with alacrity to President Adams's order to ready two thousand New Jersey militiamen to march. His prompt, decisive action brought one Philadelphia militant Federalist newspaper's praise: "What a charming thing it would be if every state had such a governor as New Jersey! . . . It will be long, very long indeed, 'ere Poor Pennsylvania will see a Howell in her chair of state."

Howell's last term in office ended in October 1801, when the Federalists lost the state. Disgrace and death followed in quick succession. As soon as the Republicans had taken office, the legislature accused Howell of failing to account for all monies spent on military preparedness and ordered him to give the state treasurer the unexpended monies and a statement of expenditures. The investigation was incomplete in April 1802, when Howell died with a clouded reputation— at least in Republican minds. In his obituary, the Republican press stated that he was possibly guilty of embezzling funds. The Federalists answered that Howell's failing health had prevented him from maintaining proper accounts.

At the end of Howell's long tenure as governor, six months before his death, the Federalists acknowledged publicly that he had not been a statesman of the first magnitude. His popularity with his electors, the members of the Federalist-dominated New Jersey legislature, surpassed his effectiveness as governor.

[Agnew, Daniel.] *Major Richard Howell of New Jersey.* [Philadelphia]: n.p., 1876. Rutgers University Special Collections, New Brunswick, N.J.

New Jersey Letters, Rutgers University Special Collections, New Brunswick, N.J.

Timothy Pickering Papers, Massachusetts Historical Society, Boston, Mass.

Anthony Walton White Papers, Rutgers University Special Collections, New Brunswick, N.J.

Pasler, Rudolph J., and Margaret C. *The New Jersey Federalists.* Rutherford, N.J.: Fairleigh Dickinson University Press, 1975.

Rudolph J. Pasler
Margaret C. Pasler

JOSEPH BLOOMFIELD (October 18, 1753– October 3, 1823) was the fourth governor of the state (1801-2; 1803-12) and the first Jeffersonian-Republican to hold the office. He was first elected in 1801, then successively each year from 1803 to 1812. Described by a contemporary as "rich," and taking great pride in his occasional military service (he preferred to be called "General" rather than "Excellency"), Bloomfield managed to combine the roles of governor and party leader during his long tenure in office. This accomplishment was all the more pronounced because the governor's office possessed but few constitutional and appointive powers and no popular mandate: the post was filled by the joint meeting of the New Jersey Legislature and not by popular election until after 1844. Despite the office's inherent weakness in an era of legislative domination, Bloomfield remained a powerful figure in New Jersey for nearly a quarter century.

Bloomfield was born in Woodbridge into a notable family of English origin. His father, Moses Bloomfield, a well-to-do physician and a political figure, served in both the colonial New Jersey Assembly and the Provincial Congress that replaced it at the beginning of the American Revolution. Joseph was educated at an academy in South Jersey, and he had almost finished reading law when the Revolution began. He dropped his studies to accept a captain's commission in the new Continental army, where he served with distinction in the New Jersey Brigade and other units, resigning in 1778 with the rank of major. In that year he married Mary McIlvaine, settled in Burlington, and was admitted to the bar. The Bloomfields had no children, but adopted their nephew Joseph McIlvaine and raised him.

His elite background, revolutionary service, inherited wealth and urbanity all propelled him toward political leadership at a time when many of his class had chosen to side with the Loyalists. After a period of indecision, Joseph Bloomfield emerged as one of the few genuine landed "aristocrats" in New Jersey to join the Jeffersonian cause instead of the more mainline Federalist party in the decade following the ratification of the federal Constitution in 1788.

At first, there was little to indicate that Bloomfield was anything but a good Federalist supporter of Washington's. He was a presidential elector for Washington in 1792, and as the general commanding the New Jersey militia he accepted the president's call to lead the state's troops in helping to suppress the Whiskey Rebellion. Jay's Treaty with Great Britain in 1795 and, a year later, Washington's announcement that he would retire and support John Adams to replace him, however, gave the prominent militia general cause to ponder his future allegiances. In 1796, as politics in New Jersey became heated for the first time since ratification, rumors of his defection to the Anti-Federalists (budding Jeffersonian-Republicans) began to circulate. He protested, "I am a friend of the President and Government, [as] I have already evinced . . . in 1792 and . . . 1794." In July of 1797, moreover, Bloomfield wrote to his friend and New Jersey compatriot Jonathan Dayton, Federalist Speaker of the House of Representatives, recommending an office seeker "as a good federalist."

Bloomfield finally surfaced as a Jeffersonian later that year, but his Federalist ties haunted him throughout his political career. When he appointed a Federalist to office in 1801, for example, one Republican congressman commented that it was "just like him." A year later another congressman commented that Bloomfield was still susceptible to "Federal *Flattery* and *Deception.*" As late as 1811, after Bloomfield had spent a successful decade as the Jeffersonian-Republican governor of New Jersey, still another party manager wrote cynically, "I did not suppose that any one expected [sic] Bloomfield of belonging to the Republican party from principle."

Despite such lingering suspicions Bloomfield had been a key figure in cementing the Jeffersonian party organization in the state in the years 1796–1800. He continued to identify with Republican party issues, opposing both the foreign policies of John Adams and the Alien and Sedition Laws of 1798

Parvenu New Jersey Jeffersonian politicians—they were often "new men" brought forward politically by the Revolution—were flattered by invitations to caucus at the Bloomfield family residence in Burlington, with its "fine library and many curiosities." In 1800, after Bloomfield was named chairman of the first statewide Republican nominating convention, a party device introduced to cultivate unity for the pending congressional and presidential elections, he emerged as the titular leader of the party. The New Jersey Jeffersonian Party's efforts in these elections marked its coming of age, and in 1801, for the first time, it captured control of the state. Bloomfield's leadership was instrumental in achieving the victory, and the Jeffersonian legislative majority elected him governor for the constitutionally prescribed one-year term. A legislative deadlock prevented the election of a governor in 1802, but in 1803 and successively through 1811 Bloomfield was reelected with awesome regularity.

Although he had almost no constitutional authority, Bloomfield used his position as party leader with surgical precision to strengthen the governor's office. The state legislature, dominated by a Jeffersonian-Republican majority, introduced the institution of the caucus to encourage party regularity; as a state institution, the caucus has survived the hazards of almost two centuries, down to the present. Bloomfield came to be a fixture in the caucus, which, while he remained governor, was not limited to legislators but included other representative party leaders. He combined this personal authority with the prestige he commanded in Washington, D.C., as an important spokesman for the state party to the Jeffersonian administration. As a result, his was a strong voice in dispensing patronage in the state. He wrote to President Jefferson outlining New Jersey's appointive priorities under the new national administration, and Jefferson chided him for his long shopping list: "It is the case of one loaf and ten men wanting bread." But Bloomfield delivered the federal offices in 1801 and thereafter, and Jefferson seldom afterward treated him lightly.

As governor, Bloomfield used his moral and political leadership to initiate the gradual emancipation of slavery in New Jersey. His father before him had staunchly opposed bondage, freeing fourteen slaves at the time of the Revolution. Joseph himself was a longtime leader of the New Jersey Society for the Abolition of Slavery. A potent lobbyist, he was instrumental in promoting a considerable measure of Republican unity against slavery. Although he was accused of turning his back on his elite ties and background, he also favored controversial legislative reform measures to tax dividends from private bank stock and the creation of state-chartered banks to thwart monopolistic private banking interests in New Jersey.

During his last years in office, from 1808 to 1812, Bloomfield—like Republican officeholders everywhere—was caught up in defending unpopular foreign policy measures emanating from Washington. In an effort to protect American sovereignty while keeping the nation out of war with England, the Jefferson and Madison administrations had introduced successive measures embargoing trade with England, inevitably interrupting commerce with all of Europe. The consequent economic recession and the popular emotional reactions to continuing impressment of American sailors on the high seas placed New Jersey's Republicans on the defensive and caused a division in party ranks. Bloomfield contended expertly with these political difficulties, defending his party against allegations that it was "the party of war." In the five years before the War of 1812, Jeffersonian-Republicans were hopelessly divided by foreign policy questions and Federalists were revitalized by them, but even so Bloomfield managed to gain reelection in the joint meeting of the legislature each October. When war was finally declared in June 1812, Bloomfield promptly resigned as governor in midterm to accept President Madison's nomination as brigadier general in the rapidly expanding United States Army.

Evidence of Bloomfield's personal popularity and of the unifying strength of his party leadership became all too clear in the succeeding legislative election for governor in October 1812; for the first time in more than a decade a Federalist was named to fill the chair vacated by "the General." Although his military service was much more prosaic than colorful slogans would suggest (he spent his three years in the military organizing and supervising training and defense establishments in New York and Pennsylvania), he must have been touched by the thoughts of those Republican celebrants who toasted him at a party gathering on the Fourth of July, 1812: "When in the camp, on the march, or under the walls of Quebec, may he never want the genuine character of a Jersey Blue."

When the war ended in 1815, General Bloomfield retired to his mansion in Burlington. His ease was short-lived; his personal popularity and ability to unite warring factions of the party resulted in his election to two terms in the House of Representatives, in 1816 and 1818. Only in 1820, in his sixty-seventh year, was he allowed to decline renomination and retire again to his estate in South Jersey. There he died in 1823, overshadowed in history by the founding fathers, to whom he was contemporary, but bound to them by his able service to the causes that had rendered them immortal.

Joseph Bloomfield Letters, Rutgers University Special Collections, New Brunswick, N.J.

Emmet Collection, New York Public Library, New York, N.Y.

Gratz Collection, Historical Society of Pennsylvania, Philadelphia, Pa.

Thomas Jefferson Papers, Library of Congress, Manuscript Division, Washington, D.C.

New Jersey Broadsides Collection, The New Jersey Historical Society, Newark, N.J.

Samuel L. Southard Papers, Princeton University Special Collections, Princeton, N.J.

John W. Taylor Papers, The New-York Historical Society, New York, N.Y.

Oliver Wolcott Papers, Connecticut Historical Society, Hartford, Conn.

Fee, Walter R. *The Transition From Aristocracy to Democracy in New Jersey, 1789–1829.* Somerville, N.J.: Somerset Press, 1933.

Prince, Carl E. *New Jersey's Jeffersonian Republicans, 1789–1817.* Chapel Hill: University of North Carolina Press, 1967.

Carl E. Prince

AARON OGDEN (December 3, 1756–April 19, 1839), a man of impressive physique and a craggy and truculent countenance, had a character to match. To a distinguished family name he added a lustrous military service during the Revolution and a solid reputation among New Jersey lawyers.

The family had deep roots in New Jersey. John Ogden, who built a house in Elizabethtown in 1664, was one of the original settlers of that community. He moved there from Long Island, to which he had emigrated in 1640 from Hampshire, England. Aaron's father, Robert Ogden, had been speaker of the New Jersey lower house on the eve of the American Revolution. Aaron graduated from the College of New Jersey (later Princeton University) in 1773. There he met many of the state's future leaders, with whom he worked and fought in the Revolution and later in the state's courts and in the political arena. In 1787 he married Elizabeth Chitwood, daughter of another prominent family, who bore him two daughters and five sons.

He capitalized on his assets to become one of New Jersey's leading Federalists and to build a long and impressive political career. During the early national period, however, political success in New Jersey depended on party victory, not individual ability. Federalist Aaron Ogden could never overcome the Jeffersonian-Republican party's control of state politics to achieve sustained political success. He served two years (1801–1803) in the United States Senate, completing the term of James Schureman, who had resigned. From 1803 to 1812 he was elected annually to the state's general assembly, where he was the leader and the workhorse of the ineffectual Federalist minority. During these years Ogden's Federalist colleagues nominated him for the governorship whenever they wanted to challenge the Republican majority, but this was only a token action. The governor was elected by the legislature, and the Republican majority elected Joseph Bloomfield every year from 1803 to 1812.

In 1812 New Jersey Federalists shared in the nationwide Federalist revival brought about by the opposition to the national administration's maritime policy and the declaration of war against England. They won a majority in the legislature and elected Ogden governor. In 1813 the Federalists lost their majority and with it the governorship, beginning their slow decline to dissolution. Ogden dropped out of active politics to pursue a career in banking and steamboating. His permanent claim to fame, in fact, rests on his efforts to promote steam navigation, not on his political career. He is the Ogden in the landmark Supreme Court decision *Gibbons* v. *Ogden,* which ended private monopolies in interstate commerce.

In his year as governor, Ogden led the Federalist majority without being its captive. He showed an ability, integrity and independence which the state could have put to good use had partisanship not so dominated its elections. The most immediate issues Ogden faced during his term involved defense against possible British attack, coastal defense in cooperation with the governors of nearby states,

and relations with the national government.

On January 21, 1813, Ogden informed the legislature that though the state militia was willing and anxious to take the field in defense of the state, its arms and munitions were deficient for active service. The legislature appropriated a sizable but insufficient sum to remedy this defect. The national government also provided inadequate and deficient arms, having more immediate use for the little equipment it had. Ogden devoted enormous energy to solving this problem, to no avail. The Federalist legislature, which had passed some vitriolic resolutions condemning the war and its "wasteful and disastrous" conduct, refused Ogden's request for adequate appropriations. Diehard Federalists, hoping to drive Ogden to a position totally against the war, condemned the national government for not supplying the New Jersey militia or adequately providing for the state's defense, but he refused to be driven.

Ogden's general orders of November 16 and December 1, 1812, placed portions of the state militia in federal service under federal officers. In a speech at Newark he pledged the state's cooperation with the government's war efforts. He worked out a plan with Governor Daniel D. Tompkins of New York for the joint defense of New York harbor, and with the governors of nearby states on plans for coastal defense. Even though Federalists complained that his exertions were contrary to the party policy of opposing the war effort, Ogden won high praise from moderate Federalists and from his Republican opponents. Under the headline "Honor Where Honor is Due," the Trenton *True American,* the state's leading Republican newspaper, complimented Ogden on the "patriotic stand he has taken in defense of his country." His conduct, the paper said, was distinctly different from "the anti-American conduct of the friends of peace." The article concluded that Ogden "knows the value of liberty too well to sacrifice it on the altar of faction." The Madison administration appreciated his cooperation so much that Secretary of War John Armstrong offered him command of the New York–New Jersey military district. Ogden refused because Armstrong insisted that to accept the post he would have to resign as governor. When Republican Governor Tompkins of New York took that command without relinquishing the governorship, New Jersey Federalists concluded that the original offer had been a Republican stratagem to remove a Federalist governor. Ogden refused to accept this conclusion and rejected all suggestions that he adopt a more intransigent attitude. Throughout his term he consistently supported the war effort and the national government's conduct of the war.

Other than controversies concerning the war, two issues dominated New Jersey politics during Ogden's term. The Federalists recognized that their victory in 1812 was the result of a peculiar set of circumstances and passed two bills through which they hoped to retain power. They changed the method of choosing presidential electors from popular to legislative election, and they passed a complicated redistricting law, hoping to gerrymander the state in their favor. The governor supported both measures and lost much of the reputation for nonpartisanship won by his attitude toward the war.

Equally partisan, but less divisive, was the issue of state banking. Federalists, with Ogden in the lead, had long advocated the expansion of the state banking system but before 1812 had made no headway against the Republican majorities. Once they had won control of the legislature, they chartered six new banks capitalized at over $2 million. Each bank was to raise its own capital by selling shares par-valued at $50 each. Half of the stock of each bank was reserved for the state, and so was the power to make some appointments to the board of directors. Ogden worked hard behind the scenes to assure the passage of this bill and even

harder to assure that the banks created by the law actually came into being. But he refused to cooperate with the Federalist majority when it tried to politicize the banking system.

The Republican legislature of 1811 had passed an act authorizing the governor to sell state-owned shares in the bank of New Jersey to the highest bidder so long as the bid was not below the state's original purchase price. A resolution by the Federalist legislature of 1812 authorized the sale of state-owned bank stock at the best price it would bring on the market. Ogden informed the legislature that the law and the resolution were in conflict. In a rare display of executive independence, he refused "to execute the commission assigned to me" until the conflict was resolved. For this action he once more won high praise in the Republican press. However, his personal popularity could not be converted into another Federalist victory.

In the elections of 1813, the Republicans argued that opposition to the war would encourage the enemy and prolong the conflict. They blamed the Federalists for the defenseless condition of the state and condemned them for the change in the election law, some polemicists arguing that the Federalists were more concerned with their own reelection than with the country's defense against attack. The Republican press did not vilify Governor Ogden. If mentioned at all, he was compared favorably to the unpatriotic New England governors and the less-than-patriotic Federalist majority in the state legislature. On this platform the Republicans gained a ten-vote majority in the legislature and by that margin elected William S. Pennington over Ogden to the governorship.

After the war's end in 1815, Ogden shifted his energies from law and politics to steamboating. His ships, the *Sea Horse* and the *Atlanta,* carried freight and passengers from Elizabethtown Point to New York City, earning substantial profits for Ogden and his partner, Thomas Gibbons. A series of personal and commercial differences forced the dissolution of the partnership and began the long and complex litigation which culminated in the landmark Supreme Court decision of *Gibbons v. Ogden* in 1824. The expense of the litigation and the loss of the steamboat franchise depleted the fortune Ogden had accumulated. In 1829 Congress created the post of collector of customs for Jersey City especially for Ogden. Though lucrative, the position did not pay enough to enable him to liquidate his obligations, and he was imprisoned for debt in New York. Fortunately, his boyhood friend and Princeton classmate, Aaron Burr, pushed a bill through the New York legislature prohibiting imprisonment of revolutionary war veterans for debt. Thus reprieved, Ogden comfortably lived out his life with his sinecure in Jersey City. He died there on April 19, 1839.

Ogden, Aaron. "Autobiography of Col. Aaron Ogden of Elizabethtown." *Proceedings of the New Jersey Historical Society* 12 (1892–1893): 15–31.

Dangerfield, George. "The Steamboat Case." In *Quarrels That Have Shaped the Constitution.* Edited by John Garraty. New York: Harper & Row, 1964.

Fee, Walter R. *The Transition from Aristocracy to Democracy in New Jersey, 1789–1829.* Somerville, N.J.: Somerset Press, 1933.

Lane, Wheaton J. *From Indian Trail to Iron Horse: Travel and Transportation in New Jersey, 1620–1860.* Princeton: Princeton University Press, 1939.

Pasler, Rudolph J., and Margaret C. *The New Jersey Federalists.* Rutherford, N.J.: Fairleigh Dickinson University Press, 1975.

Victor A. Sapio

WILLIAM SANDFORD PENNINGTON (1757–September 17, 1826), the state's sixth governor, was one of those who benefited most dramatically from the social mobility stimulated by the revolutionary war. He was perhaps the first governor of either the colony or the state who did not derive from hereditary, propertied gentry; in large measure this fact affected his outlook and his place in history.

Pennington was born into a Newark family of limited means. He was orphaned at an early age, and his formal education ended with apprenticeship to a local hatmaker. He joined the Continental army as an enlisted man when the Revolution began. Though his service record is confused by unsubstantiated claims to heroism, it at least partly shows his value to the American cause: he was made sergeant in an artillery unit in 1777, commissioned second lieutenant in the field in 1780, and, having served through the entire war, mustered out as a brevet captain. He returned to Newark to work as a hatter. By the early 1790s he was in business for himself as a retail merchant in his native town.

He typified the new, self-made elitist attracted to the Jeffersonian-Republican cause in the 1790s. Following a pattern of political involvement not uncommon in other states in the formative years of America's first party system, Pennington and his brother Aaron helped found the Essex County Democratic Society; this was part of a Jeffersonian-Republican movement emerging from popular American support for the French Revolution and encouraged particularly by the organizational efforts of Edmond Genet, French minister to the United States in 1792 and 1793. The Pennington brothers rose to leadership of the society and in 1796 used the organization as a springboard to found the first Jeffersonian newspaper in the state, the Newark *Centinel of Freedom*. This political commitment left the now successful and outspoken Anti-Federalist revolutionary veteran only a short leap from entry into active politics.

Newark provided fertile ground for men and women with Jeffersonian leanings: it was the home of several families like the

Penningtons made prominent by the Revolution. A natural rivalry developed between that growing community and Elizabethtown, the seat of a more traditional, Federalist-oriented aristocracy that included the Ogden, Dayton, Williamson and Boudinot families. By the 1790s Newark had achieved political domination of Essex County, and this along with rapid increases in its population and its growing economic centricity gave its leaders an advantage in the quest for power. The county in turn formed the vital center of Jeffersonian strength in New Jersey, its political accomplishments enhanced by the remarkable fact that from 1796 through 1807 women were permitted to vote in Essex—and they did so in significant numbers. For two decades, from 1795 through 1815, William Pennington remained a political kingpin in Essex County.

He was elected to the assembly annually between 1797 and 1799, and to the council each year from 1800 to 1804. He became a major figure in the legislature and a powerful voice in the Jeffersonian cause. As a candidate on the "Farmer's [Jeffersonian-Republican] Ticket" at the end of 1796, he was accused by one Federalist of "shouting loudly of the necessity of changing men in order to change measures." In 1798 Pennington's visibility and political stock rose enormously as a result of his moderate and successful leadership in the legisative debate over New Jersey's response to the Alien and Sedition acts.

During this period of deep involvement in politics he continued to operate his store and also plugged away at the study of law. In 1802, at age forty-five, his admission to the bar testified to his perseverance and ability. A year later he was appointed county clerk of Essex; at the beginning of 1804 he resigned from the legislature to accept an appointment to the New Jersey Supreme Court. In 1806 he was named court reporter as well as justice, and he published a *Treatise on the Courts for the Trial of Small Causes* (1806), virtually a layman's guide to the complexities of New Jersey civil law. It

was good enough to warrant republication nearly a generation later.

Pennington's service on the bench clearly did not disqualify him from quietly carrying on his political leadership. The Republican mixed caucus of Jeffersonian legislators and other party managers came close to nominating him for governor in both 1810 and 1811, but eventually it renominated Joseph Bloomfield instead. In the meantime, however, Pennington strengthened his ties to Republicans outside Essex County. In 1811, for example, the Woodbridge Jeffersonian organization resolved that as Pennington "is worthy of, so may he soon be called to the highest office of this state."

That call finally came in 1813, when a Republican legislative majority named him to a one-year term. Entering office at the low point of the War of 1812, Pennington conceived it his duty to restore unity to the state by attempting to mute the rivalry and hostility that for a score of years had separated Jeffersonians and Federalists. At first he was relatively successful at this and he was reelected in 1814, but in order to succeed he had eroded his position in both Essex County and the state by opening himself to charges of "amalgamation"—a contemporary term similar to "appeasement."

When the governor endorsed the Essex County legislative candidacy of Jonathan Dayton, a former Federalist Speaker of the United States House of Representatives, in the autumn of 1814, he drew the fire of Shepard Kollock, a longtime Essex County Republican rival who was the editor of the influential Elizabethtown *New-Jersey Journal.* At the same time the governor strongly supported Mahlon Dickerson's losing bid for a seat in the United States Senate against James J. Wilson, a powerful Republican who edited another influential newspaper, the Trenton *True American.* Not only did Pennington incur Wilson's wrath, he also undermined his own support in the Republican caucus. Worst of all, he was widely quoted as having intemperately referred to Wilson's Republican supporters as a bunch of "Clod Hoppers" who boasted "not a man of Talents or of understanding among them." This proved unforgivable in a self-made man who owed his political success to the support of New Jersey's farmers—who, after all, constituted the vast majority of voters in an agrarian state.

After the end of the war in 1815, ideological divisions in New Jersey, which had most recently been exacerbated by foreign policy issues, began to diminish. At the same time Governor Pennington, who had done much to close the rifts caused by party confrontations, found his popularity among rank-and-file Republicans decreasing, his hold on Essex County undermined, his support in the caucus threatened. In short, Pennington was almost certain to lose the next election. The party found a way out: President Madison nominated Pennington a judge in the United States District Court for the district of New Jersey and the governor accepted. By gracefully arranging this "elevation," New Jersey's Jeffersonian Republicans avoided a messy public struggle and allowed an old party wheelhorse to save face.

As for the retiring governor, he found himself in a berth that was "almost a sinecure." There were four court terms during the year but as the historian John Whitehead has noted, "they rarely lasted . . . more than a day. No grand jury was ever sworn in [Pennington's] court, nor were any indictments found." He held the office until his death in 1826. Perhaps there was some justice in his enjoying a tranquil position for the last decade of life after having paid so dearly for his successful efforts to bridge the enmities of a generation of party combat during the era of the first party system. A kind of vindication occurred posthumously when his son was elected governor in 1837.

Samuel L. Southard Papers, Princeton University Special Collections, Princeton, N.J.

Fee, Walter R. *The Transition from Aristocracy to Democracy in New Jersey, 1789–1829.* Somerville, N.J.: Somerset Press, 1933.

Link, Eugene P. *Democratic-Republican Societies, 1790–1800.* New York: Columbia University Press, 1942.

Prince, Carl E. *New Jersey's Jeffersonian Republicans, 1789–1817.* Chapel Hill: University of North Carolina Press, 1967.

Whitehead, John. *The Judicial and Civil History of New Jersey.* [Boston]: Boston Historical Co., 1897.

Carl. E. Prince

MAHLON DICKERSON (April 17, 1770–October 5, 1853), was born in Hanover Neck, Morris County, the first child of Jonathan and Mary (Coe) Dickerson. During his life, he demonstrated a diversity and longevity in political leaderhip and achievement that no other native son appears to have equaled.

Dickerson received his only institutional education as one of the twenty members of the class of 1789 of the College of New Jersey (later Princeton University), where the Reverend John Witherspoon, a signer of the Declaration of Independence, was president. Before attending college he had been tutored by educated citizens in and around Morristown. His teachers included Caleb Russell, who in 1797 established the *Morris County Gazette* (Morristown). In 1776 another tutor, Dr. Jacob Green, had argued forcibly against slavery in America. Dr. Green served at one time as acting president of the College of New Jersey, and he was the father of the college's longtime president, Ashbel Green.

After being graduated from Princeton, Dickerson read law in Morristown with his former tutor Caleb Russell, and in 1793 he was admitted to the New Jersey bar. The following year, during the Whiskey Rebellion, he rode as a volunteer cavalryman in the New Jersey militia. The militiamen saw little military action during the expedition over the mountains to Pittsburgh, but the state militia's fairly quick response confirmed the wisdom of Dickerson's lifelong reliance on citizen militias rather than standing armies.

From 1797 to 1810, Mahlon Dickerson practiced law and gained political experience in Philadelphia, then the largest and most sophisticated of American cities. While there he developed a close personal friendship with Meriwether Lewis, wrote extensively for William Duane's Jeffersonian newspapers, and was admitted to the prestigious American Philosophical Society. He was also elected to the Philadelphia Common Council, and Governor Thomas McKean appointed him recorder of the city and adjutant general of the state of Pennsylvania.

In 1810, Dickerson moved back to New Jersey, where he began to establish himself in the mining industry and in state politics. He took over his dead father's iron mine and made it one of the most productive in the nation. In the first quarter of the nineteenth century it provided ore for an estimated hundred forges from High Bridge to Hamburg. On a hilltop near Succasunna he built an estate, with a mansion that he named "Ferromonte" (Mountain of Iron), probably emulating Jefferson, who had named his Virginia estate "Monticello."

In New Jersey politics, Dickerson rose rapidly. In 1811 he was named orphans' court judge in Morris County. Like his father, Jonathan, and his brother, Silas, he was elected three times successively—from 1811 to 1813—to the assembly from Morris. In that last year, the legislature appointed him a justice of the state supreme court, a post he filled for two years. During that time his major activity, according to his diary, was holding court at Trenton and riding circuit, mainly to the northern county seats. Unfortunately, no official record exists of his activities as a justice because, on constitutional grounds, he declined a concurrent appointment as court recorder. When he was elected governor on October 26, 1815, he resigned his post as justice. Samuel L. Southard succeeded him on the bench.

Among the political issues in New Jersey during Dickerson's governorship were governmental action to combat the economic dislocations of the postwar period; the state's role in banking and internal improvements; and public education. Dickerson responded to the first by urging the passage of national tariffs to protect infant American industries. He saw them as necessary because after the Treaty of Ghent in 1815 had ended the War of 1812, the British had increased the severity of the postwar depression by "dumping" their low-priced industrial products on the American market. At the time, Dickerson was deeply involved, both as a private citizen and as governor, in the state's growing iron industry. The American iron industry, which was relatively inefficient, was particularly hard-hit by the British dumping tactics. It was not surprising that the legislature responded to Dickerson's message with a strongly worded resolution to the Congress in Washington, urging passage of protective tariffs for the iron industry. The recommendations to this end in Dickerson's first substantial gubernatorial address were his first official expressions on the topic, and they became his hallmark. Dickerson was one of the leading protariff spokesmen on the national scene for over a quarter of a century.

In the area of internal improvements, Dickerson proposed immediate attention to improving the state's roads. New Jersey's reputation for having the worst roads along the Atlantic seaboard gave the proposal a certain urgency. Instead of asking the state to build or improve roads, the new governor suggested that it encourage the further formation of private turnpike companies, which had proved successful in Pennsylvania, New Jersey and other states since the 1790s. Dickerson also pointed out the need for a canal across the state between the Raritan and Delaware rivers. Though the legislature responded by forming a public stock company, the public failed to follow with subscriptions. The canal was finally built after a private company was chartered in 1830.

As governor, Dickerson played an important role in establishing New Jersey's public school system. In the early nineteenth century the citizens of New Jersey had demonstrated a growing sentiment for the establishment of a state-financed system of public education. The first successful action toward such a school system—the passage in 1817 of a bill creating a fund for the support of free schools—took place during Dickerson's administration. An act passed in 1829 finally established the first common schools, which were partially supported by an annual appropriation of $20,000 from the income of the 1817 fund.

The most traumatic developments during Dickerson's gubernatorial years resulted from a natural catastrophe: droughts and killing frosts led to a great shortage of grass and grain. Even during July and August ice formed in the Hudson River and in waters throughout the state. Because of the unique weather and the resulting widespread distress, 1816 was known well into the twentieth century as "the year without a summer." As a Jeffersonian dedicated to minimal governmental activity, Dickerson could not contemplate official action to relieve the public distress. In a message to the legislature, he noted the shortages but looked for a positive element: he piously hoped that the rising prices would discourage distillers from making "poison" out of what was "intended by the bounty of Heaven to man for his nourishment." In 1817 the weather returned to normal.

Dickerson left the governorship for the United States Senate in 1817. Twice reelected unanimously, he served sixteen years. In Washington he made his presence felt mainly by his stands on the tariff. At that time, Americans saw the tariff issue as equal in importance to the increasingly troubling issue of slavery. Toward resolving the latter issue

Dickerson could contribute little. As the 1832 presidential election approached, he was seriously considered to replace the out-of-favor vice-president, John C. Calhoun. But the shrewd and politically adroit Martin Van Buren was selected as Andrew Jackson's second vice-president and, subsequently, as the eighth president of the United States.

Jackson, however, rewarded Dickerson for faithful service to him and to the Democratic party by offering him the cabinet post of secretary of the navy; he accepted, and served for four years remaining in office during part of the Van Buren administration. His performance as a cabinet member clearly reflected his personal charm and his ability to work with people individually. Again, as during his years in the Senate, he demonstrated his dedication to public service by seldom being absent from his duties. Ironically, he may have performed most notably in calming Baltimore and Washington in the early 1830s when antiblack riots completely disrupted the two cities. Because he was on the scene while the secretary of war and President Jackson were absent, Dickerson took charge as acting secretary of war. His years in the cabinet were marked by his success in maintaining law and order during the racial disturbances, his frequent demonstration of personal attractiveness, and, mainly, his command of administrative routines which had fallen into near chaos.

Dickerson was sixty-eight years old when he retired as secretary of the navy. Through the last fifteen years of his life he remained interested and active in politics. His iron-mining business was affected by the economic depression of the late 1830s and early 1840s, but it prospered even in those years, mainly through his personal efforts and attention. After he returned from Washington, he continued to be an outstanding spokesman for protective tariffs. He was elected president of the protectionist American Institute in 1846, and he gave speeches, wrote articles, and published newspaper propaganda for the cause of higher tariffs.

Dickerson never married. The name most commonly linked to his is that of Philemon, his younger brother, who served as Democratic governor in 1836 and 1837. The elder Dickerson served as judge of the United States District Court for New Jersey from August 1840 to February 1841, and when he resigned his friend President Van Buren appointed Philemon to the vacant seat.

Mahlon Dickerson performed his last public service in 1844 as a member of the state constitutional convention in Trenton. He was elected vice-president of the convention and appointed chairman of the committee on the governor's powers of appointment and tenure of office. He died October 5, 1853, and is buried in the Presbyterian churchyard in Succasunna, New Jersey.

Mahlon Dickerson Diary, The New Jersey Historical Society, Newark, N.J.

Mahlon Dickerson Diary, Rutgers University Special Collections, New Brunswick, N.J.

Mahlon Dickerson Papers, The New Jersey Historical Society, Newark, N.J.

Beckwith, Robert R. "Mahlon Dickerson of New Jersey, 1770–1853." Ph.D. dissertation, Columbia University, 1964.

Fee, Walter R. *The Transition from Aristocracy to Democracy in New Jersey, 1789–1829.* Somerville, N.J.: Somerset Press, 1933.

Pumpelly, Josiah C. "Mahlon Dickerson, Industrial Pioneer and Old Time Patriot." *Proceedings of the New Jersey Historical Society* 11 (1891): 131–56.

Taylor, George Rogers. *The Great Tariff Debate, 1820–1830.* Boston: D. C. Heath, 1966.

Robert R. Beckwith

ISAAC HALSTED WILLIAMSON (September 27, 1767–July 10, 1844), governor of New Jersey from 1817 to 1829, was born in Elizabethtown, the youngest son of Matthias and Susannah (Halsted) Williamson. In 1808 he married Anne Crossdale Jouet and they had two sons, Benjamin and Isaac Halsted.

Although he received only a common school education, he studied law as an apprentice to his brother Matthias, a well-known lawyer in the state. After his admission to the bar in 1791, he began a practice in Essex County that flourished and soon extended to Morris County, growing with his reputation for a thorough understanding of the law.

Initially a Federalist, Williamson broke with the party over its formal opposition to the War of 1812. When elected in 1815 as a Democratic-Republican to the general assembly, he proved himself to be an able legislator. Legislative leaders indicated their respect for his legal acumen by choosing him to serve on committees that dealt with complex legal questions, including proposals concerning laws for indebtedness and the status of free blacks. During his term in the assembly Williamson also made recommendations on divorce, which was handled by the legislature at that time. He served in the assembly for part of the 1816–17 term, but when Mahlon Dickerson's resignation created a vacancy in the governorship, the legislature chose Williamson as his successor. The support which other representatives from eastern New Jersey gave Williamson was a crucial factor in his selection over his main competitor, Joseph McIlvaine, a Burlington County lawyer who was West New Jersey's candidate in the election.

The constitution of 1776 provided for a strong legislature and a weak governor. Elected annually by a vote of the legislature, the governor lacked the power of veto, and Williamson did little to strengthen the feeble powers the constitution accorded him. He dropped the traditional practice of giving an annual message to the legislature and thereby inadvertently weakened his influence.

As governor, Williamson actively supported the construction of canals in the state and closely observed New York's achievement in opening the Erie Canal. After the 1820 failure of a private attempt to build the proposed Delaware and Raritan Canal, Williamson recommended that the state build it; but the weakness of his office hampered him, and he could not influence the assembly to act. By 1826 the issue had become divisive within the Republican party. Finally, at the end of his last term as governor in 1829, the legislature authorized Williamson to initiate a study of the benefits the canal might provide. He commissioned John Simpson to ascertain the amount of shipping between the ports of Philadelphia and New York and seized on Simpson's estimates to persuade the legislature to act. Williamson felt that "such a canal cannot fail to be of immense advantage." Its benefits would "not be confined to its immediate neighbourhood, but would be felt in every part of the state, and greatly increase her importance in the Union." The legislature chartered the canal in 1830, and by 1834 it was completed.

Under the constitution of 1776 the governor served in a dual capacity as chancellor and governor. Perhaps because of the limitations of the governor's role, Williamson put much of his energy into his work as chancellor. He reordered the rules of the court and drafted new procedures for collection when debts were secured by mortages. As a result many of the cases considered by Chancellor Williamson dealt with liens on mortgages. He refused to grant an injunction to the Paterson Society for Useful Manufactures against the Morris Canal Company for its proposed use of water from the Rockaway River. In his opinion, the society had no legal basis for a complaint since water had not yet been diverted to the canal; therefore the society sustained no damage. Ironically, during this important case, he was able to do more for the canal movement as chancellor than as governor.

Contemporaries regarded Williamson as a poor speaker and only a fair writer. However, they rarely questioned his judgment in legal cases. In the realm of

ethics Williamson, like many others, could separate his public views from his private life. For example, as governor he apparently supported the state legislature's position against the spread of slavery when the Missouri Question was being debated. However, a bill of sale dated April 13, 1826, lists Williamson as the purchaser of two slaves and their children.

Although Williamson rarely used the governor's office as a forum for political speeches, he supported John Quincy Adams in the elections of 1824 and 1828. Andrew Jackson carried the popular vote in New Jersey in 1824, but the legislature remained anti-Jacksonian.

Jackson's forces grew steadily in number during the 1824–28 period, and the decisive national defeat of Adams in 1828 weakened the morale of New Jersey Republicans. This led directly to Williamson's defeat one year later by the Jacksonian candidate, Garret D. Wall, with a 37–15 vote in joint meeting. Wall declined the office and a Jacksonian successor, Peter D. Vroom, Jr., was chosen in his stead.

From 1830 to 1833 Williamson served as mayor of Elizabeth, and in 1831–32 he represented Essex County in council. In 1832 he declined an appointment to be chief justice of the state supreme court in order to continue his increasingly lucrative law practice.

In the years from 1833 to 1844 Williamson, by 1833 a Whig, kept himself embroiled in most of the state's noteworthy legal battles. In a remarkable reversal, he became the legal counsel of the Camden and Amboy Railroad, which he had criticized while governor. In an 1834 legal battle, he skillfully attacked the Delaware and Raritan Canal Company's claims that their charter permitted them to construct a railway line along the canal. A year later he argued similarly for the Camden and Amboy against the Trenton and New Brunswick Turnpike Company.

In 1844 Williamson was chosen to be a member of the convention which met to design a new constitution. Unanimously elected convention president, he fought hard to replace the constitution that had limited him as governor with one creating a more balanced government by increasing the power of the governor and diminishing the authority of the legislature. The governor would serve a term of three years instead of one, he would be elected by the people, and he would have veto power over legislative acts.

Illness forced Williamson to resign just before the close of the convention to "prevent any delay occasioned by my abscence." He expressed "great confidence" in the new constitution, which would supersede the "radically defective" 1776 document. On July 10, 1844, only a few weeks after his resignation from the convention, he died at the age of seventy-seven in Elizabethtown. His son Benjamin, who continued his successful legal practice, was himself appointed chancellor of New Jersey in 1852 under the revised system of government.

Mahlon Dickerson Papers, The New Jersey Historical Society, Newark, N.J.

Peter D. Vroom Papers, Rutgers University Special Collections, New Brunswick, N.J.

Isaac Williamson Papers, The New Jersey Historical Society, Newark, N.J.

Isaac Williamson Papers, New Jersey State Library, Bureau of Archives and History, Trenton, N.J.

Isaac Williamson Papers, Rutgers University Special Collections, New Brunswick, N.J.

Ershkowitz, Herbert. "New Jersey Politics During the Era of Andrew Jackson, 1820–1837." Ph.D. dissertation, New York University, 1965.

Halsted, Oliver S. Address upon the Character of the Late, the Honorable Isaac H. Williamson, Delivered before the Bar by Oliver S. Halsted. Newark: A. Guest, 1844.

Opinion of I. H. Williamson esq. and Garret D. Wall, esq. in Relation to the Corporate Powers of the Trenton and New Brunswick Turnpike Company. Trenton: Joseph Justice, 1835.

Frank J. Esposito

PETER DUMONT VROOM (December 12, 1791–November 18, 1873), governor of New Jersey (1829–32; 1833–36), was born in Hillsboro Township, Somerset County, New Jersey, the son of Colonel Peter Dumont Vroom and Elsie (Bogert) Vroom. Colonel Vroom (1745–1831), of Dutch and French-Huguenot descent, moved to New Jersey from New York. During the revolutionary war, he served in the Second Battalion of the Somerset County militia. Subsequently, he occupied almost all the offices in the county, including those of sheriff, justice of the peace, member of the General Assembly (1790–98; 1813–17) and member of the Legislative Council (1798–1804).

The colonel's son received his education at Somerville Academy, and in 1808 he was graduated from Columbia College, New York. After reading law in Somerville, he was admitted to the bar in 1813. He practiced in Sussex and Hunterdon counties and gained some eminence as a lawyer before moving back to Somerville, where Attorney General Theodore Frelinghuysen appointed him prosecutor of the pleas. Vroom married twice: on May 21, 1817, Ann V. D. Dumont; and after her death, Senator Garret D. Wall's daughter Maria Matilda, on March 4, 1840.

Like his father, Peter D. Vroom began as a Federalist. During Vroom's early adulthood, however, Jeffersonian-Republican domination of the state left him little chance of achieving anything more than a local office in Somerset County. But the election of 1824, which split the Republican party, changed that. Like a number of other Federalists in the state including ex-governor Aaron Ogden, James Parker, and Garret D. Wall, Vroom supported Andrew Jackson. As a Jackson partisan and the advocate of state construction of a canal from th

Delaware River to the Raritan, Vroom was elected to the general assembly from Somerset County in 1826 and 1827. Following Jackson's victory in the election of 1828, his supporters (called Democrats after 1834) in New Jersey dominated the state politically through 1837. When, in 1829, they gained control of the legislature, Garret D. Wall was elected governor. He refused the position, and Peter Vroom was elected, ending the thirteen-year rule of Isaac Williamson.

An able governor, Vroom achieved considerable popularity during his six years in office (1829–32; 1833–36). He believed in increasing the powers of the executive branch to make it coordinate in power with the legislature. To accomplish this goal and stay within the limitations of the 1776 constitution, Vroom reintroduced the practice of regularly sending a message to the legislature and meeting with his party's legislative caucus to influence its decisions on legislation and patronage. His efforts gained his administration an impressive list of accomplishments, especially in the areas of prison and militia reform, education, and internal improvements.

After becoming governor, Vroom worked to improve New Jersey's penal system. Responding in his first message to reform groups who criticized the New Jersey prison at Lamberton, Vroom proposed building a new institution modeled after the Eastern Penitentiary in Pennsylvania. Although the legislature withheld its approval until Samuel Southard's term in office, the prison was completed during Vroom's second tenure as governor. Vroom also proposed the abolition of imprisonment for debt, another concern of reformers. The legislature enacted a partial repeal during his first term, though it did not enact total repeal until 1842. Governor Vroom also urged the legislature to reform the militia system, under which every able-bodied man between eighteen and forty-five had to train regularly with a unit. The training meetings, which accomplished little, ended in 1834 at Vroom's urging. Vroom also pushed the

legislature toward school reform. During his first term, the legislature distributed part of the money in the school fund to local townships to support public education. Although the law was inadequate and Governor Vroom consistently sought to reorganize and secure greater public financing for public education, the 1829 act was a milestone in the development of public education in New Jersey and the first step in the creation of a state-supported school system.

During Vroom's administration nothing generated more controversy than the construction of a canal and a railroad through central New Jersey. At the beginning of the 1829 session of the legislature, Vroom proposed chartering a private company to build the Camden and Amboy Railroad and left the method of building the canal to the legislature. Consequently, the Delaware and Raritan Canal Company was chartered at the same time as the Camden and Amboy Railroad Company. One year later, to secure financing for the canal, Vroom supported merging the railroad and the canal into the so-called Joint Companies. The charter guaranteed the companies a monopoly over all canal and rail transportation between New York City and Philadelphia, but even this measure failed to secure capital for the canal, and Vroom proposed taking the necessary money from the school fund and lending it to the canal company.

After 1834, the growing concern among political leaders about the power the Joint Companies exercised in the state led Vroom, during his last term in office, to suggest that the state purchase them to eliminate them as a partisan issue. However, the companies' president, Robert F. Stockton, made an offer that Vroom and most legislators found unacceptable. The sale went unconsummated and the state had a political issue that periodically caused great controversy. But despite the political problems that they created, the canal and the railroad, both operating by Vroom's last term in office, contributed greatly to the state's economic development. A transit duty the Joint Companies paid the state also reduced state taxes and defrayed the construction costs of the Trenton Prison.

Despite his support of the Delaware and Raritan Canal Company, Vroom generally acted with the anticorporation wing of his party. As governor, he urged the legislature to desist from issuing new bank charters in the state and from granting other corporate charters that did not contain strong safeguards. Until his last term in office, Vroom generally succeeded in persuading the legislature to restrict the other uses of the corporate form. Nonetheless, during his last year in office, a combination of Whigs and procorporation Democrats succeeded in creating a number of banks.

As governor, Vroom also served as chancellor of the court of chancery. Because the opinions of the earlier chancellors were unpublished, Vroom's decisions set important precedents for future courts. His decisions on corporations, which were playing an increasing role in New Jersey's economic activities during his administration, were especially significant. In *Suydam* v. *Receivers of the Bank of New Brunswick,* Vroom ruled that legislative acts regulating banking corporations could be applied to previously chartered institutions without being considered ex post facto. In several cases Vroom ruled that the state legislature, to perform public services, had broad powers to delegate its rights of eminent domain to private companies. (See *Scudder* v. *Trenton Delaware Falls Company* and *Society for Establishing Useful Manufactures* v. *Morris Canal Company.*) But Vroom's most controversial case, *Joseph Hendrickson* v. *Thomas L. Shotwell,* grew out of a schism between Hicksites and Orthodox Quakers. In an opinion that had political as well as legal ramifications, Vroom upheld the decision of Chief Justice Charles Ewing and Justice George K. Drake of the supreme court, awarding the school property of the Chesterfield Meeting to the Orthodox Quakers as the sect having the greater theological link to the original Friends who founded the

Chesterfield Meeting. Hicksite resentment over the decision led the branch to seek redress from the legislature. Finding their greatest support in Vroom's party, the Hicksites secured the passage of a law dividing church property equally in the case of a schism.

In 1836, after his party had won control of the joint meeting, Vroom declined to stand for reelection on account of ill health. Fellow Democrat Philemon Dickerson replaced him.

Vroom continued to alternate between private legal practice and governmental service. In 1837 President Martin Van Buren sent him to Mississippi as a commissioner to adjust land claims arising from the removal of the Choctaw Indians from the state. In 1838, as one of the five Democratic candidates for Congress, he became involved in the famous "Broad Seal War." Conflict over the accuracy of Monmouth County's returns caused the House of Representatives to challenge Governor Pennington's certification of a Whig victory. The House of Representatives, with a small Democratic majority, seated Vroom and the rest of the Democratic ticket. This allowed them to choose a Speaker and to control committee appointments.

After his defeat for reelection in 1840 Vroom remained in active Democrat. He assumed the role of an elder statesman in the party, generally supporting a moderate view against the threats to the union from abolitionists on one side and secessionists on the other. In his elder statesman role, Vroom ran as an elector for Pierce in 1852 and for Breckenridge in 1860. During the Civil War, Vroom urged moderation and played a large role in preventing disturbances in New Jersey over the draft law, an act which he regarded as unconstitutional. His desire to seek moderate solutions led him to give strong support to General McClellan against Lincoln in 1864.

After 1840, Vroom also served in a number of important governmental positions. He played an active role in the New Jersey Constitutional Convention of 1844. Relying on his experiences in office, he urged the convention to increase the power of the executive, especially by providing for the governor's direct election, increasing his patronage powers, and giving him a limited power of veto over legislation. At this convention Vroom also stated again the anticorporation and antibanking sentiments he had expressed as governor.

In 1846 Vroom, with Chief Justice Henry W. Green, Stacy G. Potts, and William L. Dayton, revised the statutes of the state to bring them into compliance with the new constitution. In 1853, President Franklin Pierce appointed him ambassador to Prussia, where he remained until 1857. Serving in Prussia during the Crimean War, Vroom dealt with a number of issues arising from the conflict, but his major problem as an American minister developed out of the large German emigration to the United States during this period. Vroom served early in 1861 as a commissioner to the peace conference called by Virginia to try to avert a civil war. In 1865, he replaced his son, John P. Vroom, who had died several months earlier, as a law reporter of the New Jersey Supreme Court, and served in this capacity until his death in 1873.

In summary, Peter Dumont Vroom left an important mark on the politics of New Jersey. He helped restore the governorship to a position of prominence; he helped to codify the laws in the state; he was one of the founders of the New Jersey Democratic party; and he helped rewrite the state constitution.

Charles A. Philhower Collection, Rutgers University Special Collections, New Brunswick, N.J.

Ferdinand S. Schenck Papers, Rutgers University Special Collections, New Brunswick, N.J.

Samuel L. Southard Papers, Princeton University Special Collections, Princeton, N.J.

Peter D. Vroom Papers, Columbia University Library, New York, N.Y.

Peter D. Vroom Papers, The New Jersey Historical Society, Newark, N.J.

Peter D. Vroom Papers, Rutgers University Special Collections, New Brunswick, N.J.

Garret D. Wall Papers, Princeton University Special Collections, Princeton, N. J.

Birkner, Michael J. "Peter Vroom and the Politics of Democracy." In *Jacksonian New Jersey*, edited by Paul A. Stellhorn. Trenton: New Jersey Historical Commission, 1979.

Ershkowitz, Herbert. "New Jersey Politics During the Era of Andrew Jackson, 1820–1837." Ph.D. dissertation, New York University, 1965.

Levine, Peter D. *The Behavior of State Legislative Parties: New Jersey, 1829–1844.* Rutherford, N.J.: Fairleigh Dickinson University Press, 1977.

Proceedings of the New Jersey Constitutional Convention of 1844. With an Introduction by John E. Bebout. Trenton: Federal Writers' Project, 1942.

Herbert Ershkowitz

SAMUEL LEWIS SOUTHARD (June 9, 1787–June 26, 1842) was governor of New Jersey for barely four months. His service was a brief though eventful interlude in a lengthy, varied, and distinguished political career. He was born in Basking Ridge, Somerset County, to Henry Southard, one of the founders of the Jeffersonian-Republican party in New Jersey, and Sarah (Lewis) Southard. Educated in a classical school run by the Reverend Robert Finley in Basking Ridge, he entered the College of New Jersey (later Princeton University) in 1802. Following his graduation in 1804, Southard taught school in Mendham, Morris County. Less than two years later, a Virginia congressional colleague of his father's, John Taliaferro, offered Samuel a position as tutor to his sons and nephews. He accepted and for five years lived at the Taliaferro plantation, "Hagley," in King George County. There he studied law with the eminent Fredericksburg jurist Francis T. Brooke. In 1809 Southard was admitted to the Virginia bar, and in 1811 he returned to his native state to establish a practice. Shortly after his return to New Jersey Southard married Rebecca Harrow, the daughter of a deceased Episcopal clergyman from the Northern Neck of Virginia. In 1812 the Southards established a residence in Flemington, the seat of Hunterdon County. They moved to Trenton in 1817.

From the outset of his adult life in New Jersey Southard was deeply involved in politics. As a young lawyer he wrote anonymous newspaper articles for the New Brunswick *Fredonian* and other leading Jeffersonian papers, and, during the War of 1812, began his lifelong role as a party organizer and spokesman. His evident talents, in combination, no doubt, with his name, enabled him to exert considerable influence in state politics during the period between the collapse of the first party system and the emergence of a new system organized according to loyalty or opposition to Andrew Jackson. This influence he used not merely in patronage dispensation or as a force in making nominations for elected offices, but also to secure lucrative and prestigious public positions for himself. Before reaching the age of thirty-seven, Southard served as assemblyman, justice of the state supreme court, United States senator, and, beginning in 1823, secretary of the navy under James Monroe—the first Jerseyman ever appointed to the cabinet. Invariably, he no sooner took one post than he began to look to others.

Officeholding was not his only concern. Adhering to an evolving and progressive Jeffersonian philosophy of government, Southard supported the Republican party and such causes as internal improvements, public education, the colonization of free blacks, prison reform, and fair treatment of Indians. The presidential campaign of 1824 forced him to choose among five major Republican candidates with somewhat disparate understandings of the Jeffersonian creed. Southard's support for the policies of President Monroe, as well as his cordial personal relations with his cabinet colleague John C.

Calhoun, led him to support the young Carolinian for president. Southard effectively organized Calhoun's campaign in New Jersey, and by late 1823 it was widely believed that Calhoun would run well in the state as a "Southern man with Northern principles."

The collapse of the Calhoun movement in March 1824 left Southard adrift. William H. Crawford's views were unpalatable, Andrew Jackson was in his view unqualified, Henry Clay's following in New Jersey was insubstantial, and the men running John Quincy Adams's campaign were not his political friends. Hence Southard professed neutrality, though privately he had little difficulty supporting Adams as the man most qualified and congenial to his own political notions, and most likely to keep him in the cabinet if elected.

Jackson won a plurality in the general election, but Adams triumphed in the House of Representatives and retained Southard as secretary of the navy. Southard devoted himself to strengthening the department, as he would continue to do in the Senate in the 1830s. The leading student of national public administration, Leonard D. White, has called Southard "a vigorous and effective secretary," "perhaps the ablest" of any who served during the Jeffersonian era (1801–29). As navy secretary Southard maintained close communication with administration supporters in New Jersey and deepened his commitment to the progressive Jeffersonianism he believed Adams represented. He served as the chief conduit for both patronage and intelligence between state and national capitals.

Southard played a major role in New Jersey in the presidential campaign of 1828, in which Adams carried the state. Jackson, however, won a convincing national triumph, and Southard was out of a job. Because Adams's supporters controlled the state legislature, Southard had expectations of a return to the United States Senate. However, a schism within the anti-Jackson ranks in joint meeting resulted in a setback even more mortifying because it was his bitter political rival, Mahlon Dickerson, who defeated him.

Southard was able in 1829 to win election as state attorney general. In this post he assumed leadership of the National Republican party in New Jersey; from it he rose to the governor's chair in 1832, when his party regained control of the state after three years of Jacksonian dominance. His election was a case of the office seeking the man rather than the man the office. The governorship conferred prestige and a measure of control over patronage (no inconsiderable factor in the party battles of this era), but the opportunity for leadership and national reputation lay in the United States Senate. His party, however, lacking a candidate of stature for the governor's office, entreated Southard to accept it and he reluctantly acquiesced.

Southard served as governor for only four months. During this period, he presided over a wholesale purge of Jacksonians from state, county, and local posts, demonstrating that in New Jersey at least, anti-Jacksonians were as adept as their partisan counterparts in distribution of political patronage. On state issues, however, the parties had few differences at the time. Perhaps the most significant issue was whether the state should erect a new prison (and remove the state arsenal from the capitol building to the old prison) at a cost of $150,000. A bipartisan committee of the legislature agreed with the governor that "long experience has shown, that our present building, and the system of discipline necessarily connected with it, can neither be reconciled with the principles of a just economy, nor with the great purposes of human punishment." The legislature voted the funds for the project, and the new prison was erected during Peter D. Vroom's second tenure as governor.

In areas aside from the prison question, Southard's recommendations had less impact. No doubt impressed as governor by the weakness of his office, Southard urged that the constitution be amended to permit popular election. He also sought to divest the office of its judicial duties, believing that they inhibited the election of any but lawyers and imposed intolerable political pressures in legal proceedings. In his message of January 11, 1833, Southard also supported curbs on the influx of "colored persons" into the state, though he made no specific recommendations, and favored altering the poorly functioning militia system by making service voluntary; those who did not wish to serve would pay a tax which could be used for public education or some similar purpose. A voluntary system was enacted, but not during Southard's tenure.

In his annual message to the legislature Southard, speaking less as a state administrator than a party leader, injected his —and presumably his party's—credo on national issues. He supported "a tariff which shall protect the industry of the country"; a "sound currency"; "internal improvements"; and "the independence of the judicial power, which was intended to possess and to exercise jurisdiction on constitutional questions and controversies between states." He alluded to the failures of the Jackson administration in each of these areas, with special emphasis on the Jacksonians' war against the Bank of the United States—a war that Southard believed would mean the ascendancy of state and local banks "similar to those which once scattered ruin and distress over the country and affected even the national Treasury."

As governor, of course, Southard could have little influence on the resolution of these highly charged national issues. But on the most emotional question of the moment, the nullification crisis, he was able to present his views at some length. Responding to the Tariff of 1832, South Carolina called a convention and, on November 24, passed an Ordinance of Nullification. South Carolina's challenge to the administration (and implicitly to the North) on this issue provoked a firestorm of controversy. President Jackson,

himself a slaveholder and strict-construc-
tionist Jeffersonian, astounded his
erstwhile enemies in his December 10
proclamation to the people of South Carolina by coming down firmly against
nullification and threatening to coerce
that state into submission if necessary.
Northern state legislatures expressed support for the president's forceful message
and sent documents calling on New Jersey to join this coalition. Southard introduced these documents to the legislature on January 11, 1833, with his most
noteworthy state paper as governor, a
scholarly yet impassioned disquisition on
nullification's genesis, sophistries, and
potential ramifications.

Several themes surfaced in the eigh-
teen-page analysis. First, the supremacy
of law and the need to adjudicate constitutional disputes through normal chan-
nels—that is, the court system. Nullification, Southard stressed, was an illegitimate effort to circumvent the system established by the framers. "The
provisions which have been received in
the South Carolina Ordinance of
Nullification," he wrote, "are utterly repugnant to the spirit and existence of all
our institutions, and to the rights and
privileges under them, of the minority of
the people of that state. Their enforcement would, of itself, sever the Union—
break the bonds of connection between
the states—and render them separate
powers. That which was proposed as a
peaceful remedy leads, inevitably, in the
end, to war."

Second, secession was both unjustified
and intolerable. It was "revolution and
disunion" entirely unsanctioned by the
Constitution and unacceptable to the
other states. Observing that Jackson's
determination to uphold the laws of the
land was "the language of duty, of office,
and of the constitution of the United
States," Southard made it clear that New
Jersey would contribute whatever might
be asked of it in a clash between federal
authority and South Carolina.

Partly out of longstanding personal dis-
like of Jackson and public opposition to
Jackson's politics, Southard had to qualify his words of support for the president.
He expressed regret that Jackson's language should be so violent as to encourage
defiance by the Carolinians. Moreover, as
he would explain in another message to
the legislature (January 28, 1833), he disagreed with Jackson's constitutional interpretation in a key particular. Although
he reiterated his rejection of nullification,
he insisted that the Constitution did not
sanction coercion of a state; it provided
that the federal government should act
directly only on individuals. "Both the
coercion and the right of resistance
spoken of, are opposed to the theory of our
institutions"—a theory upon which he
elaborated at some length.

The language was constitutional, but
the purport was in large measure political. Southard was only too happy to join
in flailing the dragon of nullification. But
he did not wish to be locked in embrace
with his enemy of long standing. Hence
the stress on constitutional differences
even as he upheld the substance of Jackson's position. The apparent awkward-
ness of this stance (though in fact the
constitutional argument was quite orthodox) led to some political jibes from
the Jackson press. The Newark New-
Jersey Eagle claimed that in staking out a
position apart from President Jackson's,
Southard had joined forces with John C.
Calhoun, for whom (recalling his friendship with Calhoun during the 1820s), he
"has not yet lost his partiality." Should
the two men ever again meet in the Senate, the Eagle's editor suggested, "both
advocating the doctrine of state supremacy, over the powers of the General Government, who will venture to foretell the
consequences? Let the people of New Jersey look to it." To this distortion of
Southard's position the National Republican press replied at length and with
vigor.

Soon after, however, the controversy
died; Congress passed a compromise
tariff, and South Carolina, realizing its
isolation on the issue, relaxed its defiant
posture. Southard viewed the denoue-

ment of the crisis not from Trenton but from Washington. The joint meeting of the legislature elected him to the Senate on February 23, and he resigned on February 27 to join his fellow Whigs in Washington to debate the tariff, bank, Indian, and land issues. He was succeeded as governor by Elias P. Seeley.

Southard remained in the Senate for the rest of his life. He won a measure of acclaim for his attacks on Jacksonian economic and social policy and respect for his chairmanship of the Senate Committee on Naval Affairs. He was elected president pro tem of the Senate in March 1841, and he became the permanent presiding officer of that body less than a month later when President William Henry Harrison died and Vice-President John Tyler succeeded him.

When not engaged in politics, Southard was an active member of the New Jersey bar and occasionally argued before the United States Supreme Court. During the 1830s he was counsel for the Joint Transportation Companies in their legal battles with rival railroads. He served other corporations as well. One of them, the Morris Canal and Banking Company, named him president in 1837, compelling him and his family to move from Trenton to Jersey City. He served as president of the company for little more than a year and resigned in 1839 when his Senate responsibilities and other business interests prevented his giving full attention to the corporation. He remained, however, on retainer to the Morris Canal and Banking Company until his death.

As a lawyer, Southard participated in a number of significant cases, including the hearing before the New Jersey legislature in January 1815 about the monopoly of Aaron Ogden's steamboat line. Another was the "Hicksite" case over the division of properties between contending factions of West Jersey Quakers.

A handsome, impressive-looking man who tended toward corpulence in his later years, Southard suffered increasingly from ill-health. His final illness made him, according to one contemporary, "a

mass of gouty afflictions," and forced him to resign from the presidency of the Senate on May 31, 1842. He died in Fredericksburg, Virginia, on June 26, 1842, aged fifty-five, survived by his wife and three of their seven children.

Samuel L. Southard Papers, Princeton University Special Collections, Princeton, N.J.

Samuel L. Southard Manuscripts, Library of Congress, Manuscript Division, Washington, D.C.

Ershkowitz, Herbert. "Samuel L. Southard: A Case Study of Whig Leadership in the Age of Jackson." *New Jersey History* 88 (Spring 1970): 5–24.

———. "New Jersey Politics During the Era of Andrew Jackson, 1820–1837." Ph.D. dissertation, New York University, 1965.

Fallaw, W. Robert. "The Rise of the Whig Party in New Jersey." Ph.D. dissertation, Princeton University, 1967.

Michael J. Birkner

ELIAS PETTIT SEELEY (November 10, 1791– August 23, 1846), governor of New Jersey for seven months in 1833, was born in Deerfield Township (later Bridgeton), the son of Ebenezer and Mary (Clark) Seeley. His father, a merchant and a life-long Cumberland County resident, served for many years as a Jeffersonian-Republican legislator.

Elias Seeley was educated informally. After studying with a local attorney, Daniel Elmer, he was licensed as a lawyer in 1815. According to Lucius Q. C. Elmer, a contemporary from Cumberland County, the younger Seeley "never attained much celebrity as an advocate, but had a good local practice as an attorney and Conveyancer."

On March 6, 1816, Seeley married Jane E. Champneys. The couple had two children, Elias P., Jr., and Rebecca. Until the late 1820s, when he ran successfully as an anti-Jacksonian for the legislative council from Cumberland County, Seeley was not active in politics. Reelected three times, he was named vice-president of the council late in 1832, when the National Republicans gained power. When his party's governor, Samuel L. Southard, left office for the United States Senate, in February 1833, the legislature designated Seeley to succeed him. Along with Seeley's name, the National Republicans' lack of certified state leaders, especially from West Jersey, dictated the selection.

No one could claim that Seeley had the political stature of his gubernatorial predecessor. Introducing him to the public, the National Republican *Newark Daily Advertiser* called Seeley "an amiable man," a characterization the Jacksonian press exploited in the weeks subsequent to the appointment. The Trenton *Emporium & True American* expressed satiric delight that the new governor was "amiable," and proceeded to inquire whether this "amiable" man was capable of performing his duties on the court of appeals, of negotiating the loan of $30,000 the legislature had authorized for a new prison, or of serving effectively as a trustee of the College of New Jersey (later Princeton University). The Newark *New-Jersey Eagle* was more pointed; it cited his "total unfitness" for the office. For this, *Emporium & True American* editor Stacy G. Potts offered, "the party is condemned, not Mr. Seeley," since Seeley had achieved the governorship "not through his own ambition but by the force of circumstances."

As governor, Seeley was more a political target than an active public administrator. Since he was not elected until the close of the legislative session, he was limited as chief executive to making certain appointments (for example, negotiators in a boundary dispute with New York State and compilers of civil and criminal laws in New Jersey), serving on the final appeals board of the state, and preparing an address to the legislature after the October elections.

In fact, Seeley participated in one important case as presiding officer on the court of appeals (composed of the legislative councilors and the governor): the Hicksite case, a dispute between competing factions of the Society of Friends. For several years New Jersey Quakers had been at odds over matters of doctrine and discipline, and by the late 1820s the contending forces had reached a point of no return. Quaker liberals, or "Hicksites" (a derivation from Elias Hicks, a notable Quaker liberal), broke away from the orthodox establishment. This involved a financial settlement and led to the case decided in 1833 by Seeley and the court of appeals. Although the wrangling in court and out was prolonged, the facts of the case are relatively simple to abstract. The Hicksites in Crosswicks demanded the remittance of their share of the contributions to a school trust fund administered by the Society of Friends. The orthodox, maintaining that they needed to make no concessions to schismatics, refused. Hence the court test. The case was first argued before Chief Justice Charles Ewing and Associate Justice George K. Drake of the state supreme court, sitting as masters in chancery. George Wood, perhaps the state's leading attorney, and former Governor Isaac H. Williamson argued for the orthodox, while Garret D. Wall, a leading Jacksonian attorney and politician, and Samuel L. Southard, New Jersey's preeminent anti-Jacksonian politician, argued the Hicksite cause. After lengthy proceedings in a packed courthouse (the "Quaker Case," as it was called, was followed widely in New Jersey and Pennsylvania), the justices decided in favor of the orthodox. They concluded that since the Hicksites were in fact "seceders," they were entitled neither to be considered Quakers nor to regain their school fund contributions.

Matters did not rest there. The decision was appealed to the court of last resort in New Jersey, the court of appeals, with Governor Seeley presiding. In the arguments before this body, Theodore Frelinghuysen replaced Williamson as advocate for the orthodox. The other attorneys and the end result were the same. With a 7-4 vote (across party lines), the court affirmed the decision of Justices Ewing and Drake. In a statement issued with the decision, Seeley, who had voted with the majority against the Hicksites, expressed regret that such "religious controversies" should be brought into the court, and urged both parties to seek some accommodation on their own.

The decision had important political ramifications. The New Jersey Quakers, with a clear majority of liberals, had been staunchly anti-Jacksonian since 1824, and thus were a bulwark of the National Republican organization in the state. Having taken their case to a body controlled by their longtime allies, the Hicksites were grievously disappointed at the outcome. It broke their allegiance to the National Republicans, especially when Jacksonian politicans in West Jersey, where Quakers were most numerous, identified with the Hicksite cause. This strategy, with excellent organization, paid off for the Jacksonians in the 1833 legislative elections. They won an overwhelming, statewide triumph, including victories in Burlington, Monmouth, Salem, and Gloucester counties—all National Republican strongholds. Seeley's failure to "inspire confidence" among East Jersey Whigs, according to one historian, also helped reduce the turnout of traditionally anti-Jacksonian voters and therefore figured in the Jacksonian victory in New Jersey.

Once in control of the joint meeting, the Jacksonians wasted no time replacing Seeley as governor with Peter D. Vroom, Jr. Seeley ended his term with a message on the state of the state. In it, he commented ably on the results of the operations of the state prison, the increase of the school fund, the treasury accounts, and the progress of the construction of the new penitentiary. He offered the usual litanies on the value of public education, suggested legislation (not detailed) to relieve problems resulting from the influx of "coloured persons" in the state and, like

his two most recent predecessors, urged that the current militia system be replaced by a volunteer system with inducements. Seeley's strongest words opposed public executions. "The oftener a person frequents these public exhibitions," he observed,

the less impression they make on the mind; and they can witness the melancholy spectacle with less dread and horror, and in a little time can follow their fellow men to the gallows and witness the death scene with perfect composure. It would be better for many other reasons that might be named, that public executions should be dispensed with, and the law be so amended or modified; that in the future they shall take place within the walls of the prison yard, in the presence of the sheriff and the Officers of the Court.

The newspapers of both parties endorsed Seeley's words on public executions, and the National Republican press widely hailed his message in general. The *Hunterdon Gazette* called the address a "plain sensible document," while the editor of the Trenton *New-Jersey State Gazette* observed that

the manner in which this respectable man was treated by some of the low party papers, during the time he served as Governor of the State, cannot but recur to the minds of many of our fellow citizens, at this time, with regret. The duties which devolved upon him by the constitution and the laws, he certainly discharged with ability and success. His conduct throughout that period was modest, dignified and impartial, and has left a very favorable impression upon the minds of many of his fellow citizens.

It is perhaps ironic that in performing his one notable act as governor—casting a nondecisive vote consistent with his concern for the public welfare in the "Quaker case"—Seeley greatly damaged his party's chances of maintaining control of the state in 1833. No one, however, seems to have blamed him. With the change in political control in Trenton, Seeley returned to the private practice of law, and he later served several terms in the legislature with no particular distinction. He died of cancer in 1846 at the age of fifty-five. At the outset and the end of his brief period in the political limelight, he was a decent man who was less a shaper than a creature of circumstances.

Ershkowitz, Herbert. "New Jersey Politics in the Era of Andrew Jackson, 1820–1837." Ph.D. dissertation, New York University, 1965.

Fallaw, W. Robert, "The Rise of the Whig Party in New Jersey." Ph.D. dissertation, Princeton University, 1967.

Levine, Peter D. *The Behavior of State Legislative Parties in the Jacksonian Era: New Jersey, 1829–1844.* Rutherford, N.J.: Fairleigh Dickinson University Press, 1977.

Michael J. Birkner

PHILEMON DICKERSON (June 26, 1788–December 10, 1862), the twelfth governor under the consitution of 1776, served only one year in the office, from the fall of 1836 to the fall of 1837. Although he was involved in state politics for many years, he spent his entire political career under the shadows of his older brother Mahlon (who served as governor, United States senator, and secretary of the navy) and the two leaders at the center of real power in the New Jersey Jacksonian party, Garret D. Wall and Peter D. Vroom, Jr. Philemon Dickerson, in fact, attained the governorship only when Vroom, in poor health, declined election by the Democratic legislative majority to a seventh one-year term.

Philemon and Mahlon Dickerson were among those attracted to the Jacksonian cause from the ranks of Jeffersonian Republicans. They were somewhat exceptional, since most New Jersey Jacksonian leaders had been notable Federalists. The Dickerson brothers entered the Jacksonian movement during the presidential campaigns of 1824 and 1828 primarily out of personal hostility to John Quincy Adams and Henry Clay. They were to be influential in the Jacksonian party until the late 1830s; the decline of their influence would coincide with the beginning of a long period of Whig dominance in the state.

Philemon Dickerson was born at Succasunna, in Morris County, a descendant of the Philemon Dickerson who had been part of the great Puritan migration to Massachusetts Bay in 1638. The earlier Philemon left Salem, Massachusetts, for Southold, Long Island, in 1672. The founder of the New Jersey branch of the family, Jonathan Dickerson, moved from Long Island to New Jersey in about 1745.

Philemon Dickerson received a classical education at the University of Pennsylvania and studied law in Philadelphia at the instigation of Mahlon, eighteen years his elder. In 1813 he received his license to practice law in New Jersey, established a law practice in Paterson, and married Sidney Stotesbury, daughter of Colonel John Stotesbury of New York. He became a counselor-at-law in 1817 and a sergeant-at-law in 1834. He served in the state assembly, 1821–22.

Dickerson saw the Jackson party in New Jersey in the 1830s as a true embodiment of Jeffersonian principles, particularly in the causes of limited government and a balanced program favoring both industrial and agricultural development. Yet, like most New Jersey politicans, he considered a protective tariff and internal improvements, such as the Camden and Amboy Railroad and the Morris Canal, necessary and beneficial.

The Dickerson family's interest in iron mines near Succasunna and its close identification with the commercial life of northeast New Jersey created some antagonism among Jacksonian "agrarians" in the southern and western parts of the state who were not so firmly protectionist. Despite these differences and the ambiguity of President Jackson himself on the tariff and internal improvements, Philemon Dickerson remained loyal to the general and to his successor, Martin

Van Buren. He distrusted the "unprincipled" leadership of the opposition Whigs, claiming they promoted no program at all. Elected to two terms in the United States House of Representatives in the mid-1830s, he supported the Jacksonian program straight down the line.

When Vroom declined the governorship in the fall of 1836, the Jacksonian majority in the legislature, seeking to replace him quickly with a man of proven loyalty, turned to Dickerson, and he resigned his seat in Congress to accept the position. His term as governor was filled with acrimony and party warfare. Growing economic troubles, culminating in the Panic of 1837, combined with President Van Buren's personal unpopularity to depress the party spirit of New Jersey Democrats and stimulate a new Whig challenge for dominance in the state.

Under the 1776 constitution, many appointments to local and state office were made by a joint meeting of the council and assembly, with each member having one vote. The Whigs, who had the majority in the council, were determined to prevent the Democratic majority in the assembly from controlling the appointments, but they realized that public opinion might be unfavorable if they blocked the joint meeting. They initially seemed to hope that they could make some kind of deal in advance of the joint meeting to share the offices with the Democrats, and soon after Dickerson's accession as governor they advanced the unprecedented claim that the council's voice in the joint meeting should equal the assembly's because the legislature consisted of two equal bodies. The two sides reached no agreement, and the Whigs on the council prevented a joint meeting. State and local officeholders whose terms were to end during this legislative sitting hesitated to act since their authority was so questionable. The new counties of Atlantic and Passaic, created in February, were without either administrative or judicial officers. Neither side would give in; on March 16, 1837, the legislature adjourned without having held a joint meeting.

Governor Dickerson called a special extra sitting on May 22, ostensibly to deal with the "existing 'public exigency' and devise measures for relief." But the only accomplishment of this sitting was a joint resolution authorizing the state treasurer to borrow up to $15,000 for state debts incurred during the expansionist period of easy money; other relief bills were victims of the impasse over the joint meeting. The Whigs, who had controlled the council eight to six during the earlier sittings, lacked a council majority because one of their councillors was ill and another was "held up." Since Governor Dickerson could break the six-to-six deadlock in the Democrats' favor, the Whig councillors had only one remaining weapon: they would have to walk out and leave the Democrats without a quorum. These circumstances led to an unvarying daily routine. The Whigs would propose relief measures, and the Democrats would vote them down. The Democrats would then raise the assembly's joint meeting request; the Whigs would move to table it, lose, and stalk from the chamber. The Democrats had tied the two issues together: they refused to consider relief measures until the Whigs allowed a joint meeting without any deals.

The parties accused each other of disgraceful conduct and blamed each other for the lack of relief measures. Governor Dickerson's administration and the Democrats suffered most, though; they took the brunt of public blame, and when the fall election of 1837 put the Whigs firmly in control of the state legislature, Philemon Dickerson was turned out of office.

Dickerson's short and inconclusive term as governor was but a prelude to other political troubles. Along with four other Democrats and one Whig, he was elected to the United States House of Representatives for the session of 1839–41, but the "Broad Seal War" delayed his taking office for a year and a half. The strength of the parties in the House was so even that control depended on the makeup of the New Jersey delegation. The Whigs made charges of illegal voting and Whig Governor William Pennington rejected returns from two townships and certified the Whigs' entire slate with the great seal of the state. The House overruled this action on July 16, 1840, after a bitter partisan battle, and seated the original winners. But Dickerson's second congressional career was not noted for important activity.

Beset by continued Whig attacks on the Democrats' economic policies, Dickerson was defeated for reelection to Congress in 1840. He had seen a chance to leave the unhappy atmosphere of the House even earlier, when the United States judge for the District of New Jersey, William Rossell, died. He pressed President Van Buren for the appointment. But the president, anxious to preserve the slim Democratic House majority in the climax of his fight for the independent treasury, would agree to the appointment only when Mahlon arranged to come out of semi-retirement and hold the judgeship for Philemon until after the election. In March 1841, Mahlon yielded the judgeship to his brother.

Philemon had a rewarding career on the federal bench from 1841 to his death. He approached the work with enthusiasm, dignity, and self-conscious impartiality. The volume of work was small until the Civil War, when a large number of constitutional questions piled a heavy load on the court. Dickerson's health broke under the strain, but he remained on the bench. He died at Paterson on December 10, 1862.

Dickerson was involved in no precedent-setting decisions on the court but was popular with the bar and with other judicial officials. He remained a leader in state Democratic party councils until the growing sectionalism of the 1850s pushed his sympathies toward the Republicans. He took a great interest in the affairs of Paterson; he was instrumental in procuring its city charter in 1851 and wrote *A Lecture on the City of Paterson, Its Past, Present, and Future* . . . (1856). His second son, Edward Nicoll Dickerson, became a prominent member of the New

Jersey bar, a scientist, and an inventor.

For two decades Philemon Dickerson was an important figure in the politics of New Jersey. He was not a kingmaker at the center of political power, and much of his career was adjunctive to that of his more influential brother; still, he helped build the party system in an era of transition.

Philemon Dickerson Papers, The New Jersey Historical Society, Newark, N.J.

Ershkowitz, Herbert. "New Jersey Politics During the Era of Andrew Jackson, 1820–1837." Ph.D. dissertation, New York University, 1965.

Fallaw, W. Robert. "The Rise of the Whig Party in New Jersey." Ph.D. dissertation, Princeton University, 1967.

Pitney, Henry C., Jr., ed. *A History of Morris County, New Jersey, Embracing Upwards of Two Centuries, 1710–1913.* 2 vols. New York: Lewis Historical Publishing Co., 1914.

W. Robert Fallaw

WILLIAM PENNINGTON (May 4, 1796–February 16, 1862) was born in Newark, the son of Phoebe (Wheeler) and William Sandford Pennington. After attending Newark schools, he earned a degree from the College of New Jersey (later Princeton University) in 1813 and then studied law with Theodore Frelinghuysen. In 1817 he was admitted to the bar, and he began to practice in his native city. Pennington became a licensed counselor in 1820 and a sergeant-at-law in 1834. Between 1817 and 1826, during the judgeship of his father, he served as clerk of the federal district and circuit courts in New Jersey.

William descended from a long distinguished line. His father was the grandson of Judah Pennington and the great-grandson of Ephraim Pennington. Ephraim, originally of New Haven, Connecticut, had moved to New Jersey as one of the founding fathers of the town of Newark. William's wife, Caroline, was a member of another important and distinguished family. Her grandfather, Dr. William Burnet, was a member of the Continental Congress eminent for his services in the revolutionary war, and her father, the younger Dr. William Burnet, was surgeon general of the Continental army.

As founders and leaders, the Penningtons were inevitably and consistently involved with the political and economic growth of the new town and its surrounding area.

By 1800 William's father and uncles had achieved political prominence as organizers and leaders of the new Jefferson-Republican party in Newark and in Essex county. Before President Madison appointed the elder William a judge of the New Jersey district court, he had served as a state assemblyman, council member, and governor. In 1824 the Pennington family supported John Quincy Adams for president, largely out of anger at Secretary of the Navy Samuel L. Southard, the leading New Jersey supporter of John C. Calhoun. Southard had used his influence with President Monroe to secure the district attorneyship of New Jersey for Lucius Q. C. Elmer of Cumberland County. The younger William Pennington, who had wanted the post, never forgave Southard. In 1828 Pennington was chosen to represent Essex County in the state assembly, and he became a leader of the National Republicans in the state. When the National Republicans and other anti-Jackson politicians coalesced to form the Whig party in 1834, Pennington emerged as their leader in Newark.

The victory of the Whigs over the Democrats in the congressional and state elections of 1836 opened the way for Pennington's rise to the governorship in 1837. He proved a popular governor, and until 1843 he was reeelected annually to the post. In his views and acts Pennington embodied a thoroughly Whig philosophy

of government. He believed that the government's chief duty was "to protect the rights of property and the tranquility of society; to secure and support the feeble against the strong, the peaceful against craft and oppression." It seemed obvious to him that the good of any society rested in a harmony of social interests, with mutual dependence and cooperation among the groups and classes. He believed that the legislative power belonged exclusively to the representative body of the government, that the executive branch should have no veto power, and that states' rights should be guarded jealously from federal encroachments. These principles underlay his hostility toward such national Jacksonian measures as the Independent Treasury Act, the Militia Act and the Bankruptcy Act, which he saw as undue extensions of presidential power at the expense of the states. They also explain his insistence that the proceeds from the sale of public lands should revert to the states.

As governor, Pennington fulfilled his dual role as chief executive and chancellor of the state with remarkable skill. His judicial decisions usually pleased the courts and the petitioners; the court of appeals overruled only one of his decrees, and in that instance legal opinion was divided. He was no less distinctive as chief executive. He contradicted the traditional image of the New Jersey governor as a weak executive. The office had limited authority, for it lacked the powers of veto or appointment and its occupant's annual election by a joint meeting of the houses depended on his party's continued dominance in the legislature; the governor's duties lay mainly in signing bills into law and apprising the legislature of general conditions in the state. Pennington's character and personal influence, however, enabled him to overcome the inherent weakness of his office and to exercise an effective, positive leadership. His annual messages, like those of his predecessors, pointed out which conditions needed attention and indicated the priorities for immediate legislative action, but he often adroitly used them as vehicles to propose his own solutions to specific problems as possibilities to be explored. In this way he encouraged and even directed much of the legislation passed in his administration.

His accession to office came in the wake of the disastrous Panic of 1837. The preceding legislature had seemed unable or unwilling to cope with the economic distress. Even a special session called by Governor Philemon Dickerson had failed to produce a program of relief, largely because of a deadlock between the parties in the legislature. This situation changed with a convincing Whig triumph in the state elections of 1837 and the elevation of Pennington to the governorship. As governor Pennington worked with the predominantly Whig legislature to restore public confidence in the economy. He also expressed strong moral and humanitarian concerns. He brought about a major reform of the judiciary to improve the administration of justice. Orphan courts were established to protect children from exploitation and from being deprived of their inheritances. Under him the state initiated action to establish institutions for the care of deaf-mutes and blind children and an asylum for the insane. It inaugurated prison reform, improving health and work conditions, increasing medical care for the prisoners, and providing more humane treatment for their rehabilitation and moral guidance. Pennington's administration abolished imprisonment for debt and reduced the number of crimes specified for capital punishment.

Governor Pennington refocused attention on the common school question. Joining his predecessors, he repeatedly urged legislation to provide an effective and efficient school system, for he viewed education as "a branch of public service." He urged the establishment of a state normal school to train well-qualified teachers and the appointment of a state superintendent. Although legislation passed in 1838 establishing public schools fell short of these objectives, Pennington continued to press for them and for the creation of free public libraries in every school district as well. Public apathy and the political influence of private interests delayed the reforms for another decade, but Pennington's sustained support quickened their momentum.

Pennington staunchly championed and defended states' rights and conservative economic interests. Early in his term, he figured prominently in a political incident which assumed congressional import. A routine executive act erupted into a full-scale political fracas known as the "Broad Seal War." In the close congressional elections of 1838, the governor threw out the returns from two Democratic townships on the grounds that they were questionable. Since the governor had no power to take measures for correcting questionable returns, he argued, he had no choice but to disregard them. Doing so turned the election in favor of the Whigs, and Pennington commissioned all six Whig candidates to represent New Jersey in the House of Representatives. Five Democratic candidates, among them two former governors, Philemon Dickerson and Peter D. Vroom, Jr., contested the decision. When Congress assembled in December, two delegations from New Jersey presented themselves—one with the usual credentials under the broad seal of the state, bearing the governor's signature, the other with a certificate of election signed by the Democratic secretary of state. Because the House was almost equally balanced between Democrats and Whigs, the New Jersey delegation was crucial to its organization and to the determination of the majority party. Ignoring the sealed commissions, the House refused to seat the delegation sanctioned by Governor Pennington. After days of disorder and stormy debate, Congress organized itself without five of the six New Jersey representatives. More than a year of intense debate and investigation followed, and finally the House admitted the Democratic claimants by a strictly partisan vote. Pennington, though he admitted Congress's right to investigate the credentials of its members, excoriated it for violating the great seal and for trampling on states' rights by arbitrarily admitting the protesting delegation without ascertaining the legality of the votes in the two questionable townships. The governor himself was highly criticized by his political opponents for granting the Whig commissions, but the supreme court later upheld him. The case made the need for a new election law obvious, and in 1839 the legislature passed a comprehensive act to regulate elections that remedied the defects of the old law and decreased the possibility of a recurrence of the incident.

Pennington was the first governor to bring effective action against the Joint Companies, the Camden and Amboy transportation monopoly. By virtue of special privileges granted them by the legislature in 1831, they had become so powerful that they practically dominated the state's political and economic life. In 1839, when a dispute arose in the legislature over transit duties owed to the state, the governor used his personal and official influence against the companies, which were dominated by Democrats. When the state referred the case to the supreme court, the companies paid the duties. The companies' setback, however, increased their political activity and eventually helped to restore the Democrats to power, in 1843, unseating Pennington after six years in office.

In spite of his progressive views in some limited areas, Pennington did not favor much-needed constitutional reform. The only reform he advocated and endorsed fully was the separation of the judicial and executive functions of the governor. Ironically, his proposal in 1840 that this basic flaw in the original constitution be removed by legislative action renewed agitation for constitutional revision. Failing to exercise vigorous leadership in the reform movement proved a tactical blunder that lost the Whigs the initiative and contributed heavily to their defeat in 1843. When the new governor, Daniel Haines, a confirmed revisionist, called for a constitutional convention in 1844, leading members of both political parties were elected delegates to the convention, but Pennington was not among them.

Pennington's active political career came to a temporary end with his defeat in 1844, brought on not only by his conservative position on constitutional reform but also by the machinations of politically ambitious Whigs who harbored personal resentments against the "Pennington clique" and entered into collusion with the Camden and Amboy monopolists.

Pennington returned to private law practice and never again held an important state office. His hope of becoming chancellor under the new constitution did not materialize; nor did his hope of becoming a minister to Europe. President Fillmore offered him the posts of governor of Minnesota and claims judge under the Mexican treaty, but he declined both.

Persuaded to run for Congress in 1858, Pennington made a brief but spectacular political comeback. He was elected as a Republican. The political ferment and confusion building toward the Civil War made the peaceful organization of the house difficult. After a bitterly hostile contest lasting two months, Pennington was chosen speaker. It was conceded that despite his ignorance of the technicalities and complicated rules of the House, Pennington presided in this period of high emotional and political stress with fairness, impartiality and wise conciliation. In 1860, he ran again as a Republican, but lost. He died two years later, survived by his wife and by four children, William S., Henrietta, Mary and Edward R. Pennington.

Lane, Wheaton J. *From Indian Trail to Iron Horse: Travel and Transportation in New Jersey, 1620–1860.* Princeton: Princeton University Press, 1939.

Levine, Peter D. *The Behavior of State Legislative Parties in the Jacksonian Era: New Jersey, 1829–1844.* Rutherford, N.J.: Fairleigh Dickinson University Press, 1977.

Nixon, John T. "The Circumstances Attending the Election of William Pennington . . . as

Speaker of the Thirty-Sixth Congress." *Proceedings of the New Jersey Historical Society* 2 (1872): 207–20.

Weart, Jacob. "Speaker William Pennington." *New Jersey Law Journal* 20 (July–August 1897): 230–39.

Sister Serafina D'Alessio

DANIEL HAINES (January 6, 1801–January 26, 1877), the last governor elected by the legislature, was born in New York City. His ancestors had left England in 1637 to settle in Salem, Massachusetts. Later they moved to Southold, Long Island, then left this homestead to join the first settlers of Elizabethtown. While living there, Haines's grandfather, Stephen Haines, played a distinguished role in the American Revolution. One of his sons, Elias, was the future governor's father.

Elias Haines was a well-known and successful New York City merchant. He married Mary Ogden, who was the daughter of Robert Ogden III and the niece of Governor Aaron Ogden. The couple had four daughters and three sons. It was their first child who would become New Jersey's chief executive.

The young Haines's early education took place at a private school in New York under the celebrated instructor Edmund D. Barry. After completing his preparatory education at the academy in Elizabethtown, he was graduated from the College of New Jersey (later Princeton University) in 1820. Haines then entered the law office of his uncle, Thomas C. Ryerson, in Newton, Sussex County. In 1823, after three years of study, he was admitted to the bar, and he began to practice law in Hamburg, Sussex County.

During the election of 1824, Sussex County was strongly pro-Jackson. A Federalist who became an ardent supporter of Andrew Jackson, Haines began his political life by securing Jackson all the votes cast in the small township of Vernon, in which he resided. For the rest of his political career, he continued to work within the Democratic party.

After fifteen years of private law practice, Haines was elected to the legislative council in 1839 by a large majority. He immediately became involved in the political controversy known as the "Broad Seal War." A dispute over the results of the 1838 congressional election had triggered this intensely bitter, partisan contest. In the legislative session of 1839–40, the Whigs introduced a series of resolutions to denounce the action of the House of Representatives, which had failed to support their candidates. Amzi Armstrong of Essex County and Jacob W. Miller of Morris County were the principal Whig advocates of these motions in the council. In the debates that followed, Haines led the opposition, which questioned the legislature's right and fitness to pass the Whig resolutions. Though he failed to prevent their passage, Haines debated with an ability and tact that contributed to his emergence as a political leader and, ultimately, to his election as the state's chief executive.

The Democratic caucus nominated Haines for governor on October 27, 1843, and since the Democrats had just regained control of the joint meeting after six years in the minority, Haines's election was assured. His major achievement during the first of his two terms in office was the adoption of a new state constitution in 1844. Besides being instrumental in bringing about the convention called to frame it, Haines convinced his contemporaries that the state's original fundamental law had "provisions which are at least inexpedient if not wholly incompatible with the spirit of the present age." The anachronistic unity of the offices of governor and chancellor and the chief executive's election by the legislature instead of the people became two of his chief concerns. Moreover, Haines pleaded successfully for a bipartisan convention, believing the constitution to be "a measure which is too momentous to be made the subject of party difference."

Educational reform and the creation of an efficient militia system received Haines's attention also. He told the legislature that the revision of the common school law was "one of [its] most important duties." Under the permissive sections of the 1838 law, local authorities could easily avoid both the responsibility of reporting on the condition of their schools and the obligation to visit and examine them. To insure that local government supervise educational matters properly, Haines suggested that the council and assembly "inquire into the expediency of appointing a general superintendent" of schools. Only a year later, Theodore F. King became the first state superintendent of schools.

The militia system was another area of concern for Haines, and in his second annual message he announced that it "seems to have fallen in great disrepute." Insufficient reports from the brigade officers prevented the state from furnishing the national government the militia statistics it needed before it could issue arms and equipment. Consequently, the state sustained an annual loss of military supplies. In addition, Haines complained that the state's troops were poorly disciplined, and that "the ordinary militia musters . . . are generally admitted to retard rather than to promote improvement; and to be a tax upon the time and service of the citizen without any corresponding benefit."

Under a special provision of the new constitution, Haines continued in office until the inauguration of his successor, Charles C. Stratton, on January 21, 1845. The last governor under the old constitution, Haines might have been the first under the new had he not peremptorily declined the nomination. However, only a few years later, on September 22, 1847, the Democratic State Convention nominated him for governor on the first ballot. In November, he defeated his Whig opponent William Wright, a former mayor of

Newark and a congressman. The Whigs' triumph in the legislative race made his victory all the more impressive.

On January 18, 1848, Haines became New Jersey's chief executive a second time. His term under the new constitution was three years instead of one. During this tenure, he continued his crusade for educational reform, telling the legislature that the cause of education should be its major priority since "not many more than one half of the children in the state receive instruction in the schools [and] . . . a very large proportion must be growing up in ignorance." To improve the quality of instruction in New Jersey, Haines suggested that the state create a normal school to furnish competent teachers, introduce free public education, and increase the money raised to support schools at the state and local levels.

Besides being committed to education, Haines was deeply interested in the welfare of prisoners, and he became an active agent to improve their condition. He was particularly concerned about the "want of suitable arrangements" in county prisons. Because of the lack of means to separate the prisoners, "the hardened villain and the juvenile delinquent" often occupied the same cell. The prisons also lacked any facilities that would allow the inmates to spend time usefully engaged in labor. Such conditions, Haines believed, made the county prisons "schools for vice, whose youngest pupils may become the ripest scholars and most finished rogues." To correct the situation, he urged the establishment of workshops in the county prisons, the creation of separate cells for the older and younger prisoners, and even the construction of a state reform school for juvenile offenders.

At the end of his term, on January 21, 1851, Haines resumed his law practice in Hamburg and worked on a number of important cases. In one involving the Goodyear Rubber Company's right to vulcanize India rubber, he worked with Daniel Webster. In 1852, Governor George F. Fort, his successor, nominated Haines associate justice of the state supreme court, and he took his seat on the bench in November after the senate's confirmation. He was reappointed in 1859, and in 1866, when David A. Depue replaced him after his second seven-year term, he retired. Commenting on Haines's years as the associate justice responsible for the difficult Newark circuit, his friend Lucius Q. C. Elmer said, "few judges were ever freer from the influence of passion or prejudice."

In 1860, Haines supported the candidacy of Stephen A. Douglas because he feared "that the election of Lincoln as a sectional candidate might precipitate war." After Lincoln's election, he continued to oppose every measure that might produce hostilities, but once Fort Sumter had been attacked, he actively supported the Union cause. During the war, he assisted by helping to raise troops for the Northern army. Still, in 1864, he voted for George B. McClellan instead of Lincoln because he felt that "the measures of the administration tend to protract the war." Four years later, he supported Horatio Seymour rather than Ulysses S. Grant because he was "steadily opposed to most of the measures of reconstruction adopted by the Republican party."

The former governor's involvement in public life was quite extensive. He was a trustee of many public institutions. In the Presbyterian Church, he was a ruling elder, a president of the Sussex County Bible Society, and a member of the committee that brought about the reunion of the church after the Civil War.

His special interest in prison reform led the legislature to appoint him in 1868 to study prison systems in New Jersey and other states. In 1870, Governor Theodore F. Randolph named him delegate to the National Congress on Penitentiary and Reformatory Discipline at Cincinnati. The congress named him to a committee to organize a national reform association and to prepare for the International Convention of Prison Discipline and Reform that met in London in 1872. He was a delegate to that meeting, and he served during the same year as the vice-president of the National Prison Association of the United States.

Ann Maria Austin of Warwick, New York, was the first of Haines's two wives. They were married on June 28, 1827, and had three daughters and two sons. One of the sons, Thomas Ryerson Haines, died at the battle of Harrisonburg in Virginia during the Civil War. Ann Maria died on December 8, 1844, and Haines married Mary Townsend of Newark on July 6, 1865. On January 26, 1877, he died at his home in Hamburg.

Alumni Biographical Collection, Seeley G. Mudd Library, Princeton University, Princeton, N.J.

Herrmann, Frederick M. "Stress and Structure: Political Change in Antebellum New Jersey." Ph.D. dissertation, Rutgers University, 1976.

Snell, James P., et al. *History of Sussex and Warren Counties, New Jersey.* Philadelphia: Everts and Peck, 1881.

Frederick M. Herrmann

The Constitution of 1844

CHARLES CREIGHTON STRATTON (March 6, 1796–March 30, 1859), the first popularly elected governor and the only working farmer to serve as chief executive, was born in Swedesboro, Gloucester County. His family had emigrated from England to New England in the seventeenth century, moved to East Hampton, Long Island, in 1648, and arrived in New Jersey about fifty years later.

Stratton's father, James, a judge and physician, served at the battle of Princeton as an assistant surgeon. His mother, Mary Creighton of Haddonfield, participated as a nurse in the Revolution. The couple had seven children, of whom six survived. Charles was the second.

Stratton received a common school education, attending the academy that was the forerunner of the Swedesboro public school. He and his elder brother, Samuel, attended Queens College (later Rutgers University), and were graduated in 1814; Samuel became an Episcopal minister, and Charles spent the next seven years farming.

Charles Stratton served in the General Assembly in 1821 and 1823 and from 1828 to 1829. Between 1829 and 1836, he was a chosen freeholder from Woolwich Town-

ship in Gloucester County, and, in 1835, he also served as a county trustee of the poor. He was elected as a Whig to Congress in 1836. Two years later, he gained notoriety as one of the five members of his party that the House of Representatives declined to seat in the Twenty-sixth Congress during the "Broad Seal War." He was reelected and seated in 1841. On March 18, 1844, the inhabitants of Gloucester County named Stratton one of their two delegates to the constitutional convention. He became an active member of the important committee on the legislative department and demonstrated his strong faith in democracy by opposing the suggestion that paupers be excluded from voting. He was aghast that some of his colleagues believed that "a pauper has not only lost his property, but he has lost his liberty."

He protested government ownership of internal improvements with equal ardor. Fearing the potential for corruption, he supported private control of public works projects. To prevent the state government from becoming too deeply involved in such projects, he supported reducing the proposed thirty-five-year period of state loans for internal improvements to ten years. Many delegates opposed this plan, saying it relinquished forever New Jersey's right to purchase such works regardless of the advantages. Stratton's proposal lost, forty-five to five.

On September 10, 1844, the Whig state convention nominated Stratton to run for governor in the first popular gubernatorial election. His opponent was Democrat John R. Thomson, the secretary of the Joint Companies and a leading lobbyist for them. Stratton's supporters labeled Thomson "the monopoly candidate." The election, the Whigs claimed, would decide whether the people "will govern themselves for three years to come, or be governed by a domineering company of monopolizing aristocrats, with a capital of millions in their hands." One zealous Whig from Cape May summarized his party's position by arguing that the crucial question to be decided at the polls was "whether we shall have Charles C. Stratton, the Jersey farmer to rule over us, or John Railroad Thomson." In October, after a dynamic Whig campaign, Stratton defeated Thomson by 1,358 of the 74,540 votes balloted.

The new governor took office on January 21, 1845, and immediately assumed the responsibility for guiding the state's transition to the new constitution, reminding the legislature that "the circumstances under which we are assembled, mark the commencement of a new era in the political history of the State." The fundamental law of 1844, Stratton continued, required the senate and assembly to enact laws carrying out its principles and to modify existing statutes that conflicted with its provisions. He suggested, therefore, that the time to condense the laws of the state had arrived. The governor noted that the last revision had taken place twenty-five years earlier, in 1820, and that the state's laws were to be found in that year's revised statutes and in annual pamphlets from the various following legislatures. "To the gentlemen of the Bar," he exclaimed, "this may not be a serious inconvenience, but to others less conversant with the legislation of the State, it is a source of constant embar-

rassment." During the legislative session of the next year, an ad hoc commission reported about 120 revised laws. The state published them in 1847.

Stratton was also influential in aiding the establishment of the first state mental hospital. Under an act of March 26, 1845, he appointed three commissioners to contract for the erection of a hospital and to superintend its construction. When the design proved much more expensive than originally estimated, Stratton helped persuade the legislature to appropriate an additional $50,000. This would build a structure large enough to separate the manageable patients from the unmanageable ones, a division "indispensable to their proper treatment and cure."

The Mexican War created additional challenges for New Jersey's chief executive. On May 22, 1846, Stratton received a requisition from President James K. Polk for one regiment of volunteers. He issued an immediate proclamation "calling on the organized uniform companies and other citizens of the state to enroll themselves," and the companies promptly responded to the request. However, to the governor's chagrin, "not one of them had the number of rank and file required by the memorandum accompanying the requisition; and consequently could not be accepted."

Stratton ascribed this failure to "the defective and prostrate condition of the militia system of the state," admitting that "had the circumstances been different; had the call been to suppress insurrection or repel invasion, we should have been found alike unprepared." The governor appealed to the legislature to extend "encouragement in some way to the volunteer companies" and to adopt "some simple mode of ascertaining the number of the militia of the state" so that New Jersey could receive its proper share of the issue of arms and equipment from the national government. Nevertheless, in 1847, when the War Department called on the state to raise a battalion, New Jersey could provide only four of the five required companies and took over five months to do so.

On January 18, 1848, Stratton left office to devote the last years of his life to agricultural pursuits on his farm in Swedesboro. He married Sarah Taggart of Philadelphia on February 1, 1854. Although he had no children, two of his nephews achieved fame. Thomas Preston Carpenter was an associate justice of the state supreme court, while Benjamin Franklin Howey served in the Forty-eighth Congress. Because of ill health, Stratton lived in Europe in 1857 and 1858. He died in Swedesboro on March 30, 1859.

Biographical Collection, Rutgers University Special Collections, New Brunswick, N.J.

Herrmann, Frederick M. "Stress and Structure: Political Change in Antebellum New Jersey." Ph.D. dissertation, Rutgers University, 1976.

Proceedings of the New Jersey State Constitutional Convention of 1844. With an Introduction by John E. Bebout. Trenton: Federal Writers' Project, 1942.

Frederick M. Herrmann

GEORGE FRANKLIN FORT (1809–April 23, 1872), physician, politician, and judge, who was the uncle of Governor John F. Fort (1908–10), was born near Pemberton, New Jersey. The eldest son of Andrew Fort, a wealthy farmer of New Hanover Township in Burlington County, Fort was educated in the common schools at Pemberton and at the University of Pennsylvania Medical College. After graduation in 1828, he entered the office of Dr. Jacob Eghert of Pemberton. Later that year, he moved to Dr. Charles Patterson's office in New Egypt, located then in Monmouth County. In 1830, Fort opened his own practice at Imlaystown, where he married Anna Marie Wright, the daughter of Samuel G. Wright, an iron manufacturer and future Whig congressman. A year later, he returned to New Egypt and extended his practice to southern Monmouth and western Burlington counties, as well as the area which in 1850 became Ocean County.

George F. Fort's public career began when he was elected to the 1844 New Jersey constitutional convention as a Democrat from Monmouth County. His election was made possible by the county Democratic party organization's refusal to agree to the bipartisan ticket advanced in all other counties. This resulted in a thoroughly Democratic Monmouth delegation and gave the Democrats a voting majority at the convention. During the proceedings, Fort supported universal suffrage, open eligibility for office, abolition of the freehold qualification for public office, and the popular election of all state and county officials.

In the state elections of 1844, Fort was elected to the general assembly, well ahead of his ticket, with a majority of five hundred votes. After a term in the assembly, where he served on the judiciary committee, he was elected to the state senate and once more appointed to the judiciary committee. He also served on the committee for education and the Plainfield Bank Investigating Committee and acted as one of three commissioners for ascertaining the value of state lands under water at Jersey City. Fort's reputation as a reformer originated when he sponsored a bill to insure township support for public education and created the Manufacturing Incorporation Law, which eliminated private incorporation acts for specific industries.

In 1850, George Fort was widely endorsed for the Democratic gubernatorial nomination, with the moderately influential *Monmouth County Democrat* advancing his name two months before the Democratic state convention. He was nominated on the fifth ballot over John Summerhill of Salem County, John Cassedy of Hudson County, and Henry A. Ford of Morris County. The Whigs nominated John Runk, a former congressman from Hunterdon County.

The state campaign focused on the power and influence of the Joint Companies, on the Democratic party of New Jersey and, through that party, on the state. In the first popular gubernatorial election in 1844, the Democratic candidate had been John R. Thomson, secretary of the companies. Thomson was the brother-in-law of Robert F. Stockton, the majority stockholder and president of the Camden and Amboy Railroad. Stockton supported Fort for governor in 1850 and was elected to the United States Senate in 1851. Thomson, the initial Democratic caucus nominee for the Senate in 1851, was elected to the seat when Stockton left it in 1853.

Fort was strongly associated with the monopoly interests. When the Camden and Amboy Railroad was incorporated, his father-in-law was named as a commissioner to sell stock in the company. During his administration, Fort suggested that the state government relinquish its right to purchase the works of the Joint Companies in return for a larger guarantee of revenue, arguing that an attempt to annul the exclusive privileges of the companies would constitute a violation of the state constitution. Seven weeks later, on February 28, 1854, Fort was named one of nine corporators in an act incorporating the Camden and Pemberton Agricultural Railroad Company, a trunk line of the Camden and Amboy. The Whigs attempted to label Fort and other Democrats puppets to the interests of the Joint Companies. Their charges, in substance, accused the companies of subsidizing Democratic candidates for governor in return for the appointment of friendly judges to the state judiciary. Indeed, during Fort's administration, the antimonopoly banner was constantly unfurled in elective battles with the Democratic party. During the 1850 campaign, as evidence of his antimonopoly sentiments, Fort and his supporters emphasized his sponsorship of incorporation laws.

The monopoly issue never proved effective in defeating the state's Democracy. More important in the 1850 elections for governor and congress was dissension within Whig ranks over the compromise measures of 1850. Leading Whig newspapers condemned the Fugitive Slave Law as "infidelity to the fundamental principles of the Constitution and Liberty, . . . an exhibition of faithlessness by Northern Representatives to the cause of Northern Rights." They portrayed the Democrats as allied with slave power, favorable to the unlimited expansion of slavery, and devoid of principle—demagogues "stimulating here a base and wicked Popular Prejudice against one portion of our inhabitants [blacks], refusing to consider them as entitled to the privileges of man."

The Democratic press countered, charging Whig leaders with "seeking to make the State of New Jersey an Abolition State." Democrats were not proslavery, and devoid of principle—demagogues "stimulating here a base and augural address when he argued that it was the duty of "every citizen to sustain and carry out" the Compromise of 1850. Fort maintained that the Fugitive Slave Act was binding on northern states because it was "in accordance with the evident intentment of the constitutional compact." Peace, stability, and union depended upon its enforcement in Fort's view, and if New Jersey was to remain loyal to the Union, her officials were compelled to enforce the provisions for the rendition of "fugitives from labor."

Procompromise Whigs found themselves closer to Democrats on the slavery extension issue than to fellow Whigs willing to take the stand in defense of the "Liberty" the *State Gazette* (Trenton) and the *Newark Daily Mercury* demanded. Some, like William Wright, the 1846 Whig gubernatorial candidate and a Democratic United States Senator from 1853 to 1858, simply switched parties. Their disaffection with the Whig party began in 1850 when Whig senators William L. Dayton and Jacob W. Miller voted against the compromise, and they began the process of defection to the Democratic party by exhibiting apathy and lack of enthusiasm during the 1850 campaign.

Other procompromise Whigs attempted to develop a campaign theme that omitted the controversy over the expansion of slavery. The Morristown *Jerseyman*, for example, tried to convert the tired tariff issue into a nativist platform, arguing that the Democracy's tariff of 1846 was decidely pro-European. "It is important," the editor wrote, "that we become independent of foreign nations," through a resurrection of protective features in the tariff of 1842 and the passage of stiffer naturalization laws. The schism between nativist sentiments and anti-slavery extension forces that would plague political opposition to the Democracy until 1860 had begun to work for the Democratic party even though no open conflict took place until 1854 with the passage of the Kansas-Nebraska Act.

The Whig party's failure to unify the themes of its gubernatorial campaign in 1850 led to a stunning Democratic victory. Fort garnered 53.9 percent of the popular vote, the largest percentage any statewide Democratic candidate amassed before the Civil War. More important, Democrats triumphed in Camden, Mercer, Morris, Passaic, and Salem counties for the first time since the 1843 congressional elections, marking a major voter shift. The change secured statewide dominance for the Democratic party, which did not lose a state election until the 1856 victory of the "Opposition" party candidate for governor. In the senate, Democrats gained one member, in the assembly five, achieving a majority in the lower house for the first time in seven years. By 1854, the number of Whig legislators dwindled to twenty-one, while Democrats held fifty-three seats.

During the Fort administration, expenditures for common school education increased substantially, drawn from the income of dividends paid on state-owned Joint Company stock. Major reform legislation created the ten-hour work day and protected child labor. A homestead exemption act was passed, exempting a family homestead from sale for debts totaling less than $1,000. Administration bills for the regulation of banks were secured, consistent with the "hard money" position of the Democratic platform. The system of representation in the general assembly was altered to provide for a district system to replace the old county-wide general elections. General incorporation acts applying to banks, insurance companies, and plank roads were secured, but the old system of private acts to incorporate railroads was retained. The influence of the Joint Companies continued unchecked as two United States senators were elected at their behest, and the conflict over monopoly in a democratic, free-trade economy remained unresolved.

At the expiration of Fort's gubernatorial term, his Democratic successor, Rodman M. Price, appointed him a judge of the court of errors and appeals. After a term on the bench, Fort retired from public life and resumed the practice of medicine in New Egypt. He continued to serve on the board of trustees at Bordentown Female College, and he was a trustee of the Zoar Methodist Episcopal Church in New Egypt. He spent his last years writing a laudatory history of Freemasonry in the United States, published three years after his death on April 23, 1872.

Philip C. Davis

RODMAN MCCAMLEY PRICE (May 5, 1816–June 7, 1894), naval officer and politician, the son of Francis and Ann (McCamley) Price, was born in Frankford Township, Sussex County. His forebears, migrating from Connecticut to the Sussex foothills in the 1740s, became established leaders in the county squirearchy. The governor's grandfather and great-uncle quartermastered for the Continental army and later marketed cattle, timber, and distilled whiskey to the port of New York. Sharing the privileges of his class, Rodman Price attended the Presbyterian academy at Lawrenceville and may have entered the College of New Jersey (later Princeton University), remaining there until illness forced him to drop his studies. He read some law but never practiced, choosing instead to enter the commission business in New York City. In 1840 he used family connections with the expiring Van Buren administration to secure an appointment as a purser in the United States Navy. Price would always find preferment easier with national Democrats than with party patrons at home.

Price married Matilda Decatur Trenchard, the daughter and the sister of navy men, and settled in Brooklyn Heights, comfortably berthed in the peacetime navy. After routine coastal cruises on the sidewheeler *U.S.S. Fulton,* he sailed with the ten-gun frigate, *U.S.S. Missouri,* one of the first warships to cross the Atlantic under steam, in July 1843. While recoaling off Gibraltar, an accident gutted the *Missouri,* and her officers spent some time as guests of the British Consul. Price struck an acquaintance with the American ambassador to Madrid, Washington Irving; toured Iberia, using his smattering of Spanish to collect documents for Irving's biography of Columbus; and later jaunted to Paris. Back on duty, he joined the sloop of war *Cyane,* part of Commodore John Drake Sloat's Pacific Squadron. He spent his time mainly with payrolls, occasionally going ashore at Monterey, Matamoros, or Lima to provision and bargain with local merchants. On July 7, 1846, at the onset of the Mexican War, the *Cyane* ferried a detachment of marines which seized Monterey, California. That day, Sloat named Price prefect and *alcalde* (magistrate) at Monterey, where for a month he helped administer an occupied zone.

California proved a giddy experience that dogged Price's reputation the rest of his life. With other magistrates whose duties included recording land titles, Price joined the hunt for choice rancheros, becoming Sloat's investment agent and partner in Monterey and other townsites around San Francisco Bay. In late 1848, back in New York, "buisey [sic] president making," he engineered an appointment as purser for the Pacific Squadron from the Polk administration. With headquarters moved to his own waterfront property in bustling San Francisco, Price became provisioner and payroller for ships and depots from Monterey to Honolulu, a frustrating, highly speculative operation. While gold strikes inflated commodity prices and merchants warily discounted United States bills of exchange, the navy expected Price to supply the "California Station" and establish the hegemony of American credit that would prevent the drain of gold bullion to London. He emerged a real-estate "tycoon," a booster of the city's pioneer "Long Wharf," a Democratic delegate to the territory's constitutional convention, and a member of San Francisco's first common council. But he also made unauthorized drafts on specie in the United States Customs House and neglected quarterly returns on expenses. For this, in August 1849, he was "detached" from the squadron and ordered to Washington to render account. On his return, his steamer, the *Orleans St. John,* burned on the Alabama River, destroying, he claimed, his payroll vouchers. The disaster muddled his ledgers, but provided years of litigation when the navy sued for $88,000 in unaccounted funds.

Back East, Price bought a mansion and grounds in Hoboken, entered a Wall Street banking partnership that speculated in the California trade, and looked after his absentee holdings. In 1850 the Hudson County Democratic organization, influenced by Price's father, "Judge" Francis Price, a Weehawken resident and speculator, and by Commodore Robert Field Stockton, the Jerseyman who had been military governor of California while Price was there, sought Price out for his California luster. Safely removed from debates on the issues, Price received the congressional nomination, in the words of one Democrat, J. R. Riggs, "without the least expectation of his success" but with every confidence that he could pay his own way. But the division of Whig strength in Essex handed him a narrow victory.

His mind distracted by California deals, Price served an uneventful term in the Thirty-seventh Congress. He proffered the usual private bills from home voters, like Methodist appeals to end liquor imports and proposals from Jersey City Irish Catholics for subsidized mail packets to Galway, Ireland. He was a responsive if not particularly eloquent agent for Newark harbor masters, Paterson manufacturers, the Stevens shipyards in Hoboken, and the Pacific mail steamships, all anxious for federal protection. He scarcely participated in House debate, save once as "the most immediate and direct representative the Navy has ever had upon this floor" to urge recodification of martial law aboard ship. Price's faith that traditional flogging made a "well-ordered, well-disciplined ship," was balanced by a proper Jacksonian demand that summary courts-martial supersede the captain's powers to punish at sea. Such contributions ended abruptly when he lost reelection in October 1852 and retired to his New York firm to nurse his California property and his claims on the Navy.

In 1853, as the party wrangled to tailor a gubernatorial candidate for its antimonopoly stance, many Democrats remembered Price. They reached for the ex-congressman, a figure inconspicuously tied to the privileged "Joint Companies," the Camden and Amboy Railroad and Delaware and Raritan Canal. While Whigs taunted the free-spending "California" candidate as the puppet of the Camden and Amboy and argued that western residence disqualified him under the state constitution's five-year require-

ment, Democrats campaigned as the anti-monopoly party, promising "reform" all around. According to Charles Parker, "Many [Democrats] remained at home & others went to the poles feeling little interests in the result, and but for the money used Mr. Price could not have been elected." Although Price's majority was less than his immediate Democratic predecessor's, the party rolled up a two-to-one victory margin in the new legislature.

A Hoboken interloper, vaguely suspect as a tool for New York commerce, the new governor enjoyed little real influence against the state's great oligarchs and entrenched county machines. Except for indulging a few private visions quite beyond his gubernatorial reach, Price hewed to the safe conservatism of the Democratic party, which had to meet growing unrest in the urbanizing northeastern counties. He rooted his politics in tried-and-true Jacksonian attacks against unbridled corporate power. His annual messages effused orthodox hard-money homilies and denounced "unsettling" competition for special corporate charters. Price vowed to retire all paper bank notes under twenty-five-dollar denominations gradually. His 1855 veto of the Newark Plank Road and Bridge bill, which aided Passaic River commerce and pleased Newark boosters, used classic antimonopoly rhetoric reminiscent of Judge Taney's Charles River Bridge decision.

When the 1853 "reform" pledges fell due, the governor maneuvered to placate antiestablishment voters. The inefficient state court system had long angered the people, and Democrats responded with a Law Reform Commission to reorganize the judiciary. Agreement for more judgeships, however, foundered over the appointment of Whigs to the bench. Persuaded by Democratic leaders that moderation "might save a judge," Price parceled out nominations to the deserving of both parties. He faced a far more difficult chore in cutting the umbilical cord that tied the Democrats to the Joint

Companies—a patronage empire that affronted antimonopoly Democrats and proved a liability in Hudson and Essex counties, where Whigs harangued against "the monster." Democrats in the 1853 legislature considered a state sinking fund to buy the transportation system when its exclusive charter expired in 1864. But the Camden and Amboy president, Robert F. Stockton, bargained for an extension of the Joint Companies' exclusive privileges in exchange for eventual state takeover. In the end, Governor Price, with most of his party, remained a supporter of "Jersey enterprise" and the $200,000 which the monopoly paid annually into the state treasury. He signed a compromise bill which fixed the maximum freight tariffs. But it also extended the corporation's privileges, essentially untouched, until January 1869, with the option of state takeover in twenty years.

As a patron of education, the governor rode the crest of two decades of agitation for public schools. In 1846, the legislature established matching state school-district funds for education, and Governors George F. Fort and Daniel Haines committed the Democratic party to a system of public education that included the idea of normal schools. By 1853, school reformers had made the "teachers institutes" a part of the educational establishment. Half lyceum and half itinerant camp meeting, the institutes brought the latest pedagogy to the county level, turning an emerging teacher professionalism into a powerful statewide lobby. Price participated in the 1854 Sussex Institute and urged state support to extend the institutes' work to all counties. In January 1855, he called for the establishment of a state training school, and that autumn he and School Superintendent John H. Phillips drafted the bill that established Trenton Normal School.

A cultivated cosmopolite with a taste for European grandeur, Price was also active in the realm of commerce. Jersey shippers, alarmed by booster claims of the New York City Chamber of Commerce and the rapid expansion of Manhattan's wharves into the Hudson River, appealed to Trenton for redress. Price and New York Governor Myron Clark appointed a harbor commission to investigate whether pier construction obstructed river flow and to recommend official bulkhead lines—the first such venture in bistate port regulation. Price also appointed New Jersey's first pilots' board, which protected the Newark and Jersey City tug operators struggling to stave off New York's encroachment of the Liverpool trade. From tidewater the governor looked landward and created a state geological survey, urged first by agricultural societies in search of cheap phosphates, then by industrialists anxious to exploit the zinc, franklinite, and other ores locked away in the northern counties. To head the corps of surveyors Price chose William Kitchell, the Newark geologist committed to the city's exploration of its mineral hinterland. Price took "personal interest" in the survey as it began in Sussex, pleased that the sales of engraved maps to European collectors might help defray expenses. His rationalist bent surfaced in continued proposals to scrap the patchwork of town highway commissioners with one road administrator per county—mere grandiloquence, however, when road building was the patronage staple of local politics.

As state commander in chief, the governor tried to invigorate a militia that had decayed into ragged disorder, swollen by Irish and German companies whose foreign ways appalled nativists in the officer cadre. With the governor's hearty support, Adjutant General Thomas Cadwalader held more division parades and used county brigade boards to discipline local formations. He requested, but failed to receive from the legislature, a fifteen-cent tax on all able-bodied males to subsidize the growing number of elite "uniform" companies. In 1856, the governor sent Cadwalader on a fact-finding tour of European arsenals, a frivolous assignment given the state's primitive readiness. Apart from cosmetic improvements, Price presided over a subtle revolution in the ranks and signed, despite protests from nativists, the commissions of numerous ethnic officers.

Governor Price kept the Jersey Democracy steered on a "middling" course during the agitation over various issues in the 1850s. Sidestepping demands by Protestant nativists to limit Irish-Catholic votes, Price suggested that the legislature enact a limited moratorium on the naturalization of foreigners before elections. Amidst fierce debate on the Maine prohibition law, he left the saloon issue to the legislature, provided the lawmakers uphold "constitutional rights." A conservative Democrat, unmoved by the antislavery revolt in party ranks—and to some degree a Californian, in any event—Price preferred the southern-oriented, "territorial" solution to the slavery crisis. At the 1856 state party convention, he wielded patronage and money to keep the state platform resolutely favorable to local control of slavery in Kansas. Later, in the presidential canvass, Price stumped the state for James Buchanan, then crossed to New York City for yeoman service with Fernando Wood's "Administration" machine.

Since the New Jersey constitution barred a second term, in spring 1857 Price unsuccessfully sought the ambassadorship to Mexico. Then he plunged into business ventures that had blossomed under his gubernatorial patronage. As early as 1855, he had joined Horace P. Russ in quarrying stone from "Judge" Price's property along the Hackensack River. With contracts for Russ pavement in New York, Brooklyn, and Philadelphia, the partners began a flourishing barge commerce on the inland waterways of Greater New York. While still in office, the governor joined his father in a ferry business to Forty-second Street in Manhattan. By January 1859, the Weehawken Ferry Company, with its flagship *Rodman M. Price,* was providing regular service across the Hudson River. The two also speculated on lots on Bull's Head Road, expecting the ferry to enhance the suburban appeal of the South Bergen hills.

Comfortably settled on his father's property in Ramapo, the retired governor stood aloof during the Civil War. During the secession winter he was one of the nine-man New Jersey delegation to the Washington "Peace Conference" which futilely debated John J. Crittenden's resolutions to avert war. In the *Newark Evening Journal,* April 4, 1861, he exhorted Jerseymen not to take up arms against the South; this appeal was congenial to many local merchants worried about their southern markets. Otherwise, Price stuck to business; with his father as security, he temporarily climbed out of debt.

After the war, as a Bergen gentleman farmer, Price lapsed into a political oblivion, stirred occasionally by humiliating appearances in bankruptcy court. Dubious financing forced the Weehawken Ferry into receivership in 1866. After his father's death, he so mismanaged the family estate that in 1873 the court of chancery removed him as executor. Badly in need of money, he again pursued his claims with the navy and later with the United States Court of Claims. In what appears an act of charity, in 1890 the United States Congress approved a relief bill, providing a windfall settlement. He never enjoyed the money, for chancery immediately attached it to settle another bad debt arising out of a San Francisco property sold four decades before. A broken man, Price eluded process servers on both sides of the Hudson and spent time in the Hackensack jail before his health finally gave out. He died a curious relic of "Young America," faintly remembered by a state busy building for the new century.

Rodman M. Price Papers, Huntington Library, San Marino, Cal.

Rodman M. Price Papers, Rutgers University Special Collections, New Brunswick, N.J.

Rodman M. Price Papers, University of California, Berkeley, Special Collections, Berkeley, Cal.

Knapp, Charles M. *New Jersey Politics During the Period of the Civil War and Reconstruction.* Geneva, N.Y.: W. F. Humphrey, 1924.

Lane, Wheaton J. *From Indian Trail to Iron Horse: Travel and Transportation in New Jersey, 1620–1860.* Princeton: Princeton University Press, 1939.

Snell, James P., et al. *History of Sussex and Warren Counties, New Jersey.* Philadelphia: Everts and Peck, 1881.

Joel Schwartz

WILLIAM AUGUSTUS NEWELL (September 5, 1817–August 8, 1901) was born in Franklin, Ohio. His parents, James H. and Eliza (Hankinson) Newell, both of old Monmouth County families, had moved to Ohio shortly before his birth; they returned to New Jersey in 1819 when he was two years old. Settling in New Brunswick, James Newell worked as a civil engineer and mapmaker. William Newell attended the district public schools, graduated from Rutgers College in 1836, and studied medicine locally. He married Johanna Van Deursen, the daughter of his mentor. They had three children. After completing medical studies at the University of Pennsylvania in 1839, Newell entered practice, first with an uncle at Manahawkin and then alone at Imlaystown. In 1844 he moved to Allentown, which was to be his New Jersey residence for the rest of his life.

Two years later, Newell combined politics with medicine when the Whigs of the Second Congressional District nominated him for Congress. He was elected by a narrow margin and reelected in 1848, but in 1850 he refused a third nomination. During his first term in Congress he accomplished what he always considered his most important and lasting achievement: the founding of the United States Life Saving Service. In 1848 he steered through Congress a measure appropriating $10,000 to found a series of lighthouse stations between Sandy Hook and Little Egg Harbor, a treacherous stretch of coast that had been the scene of many wrecks. Each station had a cannon to shoot a line to stranded ships so that a small car could be pulled from shore to ship and back again, removing passengers. The service soon extended from Long Island to Cape May, and after 1850, when the apparatus saved two hundred passengers and crew members of the Scottish brig *Ayrshire*, it spread over the entire Atlantic coast.

Although the founding of the service enhanced Newell's reputation, it did not lead immediately to higher office. During the 1850s, after the Whig party foundered, Newell allied with the new American, or Know-Nothing party, which sought to limit the immigrant role in American politics. In 1856 the Americans and the Republicans attempted to cooperate at the state level and agreed to run a common gubernatorial candidate to defeat the dominant Democrats. Calling themselves the "Opposition," the Americans and the Republicans nominated Newell at a joint convention in Trenton. As a Know-Nothing who opposed the extension of slavery in the territories, he was acceptable to the majority in both parties, although German Republicans in Newark and Jersey City who opposed the Know-Nothing movement tried to nominate a Republican not associated with nativism.

The American and Republican parties jointly supported Newell for governor, but each supported its own presidential candidate. The Americans adhered to Millard Fillmore and the Republicans to John C. Frémont. By taking care not to antagonize either faction, Newell defeated William C. Alexander, the Democratic candidate, by less than three thousand votes. The Democrats, however, won control of both houses of the legislature.

In his inaugural address in January 1857, Newell set the tone of his administration. He believed a governor should follow rather than lead the legislature and should use the veto sparingly. He urged strict economy and an end to state indebtedness. He promoted improvements in the school system and limitations on the sale of liquor and on the use of corporate influence. He opposed a New York plan to move its quarantine station to Sandy Hook and called for improvements in the coastal life-saving system. He also advocated stricter naturalization procedures, restrictions on the suffrage of naturalized citizens, and voter registration laws for the electorate of incorporated cities.

In subsequent annual addresses, Newell returned to each of these themes, stressing the need for economy in particular and the desirability of restricting immigration and curtailing the influence of immigrants. One issue that was not a state matter intruded in each message. Newell could not avoid the increasingly important slavery controversy. While he opposed the extension of slave territory, he saw abolitionism as an equal threat to the Union. By 1860 Newell was devoting more space in his annual message to this essentially national issue than to any other subject, urging that a course be found to save the union from northern and southern extremists.

As the slavery issue forced political realignments, Newell worked to unite the American and Republican wings of the New Jersey Opposition into one harmonious party to work with the Republicans nationally. He divided the patronage and encouraged fusion at the local level. Not always successful, he saw some of his early appointments—such as that of Charles D. Deshler to clerk of the supreme court—defeated by continued factionalism among Opposition legislators.

While no bills of great importance became law during Newell's administration, there were many enactments related to New Jersey's rapid evolution into an urban, industrial state. The legislature carved Union County out of Essex County and granted city charters to Elizabeth,

Rahway and Egg Harbor. It authorized Hoboken and Trenton to improve their water systems and granted Jersey City permission to build a workhouse. Newark, Jersey City and Hoboken received charters for horsecar street railway companies, and the Erie Railroad consolidated its New Jersey trackage. Granting corporate charters continued to constitute a major portion of the legislative workload.

Since Newell considered the executive function of government secondary to the legislative, he made no attempt to provide strong leadership. However, he vigorously defended the prerogatives of the office when he perceived them to be under legislative attack. When Chancellor Benjamin Williamson's term expired in 1859, Newell nominated Abraham O. Zabriskie from the Republican wing of the Opposition. The Democratic senate denied confirmation and demanded that he reappoint Williamson. Refusing to bow to legislative dictates in the matter of appointments, Newell sent eight more names to the senate, each of which was rejected. Rather than reappoint Williamson, Newell allowed the office to remain vacant; it was not filled until 1860, when Governor Charles S. Olden appointed Chief Justice Henry W. Green.

As governor, Newell presided over the court of pardons, and in late 1857 a case came before that body that greatly affected his post–Civil War political career. James P. Donnelly, a medical student from a New York City Irish family, was convicted of murdering Albert S. Moses over a gambling debt at the Sea View House in Navesink, and was sentenced to death by a Monmouth County Court. Donnelly unsuccessfully appealed the decision through the state courts, and finally sought a commutation to life imprisonment from the Court of Pardons. To the Irish Catholics of New Jersey, Donnelly had been convicted by a Protestant jury before Protestant judges on doubtful evidence. A question of law quickly became a socially and politically significant issue, and petitions in Donnelly's favor circulated in the Irish communities of many northeastern cities. The Court of Pardons voted six to two against commutation, with Newell among the majority. In a two-hour address to the crowd before his public hanging, however, Donnelly claimed that the court had been evenly divided and that Newell, acting on nativistic prejudice, had cast the tie-breaking vote which would cost Donnelly his life. In Newell's subsequent campaigns the Irish remembered Donnelly's accusation.

When Newell left office in January 1860, the Opposition was more unified at all levels, although the Americans and Republicans continued separate organizations in several areas of the state. Newell moved firmly into the Republican ranks, attending the party's national nominating conventions in 1860 and 1864. Soon after President Abraham Lincoln took office in 1861, he appointed Newell superintendent of the Life Saving Service for New Jersey. Newell held this office until returning to Congress in 1865, regularly inspecting all life-saving stations and urging their improvement.

In 1864, Newell received the Republican nomination for Congress from his district and won election on a platform supporting the administration and its war policy. As a congressman he voted for radical reconstruction of the South, although he was not in the vanguard of the reconstruction movement and did not favor extreme measures any more than he had as governor.

Newell was not reelected in 1866. Out of favor with state party leaders, he was renominated but unenthusiastically supported. Furthermore, remarks unfriendly to immigrants from his gubernatorial messages were circulated in German, and a distorted version of his role in the Donnelly case was spread among the Irish. Newell blamed his defeat in part on the "base and ungenerous appeal to the passions and prejudices of a large class of voters, by misrepresenting my motives and action in the discharge of solemn and painful executive duty."

Newell returned to the practice of medicine. In 1868 he once more sought the congressional nomination, but without success, and in 1870 he received the nomination but lost the election. He ran for governor again in 1877, opposing George B. McClellan, the popular Civil War general nominated by the Democrats. Newell ran an inept campaign, alienating many regular Republicans, and he lost with 46 percent of the vote. Once again his role in the Donnelly case became an issue, with the Irish-oriented Jersey City *Argus* declaring that "Newell's action toward poor Donnelly" had been "prompted by his intense hatred of foreigners."

Newell continued to practice medicine in Allentown until 1880, when President Rutherford B. Hayes appointed him territorial governor of Washington. Supporting measures similar to those he had sponsored as governor of New Jersey, he urged strict economy, lower taxes, laws to prevent intemperance and desecration of the Sabbath, the forced acculturation of the territory's Indian population, and an improved life-saving service on the Pacific coast.

Newell served as territorial governor until 1884. He then served as a United States Indian inspector in the northwest for one year. He resumed the practice of medicine in Olympia in 1885 and remained in Washington for fourteen more years, returning to New Jersey only after his wife's death.

In 1899, at the age of 82, Newell returned to Allentown. He practiced medicine and took an active role in the Monmouth County Historical Association, delivering two papers, one dealing with the founding of the United States Life Saving Service. He died at the age of 84 and was buried in the Allentown Presbyterian cemetery.

Knapp, Charles M. *New Jersey Politics During the Period of the Civil War and Reconstruction.* Geneva, N.Y.: W. F. Humphrey, 1924.

Nelson, William, ed. *The New Jersey Coast in*

Three Centuries. 2 vols. New York: Lewis Publishing Co., 1902.

Platt, Hermann K., ed. *Charles Perrin Smith: New Jersey Political Reminiscences, 1828–1882.* New Brunswick: Rutgers University Press, 1965.

Vance, Alanson A. *A Political Reminiscence.* Morristown, [1902].

Douglas V. Shaw

CHARLES SMITH OLDEN (February 19, 1799–April 7, 1876) was born of Quaker ancestry in Stony Brook, near Princeton. He was the son of Hart and Temperance (Smith) Olden. He went to Lawrenceville School. Upon graduation he worked for a while in his father's store, and then for the mercantile firm of Matthew Newkirk and Company, first in Philadelphia and later, from 1826 to 1832, in New Orleans. He returned to Princeton after inheriting a large estate from his uncle, and built the house now called Drumthwacket. Olden lived the life of a gentleman farmer and became a director of the Trenton Banking Company in 1842. He married Phoebe Ann Smith of Trenton; though they had no children of their own, they adopted a daughter.

Olden was elected to the state senate as a Whig in 1844 and reelected in 1847; he served in the senate until 1851. Little is known about his senatorial career, except that he took an interest in the State Lunatic Asylum and was chairman of the Committee on Education. In 1856 Olden supported Millard Fillmore, the American party candidate for the presidency of the United States. In 1859 the "Opposition" party nominated him as their gubernatorial candidate to oppose the Democrat, Edwin R. V. Wright. The Opposition party, which had been created in 1856 to oppose the Democratic party, was made up of former Whigs, Know-Nothings and incipient Republicans. They maintained this name through the election of 1860 and later became the Union party; they took the name Republican during Reconstruction. He was also nominated by the American party. Olden had not taken part in the heated political debate over the extension of slavery during the 1850s. A conservative, he opposed the extension of slavery and supported the enforcement of the Fugitive Slave Act. His views reflected those of the citizens of the state of New Jersey, who would never have supported an abolitionist. Olden defeated Wright by a mere 1,601 votes but the Democrats won slim majorities in the general assembly and the senate.

In his inaugural address on January 17, 1860, Governor Olden said that each state had the "exclusive independent control of its domestic policy" and that slavery was "exclusively and eminently a matter of domestic policy, to be . . . controlled by each State for itself." In the presidential election of 1860, the Opposition party supported Abraham Lincoln and opposed both Stephen A. Douglas and the fusion ticket. Olden's views were more conservative than the Republicans', but he nevertheless supported Lincoln. New Jersey cast three electoral votes for Douglas and four for Lincoln.

With the election of Lincoln, South Carolina seceded from the Union, and other southern states soon followed. During this period of crisis, Olden attempted to seek a compromise between the North and the South. In his annual message in January 1861, he reaffirmed his support for the Fugitive Slave Act and called for its enforcement by all of the states. However, he did not support the right of secession, which he considered anarchy. He viewed the crisis as having been caused "by a few persons of extreme views both North and South." At this time he felt that the people of New Jersey would "stand as a unit in favor of the Union." But he also said that they would "make all reasonable and proper concessions to insure its perpetuity." At first he placed his hopes for a compromise in the United States Congress; however, fearing that the Congress would find no means to alleviate the crisis, he urged the legislature of New Jersey to adopt a resolution appointing delegates to a convention of state delegates, which would "meet and endeavor to agree upon terms by which our Union may be saved."

When Congress failed to arrive at a compromise, Virginia called on the state to send delegates to Washington, to the Washington Peace Conference, which was attended by most of the states that had not seceded. The New Jersey legislature adopted a series of resolutions known as the "Joint Resolution in Relation to the State of the Union." They supported efforts at compromise, including the so-called Crittenden Compromise and the repeal of the personal liberty laws, and they appointed delegates to attend the Washington Peace Conference. Olden signed this resolution on January 29, 1861.

Olden, elected as a delegate to the conference, was the only governor to attend. While he did not speak at the conference, he supported the resolutions for compromise, including one favoring the extension of slavery into the territories, similar to the Crittenden Compromise; one providing compensation for runaway slaves; and one prohibiting Congress from abolishing slavery in the states. At this time most Republicans were opposing any attempt at a compromise that would extend slavery into the territories.

While Governor Olden was considered conciliatory by most Republicans, his principal fear was that an armed conflict would split the citizens of New Jersey, for there was a growing sentiment for some form of secession, or at least for the view that the southern states should be permitted to secede in peace. These fears disappeared when South Carolina and the southern Confederacy attacked Fort Sumter. This act of war by the South brought forth in New Jersey an overwhelming response in favor of the Union, and many who had earlier supported compromise now favored war on the southern states. Olden was one such person; though a month after the firing on Sumter he still feared for the fate of New Jersey, he wrote to President Lincoln that "New Jersey is a border state, & it is of great importance that she stand steadfast in the great conflict."

Olden's first major problem as the war governor was to secure places in the army for the New Jersey regiments, since many more were being offered than the federal government could accommodate. Never again would there be such enthusiasm for the war in New Jersey or elsewhere in the North; before the war was over the state would have to resort to a draft to fill the military quotas.

As soon as the war began, Olden called a special session of the legislature. In his opening remarks, he expressed his fear of invasion and called for the creation of four regiments to be armed, trained, and stationed in southern New Jersey "to make provision for the defense of the State, and especially to provide for the protection of our sea coast, the coast of the Delaware, and our frontier." He later abandoned this idea in favor of federal defense of the coast. This special session, which was marked by a lack of political partisanship, borrowed two million dollars from New Jersey banks, raised more troops than Washington could accept, passed appropriations for ten thousand stands of arms, and secured a tax to raise monies for soldier's families.

Charles Perrin Smith, the clerk of the New Jersey Supreme Court, wrote in his "Reminiscences" that "had he [Olden] failed to be elected, there can be but very little doubt that New Jersey would have been forced to cast her lot with the South in the Great Rebellion which so soon followed." While this is an obvious exaggeration, Olden assumed a primary role in mobilizing the state during the first two years of the Civil War. According to John Y. Foster, "for a period of twenty-one months, he was only absent from the State capital two days and nights, and during much of this time he worked at his desk not only during the day but far into the nights, making it a rule to complete each day the duties which that day brought." Some nights he even slept in his office at the state house.

He did leave the state to attend the conference of governors in Altoona, Pennsylvania, in September 1862. Governor Andrew G. Curtin of Pennsylvania called this conference originally to urge the Lincoln administration to follow a more aggressive campaign in the war and to replace General George B. McClellan. Two events subverted its purpose: Lincoln issued the Emancipation Proclamation the day before the conference convened, and at the battle of Antietam the union army stopped the Confederate army's advance into the North. The governors adopted a set of resolutions that Olden, with the governors of Delaware, Maryland, Kentucky, and Missouri, refused to sign because they dissented from the section that approved the Emancipation Proclamation.

Olden was a diligent worker who wrote all "letters of importance" himself and "kept everything at all times under his personal supervision." The result was that New Jersey's regiments serving outside the state were relatively well equipped and, unlike many regiments from other states, were not officered by political appointees.

Little is known about the man, for he published only the messages that he delivered to the legislature, and very few of his personal letters exist. His messages to the legislature say little of a personal nature, dealing almost exclusively with routine governmental concerns. His last message, in January 1863, urged the legislature not to abandon the men fighting the war "by lending our influence in favor of vain and fruitless efforts to interpose ill-timed pacific offices between the majestic arm of a nation's law and a wicked rebellion that will be satisfied with nothing but the accomplishment of its object." This was his only reference to the

growing peace movement that would reach its zenith in 1863.

John Y. Foster, in one of the only accounts describing Governor Olden, wrote that he was a man of "incorruptible integrity, of inflexible loyalty and of indomitable will; one of those rare men who conceal under a complacent demeanor, vast inherent strength and self-reliance, which, upon emergency, produce in them prodigies of performance."

Charles Perrin Smith, who worked with Governor Olden, recorded his impressions. Smith wrote in his "Reminiscences" that "Governor Olden's financial experience and business training, united with [an] unusual degree of sagacity and untiring industry, alone enabled him to command success; while his strict probity, and unostentatious manners gained for him the entire confidence of the people. . . . Personally cognizant of his zeal and labor, and aware of the vast responsibility with which he was burdened, I could not regard his evidently failing health with[out] great solicitude, but he steadily declined to seek relaxation."

Prevented by the New Jersey constitution from serving a second consecutive term, Olden left the governorship in January 1863. He was succeeded by Joel Parker, a Democrat. After leaving office he continued to support the war. At a mass meeting in Trenton on April 16, 1863, Olden was elected president of the Loyal National League of New Jersey, which, like similar organizations in other states, attempted to unite those supporting the war regardless of political party, forming a new organization that avoided the existing political nomenclature. Its purpose was to establish a league in each county and town. This had the effect of reviving the Union-Republican party in the election campaigns of 1863 and 1864.

Following the war, Olden served as a judge of the court of errors and appeals from 1868 to 1873. He was also a member of the Riparian Commission from 1869 to 1875, and a commissioner of the State Sinking Fund. In 1872 he headed the presidential electors from New Jersey for Ulysses S. Grant. He also continued his interest in the College of New Jersey (later Princeton University); having served as its treasurer from 1845 to 1869, he was elected to the board of trustees in 1863, where he served until 1875. Olden died on April 7, 1876, in his house at Princeton.

Charles Smith Olden Papers, Historical Society of Princeton, Princeton, N.J.

Foster, John Y. *New Jersey and the Rebellion.* Newark: M. R. Dennis and Company, 1868.

Knapp, Charles M. *New Jersey Politics During the Period of the Civil War and Reconstruction.* Geneva, N.Y.: W. F. Humphrey, 1924.

Platt, Hermann K., ed. *Charles Perrin Smith: New Jersey Political Reminiscences, 1828–1882.* New Brunswick: Rutgers University Press, 1965.

Wright, William C. *The Secession Movement in the Middle Atlantic States.* Rutherford, N.J.: Fairleigh Dickinson University Press, 1973.

William C. Wright

JOEL PARKER (November 24, 1816–January 2, 1888) was born near Freehold, Monmouth County, the son of Charles and Sarah (Coward) Parker. After his father's appointment as state treasurer, the family moved to Trenton. In 1833, his father became the cashier of the Mechanics' and Manufacturers' Bank of Trenton and sent him to Monmouth for two or three years to work his recently purchased farm. Parker then attended the College of New Jersey (later Princeton University), where he was graduated in 1839. After graduation he entered the law office of Henry W. Green, who later became chief justice and chancellor. Parker was ad-

mitted to the bar in 1842, and he began to practice law in Freehold.

Active in Democratic politics, Parker campaigned for Martin Van Buren in 1840 and James K. Polk in 1844 in their bids for the presidency. In 1847 he was elected as a Democrat to the assembly, where he took an active interest in tax reform, offering a bill that equalized taxation by taxing personal as well as real property. Although the Whigs held a majority in the legislature, Parker secured the passage of this bill in 1850.

In 1851, Parker declined to run for reelection and in the same year he was appointed prosecutor of the pleas for Monmouth County, and he served in this office for five years. He was also elected brigadier general, commanding the Monmouth and Ocean Brigade of the New Jersey militia in 1857, which he proceeded to reorganize. In 1860, he served as a Democratic elector and voted for Stephen A. Douglas. When the Civil War began, Governor Charles S. Olden appointed him a major general.

At its convention on September 4, 1862, the Democratic party nominated Parker for governor. He defeated Moses Bigelow, the mayor of Newark, for the nomination. Parker was considered a "war Democrat" (as opposed to a "Copperhead," a Democrat who opposed the war and sought peace with the South). In the election Parker defeated the Republican candidate, Marcus L. Ward, by 14,394, the largest majority in a gubernatorial election to that time. The Democrats also won majorities in both houses of the legislature.

In his inaugural address on January 20, 1863, Parker outlined his attitude toward the war. Affirming his opposition to secession as a "political heresy," he upheld the principle of states' rights, stating that the states have "sovereignty over all subjects not expressly delegated to the General Government." To Parker it was "the duty of the States, as well as the duty of the United States, to assert and maintain, in a legal and constitutional manner, their several and appropriate sovereignty." Further, he argued that while "a minority of fanatical and ultra men in each section" had brought about the war, Congress had declared that it was "not for the purpose of conquest or subjugation, overthrowing or interfering with the rights of established institutions of the States—but to defend and maintain the supremacy of the Constitution, and to preserve the Union, with the equality and rights of the several States unimpaired." He insisted that the people who supported this principle "had a right to expect that their own constitutional privileges would be respected. They did not expect that in order to suppress rebellion, the inalienable liberties of loyal citizens must be sacrificed." He condemned the use by the federal government of arbitrary arrests "without due process of law"; imprisonment of New Jersey citizens beyond the state; the suspension of the writ of habeas corpus; the Emancipation Proclamation; and other "war powers" of the Lincoln administration. Parker not only opposed emancipation but felt that if it came about it should be dealt with by "the people of the States where the institution of slavery exists" and not the federal government. He favored the restoration of peace through the use of military force or through conciliation but held that it should not result in "a union of States where part are held in subjugation as conquered provinces." He challenged the Lincoln administration when he said that "whatever legal and constitutional powers are vested in the Executive of New Jersey, for the protection of the lawful rights of the citizens of the State, will be exercised during my administration." Parker saw his duties as governor through this philosophy.

In 1863 the Copperheads reached their highest degree of support and power in New Jersey, especially in the legislature, which passed the "Peace Resolutions" that condemned the actions of the Lincoln administration in terms similar to those Parker had outlined in his inaugural address. But the peace resolutions went beyond Parker's view and called on the federal government to appoint commissioners to meet with the southern commissioners to find a way to end the war. Parker signed the joint resolutions on March 24, 1863. Since the resolutions would ultimately permit the South to leave the Union peacefully, the Republicans throughout the country condemned them as nothing less than advocating secession.

While on the one hand Parker supported these "peace resolutions," on the other he still supported the war; when the Confederate army commanded by General Robert E. Lee invaded Pennsylvania and was met in battle at Gettysburg, Parker was among the first to raise troops to assist in the defense of that state. He induced several regiments whose enlistments were ready to expire to reenlist and raised additional thirty-day troops for this emergency. His actions won him the thanks of both Governor Andrew G. Curtin of Pennsylvania and President Lincoln. He also became involved in the welfare of the troops on the battlefield and in the hospitals, as well as those that had returned home. He was a principal supporter of the Soldiers' Home. Through providing bounties, he prevented the use of conscription to fill military quotas in 1863; but in 1864 he was unsuccessful, for the draft went into effect that year.

Of all the nation's governors, Joel Parker was one of the Lincoln administration's most outspoken critics. However, while he attacked the administration's handling of political issues and its use of "war powers," he could not bring himself to call for a halt in the fighting. While the North continued to fight he hoped for some form of conciliation with the South. Even though he had signed the "Peace Resolutions" the previous year, he felt that any halt in fighting would permit the South to leave the Union. In his first annual address, delivered on January 13, 1864, he continued to attack the Emancipation Proclamation and the other Lincoln administration measures he considered unconstitutional. Yet he agreed with the president that it was "the duty of the State authorities to furnish the men necessary to destroy the armed power of the rebellion, and it is equally the duty of the general government to accompany the exercise of the power entrusted to it with proper terms of conciliation."

In 1864, the federal government attempted to establish a railroad route from New York to Philadelphia other than the Camden and Amboy Railroad, which had been given a monopoly for transportation between the two cities. The legislature adopted a joint resolution signed by Parker that condemned the Congress's actions. Parker reacted in accordance with his strong states' rights position, declaring that "the General Government has no right to build a foot of railroad or to charter a corporation to construct the same, in any of the States, for the purpose of carrying passengers or freight for compensation. . . . No power can make the creator superior to or independent of its creator." Though the United States House of Representatives approved the bill, the Senate never voted on it.

In his strongest speech against the Lincoln administration, delivered in Freehold in August 1864, Governor Parker called for a peaceful settlement to the war and stated that the "majority of the people, without respect to party, wanted peace, and desired compromise, but the Republican leaders would not consent to fair terms, and refused to submit the momentous issue to the people." He condemned conscription, confiscation and the federal government's abolition of slavery. Again, while he criticized the administration, he continued to support the war by supplying troops to serve for thirty days in July 1864 when the Confederate army invaded Maryland. At this same time, in his second annual address in January 1865, Governor Parker opposed the passage of the Thirteenth Amendment, which abolished slavery, and he expressed himself in favor of gradual emancipation by the states. He also condemned as illegal the establishment of the reconstruction governments in the southern states.

In his final annual address in January 1866, Parker opposed black suffrage and called for the "speedy resumption of the relations of all the States with the federal government." He also proudly proclaimed that "not a single right of the State of New Jersey has been yielded, and not one of her citizens, during my administration, has been deprived of his liberty without due process of law." At the end of his term he left a surplus in the treasury, a phenomenon that had not occurred for many years.

When Parker left the office of governor in 1866 he returned to his law practice. In 1868, 1876 and 1884 he was the favorite-son presidential candidate of the New Jersey delegates at the National Democratic Convention.

In 1871, Parker was once again elected governor, this time by a majority of six thousand votes, thus becoming the first person to be elected twice to the governorship by the people. During his second term in office, he continued to voice his earlier positions by calling for an end to reconstruction and by expressing himself in favor of states' rights. He also continually spoke out against corruption in government. The legislature enacted more laws during his second term than in any previous three years. Among them was the General Railroad Law. Parker also used the veto on fourteen occasions. As governor he entered into the dispute with the state of Delaware over its boundary. He also ardently supported the Centennial Exhibition to be held in Philadelphia in 1876 as a part of the commemoration of the Centennial of the American Revolution.

During his second term Parker was instrumental in securing the first group of amendments to be made to the New Jersey constitution of 1844. They included salary adjustments and an oath for legislators, guarantees of a free education, prohibition of the passage of certain special or local laws, and line-item veto in appropriation bills.

After leaving the governorship for the second time, Parker served as attorney general in 1875, as a presidential elector in 1876, and as a justice of the New Jersey Supreme Court from 1880 until his death. He was also a leading figure in the construction of the Battle of Monmouth monument in Freehold.

Parker married Maria M. Gummere of Trenton in 1843, and they had two sons and one daughter. He died in Philadelphia on January 2, 1888.

Knapp, Charles M. *New Jersey Politics During the Period of the Civil War and Reconstruction.* Geneva, N.Y.: W. F. Humphrey, 1924.

Personal and Political Sketch of Hon. Joel Parker. Freehold: Monmouth Democrat, 1871.

The Presidency. Sketch of the Democratic Candidate, Joel Parker. n.p., [1876].

Yard, James S. "Joel Parker, 'The War Governor of New Jersey.' . . ." *Proceedings of the New Jersey Historical Society* 10 (1888–89): 57–92.

William C. Wright

MARCUS LAWRENCE WARD (November 9, 1812–April 25, 1884), governor of New Jersey from January 1866 to January 1869, was a descendant of John Ward, one of the founders of Newark in 1666. His father, Moses, was a prosperous candle manufacturer in Newark. His mother was the former Fanny Brown. Marcus Ward eventually became a partner in the family business, where he put together a considerable fortune. By the 1840s he was devoting his interests to Newark civic affairs and charities and serving as director of the National State Bank and chairman of the executive committee of The New Jersey Historical Society. He was also a founder of the Newark Library Association and the New Jersey Art Union. Thus, as a young man, he gained a reputation as a successful businessman and philanthropist.

Ward did not enter politics until 1856, at the relatively late age of forty-four. It is difficult to determine the precise reason for the start of his political career. Most biographical accounts mention his strong antislavery convictions, which produced enthusiasm for the Republican party. In view of his interest in social and moral improvement this seems a logical explanation. Though he was concerned enough about slavery to go to Kansas in 1858 to support the free-state cause, he soon returned to Newark and business affairs. The political climate of New Jersey in the late 1850s was not conducive to strong antislavery stands, and it is hard to believe that Ward would have entered politics solely on that issue. Obviously, other state politicians did not consider him a maverick since they chose him as a delegate to the national Republican convention of 1860 in Chicago.

During the Civil War Ward's expanded philanthropic activities gained him a statewide reputation as "the soldiers' friend," a nickname that would serve him well politically. The welfare of the New Jersey soldiers in the field became his major interest. With his own funds he set up an office in Newark. Presided over by several clerks, it handled an elaborate scheme either to forward soldiers' pay to their families or place it in special savings accounts. If a soldier was killed, Ward's office made sure his pension was paid regularly to his survivors. Ward was also interested in the soldiers' medical needs; he made frequent visits to battlefields to oversee hospital service, and, again with his own money, established the Soldiers' Home in Newark as a hospital for wounded veterans. In later years these activities provided grist for political party controversy. Democrats spread the story that Ward made great personal profit through overseeing the soldiers' pay, and Republicans made hearty denials. No solid evidence ever supported the Democratic claims.

However honest the motives may have been, no one can deny that Ward's projects were politically sound, and they provided the springboard for his entry into gubernatorial politics. In a state where the two political parties were extremely evenly balanced and where there was also much resistance to the nationalizing policies of the Lincoln administration (particularly emancipation), Republicans saw Marcus L. Ward as someone whose appeal would transcend partisanship. Nominated first in 1862, he lost to Democrat Joel Parker. Antiemancipation sentiment in New Jersey was too strong. Since there was no provision that year allowing soldiers to vote in the field, he lost what would have been his greatest source of support.

By 1865, however, the atmosphere was ripe for a Republican victory, even in New Jersey. The war had been won, the Union preserved, and the slaves freed. A sense of thanksgiving abounded, with the general recognition that it was the Republican party that had brought about these good things. The question was not so much whether a Republican would win the governorship as which person would receive the nomination.

Two major aspirants were in the field: Ward, representing Newark and East Jersey interests as well as those of the soldiers, and Alexander G. Cattell of Camden, a wealthy grain merchant who had lived outside the state for many years. The nominating convention in Trenton appeared to deadlock. A move on behalf of the war hero, General Hugh Judson Kilpatrick, was one effort to break the impasse, but Kilpatrick gave his backers no support. Largely through the endeavors of the numerous veterans who were convention delegates, Ward was nominated on the fourth ballot. The Cattell forces, led by George M. Robeson, made the choice unanimous, and all appeared to be harmonious. Although any Republican probably could have been elected in 1865, the soldier vote, which

has generally been considered the decisive factor in his victory, greatly enhanced Ward's large majority. In addition, the Republicans won both houses of the legislature.

As governor, Ward was perhaps best known for his role in bringing New Jersey into the forefront of the Reconstruction process. For example, the previous legislature, under Democratic control, had done nothing toward ratifiying the thirteenth amendment, and the amendment, as a result, became law without New Jersey's approval. Ward devoted a considerable portion of his inaugural address to the problem, recommending that even though it would be only a symbolic gesture the state should "redeem" itself by approving the amendment. Upon its delayed ratification, Republicans facetiously welcomed New Jersey back into the ranks of the Union. A short time later, Ward and the legislature again worked in tandem to secure the ratification of the fourteenth amendment.

Ward's views on state affairs were probably of greater longterm influence in New Jersey. In this respect he was a typical nineteenth-century Republican, convinced that an active, energetic government could produce wise social and economic policies. His administration concentrated on making the operation of the state prison nonpolitical, establishing a state reform school, providing for compulsory public education and instituting a statewide uniform code of health. He also called for state action in the matter of riparian rights, asking that owners of underwater land compensate the state for the right to build improvements.

Party division over gubernatorial appointments hindered the effectiveness of Republican leadership during Ward's governorship. Charles Perrin Smith, whose reminiscences supply the only "inside" account of New Jersey politics in this period, places Ward, sought after and flattered by all sides, at the center of factional strife. According to Smith, the basic problem was the challenge the insurgency of Alexander G. Cattell and

George M. Robeson posed to the regulars. Ward apparently tried to steer a middle course, appointing Robeson attorney general and reappointing Smith clerk of the Supreme Court. On the other hand, some party leaders felt Ward gave too many favors to his Newark friends, especially after he appointed Frederick T. Frelinghuysen to the United States Senate.

By the late 1860s few doubted that practical politics was Ward's overriding interest and that, as far as he was concerned, the Republican party was the instrument of political good. Witness his remarks of November 23, 1866, to the editor of the *Chicago Tribune:* "Our State has done well and I hope and believe that we are now firmly fixed among the Republican states. The change seems great within a period of fifteen months. Two United States senators, three members of the House of Representatives, both Houses of the Legislature, all the officers of the state department Republican, are the tangible proofs that we are entirely reconstructed—the life, the energy, the spirit of an orginazation [sic] is fully aroused and we shall be armed and equipped for the next great battle." In the same year he was appointed chairman of the Republican National Committee, and in 1872 he was elected to a term in Congress.

Yet to dismiss Ward as a hack party politician would be unjust. It would be more accurate to describe him—like many who joined the Republican party prior to the Civil War—as one who saw politics as a means to material and moral progress. It appears that Ward felt a certain moral obligation to look out for the welfare of others. For example, since he felt that the soldiers would spend their money irresponsibly if left to their own devices, his overseeing their pay contained an element of paternalism.

In private life Ward was married to the former Susan Morris, and the couple had eight children. After his public life ended in 1874 with his defeat for reelection to Congress, he devoted the rest of his life to his family and personal affairs. In the spring of 1884 he contracted malaria on a trip he and his wife took to Florida. He was brought back to Newark, where he died on April 25, 1884.

Shortly after his death, Ward's son, Marcus L. Ward, Jr., used his estate to found a house in Maplewood for men and women over sixty-five who had been prominent in business and social affairs. Thus the theme of philanthropy in Ward's life reasserted itself.

Marcus L. Ward Papers, The New Jersey Historical Society, Newark, N.J.

Marcus L. Ward Papers, Rutgers University Special Collections, New Brunswick, N.J.

Knapp, Charles M. *New Jersey Politics During the Period of the Civil War and Reconstruction.* Geneva, N.Y.: W. F. Humphrey, 1924.

Platt, Hermann K., ed. *Charles Perrin Smith: New Jersey Political Reminiscences, 1828–1882.* New Brunswick: Rutgers University Press, 1965.

Shaw, William H. *History of Essex and Hudson Counties, New Jersey.* Philadelphia: Everts and Peck, 1884.

Hermann K. Platt

THEODORE FITZ RANDOLPH (June 24, 1826–November 7, 1883), governor of New Jersey and United States senator, was descended from a family that had migrated from England to Massachusetts in the first half of the seventeenth century. Born in New Brunswick, he was the son of Sarah Kent Carman and James Fitz Randolph, a member of Congress from New Jersey and publisher of the New Brunswick *Fredonian.* The younger Randolph attended Rutgers Grammar School and worked as a writer and proofreader for his father's newspaper. At age sixteen he entered a mercantile career, and he spent the next ten years as a clerk, accountant, and principal in business, primarily in the South. At twenty he went to Vicksburg, Mississippi, but in 1850 he returned to New Jersey to enter his father's extensive coal and iron business. He established his residence at Jersey City and lived there until 1862, when he purchased a ninety-acre stock farm in Morristown.

Admitted to the bar in 1848, Theodore F. Randolph became, like his father, a Whig, a states' rights advocate and a consistent opponent of the abolitionists. With the decline of the Whigs after the elections of 1852 he moved into the Democratic party. In 1860 an alliance of Democrats and Know-Nothings elected the wealthy businessman-lawyer to the general assembly from the first district of Jersey City. Appointed to the Special Joint Committee on National Affairs, he helped lead the effort to avert civil war. That effort culminated in the passage of resolutions appointing delegates to the Washington Peace Conference of February 1861.

In November 1861 Randolph was elected to fill a vacancy in the state senate, and in 1862 he was reelected for a full, three-year term. As Governor Joel Parker's chief ally in the senate, he voiced opposition to many of the war policies of the Lincoln administration but refused to endorse the extreme demands of the Copperheads. More specifically, he succeeded in thwarting Copperhead plans to limit war appropriations and helped defeat resolutions calling for an armistice in 1862. The senator's approach to racial issues reflected humanity and pragmatism. In 1865 he introduced a relief bill, which was passed, extending equal benefits and enlistment bounties to black soldiers. Whites, he explained, should not do injustice to an "inferior" race. In the same year, he opposed the adoption of the Thirteenth Amendment on the grounds that slavery was already doomed and that the measure would effectively close the door to peace negotiations. In state affairs he concentrated on monetary and fiscal

policy. As chairman of the Senate Finance Committee, the conservative Democrat began to advocate a more equitable system of corporate taxation. He successfully urged the creation of a state comptroller's office and led the opposition to a plan under which the state would assume responsibility for paying local bounties to army volunteers.

In the summer of 1865 Randolph sought the Democratic nomination for governor, but he finished second in the balloting to Theodore Runyon, a member of the party's peace faction who had just completed a term as mayor of Newark. Two years later Randolph accepted an appointment as president of the Morris and Essex Railroad. He held that post until he was elected governor in 1868.

Indicating their dissatisfaction with Republican reconstruction policies, New Jersey voters elected him governor over John Insley Blair by more than forty-five hundred ballots. Taking office on January 19, 1869, Randolph advocated prompt readmission of the former Confederate states and outlined a program that would revise election laws, develop a more equitable system of taxation for individuals, impose new taxes on corporations, and create a riparian commission. Less than a month after his inaugural address, the governor began to implement this program by urging the legislature to abandon the system of "transit duties" that certain corporations paid the state in lieu of any other "tax or impost" and to adopt a uniform tax law. Aimed especially at the monopolies of the Delaware and Raritan Canal Company and the Camden and Amboy Railroad and Transportation Company, these measures were designed both to regulate business and to increase state revenues. The legislature, still under Democratic control after the elections of 1868, repealed the parts of charters that provided for transit duties, but no uniform railroad tax was passed until 1873.

The legislature of 1869 acted more expeditiously on the governor's advice to end the exemption of certain corporations from New Jersey's general tax law. In effect, privileged companies were being assessed as if they were individual persons—namely on the value of their real and personal property rather than of their capital stock and accumulated surplus. Acting on specific suggestions from Governor Randolph, the legislature levied a tax of 2 percent on the annual earnings of corporations chartered by the state or doing business in it. The governor repeatedly tried to defend this principle of taxing corporations more heavily than individuals, but the law proved unenforceable, and it was repealed in 1872.

In justifying his tax policies, Governor Randolph emphasized that an expansion of state functions was primarily responsible for the increased cost of government. During his term expansion continued; the governor and legislature took steps to improve state facilities for correction, mental care and education. Randolph had financial as well as humanitarian motives for ameliorating the prison system. By improving the management of penal institutions and by increasing the productivity of convict labor, the governor hoped to make the state prison system self-supporting. Acting on recommendations of a special commission on prison administration, Randolph urged the legislature of 1869 to expand the Trenton State Prison and create a "House of Correction" that would employ short-term convicts at healthful and productive work in an atmosphere free from the negative influence of hardened criminals. Though the legislature made no provision for a house of correction, it approved bills to enlarge the state prison and to erect new workshops on the prison grounds. In his final annual message, Governor Randolph reported that the prison legislation of 1869 had saved the state nearly $200,000. State involvement was less pronounced in education and mental care. The free public school system was made statewide with modest financial aid in 1871, and between 1869 and 1872 the groundwork was laid for a new "lunatic asylum" at Morris Plains to supplement the overcrowded facility at Trenton. The Morris Plains asylum, however, did not open until 1876.

Although most of his proposals received prompt attention from the legislature, Governor Randolph could not secure action on his plan for election reform until March 1871. Incorporating the governor's recommendation that both corporations and individuals be punished for buying votes, the legislature passed a stringent law that disfranchised both the giver and the receiver of an election bribe and put guilty corporations in jeopardy of losing their charters. The law had little effect, however, and soon there were more complaints about election bribery than ever.

With Republicans controlling both houses in 1871, relations between the legislature and Randolph became more partisan and less cooperative. The governor vetoed more major bills in 1871 than in the previous two years combined, even though he professed to use this executive prerogative "only in such cases as were clearly unconstitutional, where unintentional mistakes had been made, or where the ends of Justice were clearly to be violated by Legislative contrivances remote from if not beyond legislative inquiry." Early in his term, Randolph used the veto to defeat bills that in his view promoted railroad expansion at the expense of individual taxpayers and property owners. Later he directed his efforts against bills that would reorganize municipal governments for partisan purposes. Although Randolph and the Democratic lawmakers had set the precedent for this type of partisan legislation in 1870, the governor unhesitatingly vetoed Republican-sponsored reorganization measures. The most important of these vetoes was of a bill allowing the Republican legislature to restructure the powerful government of Jersey City, then controlled by the Democrats. The bill was passed over his veto, however, and for the next sixteen years Jersey City was ruled by a government appointed by the state and dominated by Republicans.

Randolph's pocket veto of "An Act to

Incorporate the German Valley Railway Company" precipitated a constitutional dispute with the state court of chancery. Randolph was subpoenaed to testify in a suit charging that he had received the bill prior to the five closing days of the legislative session, but he answered that only the legislature had constitutional authority to "obtain answer" from the governor for his action or inaction. He further asserted that the governor was the sole judge of what constituted his official duties. Wishing to avoid a constitutional crisis, however, Randolph deposited the engrossed copy of the disputed bill with the state librarian.

Two other potential crises faced the governor in 1870 and 1871. The first resulted from a railroad dispute known as "The Bergen Riot." Randolph used National Guard troops to quell the riot, and the feuding railway companies settled their differences in court. In July 1871, the governor averted a threatened riot in Jersey City when he took action to prevent Irish-Americans from disrupting a parade planned by Orangemen on the anniversary of the battle of the Boyne. Although he criticized the Orangemen for reviving an "unnecessary" religious and political feud, the governor issued a proclamation declaring his intention to guarantee the right of peaceful assembly to all citizens. He followed the proclamation with an order to use up to three thousand state troops if needed. These measures proved more than ample, and civil authorities managed to cope with the situation without military assistance.

The governor's handling of the Orangemen affair prompted state and national journals to list him as a leading contender for the Democratic presidential nomination. Randolph directed his efforts toward attaining a more realistic goal—a seat in the United States Senate. In his last message to the legislature he addressed national as well as state issues, and after leaving office he played an active role in the presidential campaign of 1872. Initially a participant in the bipartisan movement to find an alter-

native to Ulysses S. Grant and Horace Greeley, the ex-governor ultimately campaigned for Greeley amid charges of a deal involving appointment to a cabinet post.

In January 1875 the Democratic majority in the legislature elected ex-governor Randolph to the United States Senate seat previously held by John P. Stockton. Randolph served in the Senate until 1881; he was a member of the Committees on Commerce, Military Affairs, Education, Civil Service Reform and the Centennial Exhibition. He also served on the special Senate committee to examine South Carolina's returns in the disputed presidential election of 1876, and for two years he was chairman of the Committee on Military Affairs. In his infrequent speeches, he criticized President Grant's use of federal troops to uphold Republican governments in the South, opposed government aid to parochial schools, argued against the remonetization of silver, and advocated an early redemption of paper currency.

In addition to his political and governmental activities, Randolph served as a trustee of Rutgers College, founded and was a president of the Washington Association of New Jersey, invented a ditching machine and a steam typewriter, and practiced philanthropy. In 1852, he married Fannie Coleman, daughter of Congressman Nicholas D. Coleman of Kentucky. He died on November 7, 1883, at his home in Morristown.

Address of Governor Theodore F. Randolph of Morris to the Democratic State Convention, Assembled at Trenton, June 26, 1872. Morristown: Louis C. Vogt, 1872.

A Brief Sketch of the Life and Public Services of Theodore F. Randolph, Democratic Nominee for Governor of New Jersey. n.p.: Democratic Committee, 1868.

Cadman, John W. *The Corporation in New Jersey.* Cambridge, Mass.: Harvard University Press, 1949.

History of Morris County, New Jersey . . . . New York: Munsell, 1882.

Knapp, Charles M. *New Jersey Politics During the Period of the Civil War and Reconstruction.* Geneva, N.Y.: W. F. Humphrey, 1924.

Leiby, James R. *Charity and Correction in New Jersey: A History of State Welfare Institutions.* New Brunswick: Rutgers University Press, 1967.

Letter of Governor Randolph of New Jersey, to Hon. Cortlandt Parker, Relating to Executive Prerogatives and Judicial Authority. Trenton: Wm. T. Nicholson, 1871.

Peterson, Kent A. "New Jersey Politics and National Policymaking, 1865–1868." Ph.D. dissertation, Princeton University, 1970.

Robert C. Morris

JOSEPH DORSETT BEDLE (January 5, 1831–October 21, 1894), as a contemporary account put it, was "an instance of a man who, at a comparatively early age, achieves the highest honors of his state, apparently without having passed through any of the highways and byways of the politician."

Certainly, having an established, influential family on both sides did not harm his career. Bedle's paternal grandparents were natives of New Jersey. His parents were Thomas and Hannah (Dorsett) Bedle. His father was a merchant, a justice of the peace for more than twenty-five years, and a judge of the Court of Common Pleas for Monmouth County. Through his mother's family, which had immigrated from Bermuda more than a century and a half earlier, the future governor was related to Garret Dorsett Wall, a Democratic party leader in New Jersey in the Jacksonian era, who had declined to serve as governor after the legislature elected him in 1829.

Born in Middletown Point (now Matawan) on January 5, 1831, Bedle was educated at the academy there. His apparently delicate health and his father's

desire to have a son engaged in commerce made him forgo the college course to work two years in a general country store. But a strong desire to study law led him to become a student for about three and one-half years in the Trenton law office of William L. Dayton, who had been a United States senator and would be the vice-presidental candidate of the newly formed Republican party in 1856 and minister to France in 1861. Bedle spent one winter at the law school in Ballston Spa, New York, and after another winter in the Poughkeepsie office of Thompson and Weeks—on his twenty-first birthday—he was admitted in New York State as an attorney and counselor. He did additional study with Matawan lawyer Henry S. Little, who was to become a member of the "State House Ring," and was admitted to the New Jersey bar the following year, 1853. For the next two years he practiced law in Middletown Point, moving to Freehold in 1855 and advancing to counselor in 1856. There, in 1861, he married Althea F. Randolph, the eldest daughter of Bennington F. Randolph, a local lawyer with an extensive practice. She was the niece of Democratic Governor Theodore F. Randolph (1869–72).

In 1865, when he was thirty-four, Bedle became the second youngest justice in the state supreme court's history. Democratic Governor Joel Parker, also a Freehold lawyer, appointed him to the largest circuit, Hudson-Passaic-Bergen. Soon afterward Bedle moved his residence to Jersey City, next door to Leon Abbett, who was to serve two terms as governor. In 1871, just before the close of Bedle's term as justice, the Democratic "State House Ring" planned to nominate Bedle for governor. The judge "himself took no steps to secure the nomination, rather discouraging the movement in his favor," reported a Newark daily newspaper; and his new neighbor and rival, Abbett, persuaded Parker to run—successfully—for a second nonconsecutive term. Bedle was reappointed to the bench in 1872.

Unanimously, the 1874 Democratic convention selected Bedle as its nominee for governor. The Republicans had chosen a former congressman from Newark, George A. Halsey, who opposed the system of state legislative commissions under which Jersey City was being misgoverned. In the Hudson County Court of Oyer and Terminer, Bedle's fervent charges to the grand jury had led to the indictment for fraud and conspiracy of the Republican ring that had seized control of Jersey City; he had later tried and sentenced the ring members. Refusing to resign his judgeship or to campaign for office, Bedle nevertheless was elected by 13,233 votes, the second greatest majority in the state until then. "The country was then very much depressed, and the times were hard, and there was a tendency in the minds of the people to select an Executive who had been out of the arena of politics," according to one explanation. By his own admission, Bedle's information on the actual condition of state affairs was "only cursory."

Pleas for economy, home rule, and general legislation marked Bedle's inaugural address in 1875. He would try "to check all tendency to extravagance," but "the great cause of complaint is not in the State appropriations," the legislature was told, but "in the taxes of municipal bodies including assessment for local improvements." The most effective remedy would to be give direct responsibility to elected officials: "To my mind the best municipal government for our people, and the only one consistent with the spirit of our institutions is that in which they govern themselves. . . . The simpler the machinery of a local government the better." Bedle hoped to see the day "when every city in this State, of a certain population, will be governed by one general law," but he acknowledged that making this practicable would probably require a constitutional change. In an attack on special legislation, he held, "corporate privileges in many matters of legitimate trade and enterprise should be open alike to all, and readily obtainable on compliance with general laws wherever the demands of business require it." Conse-

quently, his first veto killed a bill to incorporate a Newark manufacturing and trading company on the ground that the measure was special. During his first year he vetoed at least five similar bills for manufacturing companies and two measures for incorporating fraternal lodges.

A state constitutional amendment ratified in November 1875 restricted special legislation. Bedle's next two years in office therefore differed significantly from the experience of earlier governors. In 1873 his immediate predecessor, Joel Parker, had complained, "the general public laws passed at the last session are contained in about one hundred pages of the printed volume, while the special and private laws occupy over twelve hundred and fifty pages of the same book." During Parker's administration the legislature had passed 603 laws the first year, 724 the second, and 537 the third, only one-sixth of which were general. During Bedle's first year the number had descended to 454; it declined to 213 in the second year and 156 in the third with 85 percent in the general legislation category. Not until 1961 would fewer statutes—145—be enacted during a single session.

The exact interpretation of the amendment was in doubt. Bedle saw that the prohibition of special legislation did not necessarily apply to laws affecting the state's municipalities. In 1876 he declared in his first annual message that "as to cities and all other municipalities, except towns and counties, the Legislature may yet pass local and special laws, save only for 'appointing local officers or commissions' and wherever on particular subjects enumerated in the amendments it is prevented." Because it concerned local elections, that spring Bedle vetoed a bill that applied to any city "*now* wholly or partly governed by local boards or commissions, whose members are chosen by the Legislature in joint meeting" (italics added). Jersey City alone answered that description; and, besides, the public notice now required for passage of local and special bills had not been given. But only because proper notice had not been given did the governor veto two other local bills that would apply only to Newark.

Much publicity followed Bedle's 1876 veto of "An act to provide for the maintenance and education of the deaf and dumb, feeble-minded and blind persons in this State," which proposed to establish three institutions to care for these unfortunate persons without any charge, whether or not they or their parents could afford to bear any part of the expense. This bill was "intended to adopt a new policy," and this was "not the time for such a change," Bedle argued. He objected further that the bill was "not in fair compliance with that provision of the Constitution limiting bills to one object." The senate overrode the veto but the assembly failed to override in a close vote in which eight Republicans crossed party lines to support Bedle.

But in 1876 a strict party vote in both houses repassed "An act for the government and regulation of the State Prison" over gubernatorial disapproval. Bedle had argued that that measure would give a board of inspectors—statutory officers whom the legislature chose in joint meeting—powers paramount to those of the keeper, whom the governor appointed with the senate's advice and consent as required by an 1875 amendment to the state constitution. Endorsing the reasoning of its own party, the Republican *Newark Daily Advertiser* insisted that it was "partisanship which led his Excellency to veto the bill." It made no mention that the legislative joint meeting of 81 members included only 33 Democrats.

At the close of the 1877 legislative session Bedle refused to be directed by his own party's caucus. He had just approved a reform bill to establish one district court judge in each of six cities and two judges each in Newark and Jersey City to assume the civil jurisdiction of justices of the peace. The senate confirmed the nomination of Bedle's father-in-law, Bennington F. Randolph, for one of the Jersey City judgeships but rejected the governor's nomination of a Republican—an effort at bipartisanship—for the other

judgeship, creating "no end of commotion." The submission of another Republican name received like treatment. In response, Bedle sent a lengthy gubernatorial message announcing "no further reason for the detention of the Senate" and made the original GOP appointment *ad interim*. (The message received not even the courtesy of being printed in the senate's journal).

Attention to the railroads marked Bedle's administration. In January 1876 he declared, "The revenue received by the State from Railroad Companies is not near as large as it should be." Although pertinent changes in legislation were proposed then, he made no similar plea in the next two annual messages. But during the great railroad strike of 1877, Bedle called up all companies of the state's National Guard to protect the trains and the new crews of two railroads. "Failure in the use of military to suppress riots only aggravates, and futile effort is reprehensible, if possible to guard against it," he declared. For such action he "earned no end of commendation from all parts of the country," according to a leading New Jersey journalist.

At the expiration of his term, Bedle resumed his law practice, serving as legal counsel for the Delaware, Lackawanna and Western Railroad, and becoming a director of many prominent corporations. Three times he refused judgeships, and he declined presidential nominations as minister to Russia and to Austria. During the last year of his life, he served on the state's Constitutional Commission of 1894. His death followed an operation for the removal of bladder stones.

Applegate, John Stillwell. *Early Courts and Lawyers of Monmouth County.* . . . Freehold: [Monmouth County Bar Association], 1911.

Ellis, Franklin. *History of Monmouth County* . . . . Philadephia: R. T. Peck & Co., 1885.

Harris I. Effross

GEORGE BRINTON MCCLELLAN (December 3, 1826–October 29, 1885) was the son of George McClellan, a prominent Philadelphia physician. Choosing a military career, he went to West Point, from which he graduated in the top 5 percent of his class. He participated in the Mexican War and served as a military observer in the Crimean War. In 1857, for financial reasons, he resigned his commission and became chief engineer of the Illinois Central Railroad; in 1860 he became president of the eastern division of the Ohio and Mississippi Railroad. That same year he married Ellen Mary Marcy. The couple had a son and a daughter.

When the Civil War broke out McClellan rejoined the army. He quickly became one of the most prominent Union generals and received command of the Army of the Potomac, but he failed to prosecute the war to President Lincoln's satisfaction and was removed in 1862. This ended his military activities. In 1864 he ran for president as a Democrat but lost to Lincoln by a wide margin, winning only the electoral votes of New Jersey and two border states. Between 1864 and 1877 he traveled through Europe, served as a consultant on a variety of engineering projects, held the position of chief engineer of the New York City Department of Docks, and participated actively in the affairs of the Democratic party.

Highly popular in New Jersey, where he maintained his residence, he was nominated for governor by the Democratic party in 1877. His selection, however, largely resulted from the maneuverings of key members within the party who wanted to prevent the frontrunner, Leon Abbett, from gaining the nomination. At a crucial moment an unidentified delegate took the convention by surprise and put McClellan's name up for consideration; in a wild scene of well-planned enthusiasm, all other contenders were forgotten, and the ex-general received the prize by acclamation. During the campaign his Republican opponent, William A. Newell, charged that McClellan was not really a resident of New Jersey, but McClellan, who had a home in Essex County, refuted this accusation with little difficulty and won the election by a large majority. So many people sought to attend the inaugural ceremonies in January 1878 that the proceedings had to be held out of doors in front of the state house.

In spite of his highly successful campaign and widespread personal popularity, the course of events quickly diminished whatever opportunity McClellan might have had to exert strong executive leadership in controversial issues. Largely as a result of the size of McClellan's victory, the Democratic party controlled both houses of the legislature for the first time since 1870; the governor, however, quarreled with influential members of the senate over appointments and patronage and lost standing with that body. At the assembly's instigation, moreover, the legislature enacted several highly partisan measures designed to insure that the Democrats would remain in command of the state for years to come. These bills, of which one flagrantly gerrymandered assembly election districts and another disfranchised college students (who tended to vote Republican), so antagonized the voters that they elected Republican majorities to both houses for the remaining two years of McClellan's term. In general, his relations with the legislature were strained.

As governor, McClellan urged the reduction of the people's tax burden. Entering office while New Jersey still suffered the results of the panic of 1873, he announced in his inaugural address that the most urgent matter before the legislature was "to give the people of this State the greatest possible relief from their burdens during the financial depression, and to do all in our power to hasten the return of a better state of affairs." He advocated caution in expenditures so that the state

1. State Capitol of New Jersey at Trenton, ca. 1790

2. Edmund Andros

3. Daniel Coxe

4. Edward Hyde, Lord Cornbury

5. Robert Hunter

6. William Burnet

. Lewis Morris

8. Jonathan Belcher

9. Francis Bernard

10. William Franklin

11. William Livingston

12. William Paterson

13. Richard Howell

14. Joseph Bloomfield

15. Aaron Ogden

16. William S. Pennington

17. Mahlon Dickerson

18. Isaac Williamson

19. Peter D. Vroom

20. Samuel L. Southard

21. Elias P. Seeley

22. Philemon Dickerson

23. William Pennington

24. Daniel Haines

25. Charles C. Stratton

26. George F. Fort

27. Rodman M. Price

28. William A. Newell

29. Charles S. Olden

30. Joel Parker

31. Marcus L. Ward

32. Theodore F. Randolph

33. Joseph D. Bedle

34. George B. McClellan

35. George C. Ludlow

36. Leon Abbett

37. Robert S. Green

38. George T. Werts

39. John W. Griggs

40. Foster M. Voorhees

41. Franklin Murphy

42. Edward C. Stokes

43. John F. Fort

44. Walter E. Edge (driver) and Franklin Murphy (front, next to Edge). The man behind Edge is probably James F. Fielder. The photograph was taken ca. 1902.

45. James F. Fielder

46. Walter E. Edge

47. George S. Silzer, A. Harry Moore, Edward I. Edwards

48. The State House in 1981

49. Morgan F. Larson

50. Harold G. Hoffman

51. Charles Edison

52. Alfred E. Driscoll

53. Robert B. Meyner

54. Richard J. Hughes

55. William T. Cahill

tax, a revenue measure that helped to pay the ordinary expenses of government, could be cut in half; in 1880, he recommended that the tax be abolished, and noted that he saw no reason to impose it as long as appropriations were confined to reasonable levels. At the end of his term, there was no direct tax on the people for state purposes.

McClellan devoted special attention to measures he felt would help foster the state's prosperity, and his annual messages to the legislature outlined specific ideas to accomplish this end. The abolition of the state tax constituted an integral part of his overall plan, for, as he pointed out, "it is far better for us to leave the money in the pockets of the people, for by them will it be best employed in increasing the wealth of the State and in the development of its resources." More positively, he urged in 1878 that New Jersey follow the example of Massachusetts and institute a Bureau of Statistics of Labor and Industries to gather information on industrial affairs and to serve as a resource in the preparation of legislation; the agency was established during his first year in office. In 1879, he called for the creation of an agricultural experiment station to provide farmers with examples of the benefits of scientific cultivation, and the legislature followed this recommendation in 1880. McClellan felt that specific industries, such as silk culture and sugar growing, should receive the government's encouragement. Similarly, he directed the state library to purchase books on pottery and glassmaking that New Jersey artisans could use for ideas on design, and he called for the creation of a pottery museum to show the finest specimens from Europe, thereby providing actual examples of craftsmanship.

McClellan also stressed the importance of education in industrial development. The schools should, as far as possible, prepare students for their future work. In farming regions, he felt that public schools had an obligation to instruct boys not only in the basic subjects but also in the principles of agriculture; in manufacturing regions, teachers should stress the pursuits of manual labor. "It is clearly good political economy," he declared, "in the State which educates its children, to make that education tend, in some measure, at least, to the benefit of the commercial and other industries of the State." The governor realized, however, that the existing school system could not carry out such an important task without assistance. The great need, he noted, was to convert unskilled into skilled labor; the pottery industry of Trenton, for example, could not find enough trained workers to hire. To remedy this problem, which afflicted other areas of the industrial community as well, he called for the creation of technical schools throughout the state; these institutions would help to provide the skilled labor necessary for the growth and prosperity of the New Jersey economy. Although he felt that local associations should begin and operate these schools, McClellan declared that "giving State aid freely, at least in the incipiency of the system, will prove as wise an expenditure as can be made." During his term, a law was passed permitting the establishment of these schools, but McClellan's overall vision was not fulfilled.

A number of important developments occurred while McClellan was governor. An old soldier, he took a special interest in the condition of the New Jersey National Guard and helped to improve its discipline and organization; during his administration two companies were equipped with Gatling guns, regular rifle practice was instituted, a new battalion was organized, and provision was made to supply new uniforms to the troops. Under legislative authority, McClellan appointed special commissions to study the possibilities of revising the state's jumbled and confusing tax laws and of drafting general laws for governing cities; these commissions reported to the legislature, but no positive action resulted from their deliberations. Finally, in his messages, McClellan emphasized his belief in a diligent and alert citizenry as the best defense against government corruption, and in 1879 a Republican member of the senate introduced a law echoing these sentiments; the financial accounts of local officeholders were made subject to examination by experts whenever twenty-five freeholders should request such a step.

However, few concrete measures resulted directly from McClellan's actions as governor. He tended to stress issues on which most people could agree; abolishing the state tax and improving the condition of the National Guard were recommendations that met with wide popular approval. His major contribution involved suggestions for economic prosperity that in a loose sense constituted a program to foster development; few of his predecessors thought in such overall and comprehensive terms. On the other hand, his ideas in this regard, had they become reality, would no doubt have increased the level of state expenditure greatly. Although he seemed to recognize this fact, McClellan did not address himself to the problem of raising additional revenue; indeed at one point he lamented the fact that teachers, who were crucial to his plans for development, received such small compensation for their labors, but he suggested no remedy for their condition. His messages to the legislature mentioned no issue that might arouse controversy; consequently, he did not concern himself with such topics as taxing the railroads and restraining the political power of corporations. He made little effort to exert an active influence on the deliberations of the legislature, and where his suggestions became law it is highly likely that the measures would have passed without his support; the establishment of a Bureau of Labor and Industries, for example, needed little executive support. At best, his record as governor was mixed.

When his term expired in 1881, McClellan retired to private life. Apparently he found the experience as governor somewhat taxing, for he wrote that he was glad it was over "as it was becoming a nuisance to be obliged to go to Trenton in all matters." He died in 1885 of heart trouble at his home in Essex County.

Records of Governor George B. McClellan, New Jersey State Library, Bureau of Archives and History, Trenton, N.J.

Myers, William Starr. *George Brinton McClellan*. New York: Appleton-Century, 1934.

Jerome C. Reddy

GEORGE CRAIG LUDLOW (April 6, 1830–December 18, 1900) was born in Milford, Hunterdon County, New Jersey. In 1835 his family moved to New Brunswick, where he lived for the rest of his life. He was graduated from Rutgers College in 1850, and he opened a law practice in 1853. Both his father, Cornelius Ludlow, and his grandfather, Benjamin Ludlow, had been active in the affairs of the Democratic party, and he followed their example; over the next two decades he held a variety of municipal and county governmental positions. As a prominent local member of the party, he was elected to the New Jersey senate in 1876 and chosen its president in 1878. He received his party's nomination for the governorship at the convention of 1880. Although he had the background and experience to warrant the nomination in his own right, his actual selection was largely the result of an alliance between Leon Abbett, one of the most important Democratic politicians in the state, and the so-called "State House Ring," a group of office holders in Trenton determined to prevent the convention from selecting a political rival of Abbett's. The closely contested election was heavily influenced by railroad interests. Ludlow, a private counsel for the Pennsylvania Railroad, defeated his Republican opponent, Frederic A. Potts, an influential stockholder in the Jersey Central Railroad, by only 651 of the nearly 250,000 votes cast.

That was the closest gubernatorial contest in New Jersey history, and Ludlow entered office with certain handicaps. First, the Republican party controlled both the senate and the assembly during his first year as governor, and for the remaining two years of his term it had a majority in the senate. Second, although Ludlow had a widespread reputation for integrity and honesty, many felt that his connection with the Pennsylvania Railroad might unduly influence his decisions as governor; indeed, immediately following his narrow victory, rumors, probably unfounded, circulated that the railroad had thrown the election to Ludlow by ordering its employees to vote for him. Moreover, he owed his nomination in part to the "State House Ring" and quickly reappointed two of its members to lucrative positions in state government. Finally, since he was in no sense a leader of his party, he had no power base or following in the legislature to rely on in any political struggle that might develop during his term. He had little hope of providing strong executive leadership.

Those who feared that Ludlow might be too subservient to the railroads were proved wrong, for he attempted to frustrate corporate plans by using his veto power on two important occasions. During the 1882 legislative session, friends of the Central Railroad of New Jersey pushed through both houses a bill designed to allow the board of directors to increase the corporation's capital stock without obtaining the shareholders' approval; the measure was aimed at removing control of the railroad from the stockholders. When the bill reached Ludlow for his signature, he vetoed it, denouncing it as immoral and unjust. He had insufficient power, however, to make his veto stand against the wishes of the Central Railroad, and both senate and assembly voted to override by very large majorities.

During the same session, the Pennsyl-

vania Railroad quietly gained senate approval for a bill that would limit public access to large areas of the Jersey City waterfront. The state had awarded the railroad grants of land lying under water and the railroad had engaged in extensive filling operations and had constructed terminals and warehouses on the property. Erecting fences around the facilities, the railroad refused Jersey City the right to build roads over its holdings to the waterline. When challenged in court by Jersey City, the company asked the assembly to sustain it by approving the bill. When the newspapers pointed out what the bill would accomplish, a furor resulted, but despite public outcry the railroad's scheme gained the approval of the assembly. When the bill reached his desk, Ludlow defied intense pressure from the corporation and refused to sign it. In a stinging veto message, he denounced the bill as "an abuse of legislative power and a violation of the principles of fair dealing and justice." Nevertheless, the senate quickly overrode the veto by a comfortable margin. Only bribery charges and a legislative investigation prevented the assembly from taking similar action, for the session ended before a vote could be taken.

More positively, Ludlow had to struggle with the problem of balancing the state budget, and in the process he helped to pave the way for reform. Since he believed that the individual citizen and property owner labored under a tax burden that was too heavy, he called for the curtailment of all unnecessary expenditures; aggravating his problem, his predecessor had ended the state tax, a small revenue measure that had helped to fund the ordinary expenses of the government, and reinstating it would have run counter to Ludlow's beliefs and proven politically hazardous to the Democratic party. As a result, in his first message to the legislature in 1882, Ludlow advocated a host of measures designed to bring expenditures and anticipated receipts into balance by cutting costs. Unfortunately, the legislature did not adhere totally to his recommendations, and in the following year Ludlow noted that the state had spent $280,778.28 more than it had received in revenue.

In 1883, however, Ludow placed greater emphasis on increasing the state's receipts than on cutting its expenditures, and he focused on the need to tap new sources of revenue. For years, many citizens had complained that corporations in New Jersey, especially the railroads, did not pay a fair share of the cost of municipal, county and state government. Railroads, moreover, paid taxes directly to the state and were by and large exempt from local taxation; in a sense, therefore, by removing valuable property from the local tax lists they increased the tax rate of the individual citizen. A special assembly committee appointed during the 1882 legislative session to inquire into the problem of railroad taxation issued its report just prior to the opening of the 1883 session.

Recognizing that additional income was needed to balance the state budget, and perhaps sensing a good issue when he saw one, Ludlow gave special attention in his annual messages of 1883 and 1884 to the need for railroad taxation. He noted that railroad property was taxed proportionately far less than the property of private citizens; it would be unjust, he said, to subject the people to a state tax until all other options had received consideration. While some advocated drastic actions against the railroads, he declared that the problem could be resolved through a few simple measures. First, the law of 1876, which taxed railroads for state purposes at a rate of one-half percent on "true value," needed changing, and Ludlow urged the legislature to define precisely what considerations would determine the true value of a railroad. He called for the creation of a special board totally independent of the railroads to assess this value, establish the tax payments and keep up-to-date records to avoid the problem of outdated valuations. Second, he asked the legislature to repeal the law that exempted certain railroad systems from the "true value" tax. Ludlow believed that these measures, coupled with prudence in expenditures, would produce enough revenue for the state to carry out its tasks without resorting to a direct tax on the people. During the session of 1883, the legislature considered several plans to tax the railroads, but no law resulted from these deliberations. Ludlow lacked the political power to force the reluctant legislature to deal with his objective of equitable taxation for the railroads.

During his term, several other important developments took place. The first governor to devote substantial attention to the problem of keeping the water supply of the populous northeastern section of the state pure and healthy, Ludlow appointed a commission to investigate the matter. He asked the legislature to establish a Council of State Charities and Corrections to oversee the asylums, prisons, jails and alms houses in New Jersey, and he appointed the council's first members. During his term other important legislation was passed, including a law that grouped municipalities into four classifications.

Overall, Ludlow's administration can be characterized best as honest and diligent but basically unproductive. Prominent but not particularly powerful in New Jersey politics before his nomination, Ludlow had little chance of influencing a legislature divided between the parties and dominated by special interests. Like many of his predecessors, Ludlow tended to devote the bulk of his messages to the legislature to summaries of the lengthy reports of minor government officials. By using his veto power he set a moral tone that many felt New Jersey needed in the 1880s, but few positive achievements can be directly attributed to him. His most noteworthy deed was giving the sanction of the governor's office to the growing movement for equitable taxation of the railroads; by this he helped set the stage for the passage of a more effective railroad-taxing system under his successor, Leon Abbett.

Although Ludlow's administration accomplished relatively little, his actions, especially his vetoes, earned him the animosity of powerful interests. After he left the governorship, he resumed the practice of law, but he lived in relative obscurity. Contemporary opinion laid the blame for his less-then-prosperous condition during this period at the doorstep of the railroads. In 1894 he served on the special twenty-member commission established by the legislature to recommend changes in the New Jersey constitution. In 1895 Governor George T. Werts appointed him a justice of the supreme court. Five years later, he died in his home town, New Brunswick. He was survived by his wife and two sons.

Records of Governor George C. Ludlow, New Jersey State Library, Bureau of Archives and History, Trenton, N.J.

Jerome C. Reddy

LEON ABBETT (October 8, 1836–December 4, 1894) was a formidable man. He was undoubtedly the most powerful person in New Jersey during the late nineteenth century. Twice elected governor, first in 1883 and again in 1889, he proved to be a very effective leader and accomplished much while in office. An ardent Democrat in the Jacksonian spoils tradition, Abbett voiced the sentiments of the common man beset by the intransigent forces of special privilege. Affectionately known as the "Great Commoner," he was considered a man of the people. He reached out for contact, and indeed for confrontation. An eloquent speaker in the flamboyant style of his time, he charged the political atmosphere and helped produce striking policy changes that had previously been considered impossible. He was a man of action, ambitious for his state as well as for himself.

Abbett combined opportunism with principle to advance his cause. As a machine politician he often combined the admirable with the obnoxious. Not for any altruistic reasons, but for practical ones, Abbett much to his credit promoted public participation in politics. True Jacksonian that he was, he rewarded loyal Democrats with the spoils of victory. Coming to power as he did during the heyday of machine politics, he built a strong party organization and used it as a convenient excuse for centralizing power in the governor's office. With this power, he did things that none of his predecessors had ever attempted to do. His performance infuriated his critics and those people with rigorous Victorian moral standards and roused passionate hatred. Loved with equal passion, seeking improvement for the downtrodden, using his charm and wit with a flourish, he was a difficult man to beat. Yet despite the political hegemony that he and his followers established, he failed to achieve his lifelong ambition of advancing to the United States Senate.

In physical appearance, Abbett was short and stocky. Standing only five feet eight inches and weighing about 175 pounds, the governor was an image of energy, combativeness, and courage. He had a round face with a high forehead, broad shoulders, brown wavy hair, bright blue eyes, and large bushy eyebrows. Early in his career, he grew a full beard and a wide moustache to make himself look more mature. As a successful New York City lawyer might be expected to do, he dressed in a manner befitting his professional status. He usually wore a dark double-breasted suit with a vest and bow tie. In cold weather, he donned a fashionable Prince Albert overcoat and a brown derby hat.

Abbett's rise to the governorship is a classic American success story. In a day when recruitment to political office depended much on wealth and high position, he came from an urban working-class background in Philadelphia. His father Ezekiel worked as a journeyman hatter by trade, while his mother, whose maiden name was Sarah M. Howell, operated a millinery shop. She originally came from a prominent but not well-to-do family in Mauricetown, New Jersey. Young Abbett grew up a poor boy in the streets of Philadelphia during the Jacksonian era. He attended Central High School, where he met boys like Henry George and Ignatius Donnelly, both of whom were to become famous public figures. Attendance at college was something which only the most privileged families could afford, and after graduating from Central High, Abbett studied law on his own. He served as a clerk in the firm of John W. Ashmead, who was the United States attorney for the eastern district of Pennsylvania. Abbett passed his bar examination in 1857, but he found Philadelphia to be a closed shop when it came to attracting clients. A year later, he moved to New York City in search of a more lucrative practice. There he soon formed a law partnership with William J. Fuller, a distinguished patent and admiralty lawyer. With the city's expanding commercial activity, the law firm of Abbett and Fuller became prosperous, and it remained intact unil Fuller died in 1889.

Shortly after the outbreak of the Civil War, Abbett returned to Philadelphia to marry Mary Briggs on October 8, 1862. She was the daughter of Amos Briggs, a city judge. The couple initially established their residence in Hoboken, which was just a ferryboat ride from Abbett's law office in Manhattan. In the seventeen years of their marriage, they had two sons and a daughter.

Encouraged by his law partner, Abbett entered politics in his newly adopted hometown in 1864, campaigning for General George B. McClellan in the presidential race against Abraham Lincoln. In the same campaign, he was elected to represent Hoboken in the general assembly. The Civil War overshadowed his early political career. He was an intensely loyal

Democrat, aligned with the party's Copperhead wing, which vehemently opposed the war. A staunch states' rights advocate, he vigorously objected to the policies of the Lincoln administration, especially its Emancipation Proclamation. Although philosophically opposed to slavery, he went along with his party and voted against the ratification of both the Thirteenth and Fifteenth amendments. At the time, there were only eight Negroes living in Hoboken, and he did not favor their advancement. Opposing the use of federal power during the war, Abbett deplored the expanded role of that power during Reconstruction. He gained statewide recognition by defending United States Senator John P. Stockton, whom the radicals of the Republican party had expelled from Congress.

Seeking to broaden his political base in Hudson County, Abbett moved to Jersey City in 1867. He was reelected to the general assembly for the next two years, and his fellow state legislators chose him speaker. The speakership was an important leadership position which he used to great advantage. The key to his success lay in his instinctive ability to gauge what would be acceptable to his own party, to the opposition, and to Governor Theodore F. Randolph. During the 1870s he endorsed a conservative approach to public policy while devoting much of his energy to the task of building the party organization. No crusader, he was at this time a survivor. Thus he identified himself with the powerful Camden and Amboy Railroad and defended this monopoly whenever it came under attack by those outside New Jersey. Like most politicians who move into the front ranks, he discovered that the political system within which he had to operate was not only shaping his decisions but also formulating his options.

In the late 1860s, the immigrant Irish Catholics in Jersey City were gaining political power. Frightened, the militant Know-Nothing nativists subjected them to discrimination and abuse. Abbett was one of the few Protestant leaders willing to share power with the Irish. As president of the local board of education in 1869, he openly courted them by assisting in their fight to soften the Protestant tone of Bible reading and prayers in the public schools. New Jersey politicians had played ethnic politics before the 1870s, but with the advent of mass political parties, Abbett developed the strategy to a high degree. He managed nominations and distributed patronage jobs to ethnics with a deliberate intent to woo them at election time.

Many more illustrations of Abbett's cooperation with the Irish could be cited, but one will suffice. Jersey City Republicans realized that the emergent Irish were outnumbering them. To put the municipal government beyond their reach, the Republicans persuaded the state legislature in 1871 to pass the "thieves' charter," which removed the Irish intruders from city office and replaced them with commissioners appointed by the legislature. Abbett spoke out against this ripper legislation, and in 1874 he got himself elected Hudson County state senator by promising to restore home rule.

During the 1870s, the Democratic party in New Jersey was rent by factionalism. The Theodore Fitz Randolph faction, otherwise known as the "State House Ring," abhorred the Irish courtship. Conversely, leaders like Abbett and John R. McPherson, who were interested in maintaining power, realized that to win elections the party must temper its nativism and enlist broad support. Breaking sharply and completely with the State House Ring in 1875, Abbett challenged Randolph's party leadership by supporting Robert Gilchrist for the United States Senate. This abortive effort failed, but greater success followed in 1877, when Abbett backed McPherson for the other Senate seat. Abbett continually clashed with the "State House Ring" both in personality and politics.

As a state senator, Abbett kept his campaign pledge and obtained the passage of a reform municipal charter restoring home rule to Jersey City. He played subtly on the religious and ethnic issue when he sponsored his "Liberty of Conscience" bill, which allowed Catholic priests access to the state penal and mental institutions. Elevated to the senate presidency in 1877, Abbett won the applause of organized labor by sponsoring a statute that required employers to pay their workers in cash rather than in paper scrip or company store merchandise. In a similar vein, he helped the employees of the bankrupt Jersey Central Railroad try to collect their back wages by drafting a statute that made their salaries a prior lien on the assets of the company.

Abbett first sought the governorship in 1877, but the State House Ring, in an episode fraught with party intrigue, conspired to assure the nomination for George B. McClellan. Though disappointed, Abbett showed his party loyalty by campaigning for McClellan. Personal tragedy then struck. His wife died of cancer in 1879 at the age of forty. He never remarried.

Stricken with grief, Abbett temporarily dropped out of politics. Some of his close friends thought that he had lost interest. But in 1880, when he learned that his arch rival Orestes Cleveland was seeking the governorship, he roared back. As chairman of the State Democratic Convention, Abbett single-handedly steered the nomination to George C. Ludlow, a state senator from Middlesex County, who went on to win the election.

Railroads were of paramount interest in New Jersey during the Gilded Age. Governor Ludlow would have liked to tax them, but he could not break through the stalemate of forces surrounding him. To battle the railroads over state and local taxation was Abbett's calling. It struck at the heart of laissez-faire capitalism and brought him into direct conflict with the established order, which saw railroading as the lifeblood of the state's economy. Concerned because the railroads paid few taxes or none, he actually began his fight against them while serving as corporation counsel for Jersey City from 1877 to 1883.

Finally, in 1883, Abbett was nominated for governor. With railroad taxation as his battle cry, he conducted a vigorous campaign, touring New Jersey from one end to the other. Yet his hometown, Jersey City, remained the center stage of the drama. The Republicans ran state supreme court judge Jonathan Dixon, who also lived there. Abbett did not let the voters forget that Dixon had drafted the infamous "thieves' charter," which deprived the Jersey City Irish of power in 1871. Dixon also had handed down court decisions that were construed as anti-labor. Abbett's cultural affinity with urban workers and foreign immigrants accounted in large measure for his popular appeal. When the election returns were tabulated, he had defeated Dixon by 103,856 to 97,047.

Abbett's inauguration in 1884 at age forty-seven was a goal he had worked toward for twenty years. Impatient waiting and striving had whetted his appetite for the leadership opportunities that he saw in the office. Seizing the initiative, he made the rail tax issue the major thrust of his inaugural message, which the railroads interpreted as a declaration of war. During the ensuing battle, Abbett encountered all kinds of obstacles. When pressure against the passage of the tax bill intensified, he threatened to refuse to sign appropriations unless the measure was advanced. By skillfully publicizing the issue, he was able to get the bill passed—a feat that had seemed impossible. As soon as the statute had been signed into law, the railroads challenged its constitutionality in the courts. At one point, the opposition created a political smokescreen by impeaching Patrick H. Laverty, the state prison warden. Undaunted, Abbett persisted in his course of action, and the railroads finally capitulated, completely surrendering their tax-exempt status.

As governor, Abbett was one of the rare major party politicians who advocated the cause of New Jersey's black citizens. In an unusual display of gubernatorial prerogative, he intervened in a local incident of racial injustice. The body of Samuel Bass, an ex-slave, had been denied burial in an all-white cemetery in Hackensack. Abbett called for corrective action, motivated by compassion and social justice but evincing a fair and dispassionate consideration of the issues. He persuaded the legislature to pass the "Negro Burial" bill. But that was not all; he also secured the passage of the first public accommodations law. On top of this, he served as the godfather of a black child in Newark, who was baptized Leon Abbett DeKalb. An interracial baptism was an uncommon event in those days. Coming at a high tide of racism in America, these actions were particularly significant; they represented a dramatic reversal of Abbett's earlier attitudes toward blacks.

Several other reform bills were enacted to cope with the onrush of urban industrialism. The practice of using convict labor for private profit was abolished, while the laws regulating the working conditions of women and children were tightened. Aware of the disorderly and chaotic growth of nineteenth-century American cities, Abbett drafted legislation that enabled the bankrupt municipalities of Elizabeth and Rahway to regain their solvency. His appointments displeased civil service reformers. In Jacksonian fashion, he ousted holdover Republicans from office and replaced them with loyal Democrats whenever possible. In retaliation, a hostile Republican legislature stripped him of control of those appointments, but not without a fight.

Prohibited by the state constitution from succeeding himself, in 1887 Abbett sought to become a United State senator. That goal proved elusive. Retribution came, and its name was railroad power. It should be remembered that before 1913 senators were chosen by the state legislatures, not the voters. Conservative pro-railroad Democrats, who identified with the State House Ring, withheld their support from Abbett and elected Rufus Blodgett instead. Brooding, vituperative, bitter, Abbett took this defeat hard.

Meanwhile, he managed to stay alive politically. He became legal counsel for the liquor dealers' association, an important source of campaign money and financing.

Counting on his continuing popularity, party leaders prevailed upon Abbett to run for a second term in 1889. His instinct opposed seeking reelection, but he could not resist the insistence of his followers, especially since he had no attractive alternatives. After securing an agreement to raise the governor's salary from five to ten thousand dollars, he accepted the nomination. The Republicans ran Edward B. Grubb, a wealthy iron magnate and a Civil War hero. Abbett had little trouble defeating Grubb, compiling an unprecedented plurality of 14,253 votes. He would have won even without the ballot frauds perpetrated in his behalf in the Irish district of Jersey City, where the number of votes cast exceeded the number of registered voters.

Characteristically, Abbett seized the initiative and turned the election-fraud scandal to his advantage by demanding a ballot-reform law. From a friendly Democratic legislature he acquired greater control over the bureaucracy and regained the appointive powers that had been previously usurped. Never subordinate to the legislature, he now began to ask it for action on a wider and wider range of issues. He obtained a package of labor laws, free public libraries, scholarships for the agricultural college at Rutgers, highway improvements, money increases for public schools, and a department of banking and insurance. His key appointments were typically paradoxical: for some departments he chose men of high competence and integrity, for others he yielded to the demands of unsavory forces that eventually damaged his reputation. A product of the corrupt Hudson County machine, which was then run by Robert Davis, the governor could not escape being tarnished by its rampant public dishonesty.

Abbett also broke new ground in resolving industrial strife. In December 1890 a serious dispute between labor and management erupted at the Clark Thread Mills in Kearny. As it turned out, it was one of the longest and bitterest strikes in New Jersey history. Pinkerton detectives were hired as strikebreakers. Rather than exacerbate the conflict by calling out the National Guard, as governors in the Gilded Age were prone to do, Abbett cleverly defused the situation by deputizing the Jersey City police, who restored order. He then had the legislature create the first state police force and appointed John Parnell Feeney as its head. He also obtained a law that prohibited the use of private detectives in strikes.

Similarly, in 1891, the governor intervened in a labor dispute at the Oxford Iron and Nail Company in Warren County, where employees were being starved into submission by a lockout in the depth of winter. He translated the episode into the first law of any significance on mine safety. He further demonstrated his alignment with the working class by appointing labor leaders to key positions. He named Joseph P. McDonnell to the state board of arbitration and Robert O'Hara as his commissioner of mines. In truth, he never forgot his common origins or his city upbringing. He was the first urban-oriented governor in the state.

When put to the test, Abbett had the capacity to rise above politics and to do what was best for the public good. The two most controversial pieces of legislation during his second term involved legalized gambling at the horse-racing tracks and the incorporation of the Reading Railroad Coal Combine. When these bills were passed, the attendant pressures were transferred in all their intensity from the legislature to the governor. Worried about the potential adverse consequences of both bills, he vetoed them. Afterwards be successfully appealed for public support to sustain the vetoes.

But bargaining with party bosses like Miles Ross and James Smith proved costly, for they made Abbett pay heavily for his legislative vetoes. In 1893 the special interests he had antagonized once again combined to defeat him for the United States Senate. Dejected by having failed to achieve his cherished goal, Abbett finished his career by serving as a state supreme court judge. He died in his home in Jersey City on December 4, 1894, after an attack of sugar diabetes. He was buried in the family plot in the Greenwood Cemetery in Brooklyn.

By any standard Abbett was one of the ablest and most intriguing men ever to be governor. The social and economic conditions that existed in 1884 made New Jersey manipulable for someone with Abbett's sources of machine power and leadership ability. Few of his contemporaries were comparably positioned. A lifetime in politics had made him wise and ruthless in political bargaining and compromising. This experience, coupled with his determination to lead rather than follow, made him formidable. With a personality well suited for the intense partisanship of his time, he displayed great zest for party politics and party organization. Furthermore, in many ways he was considerably in advance of the times. In this sense, he was an important forerunner of a type of governor that had not yet appeared on the American political stage.

Records of Governor Leon Abbett, New Jersey State Library, Bureau of Archives and History, Trenton, N.J.

Hogarty, Richard A. "Leon Abbett of New Jersey: Precursor of the Modern Governor." Ph.D. dissertation, Princeton University, 1965.

The Record of Leon Abbett ... as Assemblyman, Senator and Governor. Jersey City: Heppenheimer, 1889.

Shaw, Douglas V. The Making of an Immigrant City: Ethnic and Cultural Conflict in Jersey City, New Jersey, 1850–1877. New York: Arno Press, 1976.

Steffens, Lincoln. "New Jersey: A Traitor State." McClure's Magazine 24 (April 1905): 649–64.

Richard A. Hogarty

ROBERT STOCKTON GREEN (March 25, 1831–May 7, 1895) brought to the governorship a commanding presence, the status of a colonial elite ancestry, and more than three decades of political experience. His greatest single asset was his family name. However, he failed to exploit these obvious advantages. As chief of state, he was a model of dignity and restraint, a symbol of integrity and social respectability; but he lacked passion for his cause or against his opponents. He was cool and dispassionate, cultured and scholarly, impersonal and logical. The press respected him; the electorate admired him but did not embrace him as it had his predecessor Leon Abbett. He lacked both Abbett's zest for the strategy and tactics of party politics and his mastery of its subtleties. Although imbued with a strong sense of civic duty, Green nevertheless was a captive of the political system and the business interests that dominated it. As such, he did not assume an activist role in shaping public policy, and he did not distinguish himself in office.

A patrician by birth and disposition, Robert S. Green could lay claim to a sterling Yankee background. He was descended from a long line of Presbyterian ministers and a family that had been politically active in New Jersey since the American Revolution. His great-grandfather, the Reverend Jacob Green, had served as chairman of the committee that drafted the first state constitution at the Provincial Congress in Burlington in 1776. His grandmother, Elizabeth Stockton, was the daughter of Commodore Robert F. Stockton, who had been a naval hero in the War of 1812; she was also a direct descendant of Richard Stockton, who had signed the Declaration of Independence. These family credentials gave Green impeccable native-born, blue-blood status. At a time when family lineage and patriotic loyalty counted heavily in state politics, Green was endowed by birth with a valuable political resource. Over the years, the gentry had held power by tradition, by law, by wealth and not, usually, through the electoral sanction of universal suffrage.

Green was born in Princeton. Not much is known about his early childhood except that he grew up in a household where religion was important, discipline strict, and the moral distinction between right and wrong clearly defined. His mother, the former Isabella McClulloh, read the Bible to her children, spun the material for their clothing, and tried to inculcate the values of honesty and ambition. Raised close to Nassau Hall, Robert received a fine education. He graduated from the College of New Jersey (later Princeton University) in 1850. The family was closely affiliated with the college. The Reverend Ashbel Green, Robert's grandfather, was a renowned theologian who had served as president of the college from 1812 to 1822. His father, James S. Green, was a member of the law faculty. James Green was a man of considerable influence. In addition to having served as a United States attorney, he had been the Democratic party's candidate for governor in 1837, losing in the legislative balloting to William S. Pennington, the Whig party nominee. He was also closely identified with the transportation interests of the state, and he served as a director of the Delaware and Raritan Canal Company as well as treasurer of the Joint Railroad and Canal Companies.

Determined to follow in his father's footsteps, Robert S. Green, entered the legal profession. As was the custom in those days, he read the law while clerking in a local firm. Admitted to the New Jersey bar in 1853, Green eventually earned repute as one of the ablest constitutional lawyers in the state. Meanwhile, he showed an early interest in politics. In 1852, he served a brief stint on the Princeton Borough Council. The family had a long-standing traditional association with the Democratic party, which no doubt helped to launch his political career.

In 1856, Green moved from his home town to the city of Elizabeth, where he promptly became involved in the political effort to establish Union County. He was also instrumental that year in securing the passage of legislation that designated Elizabeth as the county seat. In 1857 Green married Mary E. Mulligan. In due course, they raised a son and three daughters. Step by step the young lawyer from Elizabeth climbed the political ladder, from prosecutor of the borough courts to city attorney to city councilman to surrogate of Union County. In 1868 he was named the presiding judge of the Court of Common Pleas. In 1869, Governor Theodore F. Randolph chose him to represent the state at the commercial convention in Louisville, Kentucky.

While still young and ambitious, Green came to accept the concept of litigation as a form of political action. He played a leading role in the struggle to break the Camden and Amboy Railroad monopoly of transportation rights between New York City and Philadelphia. This was no small accomplishment. The railroad had amassed enormous political power since its origin in 1831. One by one, legislators came to owe fealty to the home-grown monopoly, and they often succumbed to the blandishments of its lobbyists or to fears of political reprisal. At the time of the Civil War, when rail transportation was needed for military purposes, senators in Congress derisively referred to New Jersey as the "State of Camden and Amboy." The railroad, unwilling to give up its preferential treatment and its guaranteed freedom from competition, resisted newcomers with understandable passion. In 1872, Green brought suit against the monopoly on behalf of the National Railway Company, which had started building a competing line. Although the suit was denied, it stirred a fierce battle in the state legislature and directly led to the passage of the first general railroad law in 1873. With the enactment of this statute, the monopoly was finally crushed. Only in these bold and daring attacks on the Camden and Amboy Railroad did Green win the status of popular hero.

Recognizing Green's talents, Governor Joel Parker appointed him in 1873 to a blue-ribbon commission instructed to revise the state constitution in the light of the myriad problems created for local governments by the onrush of urbanization and industrialization. Green chaired the important committee on general and special legislation. Among other things, the revised constitution forbade the legislature to pass special laws for individual cities and required tax authorities to assess property by uniform rules and according to its true value. The state legislature's unwarranted interference in municipal affairs had become a serious abuse. By identifying himself with tax reform and the home-rule movement, Green continued to improve his political standing.

For the next two decades, Green led a busy double life as attorney and state and national politician. With "railroad fever" sweeping New Jersey, Green became wealthy as a railroad lawyer. In January 1874 he became a member of the New York bar and joined the prestigious Wall Street law firm of Brown, Hall and Vanderpoel. As a Princeton alumnus he added to the firm's luster. He was later made a full partner, when the firm changed its name to Vanderpoel, Green and Cuming.

Never far removed from politics, Green served as a member of the Union County Democratic Committee, where his skills as a political organizer and campaign strategist were highly valued. In 1868, he made a bid for Congress, but he lost his party's nomination to John T. Bird of Hunterdon County by the bare margin of two votes. In 1880, he was a delegate to the Democratic National Convention which nominated General Winfield Scott Hancock, who had led the Union forces at Gettysburg. In 1884, Green finally obtained his party's nomination for Con-

gress, and he defeated the popular Republican incumbent John Kean, Jr., by a plurality of 1,848 votes.

Before his one term in Congress expired, Green decided to enter the gubernatorial race of 1886. However, he encountered considerable intraparty opposition for the nomination, mainly from the powerful "State House Ring," which backed Rufus Blodgett, manager of the New York and Long Branch Railroad. Aligned with the more progressive wing of his party, Green received the crucial support of major Democratic leaders like Leon Abbett and John R. McPherson, and he won the nomination.

The gubernatorial contest proved interesting. The Republicans ran Congressman Benjamin F. Howey of Warren County, a manufacturer of slate and roofing materials. The emotionally charged issue of temperance was soon interjected into the campaign. No other question did more to inflame religious and ethnic antagonisms. In the eyes of teetotaling, evangelical Protestants, drinking was an alien practice that posed a dangerous threat to public morality. They saw it as the root cause of crime, idleness, and poverty. As the campaign progressed, nativism and anti-Catholicism became intermingled with the temperance issue. Drunkenness was associated with immigrants, and Irish Catholics in particular were unfairly scapegoated. For his part, Green played for the Irish vote and gently embraced the liquor interests. On November 2, he defeated Howey by a vote of 109,939 to 101,919—a victory widely attributed to the surprise impact of the third-party candidate, Clinton B. Fiske, who ran on the Prohibition ticket. Advocating total abstinence as his main platform, Fiske polled 19,808 votes. Since Green only beat Howey by 8,020 votes, it was claimed at the time that Fiske's candidacy cost Howey the election.

Green's long experience as a judge and politician contributed little of direct value to him as governor. Entering the office at age fifty-six, he chose to play his role as chief of state in a subdued manner, sharing initiative and responsibility generously with any who would ease his burdens of accountability. In political circles, he was easygoing, soft-spoken and low-keyed, allowing his wry, often subtle sense of humor to mask his ambition. He was unable to lead the state legislature on the important social issues of the day. He chose to cooperate with party bosses rather than try to dominate them, and the result was a placid and relatively unproductive term.

In his inaugural message, Green paid lip service to the problem of railroad taxation, but as governor he did not do much about it. At the outset of his term, the state board of assessors revealed that the recalcitrant Morris and Essex Railroad owed the state approximately $1.2 million in back taxes. Rather than insist on payment in full, Green submitted the matter to arbitration. He did not press for a settlement, and the dispute was still unresolved when he left office three years later. He was equally lackadaisical about reorganizing the New Jersey National Guard. In spite of a Congressional mandate to do so, he preferred to leave the task to his successor.

Not surprisingly, a protracted controversy over liquor regulation dominated state politics during much of Green's administration. Temperance zealots publicized the state's failure to enforce its liquor law—at least in Jersey City, where many saloonkeepers openly defied the law and sold intoxicating beverages on Sunday. The violation outraged the Protestants, not only insulting the Christian Sabbath but also offending that sense of moralistic propriety so characteristic of small-town New Jersey. Evangelical church groups flocked to Trenton to petition the legislature to stop the flow of "pagan rum."

Intense lobbying aroused a Republican legislature to pass a stringent liquor control law in 1888. This statute mandated a system of high license fees and established a policy of local option whereby each county could decide in public referendum whether to prohibit the sale of liquor. Brushing aside his Presbyterianism for the moment, Green, who wished to preserve his good relationship with the Abbett faction of his party, vetoed the temperance law, but the Republican-controlled legislature quickly overrode his veto.

Temperance next won easy local-option victories in six counties: Cumberland, Warren, Salem, Gloucester, Cape May, and Hunterdon. Stunned German, Irish and other liquor dealers from the cities sought to overthrow what they considered a tyranical puritan blue law. The state supreme court upheld the law but the dealers demanded its repeal when the Democrats regained control of the legislature in 1889. Public opinion, however remained overwhelming in favor of its retention. Under mounting church pressure, Green stayed out of the picture, leaving other party leaders to negotiate a compromise that retained the high license fees but deleted the local option provision. His failure to lead did not pass unnoticed.

In many ways, constituents and leader were not closely attuned to each other's calculations. Although Green courted the support of urban factory workers, he did little or nothing to help them. Several bills designed to eliminate the hiring of Pinkerton detectives as strikebreakers and union infiltrators were introduced, but they failed to become laws for want of strong gubernatorial leadership. The same fate befell a ballot-reform bill strongly supported by organized labor.

Similarly, Green spurned the Irish shortly after he took office. He showed his nativism by curtly refusing to attend a mass protest rally against British rule of Ireland and the attendant abuse of human rights. Interpreting his refusal as an ethnic insult, the Irish, who consistently gave the Democrats large numbers of votes, considered him an ingrate. His leadership style contrasted sharply with Abbett's, which attempted to have the party uphold the traditional Protestant hegemony without outraging its Irish voters.

Green cooperated with the dominant business community both openly and covertly. Ideologically, he conformed to the safe, comfortable conservatism that characterized the age of industrial expansion. Under his administration, business interests were prominent and powerful. For example, he signed into law the famous statute of 1889 that legalized the holding company and allowed businesses to incorporate for almost any purpose.

Upon leaving office, Green was appointed by his successor, Leon Abbett, to the New Jersey Court of Chancery. Some observers criticized the appointment as a political payoff, but Green performed well as a judge. His temperament seemed better suited for the judiciary than the executive. He died in Elizabeth on May 7, 1895, while serving on the bench. Interment was in the Greenwood Cemetery in Brooklyn.

All things considered, Green was not an effective governor. His concept of the office lacked sufficient scope, his programs were innocuous, and his leaderhip was insignificant. The essence of the gubernatorial role escaped him both as party leader and policy leader. He found it a burden rather than an exciting opportunity. The Green administration earned the admiration of the business community, but it did not capture the passion of the times or the imagination of the electorate.

Richard A. Hogarty

GEORGE THEODORE WERTS (March 24, 1846–January 17, 1910), lawyer, state senator, supreme court justice, twenty-eighth governor of New Jersey, was born at Hackettstown, Warren County. He attended the public schools in Bordentown and completed his academic training at the State Model School in Trenton. In 1863 he moved to Morristown to study law with his uncle, the former Attorney General Jacob Vanatta. Four years later the twenty-one-year-old law clerk was admitted to the New Jersey bar. He promptly established an office in Morristown.

Over the next sixteen years Werts built a lucrative law practice and gained a reputation for integrity and skill as a trial lawyer. Although he was a Democrat in an overwhelmingly Republican community, he was elected recorder of Morristown in 1883 and mayor in 1886. In the latter year, at the age of forty, he was also elected state senator from Morris County. His political success was due in no small measure to his wife, the former Emma Stelle, whom he had married in 1872. His marriage and the subsequent births of his two daughters helped fill an important social and emotional void in his life.

During his six years in the senate Werts compiled a commendable record, highlighted by his election as senate president in 1889. His name is associated with two pieces of legislation—election reform and local liquor option—but neither statute proved more than a politically motivated and ineffectual expedient. His independent legislative record nonetheless brought him to the attention of Governor Leon Abbett. The governor's term would expire in 1893, and he had his eye on a seat in the United States Senate. Fearing that a promising young legislator with political ambitions might threaten his plans, the governor appointed Werts to the state supreme court in February 1892 to fill a vacancy on the Hudson County circuit.

Abbett had little need for concern. Werts was a party man who had previously demonstrated his loyalty by sponsoring an act that shortly before Abbett's inauguration doubled the governor's salary. In 1892, despite his earlier fears, the governor supported Werts for the Democratic gubernatorial nomination rather than allowing one of his political enemies to gain the nomination. Although the Democratic caucus had considered both Edward F. C. Young and Justice Job Lippincott,

Werts won an easy first-ballot convention victory.

His Republican opponent, John Kean, Jr., campaigned against the Abbett administration by condemning such abuses as ballot-box stuffing, the sale of political offices, and Democratic subservience to the liquor and racetrack interests. Although Werts remained inactive during the campaign and continued to sit on the bench, party chairman Allan L. McDermott ably handled Democratic strategy. He sought to divert attention from the damaging Republican charges of corruption by linking the gubernatorial race with the Democratic presidential campaign of Grover Cleveland. For in spite of the political stalemate of national politics between 1876 and 1892, the Democrats had carried New Jersey in every presidential election since the Civil War save that of 1872 and in all but one gubernatorial contest in the same period. The strategy worked perfectly.

Cleveland's fourteen-thousand-vote plurality proved enough of a cushion to carry Judge Werts into the governor's mansion by a margin of over seventy-six hundred votes.

In his inaugural address Governor Werts proposed expanding the state's prison facilities, creating a reformatory for juvenile delinquents, and passing ballot-reform legislation. He directed the bulk of his remarks at those who criticized New Jersey for not having antitrust laws. Long before the United States Supreme Court's enunciation of the "rule of reason," Werts sought to distinguish justifiable from unjustifiable restraints of trade. "The distinction appears to be," he observed, "that where the restraint of combination is . . . simply the natural consequence and not the intent, the combination is not improper; where the object is to destroy competition and obtain control of . . . production . . . such combination is unlawful." Following the initiative of earlier Democratic administrations, Werts encouraged the combination of capital through the continuation of the state's liberal incorporation laws.

The 1893 legislature distinguished itself only by its excesses in violating morality and constitutionality. The most flagrant abuse occurred in connection with legalizing gambling at the state's racetracks. For a number of years prominent Democratic officials, including Assembly Speaker Thomas Flynn, had enjoyed a profitable working relationship with tracks in Gloucester, Monmouth, and Guttenberg. The legislature's passage of the bill to legalize gambling in arrogant disregard of public opinion stimulated the emergence of an influential antiracetrack league. Though Governor Werts vetoed the legislation, racetrack critics alleged that his haste to do so prevented effective mobilization against the gambling interests and helped enable the "jockey legislature" to override the veto.

The bitterness the gambling legislation provoked was evident in the off-year election of 1893, which produced a thirty-thousand-vote majority for the Republicans and gave them control of both the assembly and senate. But gambling was only one of many issues with cultural overtones that made themselves felt at the polls. The antiracetrack crusade proved to be overwhelmingly Protestant in leadership and composition. The enthusiasm the antigambling campaign generated among evangelical Protestants and the apathy it met among Roman Catholics suggest the divergent ethnocultural attitudes that characterized New Jersey politics during the late nineteenth century. It was not coincidental that the Republicans imbued their 1893 campaign with a pietistic fervor that viewed gambling as immoral and received its most vocal support from the predominantly rural counties of South Jersey.

The GOP's success also came at the expense of urban, new-stock Democratic legislators who had supported the gambling legislation and succumbed to its moral repercussions. New Jersey's Catholic hierarchy's ill-timed attempt to obtain public approval for state aid to parochial schools further stimulated this pietistic fervor. Though Governor Werts and the

Democratic legislators tried to disassociate themselves from the church, the parochial-education issue intensified ethnocultural divisiveness. This, in addition to the impact of the 1893 depression, may account for Democratic defeats in the urban-industrial counties of Hudson, Essex and Passaic, and for the loss to the Republicans of seven of the state's ten largest cities.

Instead of accepting the results, the Democratic minority in the senate organized a rump session and refused to certify the eligibility of the newly elected GOP members. They advised Governor Werts of their decision and asked him to recognize their body as the senate of the state. Displaying the same notable absence of courage that had characterized his mishandling of the racetrack scandals, Werts acquiesced, following a policy of inactivity and neutrality that allowed the capricious, selfish, and partisan actions of this small group of Democrats to paralyze the state's political process. This tragically ludicrous episode, in which the state had two functioning senates, was resolved in March 1894 when the supreme court ruled the rump session illegal.

The substitution of a Republican majority did not materially alter the quality of New Jersey politics. The 1894 legislative session is memorable only for the GOP's efforts to dislodge Democrats from all key appointive positions. Governor Werts's inability to provide even minimal executive leadership encouraged both parties to operate in a factious vacuum rather than face the problems of mass unemployment and poverty. Trying to avoid all responsibility for the depression, the Democrats sought security in a campaign that identified their opponents with anti-Catholicism, prohibitionism, and antiurbanism. They denounced the GOP for countenancing the existence of secret Protestant societies and for using the pulpit for propaganda purposes. For their part, Republicans supported legislation that would restrict religious training in public schools to the reading of the Lord's Prayer and require all schools to fly the American flag.

Cultural divisions continued to dominate state politics. Discussion of the depression revolved solely around its political repercussions and avoided any mention of possible solutions. Although the Democrats succeeded in regaining some legislative seats in 1894, the Republicans continued to capitalize on the depressed economy to secure majorities in state and congressional contests. Indeed, the precipitous Democratic electoral failures after 1892 can best be attributed to depression-created voter realignments and to the residual effects of the antiracetrack and antigambling crusades. Issues such as aid to parochial schools, naturalization, and gambling evolved into moral questions pitting old-stock Protestant Republicans from South Jersey against the new-stock Catholic urban Democrats from northeastern counties.

In his annual message to the 1895 legislature Governor Werts simply repeated past proposals for prison expansion and ballot reform, adding a call for water conservation. The legislature enacted none of these measures. Instead, it passed the Storrs Naturalization Act over the governor's veto. This infamous statute, which was clearly aimed at new-stock immigrants and the Democratic party, prohibited naturalization one month before any election. The legislature also rejected two amendments submitted by a special constitutional commission, one to outlaw gambling and the other to give women the right to vote in local school-board elections. But the most spectacular achievement of the 1895 legislative session centered on an investigation that uncovered corruption, graft and waste in state government. Former Democratic officials were discovered to have sold pardons and accepted bribes and kickbacks from construction companies. The disclosure of Democratic corruption significantly helped the Republicans to elect John W. Griggs governor and to keep control of the legislature in 1895.

It was George T. Werts's misfortune to preside over the dismantling of the Democratic party, which had dominated New Jersey politics between 1869 and 1896. Though the governor had scrupulously avoided any personal taint of illegality, his party's corruption contributed to its repudiation by the voters. Democratic supremacy in the post–Civil War period had resulted from efficient machine control at the local level. But the 1893 legislature had shocked even the most jaded citizens with its sordid behavior in legalizing racetrack gambling. The onset of the depression only accelerated a voter realignment toward the GOP that reflected a national trend and culminated in the election of William McKinley in 1896. It is clear that the vaunted Republican majorities of that year in New Jersey had actually been over three years in the making.

The governor's failure to provide leadership and his willingness to let the focus of power rest in the legislature characterized the Werts years. While the public was trying to cope with the most severe industrial depression of this generation, Governor Werts was leaving as his most enduring legacy a budget surplus of almost $1 million. His administration was notably deficient in rebuilding the integrity of state government. Once his term ended Werts retired to private life and his Jersey City law practice. He died on January 17, 1910—the very day that Governor-elect Woodrow Wilson inaugurated a new period of Democratic control.

Records of Governor George T. Werts, New Jersey State Library, Bureau of Archives and History, Trenton, N.J.

Brooks, Noah. "George T. Werts." *Harper's Weekly* 38 (March 3, 1894): 198.

Leiby, James R. *Charity and Correction in New Jersey: A History of State Welfare Institutions.* New Brunswick: Rutgers University Press, 1967.

Link, Arthur S. *Wilson.* 5 vols. Princeton: Princeton University Press, 1947–65.

McSeveney, Samuel T. *The Politics of Depression: Political Behavior in the Northeast, 1893–1896.* New York: Oxford University Press, 1972.

Eugene M. Tobin

JOHN WILLIAM GRIGGS (July 10, 1849–November 28, 1927) had many political admirers in a life that included service as New Jersey's twenty-ninth governor, United States attorney general, and member of the Permanent Court of Arbitration at The Hague. William E. Sackett saw him as a masterful and overpowering personality, "an intellect in a mold of ice." Walter E. Edge recalled, in *A Jerseyman's Journal,* that Griggs was "an attractive man—of fine appearance, an eloquent orator, a keen thinker . . . [with] a fine sense of humor and every attribute of warmth and understanding."

Griggs was a scion of a farming family that had been settled in New Jersey since about 1733. The youngest son of Daniel and Emeline Johnson Griggs, he was born at the family homestead on Ridge Road near Newton, the county seat of Sussex County. He attended the Collegiate Institute in Newton, then matriculated in 1864 at Lafayette College in Easton, Pennsylvania. Although he had participated a year before graduation in an unruly protest against the abolition of student fraternities, he was graduated in 1868, and he returned to Newton, where he studied law as Robert Hamilton's clerk until May 1871. To complete the prescribed three-year apprenticeship, he served with Socrates Tuttle in Paterson. He received his license as an attorney in November 1871, and three years later he was admitted as a counselor. After two years of independent practice, he opened a law office with Tuttle. By 1879 he had established a clientele large and important enough to warrant opening his own office. Robert H. McCarter wrote in his memoirs that as a lawyer Griggs showed a "wonderful power of clearing up difficulties that arose in the course of protracted trials." Not surprisingly, Griggs's practice prospered.

Griggs entered state politics in 1875 as the Republican candidate from the first assembly district of Passaic County, and he was elected over the Democratic incumbent with 51.9 percent of the vote. Although at twenty-six he was the youngest member of the assembly, he served on several committees and played a key role in restructuring the election laws under the constitutional amendments approved in 1875. He was reelected in 1876 but defeated for a third assembly term in the Democratic year of 1877. During the next five years he cultivated his legal practice and served as counsel of the Passaic County Board of Chosen Freeholders (1878–79) and city counsel of Paterson (1879–82).

In 1882 Griggs returned to Trenton as a state senator, having defeated the Democratic candidate, Judge James Inglis, Jr., by only 182 votes. He spent six years in the senate serving as chairman of eight regular committees, including Railroads, Canals and Turnpikes, and Revision and Amendment of the Laws. His principal achievement came in 1884, when he was organizer and chairman of a six-member joint committee on corporate taxation. Living up to his reputation for fierce partisanship, Griggs overcame Governor Leon Abbett's "thoroughly equitable bill" for the taxation of railroads and other corporations, framing legislation he considered less punitive. Griggs's taxation bill, which became law and survived judicial review, considerably enriched the state coffers. He made an unsuccessful bid to become president of the senate in 1885 and was elected to the position in 1886.

Griggs began to set his sights on higher distinctions. In 1888 he served as a delegate-at-large to the Republican National Convention, where he nominated New Jersey Congressman William W. Phelps for vice-president. In 1889 he hoped in vain that his railroad taxation work might win him the Republican gubernatorial nomination in New Jersey. Early in 1892 President Benjamin Harrison seriously considered naming him to fill the United States Supreme Court vacancy created by Joseph P. Bradley's death. As Griggs's confidential correspondence with William T. Hunt, editor of the *Newark Sunday Call,* reveals, Griggs enlisted the aid of Senate President Garret A. Hobart and others to influence Harrison in his favor. He also tried to curb stories that criticized him in the local Democratic press. Nevertheless, he was not selected, and his political ambitions were temporarily frustrated.

The Republicans in 1895 had their work cut out. Not since Marcus L. Ward's election in 1865 had New Jersey chosen a Republican governor. On the third ballot of the 1895 Republican State Convention, Griggs finally overcame the challenge of John Kean, Jr., and received his party's gubernatorial nomination.

Throughout the subsequent campaign against the Democratic candidate, Alexander T. McGill of Jersey City, Griggs waged a battle "for honesty, for retrenchment, for reform." His campaign rhetoric charged the Democrats with eleven years of prodigal and corrupt administration perpetuated by voting fraud in Hudson County. Specifically, he pointed to the Democrats' attempts to pass the Coal Combine Bill and to their abuses in racetrack gambling; he also accused them of staffing the state prison and the state hospital at Morris Plains with political hacks. On national issues he spoke openly for the gold standard, protectionism, and a cessation of Chinese immigration. But he rarely injected such issues into the New Jersey campaign.

Public disaffection from the incumbent party joined with dissension within the Democratic ranks to pave the way for a solid Republican victory. On November 5, 1895, Griggs was elected with 52.5

percent of the 311,609 ballots cast. He had a plurality of 26,900 votes and carried seventeen counties. Interviewed after his victory, he promised "honest government, honest officials, reduction of expenses, reduction and simplification of legislation." His victory initiated a succession of Republican governors broken only by the election of Woodrow Wilson fifteen years later.

In his inaugural address at Taylor's Opera House in Trenton on June 21, 1896, Griggs called on the legislators to consider "a restriction in the volume of legislation," especially about the unmanageable mass of statutes dealing with municipal corporations; to pass no law "unless there is some public necessity demanding it"; to enact reforms for "the protection of life, limb and health" against danger from public use of the highways and streams, specifically to prevent civilian injuries from trolley cars and to guard against the pollution of New Jersey rivers by urban sewage; and to keep the state's charitable and penal institutions free from political control.

The new governor directed his first efforts toward removing recalcitrant Democratic state officials. He replaced Secretary of State Henry C. Kelsey, who had held the post for twenty-five years, with George Wurts of Paterson. Other officeholders whose careers were ended by the reform-minded administration included the "lay judges" of the courts of common pleas. On March 19 state Senator Foster M. Voorhees introduced a bill to eliminate them and reduce the salaries of county court judges; the legislature approved the bill a week later, vacating forty jobs and saving perhaps $100,000.

Griggs turned his attention to the problem of grade crossings, and an act approved on March 25, 1896, eliminated the public menace of grade crossings in Newark and Jersey City. The legislators departed from the spirit of Griggs's inaugural message and produced a series of bills that made it more difficult for the victims of trolley accidents to sue the

North Jersey Traction Company and other operators of surface lines in Essex and Hudson counties. In line with Griggs's views, in 1897 the legislature prepared a constitutional amendment proscribing all forms of gambling, especially horse-track gambling, though that had received legislative sanction only three years earlier; but the amendment was barely approved at public referendum.

Griggs, an avid hunter and fisherman, felt strongly about conservation, and during his two years in Trenton the legislature passed a series of laws preventing water pollution and protecting fish, shellfish, and wildlife. His most important environmental effort was an act approved on February 26, 1896, to curb the pollution of the Passaic River and establish a general sewage system for the area. The act authorized an expenditure of $10,000. Writing to his friend William T. Hunt on December 19, 1897, Griggs said that the real danger lay "in the indifference of the local communities outside of those that actually get the smells. They are afraid of the expense, and are not spurred by the sense of immediate necessity." The preservation of public health and safety demanded state rather than local pollution controls. Under this act, Griggs named Hunt and two physicians to consider the problem, hire consultants, and make recommendations. Fifteen years and four commissions later, however, the effort had accomplished nothing of substance.

On January 11, 1898, in his last message to the legislature, Griggs surprised both parties by recommending an investigation of criminal law administration and other allegedly corrupt Democratic practices in Hudson County. Before an investigative committee could be set up, however, Griggs resigned the governorship to become the United States attorney general. On January 25 he had signed into law an act determining the order of succession to the office of governor, and therefore there was no constitutional crisis. On February 1, 1898,

Foster M. Voorhees, president of the senate, was sworn in as acting governor until the fall elections.

Griggs had been offered the post of attorney general at the recommendation of Vice-President Garret A. Hobart, his political mentor from Paterson. He was sworn in on February 1, 1898. He shared President McKinley's political outlook, and as early as April 9, 1896, he had spoken before the McKinley Club of Hartford, Connecticut—the first McKinley club in the nation. He fully supported the McKinley administration's imperialistic policies. In fact, near the close of the Spanish-American War, he accompanied the president, the vice-president, and the secretary of war on a visit to Theodore Roosevelt's victorious Rough Riders in Cuba. His most important achievement in the cabinet was arguing the "Insular Cases" before the United States Supreme Court. These cases determined the constitutional status of the conquered lands. In them, as he later wrote to Charles Bradley, Griggs relied heavily on the "broad national views of the Constitution" that Associate Justice Joseph P. Bradley had evinced in the case of the *Mormon Church* v *the United States.* Griggs remained in the cabinet until McKinley's assassination in 1901.

Though he continued to make his permanent home in Paterson, Griggs turned to corporate law as a member of Griggs, Dill, and Harding in New York City. Soon he accepted an appointment to the Permanent Court of Arbitration in The Hague, where he served from 1901 to 1908. Yet there was still time for politics. When Senator William J. Sewell died in December 1901, Griggs emerged as a leading candidate to replace him. The Republican state legislators, however, selected John F. Dryden over him. Six years later Griggs was once again passed over for the GOP senatorial nomination from New Jersey. On October 13, 1904, he addressed a Republican campaign meeting in Paterson and exhorted party members to take up a "progressive conservative" ideal. He was hostile to New Jersey progressivism, which in 1906 he satirically termed the "New Idea." Service at The Hague did not dim his political interests, but his brand of conservatism was losing some of its popular appeal.

In 1908 Griggs once again resumed legal practice. He became a senior member in the law firm of Griggs, Baldwin and Baldwin, in New York City. His business interests included directorships of the New York Telephone Company, the Bethlehem Steel Corporation, the American Locomotive Company, and the Marconi Wireless Company. During the battle in 1908 for a public utility commission in Trenton, he testified before a senate committee against the regulation of telephone companies. He devoted the remainder of his active life to corporate law and business interests in New York City and Paterson, and he died on November 28, 1927, leaving a $1-million estate. He was married to Carolyn Webster Brandt in 1874 and to Laura Elizabeth Price in 1893. He had seven children.

Manuscript Collections, New Jersey Historical Society, Newark, N.J.

Records of Governor John W. Griggs, New Jersey State Library, Bureau of Archives and History, Trenton, N.J.

Lott, John L., and Finch, James A., eds. *Official Opinions of the Attorneys-General of the United States.* Vol. 23. Washington: Government Printing Office, 1902.

McCarter, Robert H. *Memories of a Half Century at the New Jersey Bar.* Camden: New Jersey State Bar Association, 1937.

Moffat, William D., comp. *Addresses by John William Griggs.* n.p.: privately printed, 1930.

Don C. Skemer

FOSTER MCGOWAN VOORHEES (November 5, 1856–June 14, 1927) served as the state's chief executive from 1898 to 1902. He was the youngest governor in more than four decades.

Although his career was always associated with Elizabeth, Voorhees spent both his youth and his retirement in Hunterdon County. He was born in Clinton of Dutch-English ancestors who had immigrated from Holland about 1660 and had first settled on Long Island. His father, Nathaniel W. Voorhees, a nonpracticing member of the New Jersey bar, was the cashier of the Clinton bank and a delegate to the Republican National Convention that nominated Abraham Lincoln for president in 1860. Foster M. Voorhees was educated in the local public schools and at Rutgers College, from which he graduated in 1876 as second-honor man with prizes in moral philosophy and Greek.

He taught school for a year at the Rutgers Grammar School, then studied law in Elizabeth with William J. Magie, Union County's Republican state senator, and Joseph Cross, who later occupied the same office. In 1880 Voorhees was admitted to the bar. In 1884 he became a counselor-at-law. In the same year he was elected to the board of education of Elizabeth. He represented Union County's second district in the 1888 assembly. During that session he secured passage of the legislation that enabled the recently bankrupt city of Elizabeth to solve its financial difficulty.

Voorhees quickly became a leader in the legislature. In 1889, and again in 1890, when he represented Union's first district in the assembly, he headed the Republican minority. He played a major role in framing the "Werts High License Law," which increased the cost of liquor licenses and added a quarter of a million dollars annually to the state treasury. He took an active part in the defeat of Democratic Governor Leon Abbett's bill to tax railroads at the same rate as other property. Railroads had been claiming exemption from Republican tax revision plans on the grounds that they had irrepealable contracts with the state. But the enactment of a joint committee bill greatly increased New Jersey's income from the railroads. Serving on a legislative committee that prepared election bills, Voorhees "perfected" the Werts ballot reform law, which provided for voting secretly on official ballots. At the end of his third assembly term (1890), he refused to stand for reelection. But in 1893, after the people of Union County formed a citizens league to fight corruption, he ran for the state senate and defeated James E. Martine, later a United States senator.

Voorhees's prominence increased in the upper chamber. He became the Republican leader in the "Rump Senate" in the 1894 split over the credentials of Senator James Bradley of Monmouth; when Democratic Governor George T. Werts nominated him circuit court judge, he declined so that he would not have to leave the senate during the dispute. Afterwards, the state supreme court sustained the GOP. "He saved the day for the Republicans, not only by insuring continuance of the slender majority [eleven to ten], but also by his counsel in the exciting days of that session," a Trenton newspaper said a generation later. As senate majority leader (1895–96) Voorhees successfully sponsored a measure requiring a single annual appropriation bill instead of the customary separate bills, the use of which made it difficult to tell the full amount of the annual appropriation. In 1895, Voorhees chaired the special investigating committee of the senate, which, *The New York Times* reported, "exposed the State House Frauds, arousing a storm that resulted in the election of Governor [John W.] Griggs, the first Republican Governor in New Jersey for twenty-five [twenty-seven] years." Voorhees lost the gubernatorial nomination to Griggs and supported him in the election of 1895. In 1896 he declined the position of clerk in chancery. He was reelected to the senate that year and continued as majority leader through 1897. The following year he was unanimously chosen senate president.

When Griggs was appointed attorney general of the United States a complication arose. Voorhees was in line to assume the duties of the governorship, but the "office seemed to be without title," for he would be merely the president of the senate with the added responsibility of the governor. Accordingly the legislature passed a law creating the office of acting governor and prescribing the text of his oath. Griggs signed the law on January 25, 1898. He resigned on February 1, and Voorhees became the first officially designated acting governor.

At the state Republican convention in September 1898, Voorhees was nominated for governor by acclamation, an unusual distinction. But because the state constitution prohibited a governor from succeeding himself, he resigned his senate seat on October 18 to vacate his position as acting governor. He was replaced in this role by the assembly speaker. He campaigned strenuously, accusing the Democrats of corruption and promising extensive reforms. His party charged that his opponent, Essex County Prosecutor Elvin W. Crane, was the tool of Senator James Smith, Jr., New Jersey's Democratic boss. In November, he won fifteen of the twenty-one counties (including Essex), polling 164,051 votes to 158,552 for Crane. Though small, this was a larger plurality than Griggs had received in 1895.

Voorhees's "career as Governor by his own right was not considered to be as brilliant as when he was Acting Governor," according to the *Elizabeth Daily Journal* (obituary, 1927). The Spanish-American War, it said, had "offered a fine opportunity for him to display his abilities, and his work was so excellent that it overshadowed his subsequent activities." But the Voorhees administration, the

newspaper granted, was "characterized by reforms of great and permanent value." More accurate, probably, was the appraisal of former Republican Governor Edward C. Stokes, who wrote in 1928 that Voorhees's "gubernatorial term was Coolidge-like in its simplicity, its modesty and devotion to the Commonwealth, economical, conservatively progressive."

Voorhees was notably successful in improving social conditions for the unfortunate. As acting governor in 1898, he signed a bill establishing a state village at Skillman for the care of epileptics. After a newspaper disclosed deplorable conditions at the Hudson County Poor Farm on Snake Hill, he approved a bill in 1899 establishing the State Board of Children's Guardians. That agency, "the most progressive institution of the period," took children out of filthy, ill-run almshouses and placed them with families. In 1899 Voorhees also got the legislature to fund the completion of the Rahway Reformatory. Construction, which had been "practically for more than a year at a standstill," resumed, and the reformatory opened during his term (August 1, 1901). He urged revision of the 1895 reformatory law, which he called "crudely drawn" and "obscure and conflicting in details," and as a result the law was repealed when a new one was enacted in 1901.

State revenues were increased and carefully preserved during the Voorhees administration. In his inaugural address Voorhees directed "attention to the growing surplus in the treasury" and pointed out the "little likelihood of further demands of extraordinary expenditures in the immediate future, except in one or two instances." He warned the legislature that a surplus far larger than required would "prove a constant inducement to extravagance or unwise expenditure." By 1902 he could note that the senate, which had been remitting taxes on certain portions of its revenues since 1898, was employing its surplus to reduce the burdens of local taxation.

One method of distributing the surplus,

Voorhees pointed out, had come into use in 1901 as a result of the General School Law of 1900. During his tenure as acting governor a revision commission had been appointed, and Voorhees, maintaining that "no laws were in greater need of revision than those relating to the public school system of the State," had urged careful consideration of its reports. In 1900 the legislature passed the commission's bill with amendments, and by 1902 Voorhees was claiming that the law had "established for the first time 'a thorough and efficient system of free public schools,' as the Constitution expressly empowered and directed it alone so to do." Even though the court of errors and appeals invalidated the law on several technicalities, many of its provisions were adopted later.

The subject of taxing franchises was "probably the most important that will engage your attention during the present session," Voorhees told the 1900 legislature. Corporations of a "public service" character that occupied municipal streets and highways paid taxes to the municipalities only on personal property and real estate. An act of 1900 imposed a tax of 2 percent on the annual gross earnings of the holders of such franchises; the state board of assessors distributed the funds among the taxing districts in proportion to the assessed valuation of the property along the thoroughfares.

Voorhees was also interested in constitutional change. He first spoke on the subject to the senate and assembly leaders during his ninth week as governor (1899). Three hundred or more bills had been passed, but only seventeen had been presented for his signature. The governor's right to approve bills during an unlimited period after the legislature adjourned had been recognized theoretically at least since 1879, but such authority was dangerous, Voorhees held. Believing it contrary to the spirit if not the letter of the constitutional separation of powers, he advocated eliminating it by amending the state constitution. Indeed, he was not convinced that a governor had the right to

sign a bill even one day after the legislature had ceased, and he refused to act on bills except during the sessions in which they were passed.

In the concluding paragraphs of his final official gubernatorial message (1902) Voorhees vigorously advocated amending the federal constitution to elect United States senators by popular vote instead of by state legislature. In 1911, two years before such an amendment was ratified, New Jersey's legislature would become the first in the East to acquiesce in the choice of a prior primary election—James E. Martine, Voorhees's 1893 state senatorial opponent.

The state's leading Republican newspaper, the *Newark Evening News,* appreciated but did not overly laud Voorhees's administration. At the close of the 1899 lawmaking session, the journal expressed approval that "Governor Voorhees has not been in any sense a dominating force over the Legislature" and that he had "not led nor visibly guided its sentiment and action." In 1900, whatever praise the legislature deserved was "not so much for what it did as what it refrained from doing." And in 1901, less than a dozen of the 212 laws enacted were "of a nature that will be of any general benefit or disadvantage to the State at large."

But Voorhees's "backbone" was evident in his refusal "despite extraordinary pressure" to sign Senator Edward C. Stokes's 1901 bill providing that a corporation could extend its charter for up to fifty years, at any time before it expired, simply by filing a certificate with the secretary of state. He also showed his independence in another matter that year. He refused to call an extra session to provide a common sewerage system for municipalities in the Passaic River Valley, subjecting himself, as he told the legislature upon leaving office, to "the bitter criticism of ardent advocates of immediate action." Instead, he made emergency funds available to the State Sewerage Commission to survey the pollution problem in the valley and to obtain the opinion of expert engineers. Legislation of 1902 dealt with the problem.

In 1903 the Bankers' Life Insurance Company of New York City, whose affairs were in bad shape, made Voorhees its president in an attempt to reconcile differences among its officers. In 1906, only months before the New York Insurance Department prohibited the company from doing further business, factional strife and reorganization caused Voorhees to resign and go back to his law practice in Elizabeth. In 1908 a special grand jury indicted him and the company's former secretary for perjury, charging that in 1904 Voorhees had signed a false statement that dividends worth $20,000 were not due certain stockholders. He pleaded not guilty and told the press that "it is simply a case of my signing certified reports without careful inspection." He had "reposed trust in subordinates, as is done every day by hundreds of busy men, and . . . [been] misled into signing padded documents." The indictment was dismissed in 1910.

In 1925 illness forced Voorhees to suspend his business and professional activities and retire to his farm in High Bridge for a few months. During the first six months of 1927 he had several severe heart attacks that made him discontinue daily visits to his Elizabeth law office and eventually confined him to bed. Exactly eighteen years to the day and hour after his father's death, Foster M. Voorhees succumbed to chronic myocarditis.

He bequeathed his High Bridge property to the State primarily "for forestry and similar purposes." The land is now Voorhees State Park, Hunterdon County.

Records of Governor Foster Voorhees, New Jersey State Library, Bureau of Archives and History, Trenton, N.J.

Honeyman, A. Van Doren, ed. *History of Union County, . . .* Vol. 2. New York: Lewis Historical Publishing Co., 1923.

Ricord, Frederick W., ed. *History of Union County, New Jersey*. Newark: East Jersey History Co., 1897.

Harris I. Effross

FRANKLIN MURPHY (January 3, 1846–February 24, 1920), governor of New Jersey from 1902 to 1905, was born in Jersey City, the son of Abby Elizabeth (Hagar) and William Hayes Murphy, a shoe manufacturer. He was a descendant of Robert Murphy, who settled in Connecticut in 1756 and whose son Robert, Franklin's great-grandfather, fought in the Revolution. When Murphy was ten, his parents moved to Newark, where he attended Newark Academy. In 1862, at the age of sixteen, he left the academy to enlist as a private in Company A, 13th Regiment, New Jersey Volunteers. For the next three years he was on active duty, both with the Army of the Potomac and with General William T. Sherman in the West and "from Atlanta to the Sea." He fought in nineteen engagements, including Antietam, Chancellorsville, Gettysburg, Missionary Ridge, and Lookout Mountain, and in June 1865 he was mustered out as a first lieutenant.

With capital his father advanced in 1865, when he was nineteen, Murphy established a small varnish manufacturing business in Newark. The venture prospered and became the nationally known Murphy & Company, incorporated in 1891 as Murphy Varnish Company. Over the years it established additional plants and outlets in cities from Boston to Chicago. Murphy served as its president until 1915 and as chairman of the board of directors until his death.

Meanwhile Murphy had become active in Republican politics. From 1883 to 1886, he was a member of the Newark Common Council, serving the last year as president. During his years in office the council undertook an extensive program to improve streets and parks and introduced electricity for street lighting. In 1885 Murphy went to the state legislature, where he served one term as assemblyman. In the 1890s he struggled within his party to wrest more power for the populous North Jersey counties from state Republican boss William J. Sewell, who dominated the party from his base in South Jersey. Murphy became chairman of the Republican State Committee in 1892, and, assisted by favorable population and economic trends and scandals in the Democratic regime, he helped transform New Jersey into a solidly Republican state. After being made a member of the Republican National Committee, Murphy joined its executive committee. In 1901 he received the Republican nomination for governor and easily defeated his Democratic opponent, Mayor James M. Seymour of Newark.

On assuming the governorship, Murphy, as a successful businessman, was appalled by the unbusinesslike way in which the state government was conducted. He attacked the widespread absenteeism of state officials, partly through his own example: he moved into a house in Trenton and urged the establishment of a permanent governor's mansion. He found state funds held in favored banks at no interest and secured the passage of a law requiring their deposit in interest-bearing accounts. He ordered regular audits of all departmental finances and worked for the abolition of the fee system in state and county offices.

Murphy also showed his business point of view by his strong defense of New Jersey's corporation laws, under increasing attack as breeders of the trusts, and by his action on the attorney generalship. When Thomas N. McCarter resigned as attorney general to head the giant new Public Service Corporation—a firm almost certain to become involved in litigation with the state—Murphy complacently appointed McCarter's brother Robert H. McCarter in his place.

But Murphy was no simple standpatter: he wanted business and politics conducted in a decent orderly way, and to that end he was willing to support needed reforms. Struck by the rampant corruption accompanying New Jersey's unregulated primary elections, in 1903 he strongly backed the passage of a new primary law. Although it provided direct nominations (with which Murphy had little sympathy) for only very minor offices, it carefully regulated the election of delegates to state and local nominating conventions, and it became the base on which all subsequent primary reform was built. Murphy also secured the gradual introduction of voting machines, but, proving unpopular, they were abandoned during the administration of Woodrow Wilson.

When Murphy learned that New Jersey's weak child-labor laws were virtually ignored, he forced out the incompetent state factory inspector and backed new child labor legislation that compared favorably with that of most of the other states. He helped secure New Jersey's first tenement-inspection law (although it proved weak in practice), a law establishing a state tuberculosis sanitarium, and an act establishing boards of education with fund-raising powers independent of local politicians. Concerned about the effectiveness of state charitable institutions, he urged the legislature to support them generously, as befitted a wealthy state. Murphy faced up to the perils of the dawning automobile age; and although the legislature did not heed his heroic suggestion to prohibit automobiles geared to run over fifteen miles an hour from the roads of New Jersey, it began the regulation of motor vehicles. But it turned a deaf ear to his proposal to ban billboards from railroad rights-of-way. The governor also tackled two perennial problems—the cleanup of the sewage-laden Passaic River and the abandonment of the Morris Canal—unsolved until long after his term of office.

Murphy's governorship coincided with the rise of progressivism in New Jersey, a part of the larger progressive movement sweeping the nation. Among its primary objectives was the more equal taxation of railroad property, championed particularly by Mayor Mark M. Fagan of Jersey City and his corporation counsel, George L. Record. Jersey City and other financially hard-pressed Hudson County municipalities found much of their most valuable real estate in the hands of railroads with tax rates severely limited by state law and mainstem property that paid taxes only to the state, not the municipalities. Fagan and Record also sought legislation empowering municipalities to tax public utility franchises at full local rates. Supported by other North Jersey municipal executives, they urged the Republican-dominated 1904 state legislature to pass remedial legislation, but the party leaders would have none of it. Railroad and utility interests were too powerful to challenge, and though the local taxation of mainstem railroad property would benefit municipalities, it would deprive the state of a prime source of revenue. This raised hackles in South Jersey and other areas with little or nothing to gain from the proposal, facing instead the possibility of a state tax to replace lost mainstem railroad revenues. When the legislature adamantly refused to act, Mayor Fagan in exasperation addressed a stinging public letter to Governor Murphy, charging that the railroad and utility interests controlled the Republican legislature and the party was subservient to corporate greed and injustice. Although Murphy refused to comment, the letter spurred the party to action: a commission to investigate the railroad tax issue was appointed, and the following year, under Murphy's successor, tax legislation was passed that went far toward meeting progressive demands.

Murphy's influence in the national and state Republican party did not end with his governorship. He had long held the chairmanship of the Republican State Committee, and from 1900 to 1918 he was a member of the Republican National Committee, except for a brief period in

1912 after the progressives had carried the New Jersey Republican presidential primaries. In 1897 he was offered the post of ambassador to Russia but for business reasons he declined. He was a delegate to five national conventions (1900–1916) and a contender for the vice-presidential nomination in 1908. In 1910 he tried unsuccessfully to win the Republican senatorial preference primary. Six years later, with strong organization support, he made a fight for the United States senatorial nomination but lost in an upset to Joseph S. Frelinghuysen.

Despite certain progressive aspects of his governorship, throughout his political career Murphy was basically conservative. He once described himself as "an old fashioned republican, the son of an old fashioned whig," who had "marched as a boy with the wide-a-wakes in the Frémont campaign of fifty six." He became an implacable foe of the direct primary, opposed the popular election of United States senators, expressed doubts about the civil service law, and once declared that all officeholders, including judges, should contribute annually to the party that elected them. In the growing split in the national party that culminated in the 1912 Roosevelt revolt, Murphy stood solidly with the regulars.

Murphy's public services were not limited to strictly political office. For over twenty years he was a member of the Essex County Park Commission. He long served as a member of the board of managers of the National Home for Disabled Volunteer Soldiers. He was one of the American commissioners to the Paris Universal Exposition in 1900, and in 1916 he headed the Committee of One Hundred, which planned the 250th anniversary of the founding of Newark. A member of the Methodist Episcopal Church, he was a trustee of Drew Theological Seminary. Particularly interested in patriotic societies, he belonged to a number of them and once served as secretary-general and then president-general of the Sons of the American Revolution. While governor he received the LL.D.

degree from both Princeton University and Lafayette College.

In his private pursuits, Murphy lived graciously. He was concerned with books, art and music; late in life he taught himself to play a large pipe organ installed in the music room of his Newark home. His large collection of books on art, architecture and related subjects was sold some years after his death. In 1868 he married Janet Colwell of Newark, who died in 1904; only two of their eight children survived them. In the winter of 1920, while vacationing in Palm Beach, Murphy suffered an intestinal obstruction. He underwent surgery on February 18 and died six days later.

Records of Governor Franklin Murphy, New Jersey State Library, Bureau of Archives and History, Trenton, N.J.

Noble, Ransom E. *New Jersey Progressivism Before Wilson.* Princeton: Princeton University Press, 1946.

Ransom E. Noble

Edward Caspar Stokes (December 22, 1860–November 4, 1942), governor of New Jersey from 1905 to 1908, was born in Philadelphia, the son of Edward H. and Matilda G. (Kemble) Stokes. His parents, both of whose families had lived in New Jersey for generations, soon moved back to the state, settling eventually in Millville. There Stokes attended the public schools; later he went to the Friends School in Providence, Rhode Island. He was second in the graduating class of Brown University in 1883. Returning to his home town, he took a position in the Millville National Bank, where his father was cashier.

Stokes developed an early interest in public education, serving as superintendent of schools in Millville from 1889 to 1898. He had meanwhile entered politics as a Republican, and he was elected to two terms in the state assembly (1891–1892) and three in the state senate (1893–1901). As an assemblyman, Stokes introduced and pushed to passage a bill requiring the payment of weekly wages in cash, aimed at industries that still paid in orders on company stores. As a senator he fought against the passage of racetrack gambling bills and joined the movement that led to antigambling amendments to the state constitution. When the senate Democratic majority, repudiated at the 1893 election, attempted to retain its seats and exclude newly elected Republicans, Stokes was a leader in the successful fight to thwart its efforts. At the 1895 session he served as senate president. In 1901 he was appointed clerk of the court of chancery, where he served until his inauguration as governor.

When Stokes was nominated for governor in 1904, the New Jersey progressive movement, with its animus against railroads, trusts, and old-line political machines, was well under way in the northern part of the state. The problem of equal taxation of railroad property had been a major issue in the 1904 legislature. Stokes had entered politics under the aegis of South Jersey Republican boss William J. Sewell and had, by 1904, become a bank president and railroad director. This seemed to make him vulnerable as a candidate, particularly since his Democratic opponent, Charles C. Black, had something of a reputation as a champion of equal taxation. But the Republican party showed a willingness to make concessions on the issue and united solidly behind Stokes, who won easily with a plurality of over fifty thousand.

A growing split between the regular Republicans and the progressives within the Republican party, with the latter faction soon becoming known as the "New Idea," marked Stokes's term of office. The progressives were demanding the taxation of all railroad property at full local rates for the benefit of the localities, laws limiting the terms of utility franchises and taxing them at local rates, the establishment of state public utility and civil service commissions, and legislation extending the direct primary. Stokes's political and economic background placed him in the regulars' camp; nevertheless he tried to steer a middle course, urging compromise and making overtures to the New Idea. A law was passed taxing second-class railroad property (that is, property other than mainstem used for railroad purposes) at full local rates, though legislation placing a maximum limit on such rates offset its effect considerably. Mainstem railroad property, formerly taxed at only .5 percent and exclusively for the state, was now to be taxed at the average state rate; the additional proceeds—as recommended by the governor—were to be apportioned among the counties for school purposes. A law was passed limiting new utility franchises to a term of twenty years (though a municipality could, by popular vote, grant a franchise of up to forty years); a slight increase was voted in the rate at which franchises were taxed; but efforts to establish a state public utility commission were defeated. Direct primary nominations were extended to county and municipal officials and to state legislators, and a law was passed allowing the voters of each party to indicate their choice for United States senator to the legislature. Despite a strong recommendation from the governor, legislation establishing a civil service commission was voted down.

One of Stokes's outstanding personal contributions as governor was his persistent championing of conservation legislation. By the time he left office a State Board of Forest Park Reservation Commissioners had been established, and the state had bought or contracted for over 10,500 acres of woodland; a State Water-Supply Commission had been given supervision over potable waters and their diversion from the state prohibited; and the purchase of freshwater lakes had been

authorized. Stokes State Forest was later named in the governor's honor. Stokes also worked to improve the state's jury system, continued Governor Franklin Murphy's efforts for the regulation of automobiles, and secured a law establishing a Department of Charities and Corrections.

Stokes had chaired a commission under Governor Voorhees to revise the school laws, and as governor he continued to press for educational advance. He was influential in diverting a portion of the increased railroad taxes to school purposes. He urged improved teacher training to staff the growing number of high schools, "these poor man's colleges," as he described them. He lectured the legislators, apparently with little effect, on the need for writing bills in clear English. He noted that one-fifth of the state's population was foreign born, and urged that immigrants be taught the obligations and duties of citizenship in their own languages. He called attention to the proportionally more rapid growth of New Jersey's black population, and he recommended increased industrial training.

One cherished ambition Stokes never realized—election to the United States Senate. The first opportunity presented itself in 1901 when United States Senator William J. Sewell died in office. Stokes, who also hailed from South Jersey and was looked upon as a Sewell lieutenant, immediately entered the contest but met formidable opposition from John F. Dryden, president of Newark's Prudential Insurance Company of America. When Republican legislators caucused on the issue, Stokes and Dryden tied with twenty-four votes each, and fifteen went to a third candidate. As the third man's support crumbled, enough votes went to Dryden to insure his election. In 1910, taking advantage of the new senatorial preference primary law, Stokes entered the Republican primary and eked out a slender victory over Congressman Charles N. Fowler and former Governor Franklin Murphy. But the Democrats won control of the legislature at the general election and sent the winner of their own primary to the Senate. Stokes's third and last serious effort came in 1928.

In the meantime, however, he attempted in 1913 to win another term as governor. Though he took the Republican primary easily he faced a difficult general election, opposed not only by the Democratic candidate James F. Fielder but also by the progressive Everett Colby. Fielder, who had become acting governor when Woodrow Wilson became president and had Wilson's express support, won the election, but Stokes made a creditable showing, holding down the progressive vote and making large Republican gains over the party's performance in the state in 1912.

In 1919 Stokes was chosen chairman of the Republican State Committee; during his tenure the Republicans lost three successive campaigns for governor. The Democratic party appealed to the growing number of urban residents, especially those of more recent immigrant stock; its open opposition to prohibition was especially attractive. The political implications of the prohibition issue caused Stokes to revise his own thinking; originally a temperance man from a dry section of the state, he came out against the Volstead Act in the 1920s, although he stopped short of advocating prohibition repeal.

Stokes resigned his chairmanship late in 1927 after announcing his candidacy for the 1928 United States senatorial nomination. His principal opponents were former National Committeeman Hamilton Kean and former United States Senator Joseph S. Frelinghuysen. Because of their great wealth, Stokes made an issue of the inordinate use of money in elections; when his own backers urged him to put up $50,000 for expenses, he refused, declaring he would not make it a "campaign of dollars." Kean won in a bitter campaign that left serious scars; Stokes told a United States Senate committee investigating the use of money in the primary that he had lost because of Kean's wealth and the defection of friends.

By the 1920s Stokes had become an archfoe of the direct primary for senatorial and gubernatorial nominations, claiming that it favored wealthy candidates and encouraged corruption. He continued his assaults on the Volstead Act, attacked the Federal Reserve Board as too restrictive in its credit policies, and urged the reduction of income taxes. In 1932 he served as chairman of the New Jersey Republican campaign committee, and although Franklin D. Roosevelt carried the state (owing, Stokes thought, to Hoover's stand on prohibition), the Republicans elected a United States senator, ten out of fourteen congressmen, and majorities in both houses of the state legislature. It was his last major political effort.

Along with politics, Stokes pursued his career as a banker. As early as 1899 he became president of the Mechanics National Bank of Trenton; when it merged to become the First Mechanics National Bank, he was named chairman of the board and later president as well. He was the first president of the New Jersey State Bankers Association. But Stokes never amassed a large personal fortune, and, following the 1929 crash, he suffered reverses. Learning that he was in financial straits, the New Jersey Legislature in 1939 moved to award him an annual $2,500 pension, but he refused to accept it. Later that year the legislature created the position of assistant counsel to the New Jersey Council, the state's publicity agency, and designated Stokes as the first incumbent.

Stokes never married. Once described as "a dapper little man with a ready tongue to exploit a ready wit," he enjoyed a reputation as an orator. Temple University, Rutgers University and Dickinson College awarded him the LL.D. degree. Sports, especially baseball, were among his principal interests until the end of his life. After a year or more of failing health —not long before his eighty-second birthday—he died of a heart attack in Mercer Hospital in Trenton.

Records of Governor Edward C. Stokes, New Jersey State Library, Bureau of Archives and History, Trenton, N.J.

Noble, Ransom E. *New Jersey Progressivism Before Wilson.* Princeton: Princeton University Press, 1946.

Ransom E. Noble

JOHN FRANKLIN FORT (March 20, 1852–November 17, 1920), lawyer, state supreme court justice, thirty-third governor of New Jersey, was born at Pemberton, Burlington County, the only son and eldest child of Andrew Heisler and Hannah A. (Brown) Fort. With familial roots deep in America's colonial past, John F. Fort grew up in an atmosphere in which public service was a responsibility and elective office was the norm. His father had served in the state assembly and his uncle, George F. Fort, had been the Democratic governor of New Jersey from 1851 to 1854.

After spending his early years attending local private schools in Pemberton and Mount Holly, Fort was graduated from Pennington Seminary in 1869. He completed his formal education at Albany Law School, where he shared a house with Alton B. Parker, the Democratic candidate for president in 1904. Prior to receiving his LL.B. degree in 1872, Fort taught school in rural Ewanville and clerked for a number of prominent attorneys, including Edward M. Paxson, later chief justice of the Pennsylvania Supreme Court (1889–93).

Tall, handsome, and articulate, John Franklin Fort began his law career in Newark after being admitted to the state bar in 1873. As the state's largest city and its unquestioned financial, industrial, and social center, Newark offered an ambitious young attorney the best opportunity for rapid advancement. The fact that Fort's maternal grandfather had once been a powerful force in Essex County Republican circles must also have been a factor in his selecting Newark as the site of his law practice. The Fort name soon provided access to political and financial circles denied young men with equal intelligence but less social standing. In 1874 he served as assistant journal clerk of the state assembly. As his income increased he thought of marriage. Charlotte Stainsby, a charming, intelligent, and vivacious young woman, daughter of William Stainsby, Essex County Republican leader, met Fort shortly after his arrival in Newark, and they were married on April 20, 1876. The Fort family ultimately consisted of two sons, Franklin and Leslie, and a daughter, Margretta.

Despite the fact that the Democratic party controlled the State House between 1868 and 1889, Fort's Republican ties did not prove a serious handicap. In 1878 Governor George B. McClellan appointed the twenty-six-year-old attorney judge of the First District Court of Newark, a position he continued to hold under the Democratic administrations of George C. Ludlow and Leon S. Abbett. He resigned from the bench in 1886 to return to private practice, but later served on a number of judicial commissions, including an 1895 panel investigating the need for a uniform set of laws governing divorce, bankruptcy and insurance. In 1899 he served as a member of an American committee studying European penology, and on his return he introduced the concept of indeterminate sentencing—an idea he would advocate for the rest of his life.

Fort's link to the Republican party dated back to his law-school days when he actively campaigned for Ulysses S. Grant in 1872. In 1884 he was selected as a delegate to the Republican National Convention, where he demonstrated his awareness of the importance of party regularity by supporting the organization choice, James G. Blaine. His rising stature among New Jersey Republicans became evident in 1895 when he was selected chairman of the state Republican convention. The following year brought Fort back into the public eye when he nominated his state's favorite son, Garret A. Hobart for the vice-presidency at the Republican National Convention in Saint Louis. New Jersey's first Republican governor in twenty-eight years, John W. Griggs, then rewarded Fort by appointing him presiding judge of the Essex County Court of Common Pleas. He appeared to have reached the pinnacle of his career in 1900, when Governor Foster M. Voorhees appointed him to the state supreme court, which was assuming a position of prime importance as an alternative channel of policy combat and public decision-making.

Between 1880 and 1910 New Jersey was significantly transformed by intensified urbanization, industrialization and immigration. By 1880 the state's twenty cities made up more than one-half of the total state population. Its three largest cities, Newark, Jersey City and Paterson, had populations of foreign or mixed parentage comprising over 70 percent of their total inhabitants. By 1910 New Jersey ranked third among the states in population density. Unfortunately serious growing pains accompanied the state's demographic and industrial development. Corruption and moral bankruptcy characterized the state's Republican and Democratic organizations. Widespread recognition of the evils of concentrated wealth and calls for the restoration of economic democracy led many citizens to denounce the monopoly of the state's political and industrial sectors by an alliance of bipartisan political bosses and corporate magnates. Chief among the latter were the railroads, for though their real-estate holdings represented over one-quarter of the state's property values, they benefited from preferential tax laws at the expense of individual homeowners.

By 1900 the GOP had managed to emerge as the dominant political force in the state. This was partly the result of the election of 1896 and Republican success in attracting the new-stock ethnics disillusioned by the cultural breakdown within the state Democratic party over such issues as gambling, liquor, and aid to parochial schools. It was partly due, also, to the fruition of a sociopolitical alliance with representatives of the state's railroad and utility corporations, which represented a blatant disregard of the public interest and prompted a number of progressive Republicans to protest the inherent inequalities in railroad taxation, franchise limitation, and the complete absence of economic and political democracy. This "New Idea" faction led by George L. Record and Mark Fagan of Jersey City, Everett Colby and Frank Sommer of Essex and James Blauvelt of Passaic County demanded election reform through introduction of the direct primary; the initiative, referendum and recall; and the extension of the civil service system to include a broader range of government positions.

The Republican schism between "New Idea" progressives and their conservative "Old Guard" opponents approached crisis proportions in 1907 when disclosures of malfeasance within the administration of Governor Edward C. Stokes threatened the party's statewide hegemony. The most immediate consequence of this situation was a wide-open struggle for the Republican gubernatorial nomination. Although both conservatives and progressives offered their support to a number of candidates, only one man seemed capable of uniting the warring factions. John Franklin Fort appeared to possess many of the virtues deemed essential for the coming campaign: he had a reputation for integrity and probity; he was well known among party regulars; he had no connection with the Stokes administration; he was promised the support of influential "New Idea" leaders; and his record on the controversial issues of equal taxation and Sunday saloon-closing laws was acceptable, though equivocal.

Although one segment of the "New Idea" movement supported Essex County Sheriff Frank Sommer, the outcome of the gubernatorial nomination was never in doubt as Fort outdistanced his rivals for an easy first-ballot victory. During the campaign that followed, both Fort and his Democratic opponent, Mayor Frank S. Katzenbach of Trenton, favored the creation of a public utility commission, the enactment of civil service reform and the adoption of direct primaries. If the election turned on one issue, it was the enforcement of the so-called Bishops' Sunday saloon-closing act. Katzenbach remained publicly noncommittal, though Democrats, particularly in the industrial, immigrant and urban counties of Hudson, Essex and Passaic, forcefully denounced the law. Judge Fort, who seemed to be speaking as often from the pulpit as from the platform, ultimately came out in favor of enforcement. His advocacy seemed to diminish, however, as he campaigned closer to the state's urban centers. In spite of the burdens of a divided party and charges of Republican corruption, Fort managed to squeeze into office by a slim plurality of eight thousand votes.

In his inaugural address Governor Fort proposed to implement campaign proposals for an effective rate-making utility commission, the extension of civil service reform, the adoption of direct primaries, the enforcement of the antisaloon laws, and the creation of three new departments of motor vehicles, public reports and accounts. The governor-elect further supported legislation to eliminate the retrogressive county tax boards and institute jury reform, judicial reorganization, redistricting of the state assembly, and expansion of public roads. Unfortunately, the governor would present this ambitious and comprehensive program in each of his annual messages to the legislature only to have it rejected every time.

Indeed, the history of the Fort administration chronicles the failure of reformers as they met defeat on almost every major issue. This was due partly to the obstructive tactics of conservatives within the governor's party, and partly to Fort's equivocal leadership. For although conservatives suspected his progressive leanings, reformers had similar doubts about the degree of his commitment to economic and social change. Yet Fort proved a persistent and, at times, courageous leader, sure of his convictions and cognizant of political realities. He appeared most combative and most successful in attacking gambling and liquor violations and less heroic and certainly less effective in dealing with the railroads and utilities. His willingness to accept the token compromises the conservatives offered angered the progressives, who rejected the notion of politically motivated piecemeal reforms.

The Fort administration's most noticeable failure lay in its inability to create a strong public utility commission. Here, however, the governor faced overwhelming resistance from the Public Service Corporation, the state's utility giant, and united opposition from the conservative-controlled state senate. The Public Utility Act, which was ultimately passed by the 1910 legislature, proved to be of a quality so diluted that it required complete revision one year later. A similar lack of success accompanied efforts to abolish the county tax boards, which remained bastions of undervaluation and effectively nullified earlier tax reforms.

Fortunately, there was more progress on issues such as railroad property valuation, child labor, civil service reform, workmen's compensation, factory safety inspection, old age pensions, and direct primaries. Among Fort's secondary achievements one would have to include opening an inland waterway between Bay Head and Cape May; constructing a highway linking the state's resort areas; conserving New Jersey's water resources, and maintaining a treasury balance of over one million dollars. When viewed against the successes of reformers in other states, the achievements of the Fort administration pale. Yet the years from 1908 to

1911 were not a time of inertia but a formative period that awakened public opinion to the need for an expanded economic and political democracy. In that respect John Franklin Fort's greatest contribution as governor may have been to lay the foundation on which Woodrow Wilson would build.

Fort left the governor's office in January 1911. He spent the last nine years of his life engaged in a variety of business, political and public service activities. During the 1912 presidential campaign he served as chairman of the state Progressive Committee. Though Fort was pledged to Theodore Roosevelt, he had close ties with President Woodrow Wilson that kept him in public life. In 1914 and 1915 he served as a special envoy to Santo Domingo, Haiti and the Dominican Republic, investigating the financial and political difficulties that troubled those nations. In March 1917 Wilson named him chairman of the Federal Trade Commission, a post he held until ill health forced his resignation in November 1919. After a prolonged illness John Franklin Fort died in his South Orange home at the age of sixty-eight, on November 17, 1920.

He left a legacy of moral rectitude, honesty and hard work. During a period in New Jersey history when corruption and an arrogant disregard of the commonweal characterized government, John F. Fort gave expression to those citizens demanding meaningful social change. His dilemma was simply that he could not be all things to all people. Late in life he was fond of characterizing his term as governor by telling the story of the little girl who returned from school to ask her mother the difference between hope and expectation. "Well," said the mother, "I hope to meet your father in Heaven, but I do not expect to."

Records of Governor John F. Fort, New Jersey State Library, Bureau of Archives and History, Trenton, N.J.

Blum, John Morton. *Joe Tumulty and the Wilson Era.* Boston: Houghton Mifflin, 1951.

"The Direct Primary and the New Idea in New Jersey." *Outlook* 90 (September 12, 1908): 51–52.

Leiby, James R. *Charity and Correction in New Jersey: A History of State Welfare Institutions.* New Brunswick: Rutgers University Press, 1967.

Link, Arthur S. *Wilson: The Road to the White House.* Princeton: Princeton University Press, 1947.

McSeveney, Samuel T. *The Politics of Depression: Political Behavior in the Northeast, 1893–1896.* New York: Oxford University Press, 1972.

Noble, Ransom E. *New Jersey Progressivism Before Wilson.* Princeton: Princeton University Press, 1946.

Eugene M. Tobin

THOMAS WOODROW WILSON (December 28, 1856–February 3, 1924), thirty-fourth governor, was born in Staunton, Virginia, the son of the Reverend Joseph Ruggles Wilson, D.D., and Janet Woodrow Wilson. His paternal grandparents were James and Anne (Adams) Wilson, who emigrated from northern Ireland in 1807; his maternal grandparents were the Reverend Thomas and Marion (Williamson) Woodrow, who emigrated from Carlisle, England, in 1836.

Presbyterianism, with its Calvinistic emphasis on the sovereignty of God and its covenanter tradition, was a dominant influence on Woodrow Wilson from his boyhood. His father was a leading southern Presbyterian minister, and the son almost literally grew up in the bosom of the church. His home was also a place where education and matters of the mind were highly valued. From his "incomparable father," as Woodrow called him, the boy received intellectual stimulation, the desire to excel, and his best instruction.

Educated in private schools in Augusta, Georgia, and Columbia, South Carolina, Woodrow Wilson spent his freshman year, 1873–74, at Davidson College. His father's fortunes greatly enhanced by a call to a prosperous church in Wilmington, North Carolina, in 1875, Woodrow enrolled in the College of New Jersey (now Princeton University). The next four years were a time of rapid intellectual growth for the precocious youth. Active in sports and campus affairs, he was elected speaker of the American Whig Society and editor of the student newspaper.

Wilson studied law at the University of Virginia, 1879–80, and practiced in Atlanta, 1882–83. Disillusioned by an excess of damage suits, he entered The Johns Hopkins University in 1883 for graduate work in history and political science. His published dissertation, *Congressional Government* (1885), regarded as one of the seminal works in American political science, brought him professorships at Bryn Mawr College (1885–88), Wesleyan University (1888–90), and Princeton (1890–1902). His reputation as a scholar grew with the publication of *The State* (1889), a textbook in comparative government, and *Division and Reunion* (1893), a study of the period 1829–89 in American history.

Meanwhile, Wilson married Ellen Louise Axson of Rome, Georgia, in 1885. They had three daughters: Margaret Woodrow (b. 1886), Jessie Woodrow (b. 1887), and Eleanor Randolph (b. 1889). Mrs. Wilson died in 1914.

Elected president of Princeton University in 1902, Wilson transformed that ancient college into a modern university by reforming the curriculum, revolutionizing teaching methods, and expanding the graduate program. However, frustration plagued him from 1907 to the end of his administration. He tried to abolish the exclusive eating clubs and democratize undergraduate social life but received a sharp rebuff from wealthy alumni and trustees. He also led a fight against Andrew F. West, dean of the Graduate School, over the location and character of a residential graduate college. With the aid of alumni money, West won the battle in the spring of 1910.

In the long run, the greatest significance of Wilson's struggles at Princeton was their impact on his political thought.

Until 1907, Wilson was a moderate conservative interested mainly in administrative and municipal reform and identified only peripherally with the burgeoning progressive, or reform, movements in New Jersey and the nation at large. The struggles over the clubs and graduate college convinced him that privileged wealth threatened economic opportunity and social democracy; the crucible of turmoil and defeat transformed him into a radical social democrat.

The situation at Princeton also caused Wilson to seize the opportunity to make a new career in politics. George B. M. Harvey, editor of *Harper's Weekly,* and Harvey's friend, James Smith, Jr., of Newark, boss of the Essex County Democratic machine, tried throughout the spring of 1910 to persuade Wilson to say that he would accept the Democratic gubernatorial nomination at the next state convention. Harvey, who fancied himself a kingmaker, had been touting Wilson for the presidency since 1906. Smith needed the Princetonian as a respectable front to head off a revolt against his dominance in the state party by such young progressives as Mayor H. Otto Wittpenn of Jersey City, state Senator George S. Silzer of New Brunswick, and James Kerney, publisher and editor of the *Trenton Evening Times.* After negotiations during which he was assured that he would be left free "in the matter of measures and of men," Wilson announced on July 15, 1910, that he would accept the nomination.

Antimachine Democrats charged bargain and sale, but Smith won the support of his erstwhile rival, Robert Davis, boss of the Hudson County Democracy, and achieved Wilson's nomination on the first ballot at the Democratic state convention in Trenton on September 15, 1910. Wilson electrified the convention and won the warm support of his critics by declaring that the nomination had come to him unsought and without any strings attached, and by promising to serve the people of the state "with singleness of purpose" if elected.

New Jersey was in the throes of a popular rebellion against an alliance of old-fashioned machine politicians, the Pennsylvania Railroad, the Public Service Corporation, and other corporations. Wilson moved boldly to seize the leadership of the insurgent elements in both parties. He came out for direct primaries to give the people an opportunity to select their own nominees, a public utilities commission with power to establish rates, and legislation to provide compensation for workers and their families when they were injured or killed. He promised to be the leader and tribune of all the people. In a public letter to George L. Record, progressive Republican of Jersey City, Wilson declared that the Democratic bosses were as reprehensible as their Republican counterparts and that they would not control the state if he was elected. Under this onslaught, the dazed Republican candidate, Vivian M. Lewis, could only reply that he agreed with his opponent. The result was a Democratic tidal wave on election day, November 8, 1910. It carried a Democratic majority into the general assembly and Wilson into the governorship by 49,056 votes. Republican President William Howard Taft had carried New Jersey two years earlier by more than 80,000 votes.

During the next three months, a battle over the election of a United States senator determined Wilson's success as governor, indeed his future in politics. Both parties had held nonbinding senatorial primaries in September, and James E. Martine of Plainfield had won easily in the light vote in the Democratic primary. But legislatures still elected United States senators in 1911; and once it was certain that the Democrats would have a majority in the joint session, Smith decided that he would like to return to the body in which he had served somewhat ignominiously in the 1890s.

Wilson was in a quandary. He felt deeply obligated to Smith and wanted his support for his legislative program. On the other hand, he could not countenance the election of this agent of big business, and he knew that the voters would never trust him again if he did not fight the Newark boss. His efforts at persuasion failing, Wilson went to the voters in a speaking campaign and rallied the Democratic legislators-elect behind Martine. Smith's support outside Essex Couny melted. Martine was elected on January 25, 1911, and Wilson emerged the undisputed leader of his party.

Meanwhile, Wilson had been inaugurated as governor of New Jersey on January 17, 1911, and had begun to plan his legislative program. The first item, the Geran elections bill providing for the direct nomination of all elected officials and a preferential presidential primary, aroused the fierce opposition of the professional politicians. Twice Wilson went into the Democratic assembly caucus to plead for the measure. It was the first time in the history of New Jersey that a governor had asserted personal leadership over his party members in the legislature. The Geran bill passed the assembly on March 21, the senate on April 13.

Then followed the much easier adoption of a stringent corrupt practices law, a statewide workmen's compensation system, a measure giving the Board of Public Utilities Commissioners sweeping powers over rates and services, a bill permitting cities to adopt the commission form of government, and legislation benefiting schools and labor. It was, altogether, the most productive session since the Civil War; overnight, as it were, an aggressive governor with an aroused public opinion behind him had brought New Jersey abreast of the most progressive states in the Union.

Wilson was also hard at work to change the leadership of the Democratic party in New Jersey and to secure his own control over it. With the assistance of his secretary, Joseph P. Tumulty of Jersey City, as well as that of Kerney, he used his immense patronage to reward his friends and strengthen antimachine Democrats in every county. In July 1911, when the Democratic state chairman, James R. Nugent, committed the indiscretion of publicly calling the governor "an ingrate and a liar," the state committee deposed him and elected a Wilson partisan in his stead. An intense struggle over legislative candidates in the Democratic primary followed. Wilson campaigned hard for his friends, particularly in Essex County, where a Wilson Democratic League was challenging the Smith-Nugent machine with a full slate of candidates. Wilson Democrats swept the primary on September 26, 1911, in every other county, but they could not dislodge the entrenched Newark organization. Smith and Nugent had their revenge in the general election of November 7 by not supporting their own ticket, thus assuring the election of a legislature that the GOP would control in both houses.

In his annual message of January 9, 1912, Wilson called for the reorganization and rationalization of the state's commissions and agencies, tax reform, health and welfare legislation, and the gradual elimination of grade crossings over railroad tracks. In response the Republicans in the legislature, not eager to add to a Democrat's laurels, chipped away at the major legislation of 1911, passed a grade crossing bill that Wilson thought put undue hardship on the railroads, and offered nothing by the way of constructive reform. There was much public mutual recrimination when at the end of the session Wilson sent forty-two veto messages to the legislature on one day, April 2, 1912.

Wilson had meanwhile emerged as seemingly the leading contender for the Democratic presidential nomination in 1912. He spoke frequently, and everywhere that he went idealistic, progressive Democrats responded eagerly. A group of friends conducted a publicity bureau in New York, but Wilson would not permit them to make any alliances, much less any deals, with the state organizations. For Wilson, the crisis of the preconvention campaign came with the New Jersey presidential primary on May 28, 1912; repudiation by the Democrats of his own state would have killed all his presidential hopes. Except in Essex County, however, New Jersey Democrats gave their governor a thumping endorsement, and his nomination for the presidency remained at least possible.

Though Wilson supporters constituted only about one-fourth of the delegates in the national Democratic convention that opened in Baltimore on June 25, they were fanatically loyal. They hung on even when Champ Clark of Missouri, Speaker of the House of Representatives, won a majority on the tenth ballot, but not the two-thirds then necessary; gradually wearing away the Speaker's strength, they achieved Wilson's nomination on the forty-sixth ballot. The New Jersey governor conducted a strenuous campaign on a platform demanding, principally, tariff reform and legislation to destroy industrial and financial monopoly—as Wilson put it, a "new freedom" for the American people. Even though he received only 42 percent of the popular vote on November 5, 1912, Wilson won an overwhelming victory in the electoral college because the Republicans were divided between the regulars led by Taft and the progressives led by former President Theodore Roosevelt. The split in the GOP was also crucial in the election of a large Democratic majority in the House of Representatives and a small Democratic majority in the Senate.

The Democrats also won majorities in both houses of the New Jersey legislature, and Wilson decided to remain in harness as long as possible. From mid- January to mid-February 1913, he pushed through the legislature a series of measures called the Seven Sisters, designed to prevent cutthroat competition and monopoly, as well as a new grade crossing bill, ratification of the Sixteenth Amendment establishing a federal income tax, and other legislation. The remainder of his time as governor he devoted to an unsuccessful fight to remove the power of constituting grand juries from the hands of sheriffs, often allied with corrupt machines, and to vest it in the governor. He also failed to get a bill for a constitutional convention through the rurally dominated senate. He handed over the reins of the state government to the president of the senate, James F. Fielder, on March 1, 1913, saying that serving the people of New Jersey had been the greatest privilege of his life.

Inaugurated as twenty-eighth president of the United States on March 4, 1913, Wilson proceeded with accustomed vigor to rally public opinion and Democrats in Congress behind legislation to overhaul and strengthen the national political economy. He was what historians and political scientists call a strong president. He kept careful watch over the conduct of foreign relations; indeed, during crises he conducted diplomacy personally and wrote the diplomatic correspondence of the United States on his own typewriter. Reviving the custom, abandoned by Jefferson, of addressing Congress in person, he made it clear that he intended to break down the wall that had so long separated the executive and legislative departments. He worked closely with committee chairmen and others in Congress in drafting legislation and used party discipline , patronage, and public opinion to force recalcitrant Democrats into line. Later, when the nation was fighting in World War I, Congress gave him virtual dictatorial authority. Wilson brought presidential power to its apogee, yet, withal, he ruled with restraint and deep respect for constitutional traditions.

The first item on the Wilson legislative program was tariff reduction and reform. The Underwood-Simmons Tariff Act of 1913 not only greatly reduced duties and enlarged the free list but also levied the first income tax under the Sixteenth Amendment. Wilson's victory paved the way for even more important legislation— the Federal Reserve Act of 1913. One of the most important acts in American history, it created a new currency and a system of central banking through the Federal Reserve System. In 1914 came the Federal Trade Commission Act and the Clayton Antitrust Act. They established a new agency to serve as a watchdog over competition and tightened the laws against potential monopolists. A special provision of the Clayton Act declared, for the first time in federal legislation, that labor unions were not to be construed as conspiracies in restraint of trade.

A lull followed this first surge of reform, but Wilson put through an even more significant program in 1916. It included the first federal child labor law; an employers' liability measure; a heavy increase in the income tax and the first federal estate tax; the eight-hour day for workers on interstate railroads; and a federal farm credit system. By orchestrating public opinion and leading his party members in Congress like a prime minister, Wilson in less than four years put through the most comprehensive legislative program in American history to that time. It laid the foundations of the present-day political economy of the United States.

In his foreign policy, Wilson pursued a course of idealism tempered by an understanding of practical realities. He repudiated Taft's "dollar diplomacy" (the use of private financial resources to advance national interests) in the Caribbean, yet he felt compelled to occupy Haiti and the Dominican Republic to save them from self-destruction. He was more successful in Mexico. There he contributed significantly to the triumph of a democratic revolutionary movement.

The greatest challenge to Wilson's wisdom came with the outbreak of the First World War in Europe in August 1914. His supreme ambition and the objective of all his policies toward the rival alliances was to end the carnage through American mediation. Thus he endured assaults against American maritime rights by British cruisers and German submarines while winning significant concessions from both sides. And when the Germans began to sink American and other neutral ships in early 1917, he accepted a decision for war mainly because he believed the United States could bring peace more effectively as a belligerent than as a neutral.

From the declaration of war against Germany on April 6, 1917, to the armistice of Novermber 11, 1918, Wilson mobilized a great army and the entire domestic economy in the first total war in American history. He also raised the hopes of liberal and democratic forces everywhere in a series of speeches that called for an end of imperialism, rival balances of power, and heavy armaments, and demanded a postwar international organization to promote cooperation and prevent war. The most notable of these speeches was the Fourteen Points Address of January 8, 1918.

Going to Paris in December 1918 as head of the American Peace Commission, Wilson was hailed throughout western Europe as the savior and hope of mankind. During the following months at the Paris Peace Conference, he fought with incredible tenacity for a liberal settlement. The Versailles Treaty with Germany, signed on June 28, 1919, was a bundle of compromises that in important particulars violated Wilson's ideals. However, the treaty included provision for a strong international organization, the League of Nations.

Wilson presented the treaty to the Senate on July 10, 1919. The Republicans in that body objected strongly to Article X of the constitution of the League because it guaranteed the independence and territorial integrity of member nations. Led by Henry Cabot Lodge of Massachusetts, they refused to consent to ratification without a clear avowal that the United States did not consider itself bound to support Article X. Wilson rejected ratification with that reservation, saying that it was tantamount to nullification of the treaty. He tried to break the stalemate by embarking on a long speaking tour to rally public opinion to his side. However,

he suffered a severe stroke after his return to Washington in early October. Though unable to give any effective leadership to Democrats in the Senate, he still had influence enough to prevent that body's approval of the amended treaty. Thus the United States remained technically in a state of war with Germany until a separate peace was negotiated in 1921.

Somewhat recovered by the spring of 1920, Wilson remained secluded in the White House while the ship of state drifted without a rudder. The anti-League Republican senator, Warren G. Harding, won the presidency in November 1920. Wilson retired with his wife, Edith Bolling Wilson, whom he had married in 1915, to a home on S Street in Washington. He lived there quietly in declining health. He died on February 3, 1924, and was buried in the Washington Cathedral.

Woodrow Wilson Collection, Princeton University Special Collections, Princeton, N.J.

Woodrow Wilson Papers, Library of Congress Manuscript Division, Washington, D.C.

Records of Governor Woodrow Wilson, New Jersey State Library, Bureau of Archives and History, Trenton, N.J.

Baker, Ray Stannard. *Woodrow Wilson: Life and Letters.* 8 vols. Garden City, N.Y.; Doubleday, Page and Co., 1927–39.

Hirst, David W. *Woodrow Wilson, Reform Governor: A Documentary Narrative.* Princeton: D. Van Nostrand, 1965.

Kerney, James. *The Political Education of Woodrow Wilson.* New York: Century, 1926.

Link, Arthur S. *Wilson.* 5 vols. Princeton: Princeton University Press, 1947–65.

Link, Arthur S., et al., eds. *The Papers of Woodrow Wilson,* 36 vols. to date. Princeton: Princeton University Press, 1966–.

Arthur S. Link

JAMES FAIRMAN FIELDER (February 26, 1867–December 2, 1954), governor, jurist, was born in Jersey City, the son of George Bragg and Eleanor A. (Brinkerhoff) Fielder. On his father's side his ancestors were English. On his mother's they were Dutch; among them were some of the earliest settlers of the old Bergen section of Jersey City and some of the founders of the Dutch Reformed Church in the state. His father was a member of the Fifty-third Congress. Fielder received his early education in the Jersey City public schools and at Selleck's School in Norwalk, Connecticut. In 1887, a year after being awarded his LL.B. from Columbia Law School, he was admitted to the Hudson County bar. He began to practice law in the office of his uncle, former state Senator William Brinkerhoff, and eventually became his partner. Fielder married Mabel Cholwell Miller of Norwalk, Connecticut, on June 4, 1895.

Large, powerfully built and active, Fielder was fond of fishing, hiking and golf. His associates admired him for his mild and pleasant temperament and also for his firm resolve and unshakable integrity once he had set a course.

Developing an early interest in politics, Fielder served on the Hudson County Democratic Committee. In 1903 and 1904, he was elected to the state assembly; three years later he was elected to the New Jersey senate, and he was reelected in 1910 by the largest plurality ever given a senator from Hudson County to that date. In the senate he served on a number of important committees that included Banks and Insurance, Judiciary, Riparian Rights, Passed Bills, the School for the Deaf Mutes and the Soldiers' Home. As a measure of his competence and his popularity, in January 1913 his fellow lawmakers chose him president of the senate, knowing that he would become acting governor when Governor Woodrow Wilson resigned to go to Washington. In his last message to the legislature, Wilson praised Fielder as "a man of proved character, capacity, fidelity and devotion to the public service, a man of the type to which the people of this State desire their public men to conform."

Fielder had been a loyal supporter of the Wilson administration, and as acting governor he turned immediately to the task of completing the Wilson program. Though not a dynamic executive in the Wilson mold, Fielder gained friends through his willingness to combat representatives of the Smith-Nugent machine in the legislature, as well as the state's powerful corporate interests. He vetoed a special Atlantic City bill that would have opened the way to weakening commission government in other cities; he signed the full crew bill that the railroads had resisted, which afforded maximum safety for passengers. His approval of a bill providing for widows' pensions led the state into a field previously neglected. In the fight for constitutional reform, however, Fielder's personal leadership proved insufficient to bring about the passage of a bill providing for the election of delegates to a convention scheduled to meet in the fall. The bill passed the assembly with bipartisan support but went down to defeat in the senate at the hands of senators from rural counties who feared the reduction of their power in the legislature.

The struggle for reform of the jury system was more complicated. The drawing of juries, particularly grand juries, was "notoriously subject to political influence and control," as Wilson had charged. Sheriffs, unsupervised by the judiciary or any other agency or official, drew the juries for the county courts. Frequently controlled by local machines, sheriffs could easily fix the personnel of the juries to prevent the indictment of any interest protected by the machine. The reformers intended to prevent such corruption by turning the whole process over to the judiciary. Both parties recognized the need for reform, but the Smith-

Nugent machine, the liquor interests, and the sheriffs themselves mounted powerful opposition. Despite Wilson's initial leadership and Fielder's vigorous follow-up, this coalition managed through various tactics to prevent the passage of an effective bill before the end of the session on April 4, 1913. In agreement with Wilson and other party leaders, Fielder issued a call for a special session. Before it convened on May 6, President Wilson returned to the state to help with the struggle, but his ambiguous statements and failure to back a specific plan served only to distress and confuse the reformers. Finally, on the eve of the special session, Fielder and other state leaders in conference with the president worked out a compromise bill that provided for jurors to be selected by county jury commissions composed of the sheriff and one other member appointed by the chancellor or head of the court of chancery. An amendment added in the special session required that the bill be submitted to a public referendum. In the election on November 4, 1913, the people approved the new system.

Fielder's intention to seek the Democratic nomination for governor in the fall primary was evident from the beginning. Within a week of becoming acting governor, he announced his candidacy for a full term and began to organize his campaign. For the first time, the gubernatorial candidate would be selected according to the newly reconstructed primary laws. As incumbent, Fielder enjoyed some advantage, but this edge largely depended on Wilson's publicly blessing his candidacy. Fielder's major rival was H. Otto Wittpenn, longtime progressive Democrat, mayor of Jersey City, temporary head of the party in Hudson County and strong supporter of Wilson's programs in the state and presidential campaign. Frank S. Katzenbach, former mayor of Trenton and perennial candidate for governor, was also in the race, but his support dwindled as the campaign ran on. Wittpenn was just as eager as Fielder to win Wilson's backing, but the

president, reluctant to choose between two loyal friends and backers, delayed his decision until late summer. Finally, on July 23, 1913, he wrote to Wittpenn that he thought a three-cornered fight would be "most unwise." He felt the party should unite behind Fielder, who, Wilson wrote, "backed me so consistently, so intelligently, so frankly and honestly throughout my administration and has followed, on the whole, so consistent a course that I feel I would have no ground whatever upon which to oppose his candidacy." Clearly Wilson also believed, in view of the Essex organization's antagonism to Wittpenn's candidacy, that Fielder had the better chance for victory. Wittpenn's graceful withdrawal resulted in a handy victory for Fielder over Katzenbach in the primary on September 23, 1913, by 45,229 votes. The size of the victory had been due largely to support from the Smith-Nugent machine. Even so, Fielder, emulating his predecessor, felt it necessary to declare his independence, and a week after the primary he attacked the organization, seeking to read James R. Nugent and his associates out of the party. Wilson immediately expressed admiration for Fielder's stand, but other advisors thought he had seriously weakened his chances of winning over his formidable Republican opponent, Edward C. Stokes.

Fielder campaigned vigorously, speaking throughout the state. He resigned from the senate on October 28, 1913, creating a vacancy in the governorship and evading the constitutional provision against succeeding himself. Despite some pessimism, he defeated Stokes by a solid plurality of 32,850 votes although he received only a minority of the 354,578 total cast. The Democrats retained a slim majority of three in the senate and fourteen in the assembly.

But his victory, Fielder knew only too well, was less than it appeared. Shifting loyalties within the Democratic party had already destroyed any chance of mustering the solid majorities needed to continue progressive legislation. The Smith-

Nugent machine had now recovered fully from the Wilson onslaught. It was forming a new alliance with Frank Hague, a rising young Hudson County political leader gradually emerging as boss of the old Davis organization. Together they formed a major legislative force generally obstructive or openly hostile to Fielder's progressive initiative. Meanwhile, the old-line progressives, the bulk of them originally from the Republican party, once more separately grouped behind Colby, who had taken more than 41,000 votes from Fielder in the gubernatorial contest. And before the end of Fielder's first year, the White House made it clear that it had lost interest in further promotion of the progressive campaign in New Jersey. Wilson, in fact, soon found it politically expedient to put aside old animosities and cooperate with the state organizations that had earlier drawn so much of his wrath.

In the face of these obstacles Fielder's successes were moderate. He secured repeal of the Hillery Maximum Tax law, one of the few distinctly progressive measures he had called for in his inaugural. The law had been passed to protect the railroads after equal taxation laws had brought these corporations on a par with other state taxpayers. Other legislation achieved was hardly controversial. It included the imposition of an inheritance tax, improvement in the conduct of preferential primaries in counties and municipalities, strengthening of the pure food laws, reforms in the penal system, an increase in funds allotted to agricultural research, a bank stock tax law, and a major improvement in the drafting of legislative bills by establishing a Legislative Reference Bureau in the State Library and appointing an expert bill-drafting adviser in the office of the attorney general. Three constitutional amendments were also submitted to the people. The first, which Fielder opposed, granted woman suffrage; the second simplified the amendment process; and the third expanded the power of municipalities to condemn land for public improve-

ment. All three were voted down in a referendum in October 1915.

At the end of the first legislative session of his administration, Fielder summed up his despair in a letter to Joseph P. Tumulty. "I have been up against some difficult legislative situations during my experience at Trenton," he wrote, "but this is the worst that I ever encountered. There are several factions of Democrats and at least two of the Republicans with outside influences constantly at work on each and . . . the Democratic Assemblymen, for the most part, are the most unreliable lot of men we ever had to deal with. One never knows upon whom he can count to assist in legislation."

The situation did not improve, for the Democrats lost control of both houses of the legislature in the 1914 elections. The following year the Republicans increased their lead to continue a domination that endured for more than a decade. The remainder of Fielder's term was frustrating and relatively unproductive, although the legislature enacted some laws he supported. It passed some recommendations of the Economy and Efficiency Commission to reduce the number of boards, departments and political commissions. It created a central purchasing bureau for the state and its institutions. It required advance announcement of proposed expenditures to enable the public to review them and react. It limited a woman's work day to ten hours and safeguarded factory workers from some industrial hazards and occupational diseases. But the governor had little power beyond the ability to threaten with the veto or to use it. A coalition of Democrats and Republicans had already begun to dismantle the Wilson reforms, particularly those referring to New Jersey's corporation laws.

By the end of his term, Fielder, thoroughly at odds with both parties in the legislature, charged them with failure to meet the needs of the state and vowed to have done with politics for life. In 1917, he became State Food Administrator to help the war effort. Two years later he was named vice-chancellor of the court of chancery, a post he retained for twenty-nine years. He died in Montclair at the age of eighty-seven.

Records of Governor James F. Fielder, New Jersey State Library, Bureau of Archives and History, Trenton, N.J.

Records of Governor Woodrow Wilson, New Jersey State Library, Bureau of Archives and History, Trenton, N.J.

Joseph P. Tumulty Papers, Library of Congress, Manuscript Division, Washington, D.C.

Kerney, James. *The Political Education of Woodrow Wilson.* New York: Century, 1926.

Link, Arthur S. *Wilson.* 5 vols. Princeton: Princeton University Press, 1947–65. Vol 1: *Wilson: The Road to the White House* and vol. 2: *Wilson: The New Freedom.*

David W. Hirst

WALTER EVANS EDGE (November 20, 1873–October 29, 1956) enjoyed the unique distinction of serving as governor during both World War I and World War II. Born in Philadelphia to William and Mary (Evans) Edge, Walter descended from a family resident in the Chester Valley since the eighteenth century. After his widowed father remarried in 1877, the boy moved with his family to Pleasantville, New Jersey, where his father worked for the Pennsylvania Railroad. Edge spent his boyhood in the occupations of late nineteenth-century rural youth—fishing, hunting, limited schooling, and work. His autobiography, *A Jerseyman's Journal* (1948), recalls these years with the urban American's nostalgia for the Arcadian myth. Edge's formal education ended at the age of fourteen, when he completed the equivalent of eighth grade. He began his business career in Atlantic City, as "printer's devil" on the *Atlantic Review,* and when he was sixteen he found part-

time employment with the Dorland Advertising Agency. Within two years he bought the agency and began a rapid approach to his goal of being independently wealthy.

In the best Horatio Alger tradition, Edge worked hard, and circumstances came to his aid. Most significant among them was Atlantic City's boomtown growth as a resort. He had grasped the potentialities of the development early and made himself and his business a part of the movement. In 1893 he established a social-notes paper, the *Atlantic City Daily Guest;* this proved so profitable that in 1895 it became a full-fledged newspaper, the *Atlantic City Daily Press.* His advertising agency, meanwhile, expanded to include general commercial advertising. By 1910 the Dorland agency, with offices in New York City, London, Berlin, Paris and other European cities, was grossing some $10 million annually. By the early years of the twentieth century Edge had established a financial independence in business enterprises that continued to support him comfortably over the next fifty years, while he engaged in public affairs.

Walter Edge married twice. By his first wife, Lady Lee Phillips, whom he wed on June 10, 1907, he had one son, Walter E. Jr. The first Mrs. Edge died in July, 1915. On December 9, 1922, he married Camilla Loyall Ashe Sewell of Bath, Maine. One son, Loyall, and two daughters, Camilla and Mary Esther, were born to this union. His second wife and his four children survived him.

Even while concentrating on his goal of early financial independence, Edge had always envisioned a career in politics and public service. In the early 1890s he had become active in the Atlantic City Republican party, and in January 1897 he had been appointed journal clerk of the senate as a reward for his newspaper's endorsement of the GOP candidates. From this undemanding position he observed the tactics of state politics and met its chief figures. With time out for service in the Spanish-American War, Edge served three years in this post and an additional four as secretary of the state senate. He made an unsuccessful attempt in 1904 to gain the GOP state senate nomination from Atlantic County against the candidate of the local Republican organization. In 1909 he won election to the assembly. In the following year he gained the first of two terms in the senate.

Walter Edge's service in the legislature coincided with the climax of the reform movements of the early twentieth century. But Edge was not a reformer. Perhaps chastened by his unsuccessful opposition to the GOP organization in 1904, he carefully remained with the party leadership throughout the upheavals of the "New Idea" and progressivism, though he cooperated with the reformers when their measures appeared sure to triumph. During the Republican travail of 1912 Edge demonstrated his party regularity when he and his newspapers supported William Howard Taft for the presidency and stood strongly against the insurgent Bull Moose candidacy of Theodore Roosevelt. In the following year he won reelection to the state senate, and in 1915 he was chosen president of the senate. By this time he was well known throughout the state GOP and widely recognized as one of its leading lights.

Although the "Sand Dune Senator," as Edge was sometimes called, was not a reformer, he was not a reactionary either. He supported some significant social legislation. Appointed in 1910 as an assembly representative on a commission to develop an employer's liability law, he worked diligently through the summer of that year examining American statutes and judicial decisions and going to Europe to study developments in the compensation field. As a freshman senator in 1911, he sponsored the commission's bill in the upper house and won Woodrow Wilson's acceptance of it. The measure became an early example of successful legislation on employer's liability. He pushed also for a ten-hour day for women and a measure to protect factory workers against industrial hazards. Edge de-

veloped a reputation for concern with the economy and the efficiency of state operations. As chairman of a joint legislative commission he was instrumental in shaping measures to reduce the number of boards and commissions conducting state business and to provide a rational organization of the whole. He introduced and steered to passage a budget bill to make the governor the responsible fiscal head of the state and a measure to create a central purchasing bureau to economize by bulk purchase.

On January 21, 1916, Edge announced his candidacy for the Republican gubernatorial nomination. Well known because of his prominent legislative service, he counted on his business success to win popular confidence and on his long record of party regularity to gain the endorsement of the state and county GOP leadership. In a three-way primary he defeated—by a mere three thousand votes —Austen Colgate of the Colgate Soap Company and George L. Record, prominent reform spokesman. Had Record not been in contention Edge might have lost. Since Edge was the most conservative of the three, most of Record's twenty-nine thousand votes would probably have gone to Colgate.

In the last summer before the United States entered World War I the New Jersey Democracy chose H. Otto Wittpenn as its gubernatorial candidate. A prominent Wilson supporter and former mayor of Jersey City, Wittpenn, with his close ties to the German-American community, would supposedly offset any defections resulting from the international situation. The strategy probably would have worked if the New Jersey Democrats had not been so divided between Wilson and anti-Wilson factions that they failed to develop an effective campaign or issues. The Republicans, on the other hand, had for the first time in four years a truly united party, and Edge developed early a campaign slogan and image: "A Business Man with a Business Plan." The GOP platform promised speedy revision of corporation and election laws and effective and efficient government with the governor as "the business manager, the legislature as the board of directors, and the people as the stockholders." The vigorous campaigning of Edge and the entire GOP organization returned New Jersey to its normal place in the Republican column; Edge's margin over Wittpenn was a convincing 69,647.

In his first message to the legislature, in January 1917, Edge spelled out his conception of gubernatorial leadership and emphasized the need to consolidate state boards and agencies, to improve civil service by the standardization of duties and compensation, and to find solutions to the administrative and fiscal problems of state institutions—penal, custodial and rehabilitative. He also proposed a close examination of the impact of the "Seven Sisters"—the Wilson-era corporation reform laws—on state finances, greater home rule for municipalities, an increased franchise tax on public utilities corporations and a complete reorganization of the state board to provide for comprehensive road development. By an effective combination of cajolery, arm-twisting and patronage, Edge achieved most of his program.

The legislature of 1917 enacted Edge's franchise tax on public utilities corporations, allowed greater home rule for cities, and authorized consolidation of state boards. It also created special commissions to examine the problems of civil service reform, corporation law reform and the problems of state institutions; the reports of those commissions led to significant improvements in the state institutions, especially the prisons, and to the emasculation of the Wilsonian corporation laws. The 1917 legislature also granted the governor his desired reorganization of the road department. To direct the new department and to lay the groundwork for a comprehensive system of roads, Edge secured General George W. Goethals of Panama Canal fame as state engineer. As part of the overall plan, Edge successfully initiated construction of the Holland Tunnel, connecting Jersey City

and New York City, and of the Delaware River Bridge (now the Benjamin Franklin Bridge), spanning the Delaware from Camden to Philadelphia. Although completion of these projects came well after his term, Edge secured the preliminary legislation. He also figured prominently in the bistate negotiations that led to the establishment of the Port of New York Authority. In addition, during his term he won improvements in the workmen's compensation law and in public health education, and he pushed for the creation of a state police force to provide adequate protection to rural and developing suburban areas.

The 1917 state legislature adjourned two weeks before the United States entered World War I, but the ominous shadow of war had led it to delegate emergency authority to the governor in advance. Late in March, after conferences with the war department, Edge set in motion the acquisition of the area which became Camp Dix. The New Jersey Committee of Public Safety, composed of municipal executives, was formed to coordinate action throughout the state in emergencies. National Guard units were recruited to full strength, a state militia was created to replace the National Guard, and a system of recruiting high school youths to work on farms was initiated. In his last annual message to the legislature in 1919 Edge addressed the problems of the returning veteran. He urged the state to inaugurate a transitional program of public works and road building to take up the employment slack created by the conversion to a peacetime economy, retrain and rehabilitate disabled veterans through a special program in the public schools, and establish a public health program to combat the venereal disease that had become alarmingly evident during the war. Little came of these plans, however, since the governor based them on the assumption that the federal government would be equally provident and would cooperate with the states.

By the time Edge presented his postwar

program to the legislature, he had already won election to the United States Senate in the 1918 GOP landslide. He continued as governor until May 1919, when he resigned to attend the special session of Congress dealing with the peace settlement. Though active in the Senate, Edge was not among its leaders. In November 1929, as his second term drew to a close, President Herbert C. Hoover appointed him to the post of ambassador to France, which he held until March 1933.

For the following decade Edge enjoyed a life of retirement at his homes here and abroad and served as an elder statesman of the Jersey GOP. With the outbreak of World War II he was anxious to return to some form of public service. In 1943 the state Republican organization was desperately divided and had long been out of power. Edge agreed to run for governor on condition that nobody oppose him in the primary and that the party maintain strong discipline. Other potential candidates were persuaded to withdraw, and Edge was nominated.

The Democrats ran Vincent J. Murphy, the state leader of the American Federation of Labor and the mayor of Newark. Edge, telling the voters they must choose between the program of the GOP and the domination of "labor leaders, communists and Hagueism," hammered on the theme of the power of Hudson County boss Frank Hague. On the positive side, he proposed streamlining state government and planning early to meet postwar problems, and he strongly supported the referendum Governor Charles Edison had initiated for a new state constitution. The voters chose Edge by 127,000 votes and constitutional revision by over 150,000.

Assuming office early in his seventy-first year, Edge ensured party discipline in the legislature by withholding patronage appointments until the end of the session. In the interim between his election and inauguration he set in motion the drafting of measures to fulfill his program. A liberalized servicemen's voting law supplemented the emergency wartime legislation already in effect. But Edge concentrated on measures to secure the modernization of state government and to ensure successful dealing with anticipated postwar problems. In his mind they were closely linked, for only by improving the structure of government could the state solve the problems.

First Edge attended to constitutional revision. On January 24, 1944, he submitted to the legislature a new document drafted by thirty Republican legislators, and it was approved within six weeks. It extended the governor's term to four years and amplified his powers to make him a "strong" executive, increased legislative terms to four years in the senate and two in the assembly, reorganized the judiciary, and provided for one state budget to deal with all receipts and expenditures.

Although the proposed constitution met the demands of most proponents of revision, it was politically vulnerable. Drafted by Republicans only, and passed only because Republicans controlled the legislature, it was not assured of ratification by the voters. It was also involved in the battle against Frank Hague, who stood to lose much patronage if the judiciary was reorganized. During 1944 Hague and Edge engaged in a running battle. First they fought over the allocation of $15 million in railroad taxes, which Hague eventually won for the cities where the taxed property was located. Edge won a round by obtaining legislation that required the use of voting machines in Hudson County and reduced the chance of electoral flimflam. But Hague took top honors when, a few weeks before the elections, he launched a multi-pronged attack on the new constitution. Charging that it would limit organized labor's activities, inhibit the opportunity for the advancement of returning veterans, and subject all church property to taxation, he engineered its defeat at the polls by 126,000 votes.

Despite defeat on the constitution in 1944, Edge achieved much of his program. He consolidated a number of state boards and commissions, set up a Taxation and Finance Department to handle all fiscal matters, and obtained some support for civil service reform. He also created an Economic Development Department to deal with postwar planning and began to accumulate a fund—initially $25 million—for state support of efforts to insure an orderly postwar conversion. He obtained legislation that created a state insurance program to guarantee loans to veterans who wished to establish themselves in business or in the professions, an antecedent to the G.I. Bill. After the defeat of constitutional revision, Edge sought to accomplish some of the reorganization through legislation and continued to pressure for a new revision of the constitution. In addition, in 1945 he obtained remedial legislation to improve the living conditions of migrant workers and a series of seven measures to ban racial or religious discrimination in employment, schools, hotels and elsewhere, and he sought legislation to prevent strikes in public utilities.

During Edge's last year in office problems connected with reconversion to a peacetime economy came to the fore. Demobilization brought housing shortages and unemployment. State planning agencies could give some help. Federal involvement sometimes obstructed progress. For example, although Edge complained bitterly that the federal government was using only small portions of Camp Kilmer and Camp Dix, the government refused to consolidate its activities to make housing space available. In addition to these problems, a wave of strikes led to bitter political battles and occasional street confrontations. Edge effectively used the principal state agency, the State Board of Mediation, to end most of the strikes without lengthy disruptions. But like all his contemporaries, he failed to find any effective means to preserve public services in disputes between capital and labor, especially in such instances as the Public Service gasworks strike of 1946.

As his term drew to a close in 1946, Edge had sufficient control of the state Republican organization to insure the nomination of Alfred E. Driscoll as his successor. In the election of 1946 the Republicans won easily. After his term, Edge continued actively supporting constitutional reform until the constitution of 1947 was adopted. Remaining thereafter an elder statesman of the party, he took little active part in politics. After his death in 1956 he willed Morven—the Stockton family residence, which he had purchased—to the state as an official residence for the governors.

Walter E. Edge Papers, The New Jersey Historical Society, Newark, N.J.

Records of Governor Walter E. Edge, New Jersey State Library, Bureau of Archives and History, Trenton, N.J.

Edge, Walter E. *A Jerseyman's Journal.* Princeton: Princeton University Press, 1948.

Sly, John F. "Walter Evans Edge, 1873–1956: A Tribute." *Proceedings of the New Jersey Historical Society* 79 (1961): 1–15.

Joseph F. Mahoney

EDWARD IRVING EDWARDS (December 1, 1863–January 26, 1931), a distinguished public servant, was born in Jersey City, to William W. and Emma J. (Nation) Edwards. He attended the Jersey City public schools, went to New York University from 1880 to 1882, and studied law in the office of his brother, William D. Edwards, former state senator from Hudson County. On November 14, 1888, he married Blanche Smith; during their forty-year marriage, the Edwardses had two children, Edward Irving and Elizabeth Jule.

A businessman and bank president, Edwards rose to political prominence in his native Jersey City and soon attracted the attention of the Hudson County Democratic organization. He served as state comptroller from 1911 to 1917 and Hudson County's state senator from 1918 to 1920. During this period he became a friend and close political ally of the Jersey City Mayor, Frank Hague. Hague supported him for governor in 1919.

The Democratic primary in 1919 resulted in a confrontation between Hague and Essex County Democratic Chairman James R. Nugent, who was a former state party chairman. Edwards, a supporter of the Hudson County political machine, defeated Nugent in the primary by polling 53.6 percent of the vote. He won fifteen counties and polled huge majorities in Hudson County. Hague emerged from this primary confrontation as the undisputed leader of the New Jersey Democracy, beginning a domination that lasted until the late 1940s.

The gubernatorial race occurred during an exceedingly turbulent period—a period of red scares, major labor strikes in the coal and steel industries, the Boston police strike, race riots across the nation, a Camden trolley strike, the battle for the League of Nations and the Versailles Treaty, the implementation of Prohibition, and a surge of postwar inflation. The elections of 1919 were marked by the resurgence of the Republican party throughout the United States, the destruction of the old Wilsonian coalition, and a prelude to "normalcy." The GOP won all elections in the North and the West except for Edwards's victory in New Jersey.

An Elizabeth daily newspaper appropriately labeled Edwards's campaign "The Applejack Campaign." Although Edwards was personally "dry," he ran as an avowed "wet," opposing Prohibition, defending states' rights, and demanding nullification of the Eighteenth Amendment. Despite being labeled a Bolshevik, an anarchist, a traitor and a seditionist, Edwards won a narrow victory, polling 51.7 percent of the two-party vote— 217,486 votes to 202,976 for Trenton businessman Newton A.K. Bugbee, a margin of 14,510.

Edwards won the "applejack" battle in the cities, where antiprohibition sentiment was strong. The wet-or-dry campaign produced an urban political revolution against Prohibition and its concept of Americanization. Edwards, an Episcopalian and a Mason, rolled up impressive margins in the urban, Catholic, ethnic centers across the state, especially in Hague's Hudson County. Most significant, he overcame the turmoil of 1919 and the ethnic dissatisfaction with Wilson and the League of Nations.

The urban coalition of immigrants and people of immigrant background Edwards organized in 1919 established a new majority on the state and local level. This might be called the "Edwards Revolution." Not only did these voters support Edwards, but, significantly, they remained within the New Jersey Democracy after 1919. Although they may have slipped back into their old habits enough to vote for Harding and Coolidge, they helped Edwards defeat incumbent United States Senator Joseph S. Frelinghuysen in 1922, and they cast their ballots for Democratic governors in 1922 and 1925. While other states with similar ethnic composition, such as Massachusetts, were electing Republicans during the early twenties, New Jersey elected Democrats in nonpresidential years. The "applejack campaign" had created a new political alignment. It helped prepare the way for the "Al Smith Revolution" and Franklin D. Roosevelt's New Deal coalition, which has been a mainstay of the state and local democratic organizations throughout the interwar period and beyond.

During Governor Edwards's three-year term, he faced a legislature usually controlled by lopsided Republican majorities. The state senate, dominated by rural and small-town interests, with one seat for each county, was the bastion of GOP strength in the twenties. The GOP controlled the general assembly as well, especially after the Harding landslide of 1920 (fifty-eight Republicans, one Democrat, and one vacancy). The legislature frustrated much of Edwards's program and passed most of its own legislation over his repeated vetoes.

Despite the inherent difficulties in working with a Republican-controlled legislature, Governor Edwards continued to pursue the policies first enunciated in the "applejack campaign"—antiprohibitionism, cultural pluralism, and urban ethnicity. Although he frequently lost to the legislature, he kept the support of his coalition.

In early 1920, Governor Edwards carried his antiprohibition campaign to the legislature. He succeeded in obtaining passage of a bill permitting the manufacture and sale of 3.5 percent alcoholic beverages, and he signed the legislation on March 2, 1920. He carried his "defense of ancient American liberty" further, challenging the constitutionality of the Eighteenth Amendment by joining Rhode Island's lawsuit; in *Rhode Island* v. *Palma* the Supreme Court upheld Prohibition, but Edwards's fight won popular approval in New Jersey.

In January 1921, the legislature repealed the 3.5 percent alcoholic beverages law and passed the Van Ness Enforcement Act over the governor's veto. This law denied violators the right of trial by jury, and Edwards criticized it as oppressive and unconstitutional. He also asked Congress to modify the newly passed Volstead Act to allow the sale of light wines and beer. In early 1922, the Court of Errors and Appeals set aside the Van Ness Act. In mid-March, the legislature passed the Hobart Prohibition Enforcement Act, which contained provisions for trial by jury, and it became law over Edwards's veto. The Republicans' defense of Prohibition—the Eighteenth Amendment, the Volstead Act, and the Van Ness and Hobart Enforcement Acts —weakened their appeal to the urban, Catholic, ethnic minorities.

Throughout his administration, Governor Edwards fought the Public Utility Commission and the Public Service Railroad Corporation for reduced trolley fares for the urban masses. He fired the five members of the Public Utility Commission; the courts upheld him, but the GOP legislature established a new three-member commission over his veto. Edwards also waged an intense battle for a five-cent fare, but the legislature and the courts imposed an eight-cent fare and a two-cent transfer.

Governor Edwards urged the legislature in early 1921 to defeat any blue laws that might curb outside recreation on Sunday, the day urban working families had free. He attacked blue laws as un-American legislation of morality that usurped civil liberties. He refused to stop the Dempsey-Carpentier heavyweight fight in 1921 and would have sanctioned a Dempsey-Wills fight if one had been arranged in 1922. Despite continuous attacks from conservative, religious, and rural-oriented groups, Governor Edwards steadfastly maintained his principles and programs.

Among the many bills the legislature passed over Edwards's veto was a 1921 measure creating the Port of New York Authority, which Edwards at first believed would put New Jersey in an unsatisfactory, unhappy and unprofitable marriage with New York. He later withdrew his opposition and supported efforts to link the two states.

Although Governor Edwards advocated tough anticrime policies, including surveillance over known criminals, licensing to carry weapons, and a crackdown on auto theft, he strongly opposed the legislation which created the state police in 1921. He feared that the law might infringe on home rule by allowing intervention in local law enforcement, and that the troopers might be used against labor to break strikes or harass pickets. Neither of these fears materialized; the state police assisted and supplemented local law enforcement in urban and rural communities.

The Republican-controlled legislature so frequently frustrated Governor Edwards's programs and circumvented his veto power that in 1922, when a joint committee asked at the close of the legislative session whether Edwards wanted to make a farewell statement or any further communications, he replied, "What's the use? You haven't read those that I did send." Soon he announced his candidacy for the United States Senate seat held by Republican Joseph S. Frelinghuysen. He carried his work for antiprohibitionism, cultural pluralism, and urban ethnicity from the governor's chair into the senatorial campaign.

With Harding and "normalcy," the Garden State Republican party had emerged as the party of 100-percent Americanism, blue laws, Sunday closing laws, compulsory English lessons for foreign-born adults, immigration restriction, and Prohibition. Edwards launched his senatorial campaign with the slogan "Wine, Women, and Song," demanding the repeal of the Eighteenth Amendment and the legalization of light wines and beer. As before, Edwards, Hague, and the New Jersey Democracy courted urban ethnic groups with promises of antiprohibitionism, cultural liberalism, and ethnic pluralism.

Edwards defeated Frelinghuysen by 451,832 to 362,699—a margin of 89,133. He won 55.5 percent of the senatorial vote and carried Democratic Judge George S. Silzer to victory in the gubernatorial race. The New Jersey Democracy dramatically reversed Harding's landslide victory of two years before among the urban masses; reestablishing and enlarging the "applejack" coalition of 1919, Edwards restored ethnic unity in the party and consolidated Mayor Hague's domination over it.

In 1928, Edwards campaigned for a second term in the Senate. Once again he raised the banner of antiprohibitionism, often asserting that he was "as wet as the Atlantic Ocean" and calling once again for light wines and beer. His opponent, Hamilton F. Kean, however, declared for modifying the Volstead Act and, in early October, shocked New Jerseyans by announcing that he was as wet as his opponent. The Anti-Saloon League withdrew its support from Kean, but by launching his own crusade against prohibitionism he had neutralized the issue in the senatorial race.

Edwards lost, 841,752 to 608,623—a margin of 233,129. The presidential candidacy of New York Governor Al Smith had stimulated an enormous outpouring of antagonistic rural, old-stock voters that worked against Edwards and the Democrats. Edwards ran ahead of the New York governor in both immigrant and old-stock areas, but he simply could not overcome "Coolidge prosperity," the backlash against Al Smith, and the heavy turnout for the presidential race.

After this loss, Edwards's fortunes turned downward. His wife died in 1928 and his relationship with Hague deteriorated. During the 1930 campaign, he broke with Hague and threatened to join the reform coalition against him. He desired to return to the governor's chair, but Hague's choice, former Governor A. Harry Moore, blocked his path. The Great Depression brought bankruptcy and charges of corruption and fraud. On January 26, 1931, Edwards committed suicide.

Governor Edward I. Edwards's contribution to New Jersey political history lies less in the bills approved or vetoed during his governorship than in his ability to articulate the political and cultural outcry of the new majority coalition of urban ethnics. Working with Hague, Edwards revolutionized the state's politics by starting a political realignment that helped to make the Democracy the party of urban America.

Records of Governor Edward I. Edwards, New Jersey State Library, Bureau of Archives and History, Trenton, N.J.

Stickle, Warren E. "Edward I. Edwards and the Urban Coalition of 1919." *New Jersey History* 90 (1972): 83–96.

Warren E. Stickle

GEORGE SEBASTIAN SILZER (April 14, 1870–October 16, 1940), son of Theodore C. and Christina (Zimmerman) Silzer, was born in New Brunswick, where his father owned and operated the Bull's Head Tavern. After he was graduated from the public grammar and high schools of his native city, Silzer read law in the offices of J. Kearny Rice. Admitted to the bar in 1892, he immediately opened an office in New Brunswick and, until 1914, built an increasingly successful practice. Already interested in a political career, Silzer was elected to the New Brunswick Board of Aldermen, where he served from 1892 until 1896, and then for ten years he led the Middlesex County Democracy as chairman of the county committee. Aided in part by his opposition to the Bishops' Liquor Law, he was elected to the state senate in 1906 and reelected in 1909. In 1910, he announced his candidacy for the governorship on a progressive, antimachine platform, drawing 210 votes in the state convention, which nominated Woodrow Wilson for governor.

Silzer's years in the senate saw the rise of the "New Idea" movement among Republicans and the comparable surge of reformism in his own party; he was in the forefront of Democratic progressivism. Though the Democrats were a minority in that body throughout his service in the upper house, Silzer participated significantly in the passage of several measures during the Wilson years, particularly the workmen's compensation law. He served as one of Wilson's chief lieutenants in the legislature, and in 1912 Wilson appointed him prosecutor of the pleas in Middlesex County. In 1914 Governor James F. Fielder appointed him a circuit court judge, and he served in that office until the Democrats tapped him in 1922 as their nominee for governor.

Silzer's nomination represented an agreement between leading Democrats: Frank Hague of Hudson County supported Silzer in return for Middlesex County's endorsement of the retiring governor, Edward I. Edwards, for the United States Senate. Despite numerous campaign issues the question of Prohibition dominated the scene. Silzer's opponent, William N. Runyon, a long-time "dry" and conservative Republican, insisted on full enforcement of the Volstead Act. The Democrats charged, as Silzer phrased it in his inaugural address, that the Volstead Act "goes far beyond the [Eighteenth] amendment, for the latter prohibits 'intoxicating liquor for beverage purposes,' while the enforcement act . . . prohibits the use of beverages which are not intoxicating. To say that anything over one-half of one percent is intoxicating is to enact a falsehood; it would be quite as true to say that a jackass is a camel." The press and the defeated Republicans alike almost universally interpreted the electoral results—Silzer won by a margin of 43,894 votes—as a protest against Prohibition.

The election also represented confirmation of Frank Hague's domination of the Democratic party in New Jersey. Silzer won only six counties; excluding Hudson's vote, he lost the state by some thirty-six thousand votes, but the eighty-thousand plurality the Hague machine returned in its home county put him into the governor's chair. The structure of politics in the state, however, limited the electoral influence of the powerful Hague organization. County election of the legislators meant that throughout his three years in office Silzer faced overwhelmingly Republican majorities in both the assembly and the senate, a situation that plagued him and remained to hamper Democratic governors for another generation. Unlike some of his successors, however, Silzer kept the Hudson County leader at arm's length and maintained a wary cooperation with him.

The new governor's inaugural message to the legislature in January 1923 revealed him to be still the progressive of the Woodrow Wilson era. Charging that "everywhere Special Privilege shows its ugly head," Silzer promised to "put government back into the hands of the people." To further this purpose, he asked for the stringent regulation of public utilities on the basis of physical valuation and the strict enforcement of the limitations on their charges, the enactment of new protective legislation for labor, and the re-enactment of the recently repealed elements of Woodrow Wilson's "Seven Sisters" to prevent price gouging and monopolistic practices in the coal industry. In subsequent special and regular messages to the legislature, Silzer dealt with the reform of the prison system, the expansion of institutional services for public welfare, fairer methods of taxation, the construction of a ship canal across New Jersey to tie together the ports of New York and Philadelphia, more stringent control of narcotics, measures to control pollution of the state's inland and coastal waters, effective gun control, tighter control of state monies, an effective blue-sky law (a law regulating securities sales), support for a federal anti-lynching act, and numerous proposals for improved road networks. His views were wide-ranging and, in the 1920s, forward-looking. But in most instances neither the temper of the times nor the majority of the legislature rallied to his support.

Governor Silzer began his administration with a startling action calculated to demonstrate his determination to lead the state and to conserve its interests. Six days after his inaugural he announced to the astounded legislature: "I have this day removed the present state highway commission." This was the opening gun in Silzer's attack on "special privilege." The ousted commission, which Silzer considered both subservient to political interests and incompetent, had let road contracts with specifications which could be met only by a patented material controlled by a few corporations. Despite Silzer's announced opposition in the gubernatorial campaign, a $40 million bond issue for road construction had gained the voters' approval in the 1922 elections, and the new governor feared that the monies would be siphoned off for an unjustifiably expensive road surface, to the private gain of a few men. Silzer nominated a four-man bipartisan highway commission of prominent citizens and engineers—Walter Kidde, Major General Hugh L. Scott, Abraham Jelin and Percy H. Stewart. For six weeks the Republican senate refused them confirmation while it sought to force Silzer to accept other names. But the governor carried the fight to the citizenry and finally won the acceptance of his nominees.

Silzer's concern for transportation reflected his assessment of the state's potential future development. Lying along waterways dominated by the neighboring ports of New York City and Philadelphia, New Jersey, he anticipated, would increasingly develop both commercial-industrial and residential facilities. The automobile, with its flexibility of route, would stimulate the growth of the state's population and industry. To facilitate this expansion, Silzer supported extensive road building, though he would have preferred a pay-as-you-go plan to the bond issues the lawmakers and the electorate supported. He proposed that the legislature create a Port of Camden Authority to develop the lower Delaware area; that it authorize the construction of a bridge from Fort Lee to Washington Heights in New York City (later the George Washington Bridge) and of bridges between New Jersey and Staten Island; and that it give the state highway commission the authority to lay out the state road net. He initiated the proposal to incorporate the Holland Tunnel, then nearing completion, into the Port of New York facilities. Above all, he wanted rational development. "We must also," he wrote, "have in mind scientific planning which will make such development as attractive as possible. In these enlightened days we cannot drift along and permit ugliness to dominate." To this end he strongly supported zoning laws as a tool of planning, and he advocated a constitutional amendment to ensure their legitimacy when judicial decisions appeared to overthrow them.

Though supported by many New Jerseyans, the governor's proposals won only limited success during Silzer's term. The legislature of 1923 passed over his veto a measure authorizing private interests to build tunnels under the Hudson River and to preempt sites for the purpose; only the New York legislature's refusal to adopt similar legislation preserved the sites for public development. The same legislature, again over Silzer's veto, laid out a network of state roads devised by logrolling rather than by analysis of need.

Early in his term, during the Newark trolley strike of 1923, Silzer seized a second opportunity to strike down "special privilege." A labor dispute between the Public Service Corporation, New Jersey's public utilities giant, and its employees resulted in a shutdown of the trolley system, with consequent severe hardship to residents and businesses alike. When the company's intransigence threatened to prolong the impasse, Silzer directed the state attorney general to bring suit against Public Service for failure to comply with the terms of its charter; the move would have deprived the transit giant of its rights-of-way in public streets. The governor's action brought a quick resumption of service; later he obtained legislation intended to inhibit similar interruption of service by utilities.

In the first year of his term Silzer also attacked "special privilege" on the labor front. After a long battle with the Republican legislature and by dint of indefatigable appeals to the electorate, he obtained legislation prohibiting the employment of women between 10:00 p.m. and 6:00 a.m. and placing some further restraints on child labor. He also managed to improve the terms of the workmen's compensation act and to improve payments to incapacitated workers.

Throughout his term Silzer used the rhetoric and techniques of the progressive era to gain substantially progressive ends, though it is unclear whether he did so consciously. His battles with the Republican-dominated legislature won him the sobriquet "veto governor," but neither publicity nor cajolery convinced the legislature to follow his lead. Silzer's social-welfare concerns and his opposition to special privilege nonetheless influenced many New Jersey urban voters to convert to the Democratic party.

After his term ended in January 1926, Silzer, constitutionally disqualified from succeeding himself, returned to the practice of law and also became active in banking. In 1935 he defended Arthur (Dutch Schultz) Flegenheimer in a federal income-tax case, and in 1937 he was counsel to Ellis Parker, the Burlington County detective involved in the kidnapping of Paul H. Wendel in connection with the Lindbergh kidnap case. In 1926 his successor, Democrat A. Harry Moore, appointed him to a term as chairman of the Port of New York Authority. Silzer thus presided over the groundbreaking ceremonies for the George Washington Bridge, which he had proposed as governor. In 1933 he published *The Government of a State,* an analysis of the functions and operations of state governments, illustrated by examples from his own experience. Silzer suffered a heart attack and died on a Newark street as he was returning home from his office on October 16, 1940. He was survived by his wife, the former Henrietta T. Waite, and a son, Parker W. Silzer.

Records of Governor George S. Silzer, New Jersey State Library, Bureau of Archives and History, Trenton, N.J.

Schroth, Frank D. *The First Year, Being the Record of Accomplishment of George S. Silzer, Governor of New Jersey.* Trenton: MacCrellish & Quigley, 1924.

Silzer, George S. *The Government of a State.* Newark: Soney & Sage Co., 1933.

Joseph F. Mahoney

ARTHUR HARRY MOORE (July 3, 1879–November 18, 1952), New Jersey's only three-term governor under the state's second constitution, was elected in 1925, 1931 and 1937.

Moore was a Jersey City native, born in the Lafayette section, of working-class parents, Robert White and Martha (McCoomb) Moore, of Irish and Scottish descent. Moore, known as "Red," dropped out of the local public school system at the age of thirteen to take a clerk's job at $3 per week. White-collar oriented, he continued his education in his spare time, taking courses at Cooper Union in Manhattan and developing proficiency in bookkeeping and typing. Moore also became involved in local Democratic politics, gaining from his speaking ability the sobriquet, "the boy orator of Lafayette." In 1907 his longtime friend, H. Otto Wittpenn, was elected mayor of Jersey City, and Moore entered City Hall as his secretary. In 1911, following the death of the Hudson Democratic leader Robert Davis, Moore assumed Davis's post as city collector. On March 28 that year Moore was married to Jennie Hastings Stevens, a downtown neighbor. He taught the men's bible class in Lafayette Reformed Church, where his bride taught Sunday School. The couple had no children.

In 1913, after Jersey City adopted the commission form of government, Moore ran successfully for a spot on the five-man governing body. As director of Parks and Public Property, he projected an image of "the kiddies' friend" by promoting recreational facilities and opportunities for the city's youth. Gregarious by nature as well as conviction, Moore became increasingly active in church, charitable, and fraternal affairs, and he made programs for handicapped children his area of special concern.

In 1916 H. Otto Wittpenn ran unsuccessfully for the governorship, losing to Republican Walter E. Edge. Subsequently, Wittpenn virtually retired from the political scene. Moore then reworked his cooperative arrangement with a fellow commissioner, Frank Hague, into a formal alliance. Moore led the Hague slate to a clean sweep in the 1917 city commission elections, beginning Hague's thirty-year stay as mayor of Jersey City. In 1921 and 1925, Moore led the ticket to similar municipal victories. During this period he resumed his formal education, attending evening classes at the New Jersey Law School in Newark. He passed the state bar exam in 1922 and received an LL.B. in 1924.

As early as 1921, local politicians began to boom the popular Moore for the governorship. Hague, now in control of the state Democratic organization, waited until 1925, when he easily secured Moore's nomination in an uncontested primary. Moore ran on a "wringing wet," antiprohibition platform against the Morris County state senator, Arthur Whitney, a Republican who had the support of the Anti-Saloon League. The state GOP, in turn, focused its campaign on the alleged menace of "Hagueism" in state government. Although Moore carried only three counties, Hudson's plurality of 103,995 gave its local hero a comfortable victory margin in this off-year election.

Frank Hague saw the governor's office primarily as a source of jobs for his patronage-based party machine. Moore gave the right answer when he told the press after his election: "You can say for me that in patronage matters I am strictly organization." Still, the new governor could not maximize his patronage potential unless he cooperated with the Republican senate, which had a broad advise-and-consent power. A political realist, Moore determined that a bipartisan spirit would mark his administration. His conservative political outlook, summed up in a pet phrase as "the best governed are the least governed," furthered this cooperative spirit. His style was generally accorded a friendly reception in New Jersey's legislative halls, and his confrontations with the legislators, rare indeed, came about when he assumed a more conservative stance than they.

Three items from the year 1927 illustrate the temper of Moore's first administration. The first involved improving the potable water supply for north Jersey, a priority item for both governor and legislature. Moore, a proponent of "home rule," recommended that north Jersey municipalities resolve the problem working alone or via intermunicipal arrangements. The legislature, on the other hand, approved a constitutional amendment authorizing a series of regional water supply districts organized and controlled by the state. With Moore cool and Hudson County hostile, the voters rejected the idea in a November 1927 referendum.

Land use control was another major issue. After the United States Supreme Court, in a 1926 case, approved such control in principle, the New Jersey legislature proposed that the state constitution be amended to allow municipalities to exercise zoning powers. Since only local governments were to utilize the new tool, Moore and Hague approved of the amendment, campaigned for it, and saw it accepted by the voters.

A third area of controversy was a Republican plan for a major highway construction program in New Jersey. Moore was sympathetic, believing a modern road network essential to the state's development. But the governor nonetheless refused to sign a tax bill to help fund the program, asserting that it was an undue burden on the taxpayers. The gasoline tax (which became law), coupled with a $30-million bond issue approved that autumn, set the foundation for New Jersey's first comprehensive highway system, totaling some eighteen hundred miles. Complementing this program was the work being done to tie New Jersey and New York City closer together. In 1927, Moore and Governor Al Smith of New York opened the Holland Tunnel to vehicular traffic and marked the start of construction for the George Washington Bridge. During the following year the two chief executives dedicated a pair of bridges connecting Staten Island to New Jersey—the Goethals Bridge and the Outerbridge Crossing.

In his first administration, Moore also had to cope with the social problems of the "Roaring Twenties," including prohibition. Highway crime and disorder, especially at so-called "road house" night clubs, led the governor to ask the legislature to enlarge and strengthen the state police, an agency that had been established in 1921. Little progress, however, was made. A crime of another sort brought Moore national headlines in the autumn of 1926. This was the infamous Hall-Mills murder case, an alleged crime of passion that caused a sensation in the press. Moore appointed Hudson's state senator, Alexander Simpson, to prosecute the state's case against the late Reverend Edward Wheeler Hall's widow. Following a tawdry courtroom drama played to the hilt by the prosecution, the jury failed to convict, much to the embarrassment and chagrin of New Jersey officialdom.

In 1928 the Hague organization could not prevent a Republican landslide in New Jersey; the GOP easily secured the governorship for Morgan F. Larson and retained its hold on both houses of the state legislature. But the Republicans' monopoly of power meant that they could not avoid the blame for the economic depression that followed. A. Harry Moore, waiting on the sidelines, worked hard to stay in the public eye. He maintained a rigorous speaking schedule, continued his involvement in fraternal and church activities, and even had a weekly radio program over station WOR on Saturday evenings. At the end of 1930, Moore, the unofficial but obvious Democratic choice for governor, began in earnest the long drive that led to his second term.

In 1931, Moore was a polished and hardy campaigner. He believed in emphasizing patriotic and religious themes —"stick to the broad generalities of the eternal verities"—and added color with a series of amusing and tear-wrenching anecdotes. During the campaign he berated President Herbert C. Hoover and incumbent Republican Governor Morgan F. Larson for the misery they had brought to nation and state; in counterthrust, the GOP's gubernatorial candidate, Camden County leader David Baird, Jr., could do little but cry "Hagueism." It was no contest. Improving on his 1925 campaign, Moore ran well in every county but Camden, and his plurality of 230,053 votes was the largest recorded under the 1844 constitution. Another 1931 milestone was the dedication of the A. Harry Moore School in Jersey City, an institution designed specifically to meet the educational needs of handicapped children.

Economic problems dominated the governor's second term. Moore's own approach was consistent with his conservative political philosophy: the state must reduce or postpone expenditures to enable local governments and the private sector to regenerate themselves. The 1932 legislature gave him discretionary power to curb state spending—and Moore did just that. He pruned state appropriations drastically, from a total of $34.5 million in 1931 to $28.3, $19.7 and $20.7 in 1932, 1933 and 1934 respectively. He diverted money from state programs, especially from highway construction, to keep municipal governments afloat and provide direct relief to the impoverished. Moore, a machine politician who knew the importance of the personal touch, spent long hours in Trenton listening to the woes of the jobless and trying his best to meet their needs.

The governor believed that the depression was an opportune time to reorganize state and local government. He proposed, among other things, that New Jersey's cumbersome administrative structures be streamlined and placed under the firm control of the chief executive; that the courts be overhauled; that a "home rule" amendment be added to the constitution;

and that a sales or income tax be adopted to give the state a stable revenue base. Moore's only success in these matters, however, came when the legislature provided the statutory base for a modern system of municipal finance. Overall, he could do little to accelerate the movement for constitutional reform in New Jersey.

Moore's second term was marked by more than the depression. Two items that received worldwide publicity were the Lindbergh kidnapping in 1932 and the burning of the cruise ship *Morro Castle* in 1934. Moore supervised the investigation of the kidnapping, and he personally helped direct rescue operations in the waters off Asbury Park. The repeal of prohibition also took place during this administration. The state legislature authorized a mix of state and municipal Alcoholic Beverage Control Commissions, and it was Moore's responsibility to implement the new program.

The advent of the New Deal put the governor's states' rights philosophy under some strain. Nevertheless, as FDR's program unfolded, Moore lobbied vigorously to insure that New Jersey receive her fair share of public works projects and federal relief funds. In addition to these gubernatorial duties, in 1934 Moore conducted a campaign for a seat in the United States Senate, a goal he pursued at Hague's insistence. The quest was successful. Although 1934 was a comeback year for the New Jersey GOP, which obtained the governor's office for Harold G. Hoffman, Moore moved on to the nation's capital.

He served only half his term as United States senator, and the years were not overly happy ones. True, Moore brought home a generous supply of federal projects for his city and state. (Jersey City's Medical Center and Roosevelt Stadium are prime examples.) But he was ill at ease on the New Deal team, especially after Roosevelt moved in a welfare-state direction. Moore voted against social security (the only Democratic "no" vote in the Senate), the public utility holding company bill, and the 1935 amendments to the Agricultural Adjustment Administration Act, and he opposed Roosevelt's court-packing plan. He referred to the Senate disparagingly as "a cave of winds" and—perhaps with a sense of relief—accepted Hague's invitation to run again for the governorship in 1937.

By now the Democrats' "copyright candidate," Moore faced the Reverend Lester H. Clee of Essex County. Interestingly, Mrs. Moore's sister was married to the minister's brother. Despite this relationship, the 1937 contest was bitter and hard fought. Often on the defensive, Moore claimed that he was really not a foe of Roosevelt and the New Deal and that New Jersey needed an experienced man at the helm. Hudson pulled him through, its 129,237 plurality offsetting the fact that his opponent carried 15 counties.

Clee's charge of widespread vote fraud in Hudson hung like a dark cloud over Moore's third term, but various Hague maneuvers stymied state legislative investigations and court suits. Then, when a United States Senate investigating committee attempted to reopen the controversy in 1940, it discovered that the Hudson poll books had been burned. Another source of adverse publicity was the governor's appointment of Hague's son to New Jersey's highest court, the Court of Errors and Appeals, in 1939.

During these years, the principal concern of the governor and the legislature was economic recovery. With some reluctance, Moore began his third term by diverting more road funds to meet direct relief costs. His own preference was for work-relief, via part federal- and part state-funded highway and water facility construction projects. Though Moore had some success with the WPA, he failed to move a $60-million highway bond issue through the legislature in 1939. The Republicans, who controlled both houses, opted instead for a bond issue of $21 million to finance direct relief. The voters approved the issue in a November 1939 referendum.

The governor once more promoted tax reform as receipts from railroad taxes (a major revenue source in the state for a century) declined. The principal victim of this decline was state school aid, and Moore, always interested in education, suggested that the state consider a broad-based replacement tax. The legislators, believing that new taxes would weaken New Jersey's ability to attract industry and rebuild her economy, turned thumbs down. Their alternative was to bring in new revenue via horse racing, although gambling was then proscribed by the state constitution. Hence an amendment authorizing pari-mutuel betting was presented, and the electorate approved it in June 1939.

World War II began that September, and defense problems soon assumed a prominent place on the governor's agenda. By executive order, Moore set up a Governor's Emergency Committee, the first state civil defense agency in the nation. Reorganized in the autumn of 1940 as the New Jersey Defense Council, it became the coordinating mechanism for state and local civil defense efforts. Moore also had to concern himself with the development and training of the national guard and, in October 1940, with the nation's first peacetime draft. In January 1941, he handed over his office for the last time—but, for the first time, to a fellow Democrat, the former Secretary of the Navy Charles Edison.

Since Frank Hague wanted Moore to be a gubernatorial candidate once more in 1943, he held off on a nominee until late that July, hoping that Moore would acquiesce as in the past. But Moore adamantly refused to run, and Hague turned to Mayor Vincent J. Murphy of Newark, who lost in November to Republican Walter E. Edge. The whole affair led to bitter feelings between Moore and the Hague organization for a while. But by summer 1944 matters were smoothed over, and Moore was selected as a delegate to the Democratic National Convention. In 1945, Governor Edge paid tribute to Moore's long commitment to the field of education by appointing him to a vacancy on the State Board of Education.

Although Moore continued to maintain a residence in the Lafayette section of Jersey City, during his late years he spent much time at a summer home in Mount Airy, Hunterdon County. Horseback riding was his favorite avocation. His legal practice, corporate directorships, and a multitude of speaking engagements meant that his schedule remained a busy one. Moore's last major political involvement was as campaign manager for Elmer H. Wene, unsuccessful Democratic gubernatorial candidate in 1949. That year also marked the overthrow of the Hague machine in Jersey City. On November 18, 1952, Moore suffered a cerebral hemorrhage and died while at the wheel of his automobile near his Hunterdon retreat. He was 73.

Records of Governor A. Harry Moore, New Jersey State Library, Bureau of Archives and History, Trenton, N.J.

Bloodgood, Fred L. *The Quiet Hour.* Trenton: MacCrellish & Quigley, 1940.

Connors, Richard J. *A Cycle of Power: The Career of Jersey City Mayor Frank Hague.* Metuchen, N.J.: Scarecrow Press, 1971.

McKean, Dayton. *The Boss.* Boston: Houghton Mifflin, 1940.

Richard J. Connors

MORGAN FOSTER LARSON (June 15, 1882–March 21, 1961), New Jersey's fortieth governor, was born in Perth Amboy. He was the son of Peter and Regina (Knudson) Larson. His father was a Danish blacksmith who immigrated to the United States at the age of twenty-two.

Larson's rise from obscurity to the state's highest elective office in 1929 is a Horatio Alger story in local politics. Educated in the Perth Amboy public schools, Larson later studied engineering at Cooper Union Institute in New York City. In his determination to succeed, he applied the Protestant virtues of hard work and personal sacrifice as a student. He worked in Perth Amboy during the day and commuted to New York for night classes; by 1907, when he was graduated, he had logged a total of sixty thousand miles. Larson served as Middlesex County engineer in 1907–1910 and 1923–1924. He also served as city engineer for Perth Amboy and township engineer for Woodbridge. In 1914 he married Jennie Brogger, and that union lasted until her death in 1927.

Perhaps the most revealing incident in Larson's private life took place in 1921, when his brothers Lawrence and George Larson were killed in a grade-crossing accident. Larson softened the impact of that tragedy on his brothers' seven children by taking them into his home and giving each a college education.

In 1921, at thirty-nine, Larson ventured into electoral politics and was elected state senator as a Republican from Democratic Middlesex County. He was reelected in 1924 and 1927. In 1925 he became the senate's majority leader and a year later its president.

More than any other public concern, transportation interested Larson while he served in the senate, and it provided an issue of sufficient public appeal to bolster his prospects for statewide office. The rising popularity of the automobile during the 1920s and the resultant shift of thousands of city residents to suburban communities dramatized the obsolescence of New Jersey's road system. In 1925 the engineer-turned-political-leader joined Senators William B. McKay and Arthur N. Pierson, of Bergen and Union counties, to win legislative backing for three ambitious transportation projects: the George Washington Bridge, between Fort Lee, New Jersey, and 178th Street in Manhattan; the Outerbridge Crossing, from Perth Amboy to Tottenville; and the Goethals Bridge, from Elizabethport to Holland Hook. Larson achieved his most notable success in the senate in 1927, when he sponsored legislation for a state highway system. It provided for 1,700 miles of improved roads, costing an estimated $162 million, and called for a comprehensive plan for the future construction of highways. Moreover, the highway act helped put an end to the acrimonious debates and pork-barrel highway bills that had traditionally subverted efforts to modernize the state's transportation network.

Larson's advocacy of heavy transportation expenditures and his ability to placate his fellow senators gained him increasing support in the Republican hierarchy. As senate majority leader, he reportedly "went along with the majority of the members in anything they proposed," in effect associating himself with the stronger, more broadly based Republican leaders. During the 1920s he carefully built an allegiant constituency in Middlesex County, where, one observer noted in 1928, "everybody likes him." A *Newark Evening News* reporter recalled him as "under middle height, compactly built with thick brown-gray hair and complexion tanned by much outdoor life. He is of nervous, vital temperament, full of pep, youthful in outlook, smiles often and alluringly, popular, a 'regular guy' to use the vernacular." This "regular guy" image ultimately made Larson one of Middlesex County's most successful Republican spokesmen, and his adeptness in remaining essentially unscathed by Republican factionalism set the stage for a gubernatorial bid as the 1920s drew to a close.

Larson's final test as a prospective Republican standard-bearer came in 1927, when he faced what appeared to be a stiff challenge for his senate seat from Democrat Frederic M. P. Pearse. After an unusually vigorous campaign, Larson handily beat Pearse with the largest plurality any candidate for office had gained in the history of Middlesex County.

As the gubernatorial election of 1929 approached, Republican leaders viewed Larson's candidacy as a remedy to a potentially serious breach caused by the rivalry between two Essex County stalwarts, J. Henry Harrison and Fred G. Stickley, Jr. Furthermore, Mayor Frank Hague, the Hudson County Democratic boss, eyed the senate president with curious favor. Hague had successfully elected three Democratic governors in a row; in the upcoming election, however, his machine faced outspoken opposition from one gubernatorial candidate, reform Republican Robert Carey of Jersey City. A Carey victory in the general election would undoubtedly weaken Hague in Hudson County and perhaps spell disaster for him in other parts of the state. Hague sought to spoil Carey's bid by assuring a Larson victory in the upcoming Republican primary. With the help of twenty thousand votes cast for Larson by Hudson County Democrats—an unethical though not illegal practice at the time—the senate president beat Carey and two other Republican candidates. Hague's short-term strategy had worked, for Larson appeared to be a weaker opponent than Carey. After the primary, however, the scheme backfired. Larson became a formidable adversary to Hague and to Democratic control of the governorship.

Larson's gubernatorial campaign revealed some of the problems that would trouble him after winning office. His amiable, indulgent political style preserved a fragile alliance with Republican senators and with the powerful party chairman and United States senator, David Baird, Jr., of Camden County, yet it worked against him as the party's standard-bearer. Early in his candidacy Larson made his major issues the conservation of potable water, the development of transportation, and the control of water pollution. These laudable concerns stimulated little interest in the electorate, however. Predictably, confidence in Larson's political astuteness waned through the summer and fall of 1929.

Most Republican leaders wisely thought Frank Hague the most provocative issue and urged Larson to strike out against him.

In late September, after weeks of spiritless campaigning, candidate Larson finally took the offensive. He began to lash out at Hague's bold domination of state politics, claiming that the supporters of the Democratic candidate, Judge William L. Dill of Paterson, were voting to continue Hagueism. By late October graft and corruption had become the targets of Larson's speeches. "If I am elected Governor," he told audiences, "I will enter the Capitol at Trenton through the front door and the Hague machine will go out the back door." This shift in campaign rhetoric, although it came after three months of lackluster public appearances, worked remarkably well. Although Dill was unquestionably honest and appeared to be independent of Hague, he could never completely shake the implication that he was in some way indebted to the Hudson County machine. Dill received 671,728 votes to Larson's 824,005.

From the beginning of his administration, Governor Morgan Larson encountered serious division in his party and challenge to his authority. The most evident reason for these difficulties was his inept handling of local patronage during his first year in office, but he faced a more fundamental dilemma. During the 1920s and 1930s the state legislature rarely cooperated with the long-range objectives of the governors. Larson's difficulties with the lawmakers exceeded those of his predecessors, in part because after taking office he became somewhat of a political maverick. He sought, perhaps prematurely, independence from the Republican party chieftains whose support he had cultivated as president of the senate. In the first confrontation, Larson insisted that the attorney generalship be given to Senator William A. Stevens of Monmouth County, though traditionally that office had been filled after consultation with county politicos. Later the governor

angered Camden Republican boss Baird by selecting John Drewen for Hudson County prosecutor; Baird, ever the archenemy of Hagueism, wanted Larson to appoint the avowed antimachine Republican, Robert Carey, to the position.

Following the storm of controversy over the Drewen appointment, Larson made another serious tactical blunder by nominating Mayor Clyde Potts of Morristown to another term on the state board of health. The Potts nomination dismayed many Republican senators. A senate investigating committee had implicated Potts in a scheme to suppress competition in constructing the Dover-Boonton trunk sewer. The committee alleged that Potts, in violation of state law, had permitted the use of expensive patented materials and had destroyed important records bearing on the project. The evidence against Potts was considerably stronger than the governor's rationale for nominating him: Larson called Potts a close friend and political ally, and, after examining the testimony, said that "there didn't seem to be anything that involves his work as a member of the State Board of Health." Not surprisingly, the governor's justification only intensified the opposition. Larson's critics argued that he had created an embarrassing dilemma for the senate and called on him to rescind the nomination. Finally, after receiving considerable pressure, Larson followed the advice of leading Republicans and withdrew the mayor's name.

In another episode that alienated legislators, he named Senator Clarence E. Case of Somerset County to the state supreme court. This act throttled Case's senate committee, which was investigating improprieties in state government.

Larson's first year as governor ended unsuccessfully. Although his party held majorities in both legislative houses, he never received support for his policies. He faced a defiant legislature that passed "ripper" bills, which deprived him of the power to appoint officials for state agencies and made efficient administration of the government virtually impossible by causing considerable duplication of effort and waste of public funds.

During his second year in office Larson turned his attention toward improving the state economy, which had begun to slump as a result of the Great Depression. In September 1930 he directed Attorney General Stevens to initiate an action before the Interstate Commerce Commission to end alleged discriminatory freight costs in New York harbor. The complaint, which the governor outlined in his first and second annual legislative messages, claimed the lighterage rates to be in violation of the Act to Regulate Commerce. The Commission disagreed and turned the case down.

In spite of this setback, however, the major achievements of Larson's second year as governor were in interstate affairs. Drawing on his engineering background and his experience in having drafted the first comprehensive highway act in 1927, Larson reached agreement with Governor Franklin D. Roosevelt of New York in 1930 to construct the Lincoln Tunnel under the Hudson River. Although Larson was viewed as a political liability within his own state, he was a knowledgeable spokesman for New Jersey during the talks with New York officials.

During his second year in office Larson, now forty-nine years old, married Adda Schmidt. A native of Denmark, she had been the secretary and companion of his mother.

Widespread unemployment loomed as the major crisis in the state as the Larson administration drew to a close in 1931. In his third and final annual message to the legislature, the governor gave top priority to joblessness and called on the lawmakers to devise ways "to meet the state's responsibility in the crisis." He supported the creation of the state Emergency Relief Administration, a temporary agency that dispensed $8 million in aid to county and municipal programs, but he soon discovered the need for considerably more help from the national government to alleviate the economic and social misery wrought by the collapse of capitalist markets throughout the world. The Great Depression made Larson's last year in office his most frustrating. Like many Americans he believed that the Protestant work ethic and the free-enterprise system were indisputable pillars of strength in a democratic community; the depression, however, brought these traditional beliefs into serious question.

During his candidacy for governor political pundits often compared Larson to Herbert Hoover. Both men, after all, were engineers of humble origin who had achieved success through a rugged application of the work ethic. In retrospect, another analogy seems appropriate, for the Hoover and Larson administrations both began with unbridled confidence but ended during the early depression in failure and frustration.

After leaving the governorship Larson had a mixed career. He had a modicum of success in engineering with the Port of New York Authority, but his many financial holdings in banking institutions, gas and petroleum, and real estate collapsed. In 1945 Governor Walter E. Edge appointed him commissioner of the recently created Department of Conservation, a position he held until March 1949. He remained on the state payroll as a consulting engineer with the Water Policy and Supply Council, yet never again did he enjoy notoriety and influence in public affairs. At the age of seventy-eight, Morgan Larson died in Perth Amboy.

Records of Governor Morgan F. Larson, New Jersey State Library, Bureau of Archives and History, Trenton, N.J.

Clement Alexander Price

HAROLD GILES HOFFMAN (February 7, 1896–June 4, 1954), forty-first governor of New Jersey, was born in South Amboy, New Jersey, the descendant of a family which traced its lineage to the Dutch colonial settlement of New Amsterdam.

While still in high school, Hoffman became a reporter for a Perth Amboy newspaper and an occasional stringer for the *New York Times* and the New Brunswick *Daily Home News*. Upon graduation, Hoffman joined the *Perth Amboy Evening News* as a full-time employee, and quickly rose to assistant city editor and later sports editor. A dispute with the paper's owner ended Hoffman's newspaper career, and he took a job with the Du Pont Laboratory at Parlin. Shortly after the United States declared war on Germany, Hoffman enlisted with Company H, Third Infantry, New Jersey National Guard (later part of the 114th infantry of the 29th—Blue and Gray— Division of the American Expeditionary Force). The young enlistee quickly earned the rank of sergeant and was enrolled in officers' training school. Graduating third in his class, Lieutenant Hoffman rejoined his regiment as it was about to embark for France. He saw action in the Meuse-Argonne offensive, and, at twenty-one, he was promoted to captain on the battlefield.

Hoffman returned to South Amboy a war hero and took a position as treasurer of the South Amboy Trust Company. Over the next ten years, he assumed a prominent place in South Amboy's business community. He served as vice-president of his bank, president of the Hoffman-Lehrer Real Estate Corporation, president of the Mid-State Title Guaranty & Mortgage Company, treasurer of the National Realty & Investment Corporation, and director of the Investor Building & Loan Association. Hoffman also became well known in New Jersey banking circles. In 1919, Hoffman married Lillie May Moss, daughter of a prominent South Amboy dentist, Dr. William Penn Moss.

Young Hoffman also became active in South Amboy and Middlesex County Republican politics. Beginning his political career with an appointment as treasurer of South Amboy, Hoffman entered electoral politics in 1923 as Middlesex County assemblyman. In 1925, the Republicans nominated him for mayor of South Amboy with a write-in vote, and he handily won the fall election. Hoffman continued his meteoric political career as secretary to Senate President Morgan F. Larson, and in November 1926 he defeated Democrat Fred W. De Voe for congressman from the Third District by a wide margin. He won reelection in 1928, easily defeating Democrat John R. Phillips, Jr. Though Congressman Hoffman's career in Washington was undistinguished, his success in the usually Democratic Third District earned him the chairmanship of the Middlesex County Republican party and a prominent place in the state's Republican hierarchy.

When Morgan F. Larson became governor in 1929, Hoffman was slated for a prominent position in his administration. The young congressman had endeared himself to the state's strong Republican machines, in particular the Camden County organization of David Baird, Jr., and when William L. Dill's term as commissioner of the Department of Motor Vehicles expired in 1930, Hoffman gained the four-year appointment, which paid $10,000 annually. Rightfully uncertain of Republican chances in the special election his resignation from Congress would necessitate in the Third District, Hoffman refused to step down, serving out the remainder of his term and holding the motor vehicles position at the same time.

Hoffman used the motor vehicles post to its fullest advantage, speaking at functions of all kinds throughout the state. He was a brilliant speaker, debater and campaigner, and as commissioner he had an ideal platform from which to exercise his skills. He was even able to build a rather substantial national reputation as a spokesman for highway safety, a comparatively new concern in 1930.

Hoffman always considered the visibility afforded the commissioner of motor vehicles a stepping stone to higher elected office. He built an efficient and fiercely loyal personal political organization, and his arduous campaigning for Republican functionaries from Newark to Cape May earned him the gratitude of many party workers.

In 1934, Hoffman reportedly considered challenging Senator Hamilton Fish Kean for the Republican senatorial nomination, but was persuaded instead to seek the GOP gubernatorial nomination. His primary opponents were controversial Atlantic County Senator Emerson L. Richards, Essex County Senator Joseph G. Wolber, and Robert Carey. Hoffman easily won, drawing more votes than his three opponents combined. William L. Dill, Hoffman's predecessor as commissioner of motor vehicles and now a judge of the Court of Errors and Appeals, received the nomination of the Democratic party. Dill, a protégé of Mayor Frank Hague of Jersey City, won an impressive primary victory over Monmouth County's maverick Assemblyman Theron McCampbell. In a show of backing for Dill, the Hague Hudson County machine turned out more than 110,000 votes, of which 107,000 went to Judge Dill. The Democratic nominee had previously been defeated for the governor's post in the Republican landslide of 1928.

The campaign was unimpressive. Dill, though an inadequate campaigner who avoided the public spotlight, attempted to develop issues, primarily in the area of tax reform. Hoffman, an eager and superb campaigner, remained deliberately aloof from issues. The candidates, traditionally but appropriately, accused each other of being the tools of bossism.

The election was an upset. For the first time in twenty-seven years, the Democrats lost the governorship in a non-presidential election year. Mayor Frank Hague's inability to put his candidate over would be interpreted years later as a sellout of Judge Dill in order to get the affable Hoffman, later branded a Hague Republican, elected to the governorship. Little evidence exists to substantiate this contention. Actually, the vote illustrated the continued power of the Republican county machines, especially Enoch L. (Nucky) Johnson's Atlantic County organization. It also strongly indicated a far-reaching personal popularity for the thirty-nine-year-old governor-elect. And in a period of dramatically declining Republican fortunes throughout the country, Hoffman was widely championed as a potential contender for national office.

When Harold Hoffman became governor, an estimated 650,000 New Jersey residents were directly dependent on state and local government for public relief. Many thousands more were severely affected by the deepening economic depression. In the face of rapidly declining tax revenues New Jersey's municipal governments were hard-pressed to deliver essential services. Several cities defaulted, and others verged on financial collapse. With the full effect of the New Deal depression-fighting programs still in the future, the problems of meeting the depression crisis fell squarely on the shoulders of state and local government.

As governor, however, Harold Hoffman stood only on the peripheries of many of the important developments in state and local government that took place during his tenure. Although he was deeply embroiled in controversy and constantly in the news, his influence on the direction of state affairs declined continuously during his term as governor.

One of the first problems Hoffman attempted to meet—and, owing to his heavy-handed and conspiratorial manner of handling it, the cause of his first controversy—involved increasing state revenues to meet the increased demands for services from the state. In his inaugural address, Hoffman asked for a state sales tax, an unpopular issue he had skillfully avoided mentioning during the campaign. A sales tax, or some other broadening of the state's taxes, had wide support among the state's big-city politicians. However, numerous powerful business and taxpayers' associations, as well as the majority of the governor's own party, opposed any new taxes. To these people, fiscal responsibility meant reduced expenditures and a balanced budget, not increased spending.

Actively opposed by many Republican legislators, Hoffman made the fateful decision to deal with Hague's Democratic supporters in the legislature. Amidst an uproar from his fellow Republicans, Hoffman used his newfound allies to ram through the sales tax. The Hoffman-Hague "unholy deal," coming after just six months of the new governor's term, destroyed the credibility of his leadership with much of the Republican party. It had an especially adverse effect on Hoffman's relationship with the increasingly powerful Clean Government Group, a Republican faction headed by Essex County lawyer Arthur T. Vanderbilt.

The Vanderbilt wing of the party gave lip service to liberal and reformist ideals, but though it understood that the Republican party must change its public image to win elections and influence public policy in the Democratic New Deal era it was fundamentally conservative. Indeed, the Clean Government Group capitalized on Mayor Hague's failure to give the New Deal more than lukewarm support by implying that the Clean Republicans would be the New Jersey standard-bearers of progressive politics. In reality, however, in the mid-thirties the Clean Government faction devoted most of its energies to preaching governmental cost cutting and maintenance, if not reduction, of existing tax rates.

High on the new movement's list of pariahs were the last vestiges of the old Republican organization in Essex, Camden and Atlantic counties. Hoffman, already suspect for his close ties to the state's Republican bosses (the governor virtually ignored the Clean Government faction in awarding patronage) became the Vanderbilt Republicans' public enemy number one after the Hoffman-Hague sales tax deal.

The well-organized outcry against the tax measure was deafening. Skillfully using the issue to strengthen its position within the party, the Clean Government Group, made significant inroads throughout the state in the September 1935 Republican primary. Beaten, the governor was obliged to sign a sales tax repeal the following month. With his usual flair for the dramatic, Hoffman signed the bill in red ink, symbolizing what he foresaw as an "unbalanced budget and maybe hungry people."

Hoffman's first year as governor had not ended before a second major crisis rocked his administration. In late 1935, he embroiled himself in the sensational controversy surrounding the Lindbergh kidnapping case. Bruno Richard Hauptmann, convicted of the kidnap-murder of the Lindbergh baby, was awaiting execution at Trenton State Prison when the governor decided to reopen the case. The governor believed that Hauptmann had not committed the crime alone, and in the interest of justice he made a dramatic visit to Hauptmann's death cell, hoping to induce the convicted kidnapper to name his accomplices. The circumstances surrounding the governor's bizarre behavior suggest that Hoffman was more interested in the case for its potential publicity value than, as he professed, for justice.

Just before Hauptmann's scheduled execution date, the governor granted him a thirty-day reprieve and ordered the state police to reopen their investigation. What followed was a grotesque sequence of events which featured a further kidnapping, an induced confession, manufactured evidence, and assorted other travesties of justice, in all of which Governor Hoffman was deeply implicated. Hoffman's apparent intention to grant a second reprieve was blocked and Hauptmann was electrocuted. If the governor had hoped to advance his reputation by intervening in the case, he had severely miscalculated. A hostile press pilloried his behavior, and the resultant publicity further damaged his credibility.

Nonetheless, Hoffman still entertained national political ambitions. Going into the 1936 presidential election year, Hoffman's political associates were certain that the governor was maneuvering for either the presidential or vice-presidential nomination. However, if Hoffman was to have any chance at the Republican National Convention, it was essential that he emerge from a harmonious state primary in May as the head of his party's delegation to Cleveland. He was not to do so.

First, the strong sympathy in the state party for Governor Alfred M. Landon of Kansas made an unpledged delegation impossible. Second, the Republican state committee chose three at-large delegates who were less than enthusiastic about their governor (Hoffman was designated the fourth at-large delegate). Third, Hoffman faced a strong challenge for his place on the delegation from former Congressman Franklin W. Fort, who ran a vigorous campaign managed by the Clean Government faction.

Although the governor was able to beat Fort, he came in a poor fourth, thus destroying any chance he might have had at the Cleveland convention. The hollow victory in the 1936 state primary left Hoffman on the defensive within his own party. He devoted the remainder of his tenure as governor to his future political ambitions. Events, many of which carried far-reaching significance, were little influenced by the governor, who was taking on all the early characteristics of a lame duck executive.

In 1936, the state Emergency Relief Administration was disbanded, and the responsibility for administering and partially financing the relief burden was shifted back onto the municipal governments. That year, even though the governor had expressed reservations about the propriety of federal welfare, the legislature extended the provisions of the Federal Social Security Act to many New Jersey citizens.

The governor played a peripheral role in another hotly contested issue, the question of state supervision and control of municipal finances; his foes within the Republican party dominated in the struggle. Backed financially by the state's powerful business interests and politically by Vanderbilt's Clean Government Group, the Princeton Local Government Survey was launched late in 1935. Under the direction of Princeton University President Harold W. Dodds, a group of Princeton professors was commissioned to study and draft legislation which would severely restrict the powers of New Jersey local governments to administer their own fiscal affairs. In a skillfully orchestrated lobbying campaign supported by the Clean Government Republicans, the professors pushed the Princeton Survey bills through the legislature. Although the Princeton bills did not go as far as many of their business supporters had desired, they created a strong Department of Municipal Affairs with substantial control and supervisory powers over municipal finances. The governor did not play an instrumental role in these significant developments.

In fact, Hoffman was increasingly preoccupied with his political future. His final annual message to the legislature was groundwork for a 1940 gubernatorial bid. (Hoffman was constitutionally prohibited from succeeding himself, but his vision of a second term in 1940 was not unreasonable. His predecessor and successor, A. Harry Moore, would serve three terms—a record under the 1844 constitution). Unfortunately, the governor's candidate for the 1937 Republican gubernatorial nomination, Senator Clifford R. Powell of Burlington County, was soundly defeated by the Reverend Lester H. Clee, Essex County's state senator, a Clean Government luminary who had made his opposition to Hoffman a central issue in his campaign. Clee lost a close November election to Moore.

Under the circumstances, Hoffman was

not sorry to see the Republican defeat. The former governor managed to maneuver his own appointment as executive director of the New Jersey Unemployment Compensation Commission (UCC) —a $12,000-a-year post. From there, he could run a nonstop campaign for the 1940 GOP gubernatorial nomination. In the primary that year, however, he was narrowly defeated by Clean Government Republican Robert C. Hendrickson of Gloucester County, despite the considerable, and this time apparent, assistance of Hoffman's old friend, Mayor Frank Hague. But Hoffman's substantial organization within the Republican party withheld its support from Hendrickson, and Charles Edison, businessman son of the Wizard of Menlo Park, overwhelmingly defeated him.

Undaunted, Hoffman took leave of his post at the UCC in June 1942 to accept a commission in the Army transport command. (Reportedly, he had to drop thirty-six pounds in order to pass the Army physical.) He left the service in March 1946 with the honorary rank of colonel and returned to his post at the UCC.

When the Division of Employment Security was created in the Labor and Industry Department during Governor Alfred E. Driscoll's administration, Hoffman left his UCC position to become its first director. Aside from his official business, he was much in demand as a paid speaker, under the management of Thomas Brady, Inc., of New York City. He was a frequent toastmaster for the Order of Circus Saints and Sinners, an organization of which he was honorary life president.

On March 18, 1954, Robert B. Meyner, the newly inaugurated Democratic governor, suddenly suspended Hoffman from his post in the Division of Employment Security for alleged irregularities in purchases. For weeks the charges against Hoffman remained unsubstantiated, leading his loyal followers to charge Meyner with a political witch hunt. Then on June 4, while in the New York City apartment of the Circus Saints and

Sinners, Harold Hoffman died of an apparent heart attack. The calls for Meyner to clear the former governor's name became intense.

Several weeks later the government released its well-documented case against Hoffman. A letter Hoffman had written to his daughter shortly before his death substantiated the sordid tale, which spanned most of his political career. Hoffman had embezzled approximately $300,000 from the South Amboy Trust Company, of which he was an officer, in order to pay off early campaign debts. According to Hoffman's letter, a "certain wealthy elder candidate who is now deceased" had agreed to pay Hoffman's campaign costs. The wealthy benefactor had reneged, and Hoffman had embezzled to cover his debts. From at least 1949 on, he had used state funds from the Division of Employment Security to cover his bank's shortages.

Other charges of malfeasance, misfeasance, misconduct and malconduct in office were leveled at the former governor and several close associates. In addition it turned out that another state official who had learned of the embezzlement had blackmailed Hoffman for $150,000.

"Morality, in its ultimate determination, is a funny thing," Hoffman wrote to his daughter. Indeed, for Harold Hoffman, as for many other public officials over the years, morality was not an easily comprehensible commodity.

Records of Governor Harold G. Hoffman, New Jersey State Library, Bureau of Archives and History, Trenton, N.J.

Crystal, George. *This Republican Hoffman: The Life Story of Harold G. Hoffman, A Modern Fighter.* Hoboken, N.J.: n.p., 1934.

Paul A. Stellhorn

CHARLES EDISON (August 3, 1890–July 31, 1969), New Jersey's forty-second governor, was the elder son of the inventor Thomas A. Edison by his second wife, Mina Miller. His maternal grandfather was Lewis Miller of Akron, Ohio, an inventor, industrialist, and philanthropist, and a cofounder of the first Chautauqua Assembly. Charles Edison grew up in the sheltered confines of Llewellyn Park in West Orange, and he attended the Dearborn-Morgan School in Orange, the Carteret Academy in West Orange, and the Hotchkiss School in Connecticut. He matriculated at the Massachusetts Institute of Technology because, as he said later, "Father wanted me to be able to read a blueprint." After three years, although his grades were satisfactory, he left MIT, and on the advice of his father he took a job as a fifteen-dollar-a-week helper at the Boston Electric Light Company to gain general administrative training. One year later he went to work for Thomas A. Edison, Inc.

After his return from Massachusetts, Edison became a familiar figure in the growing bohemian community of Greenwich Village. He became interested in folk dancing and folk music, wrote poetry, published a literary magazine called *Bruno's Weekly,* and helped finance a theater. He remained interested in the arts throughout his life and in 1967 published a volume of his poems, *Flotsam and Jetsam.* His artistic inclinations, however, were secondary to his involvement in Thomas A. Edison, Inc. His father had put him through a strenuous apprenticeship to school him for eventual leadership of the company. Charles exhibited nearly as much flair for management and capacity for hard work as his father, but none of the inventive genius. In 1926, he officially succeeded his aging father as president of the firm and

immediately began to revamp its structure, improve its financial position—his success enabled the company to weather the depression—and modify the paternalistic labor policies his father had instituted.

Edison first served in government during World War I, assisting his father, who was president of the Naval Consulting Board, an agency responsible for developing new naval weapons and manufacturing war materials. He also met and became a friend of Franklin D. Roosevelt, then assistant secretary of the navy. In March 1918 he married Carolyn Hawkins of Cambridge, Massachusetts. They had no children.

Although he voted for Woodrow Wilson in 1912 and 1916, Edison remained a Republican until the 1930s, when he became a strong advocate of the New Deal and the only Democrat in the Edison family. "I believe in the new experiments going on," he stated in response to fellow businessmen's criticisms. "It takes courage to try new things and it takes courage to stop them if they are not successful." His support of the Roosevelt administration and his reputation as an extremely able executive drew him into government work during the 1930s. Between 1933 and 1936 he was vice-chairman of the New Jersey State Recovery Board, state director of the National Emergency Council, compliance director for the National Recovery Administration, and a member of the Regional Labor Board and the National Industrial Recovery Board. He was also a consultant during the drafting of the Federal Housing Act, and he served as regional director of the Federal Housing Administration for New Jersey, Pennsylvania, Maryland, and Delaware; some have credited him with the original idea that led to the FHA.

Edison fulfilled one of his ambitions on November 17, 1936, when President Roosevelt nominated him for the post of assistant secretary of the navy following the death of Henry Latrobe Roosevelt. He was selected because he had a record as an effective industrialist and government administrator and because he agreed with Roosevelt that the nation should build a navy second to none. Edison assumed his new position on January 18, 1937. His tenure was noteworthy in at least two respects. First, Claude A. Swanson, the secretary of the navy, was in poor health, and Edison was, in fact if not in name, the actual secretary of the navy for the next three years. Second, the president and Congress desired to increase the size of the American navy, and Edison's responsibility was to see that the ships were built on time and in conformity with the most recent advances in naval design and technology. He also supervised the naval neutrality patrols in the Atlantic Ocean. One of his major decisions prevented the sale of a group of obsolescent destroyers for junk. These vessels later made up a substantial part of the ships turned over to Britain in the "destroyer deal."

After Swanson died in July 1939, Edison became acting secretary of the navy, and he was appointed secretary on December 30, 1939. While in the department he was an innovator. Against the advice of the admirals, he insisted on developing high-pressure steam systems for propulsion, which resulted in higher speeds and greater efficiency for all naval vessels. He was also impressed by the threat the dive-bomber posed to capital ships, and he encouraged the building of small torpedo boats, torpedo bombers, and fast destroyers. His major naval accomplishment was to supervise the most ambitious naval building program in American history during a critical period.

Edison was secretary of the navy for only half a year. On March 30, 1940, he surprised his friends and acquaintances by announcing his candidacy for governor of New Jersey, and on June 24 he resigned from the cabinet. This was Edison's first campaign for elective office. It was undertaken with Roosevelt's encouragement. Roosevelt faced a reelection campaign later in the year, and he believed that with Edison running for governor he could carry New Jersey. In addition, in view of America's deteriorating relations with Germany and Japan, Roosevelt wanted to broaden his administration by including a few Republicans in the cabinet. Edison's successor as secretary of the navy was Frank Knox, a Republican newspaper publisher from Chicago. The immediate reaction of New Jersey Republicans to Edison's annoucement was negative; they argued that the naval post was next to the presidency in importance and that the threat of war made it Edison's patriotic duty to remain in Washington.

The Republican candidate for governor, state Senator Robert C. Hendrickson of Gloucester County, called Edison a tool of Frank Hague, the notorious mayor of Jersey City and boss of Hudson County. Edison could not have been nominated without Hague's support, but during the campaign he projected an independent image, emphasizing his experience in government and business, which would enable him to bring modern, efficient, and economical management to the operations of the New Jersey government. Edison went out of his way to separate himself from Hague. He attacked the recent burning of the poll books in Hudson County as well as Hague's political use of the courts. In his first campaign speech, delivered in August at Sea Girt, Edison declared in Hague's presence his independence of all bosses. "If you elect me," he told the voters, "you will have elected a governor who has made no promises to any man." Edison's stance did not disturb Hague, who assumed that it was mere campaign rhetoric. Edison won the election by nearly 64,000 votes, but he carried only seven of the state's twenty-one counties, losing even his home county of Essex. Without the 108,000-vote plurality Hague had piled up for him in Hudson County, Edison would have lost.

Edison's term in office was not particularly successful. Effective administration was almost impossible for several reasons. The state constitution was outmoded and furthermore the governor, lacking political skill, failed to establish good relations with the state's political leaders. His partial deafness further impaired his leadership. In addition, the opposing party solidly controlled the legislature; in 1942, for example, the Republicans had majorities of seventeen to four in the senate and forty-four to sixteen in the assembly. Finally, Edison kept his word about resisting Hague, and thereby made an enemy of the state's most powerful political figure.

The struggle with Hague brought Edison national attention. Before becoming governor Edison had published a song entitled "Don't Ask Nothin' of Me." This could have served as the theme song of his administration, at least as far as Frank Hague was concerned. From the beginning Edison showed that he had meant what he said at Sea Girt. In one of his first official acts, he ripped out the direct phone line connecting the governor's office with Hague's in the Jersey City city hall. The irrevocable break came on January 21, 1941, less than two weeks after the inauguration. Edison nominated Frederic R. Colie of Millburn to the New Jersey Supreme Court, the second highest court in the state. Colie, a Republican, had led the opposition to the 1939 appointment of Hague's son, Frank, Jr., to the state's highest court, the Court of Errors and Appeals.

Edison then attempted to rid the highway department of its pro-Hague head. It took the state senate a full year to vote on Edison's nominee, and the governor won confirmation only after instituting an investigation of the activities of the department, which was a rich source of patronage for the state's political chieftains. The feud with Hague broke into the open over taxation of railroad property. During the depression the bankrupt railroads had failed to pay $34 million in taxes. With the return of prosperity Hague argued that the railroads should pay the taxes, with interest. Edison instead worked out a compromise whereby the railroads would pay back the $34 million over a twenty-year period and the state would

waive the accumulated interest. Hague accused the governor of showing favoritism to the railroads, and Edison charged Hague with using the issue to retaliate for the Colie appointment.

Roosevelt gave Edison no support in the struggle with Hague. In fact, he continued to funnel state patronage through Hague. He even nominated Thomas F. Meaney, a Hague crony, to fill a vacancy on the federal district court bench in New Jersey without paying Edison the customary courtesy of consultation beforehand. Roosevelt's lack of support noticeably cooled relations between the two men.

Edison made no secret of the fact that he was out "to separate as many Hague Democrats as possible from the state payroll and to try to keep any new ones from catching on." He also struck at the financial basis of Hague's power in 1942 by ousting the entire five-man Hudson County Tax Board from office and replacing it with a board of his choosing. The original board had taxed businesses in the county heavily, and their revenues had provided much of the money that enabled the Hague machine to function. Hague responded by having some of Edison's supporters arrested and prosecuted, and by blocking a number of the governor's appointments.

Edison was determined that the Democrats should nominate an anti-Hague candidate for governor in 1943. In February 1943, in preparation for the primary, he announced the formation of the "United Democracy," a statewide anti-Hague organization. He also denounced Hague over the radio, calling him corrupt and dictatorial. Despite Edison's strenuous efforts to destroy Hague, however, Hague controlled the convention, and the "United Democracy" quietly expired. The Democratic gubernatorial candidate, Vincent J. Murphy, mayor of Newark, drew closer and closer to Hague during the campaign; by election day, in response, Edison had adopted a stance of virtual neutrality. Murphy lost the election to Walter E. Edge by approximately 130,000 votes.

Edison's most notable activity as governor was his promotion of constitutional revision. New Jersey had been operating under the constitution of 1844, an archaic document that severely circumscribed the governor's powers and made it exceedingly difficult for him to function as a true chief executive. The constitution limited the governor's appointive power, permitted a simple majority of the assembly and senate to override his veto, restricted his term to three years and prevented him from succeeding himself. It also forced him to share his power with more than eighty boards and commissions, which had overlapping functions. The government was a bureaucratic nightmare. Moreover, the antiquated judicial structure consisted of seventeen different court systems. The need for constitutional revision was recognized throughout the state even before Edison became governor. Both Edison and Hendrickson came out in support of it during the 1940 gubernatorial race, Edison proposing a constitutional convention and Hendrickson claiming that Edison, as a tool of Hague's, could not effect the necessary changes. Edison's inaugural address made constitutional revision the first priority of his administration. Opposition was especially strong among rural Republicans, who viewed revision as a threat to their power, particularly in the state senate. When in his inaugural address Edison coupled revision with a plea for restructuring the state senate to reflect the state's population more equitably, he destroyed the possibility of a constitutional convention during his term. He also alienated Hague from the drive by describing revision as a means of curbing Hague's power.

After leaving office, Edison supported the movement for revision actively. He would witness the movement's triumph when the state adopted a new constitution in 1947. Although his maladroit political approach aborted revision during his governorship, he deserves credit for focusing public attention on the question and whipping up support for revision.

After his term ended on January 18, 1944, Edison resumed his position as president of Thomas A. Edison, Inc. The company prospered under his direction, and in 1957 it merged with the McGraw Electric Company to form the McGraw-Edison Company. Edison was board chairman of the merged firm until he retired in 1961. Meanwhile he remained active in politics, supporting John V. Kenny's overthrow of Hague in 1949. He also vigorously promoted the China lobby and Douglas A. MacArthur. Disturbed by the growth of federal power under both Democratic and Republican presidents, and opposed to the foreign policies of both major political parties, Edison officially joined the New York Conservative party in 1963.

Edison's wife died in 1963, and he spent his last years at the Waldorf Towers in New York City. He died on July 31, 1969, leaving an estate of approximately $10 million. The vast bulk of it went to the Charles Edison Fund, which he had established to promote "various charities, scientific, literary, and religious education projects."

Records of Governor Charles Edison, New Jersey State Library, Bureau of Archives and History, Trenton, N.J.

Alexander, Jack. "The Ungovernable Governor." *Saturday Evening Post* (January 23, 1943): p. 9.

Burritt, Richard D. "Another Edison Makes Some Discoveries." *New York Times Magazine* (October 12, 1941): pp. 16, 27.

Connors, Richard J. *The Process of Constitutional Revision in New Jersey, 1940–1947.* New York: National Municipal League, 1970.

Van Devander, Charles W. *The Big Bosses.* n.p.: Howell, Soskin Publishers, 1944.

Venable, John D. *Out of the Shadow: The Story of Charles Edison.* East Orange, N.J.: Charles Edison Fund, 1978.

Edward S. Shapiro

The Constitution of 1947

ALFRED EASTLACK DRISCOLL (October 25, 1902–March 9, 1975) was born in Pittsburgh, Pennsylvania, the son of Alfred Robie and Mattie (Eastlack) Driscoll. His ancestry can be traced to revolutionary Haddonfield, New Jersey. In 1906, when Driscoll was four years old, the family moved back to Haddonfield. An only child, Driscoll could attribute his interest in public affairs directly to his parents, who participated actively in the affairs of the community. His mother, a participant in many church, reform, and educational movements, including the founding of the Peddie School for Girls in Hightstown, appears to have influenced her son's development profoundly.

Driscoll displayed enormous energy and drive as a child, and these became his most pronounced characteristics as governor. He graduated from Haddonfield High School as the school's most outstanding student, receiving the Childrey Award for his reputation as a hard-working student, his performance as captain of the debating and track teams, and other achievements. At Williams College, he served as captain of the track team again, continued his commitment to debating, and became one of the college's two four-letter men.

During his college years, Driscoll satisfied a thirst for adventure and a love of the outdoors. Later he reflected: "When I was in college I had a bad case of wanderlust. I went to sea during a couple of summer vacations. I worked as a cook with an expedition to the Canadian Rockies and another time, I cooked for an outfit that went north to the arctic circle. I used to justify myself by saying that I was building windows out of which I could look after I had settled down." Besides opening "windows" for the future governor, these excursions helped mold his sense of independence, which, combined with the security of deep roots in his native state, shaped his political style. That style was already visible when, at 28, he entered politics.

Fresh from Harvard Law School, Driscoll became associated with the Camden firm of Starr, Sumerhill and Lloyd. Shortly after that, he was asked to run for the Haddonfield Board of Education to prevent the local political machine from "politicizing" a nonpartisan body. When Republican leaders informed him that he could not run because the local party had already selected its ticket, Driscoll retorted, "Until a minute ago, I didn't want to run. Now, I'm going to."

Thus, Driscoll entered politics only to keep "politics" from getting in the way of the matters he deemed important. A young man of intelligence and means, he did not need the party as a vehicle for personal, financial, or political success. It was only natural that Arthur T. Vanderbilt's "Clean Government" movement, which was beginning to enjoy success in the northern counties, looked on him as a "comer." Driscoll's disdain for "petty partisan politics" would help him secure a new constitution for the state, which others had failed to do. The same quality, however, would also eventually weaken his influence over many county leaders in the party he led.

Driscoll remained on the school board for seven years, serving for a time as its president. He resigned in 1937 to run for the Haddonfield Borough Commission. After his election he became director of revenue and finance, in which office he significantly lowered the municipality's taxes and bonded debt.

At this juncture the Clean Government faction of the Republican party approached Driscoll to oppose the entrenched Baird machine in the primary for state senator, and he did so successfully. He went on to win the election. In that year a Frank Hague favorite, A. Harry Moore, won his third term as governor. Moore defeated the Clean Government candidate, Rev. Lester H. Clee, by 40,000 votes, though he carried only Hudson and Middlesex counties. Driscoll was among the first to notice irregularities. "Funny things happened in that election," he said, "including the burning of ballots." Retaining his borough commission seat, he entered the senate determined to combat machine politics in both parties at every level in the state.

He managed Robert C. Hendrickson's ill-fated campaign in the 1940 election for governor, which Charles Edison won by 60,000 votes. The following January the thinned Republican majority selected Driscoll as senate majority leader. He spent his brief term cautiously walking a tightrope between the Hague Democrats and the patronage-hungry "old guard" Republicans from the rural counties. Analyzing his situation, he observed, "My job was to get as much as I could and to yield as little as I would." Shortly thereafter, the Republican legislature designated him New Jersey's alcoholic beverage commissioner.

In that post, Driscoll displayed the capacity for hard work and for enduring sixteen-hour days that would mark his seven years as governor. He established the reputation of a strict and impartial watchdog over an industry frequently beset by scandal.

In addition to his official duties, he immersed himself in the movement for constitutional revision and adminstrative reorganization, which gained momentum during the administrations of governors Edison and Walter E. Edge. Edge named Driscoll to the New Jersey Commission on State Administrative Reorganization, which was chaired by Charles R. Erdman, Jr., and included Senator C. Wesley Armstrong, Assemblyman Walter Jones, and public member Charles A. Eaton, Jr. The commission thoroughly investigated the existing one hundred independent spending agencies and fifty independent boards and commissions, then recommended consolidating twenty-four agencies into five principal departments. These recommendations were enacted promptly. The defeat of the 1944 constitution precluded further reorganization, but Driscoll's work on the commission gave him a familiarity with the mechanisms of state government that equipped him for his most memorable feat, engineering the ratification of the new constitution.

Supported by Governor Edge, Driscoll stopped former Governor Harold G. Hoffman's attempted comeback in the Republican primary of 1946 and then defeated the Democratic candidate, Hudson County Judge Lewis G. Hansen, by a plurality of 221,000 votes. By all accounts the gubernatorial campaign was a lackluster affair, with the Republicans seeking to capitalize on President Harry S.

Truman's unpopularity and on the close relationship between Hansen and Hague. Driscoll stressed his experience and promised strong and efficient state government. He expressed support for constitutional revision only in the most general terms.

Driscoll's inaugural address revealed that in the eleven-week transition period he had studied the Edison and Edge constitutions carefully. To the surprise of most of his listeners, he called for a constitutional convention, a remedy he had not alluded to in his campaign or post-victory press conferences. Acting in the belief that the Edison constitution had been filibustered to death by a suspicious legislature and that the Edge draft had been defeated by the partisan nature of its guidance through the legislature, Driscoll decided that a limited convention would help the cause by removing it from legislative halls and partisan politics. He gave assurance that the convention would be prohibited from entering the thicket of reapportionment, and the legislature, after wrangling about how many delegates each county would send to the convention, complied with his request. To reassure skeptics who doubted that New Jersey was ready for a new constitution, Driscoll described the 1944 referendum as a defeat for the specific proposal rather than a vote of confidence for the 1844 document then in use.

The governor was responsible for a number of measures to guarantee the orderly transaction of business during the convention and to ameliorate antagonisms that could have jeopardized the new constitution at any point between the start of deliberations in New Brunswick on June 12 and the referendum in November. He marshaled the state government's resources to facilitate the deliberations and to publicize the document. As soon as the legislature approved the convention, he commissioned a Committee on Preparatory Research, headed by state archivist Sidney Goldman, to develop material that might assist the delegates, to help prepare a tentative draft of rules for the convention, and to set up a library of important reference tools close to the delegates. He minimized procedural and partisan quibbling by encouraging county leaders to field bipartisan delegations and by procuring agreement on the convention's officers before the first session.

Driscoll kept informed of the proceedings through transcripts of committee and floor deliberations, briefings with delegate George Walton, his representative at the convention, and appearances as a witness. He intervened personally to bring about at least two compromises that helped save the constitution from the kinds of sectional and religious antagonism that had defeated its 1944 predecessor.

He issued a plea to "isolate" the emotional issue of gambling from the issue of constitutional reform; he seemed to favor leaving an open door for a future referendum on charity raffles and bingo and letting the 1939 referendum on parimutuel betting stand intact. The second intervention involved the issue of second-class railroad taxation. When it became apparent that this matter could not be resolved either in committee or on the floor, Driscoll negotiated directly with the Jersey City leaders. They wanted the constitution to prohibit the preferential tax rate that the legislature had awarded the railroads in 1941 and to provide for the assessment of local property (terminals, yards and stations) at "true value" instead. The administration held out for uniform rules with the legislature empowered to handle specific problems as they arose. A compromise was reached that in effect committed the governor to the repeal of the 1941 statute but did not mention second-class real property. The compromise also strengthened the power of the legislature without abandoning the "true-value" clause. Students of the subject cite this compromise as the saving of the constitution, for it guaranteed that Hudson County would not sabotage the document at the polls as it had done in 1944 and was threatening to do again.

The rapprochement with the Hague machine was a significant retreat for Driscoll, however, and it involved a minor risk. While in the senate, he had been one of the sponsors of the legislation Hague wished to nullify, and in yielding now to the demands of practicality he angered longtime advocates of constitutional revision such as Arthur T. Vanderbilt and Walter E. Edge.

Driscoll's unwavering support for a strengthened executive and a streamlined judiciary, which had been cited by a series of former governors as the reforms most needed in New Jersey and as the major reasons for adopting a new constitution, balanced whatever concessions he made to Hudson County in this and other instances. Other highlights of the Driscoll-inspired draft included a merit system for state employees, and a guarantee of the right of collective bargaining for persons in private employment; in abolishing segregation in the militia and in public schools, the document made New Jersey the first state to outlaw segregation constitutionally. Although Governor Edge had long advocated these measures, he had refrained from including them in his draft constitution on the grounds that they represented concessions to special interests. These deletions had made it possible for Hague to instill fear in disappointed interest groups and to encourage them to vote against any draft not specifically addressed to them. The reverse was true of the 1947 draft, which was approved by a plurality of 470,464 votes.

In 1948, the Driscoll administration continued the reorganization of state government begun by the New Jersey Commission on State Administrative Reorganization and further mandated by the new constitution. Some seventy departments were reduced to fourteen, saving the state an estimated $2 million in administrative costs. One important consolidation unified all law enforcement agencies under one administrative head; another merged all fiscal functions into one department with a single director.

The law-enforcement reforms also allowed the attorney general to supersede local county prosecutors, creating an important weapon for combating organized crime. New Jersey was the first to consolidate law enforcement and financial functions in this manner, and it was a model for the twenty-eight states that followed suit after 1948.

Another constitutional mandate Driscoll was quick to act on was the commitment to civil rights. He turned over the enforcement of the new provision to the Division Against Discrimination in the Department of Education, and threw his weight behind the legislation the division recommended. That legislation included a bill making it a misdemeanor to bar any child from the public schools or to discharge a teacher on grounds of race, religion, or national origin. He also integrated the national guard at once, preempting efforts to have the secretary of the army help it thwart integration by creating all-black divisions. He signed the Freeman Bill, which prohibited discrimination because of race, color or creed in any place of public accommodation. The bill, which predated the Civil Rights Act of 1964 by sixteen years, had been in trouble in the legislature until the governor made it part of his legislative program.

In his first three years in office Driscoll also raised minimum teachers' salaries from $1,200 to $2,200, effected a temporary disability insurance program to protect workers from accidents and illness incurred off the job, and updated the parole system.

Driscoll was reelected in 1949 by a plurality of 75,860 votes, defeating Senator Elmer H. Wene, a South Jersey chicken farmer. His victory was regarded as a fatal blow to Frank Hague, who wanted to regain at the state level the power he had lost in Jersey City. Insurgent Democrats in Hague's bastion had passed the word that Driscoll's reelection would be useful to their purpose, and as a result the governor had become the first Republican since Warren G. Harding to carry Jersey City. He won there by 16,000 votes, and he only lost Hudson County by 3,400. The $100-million slum-clearance and rehabilitation bond issue he supported in that election was less fortunate, but he later secured passage of a $41 million bond issue to build low-cost housing for veterans.

During Driscoll's second administration the New Jersey Turnpike and the Walt Whitman Bridge were opened, and the Garden State Parkway was begun. The 118-mile turnpike was perhaps the most spectactular of these achievements. The Turnpike Authority, created in 1949, issued its first bonds in 1950, and the highway was built in twenty-three months. Two of the reasons frequently cited for this record construction pace are that the authority commissioned a multitude of contractors and that the governor closely supervised the project, making countless on-the-spot inspection tours. The New Jersey Highway Authority was created to build the Parkway in 1952. The 164-mile road opened in 1954.

In his last year in office, Driscoll supervised the state's purchases of Island Beach State Park and the 110,000-acre Wharton Tract in South Jersey, which he called "a rich source of water resources and reserves for the future." He also planned the development of Sandy Hook State Park, which was considered New Jersey's future answer to Jones Beach.

Like most recent administrators, Driscoll took steps to confront the problems of organized crime, racketeering, and political corruption, which had long plagued New Jersey. With Governor Thomas E. Dewey of New York he created the Bistate Waterfront Commission in 1950 to remove racketeers from the Hudson River docks. During the same year, the state police broke up a nationwide Western Union bookmaking network and moved in on a statewide narcotics syndicate.

Two scandals erupted during the Driscoll years. Neither directly touched the governor or his close advisers or damaged the credibility of his administration, but both tarnished his reputation as a party leader. The first scandal involved the purchase of two privately owned bridges by the Burlington County Board of Freeholders from a company whose major stockholders were Republican County Chairman and National Guard Chief of Staff Clifford R. Powell and his associates. The state planned to acquire the bridges for $4,900,000 through condemnation, but the freeholders, most of whom owed their positions to Powell, purchased them for $12,400,000, selling bonds to a syndicate at a New York meeting. The courts ordered the return of the profits and the bridges, and Driscoll moved to block public purchase of the bonds. Later, acting as commander of the national guard, he removed Powell from his position in that organization.

The second scandal involved another Republican bastion, Bergen County. Learning of a major gambling scandal there, the governor sent Deputy Attorney General Nelson Stamler to supersede prosecutor Walter G. Winne. Stamler secured indictments and jail sentences against three defendants. Winne was also indicted but he was later acquitted. Stamler had further success, but before he was finished the state attorney general removed him. Later, legislative investigation revealed that the brother of one of the defendants had asked the Republican state chairman to have the heat from Trenton removed. It was also learned that another defendant had briefly been employed as a clerk in Driscoll's office. Though the scandal never brought the governor's integrity into question, it revealed his failure to keep a close enough watch over the local and county Republican organizations. The very independence he had maintained from his party throughout his career may have contributed to his negligence. It is altogether likely that Driscoll's preoccupation with policy making led him to ignore or fail to scrutinize the administrative and partisan aspects of the job of governor as closely as he would have liked.

On his retirement in 1953, Driscoll assumed the presidency of the Warner-Hudnut Company (now the Warner-Lambert Pharmaceutical Company). He continued his activity in governmental affairs, presiding over the National Municipal League, speaking for a citizens' committee for the establishment of the Gateway National Recreation Area, and serving on the 1967 riot commission. He supported a number of his successors' programs, including Governor Richard J. Hughes's ill-fated 1963 bond issue and Governor William T. Cahill's 1972 tax reform package. In 1970 Governor Cahill named him head of the New Jersey Turnpike Authority, and he occupied that post until his death. He was also an active member of the New Jersey Historical Commission.

Throughout his years as governor and concerned private citizen, Driscoll embraced a concept he called "working federalism." He argued that states should have greater initiative and should cooperate with each other more fully, and the federal government should share more functions with the states. A careful reading of his second inaugural address shows that this concept resembles the idea of revenue sharing, an innovation of the 1970s. Driscoll's denunciation of what he saw as the national government's growing detachment from the public suggests that he would have had much in common with the "anti-Washington" politicians of the contemporary era: "In our republic, it has been the traditional task of the states to protect individual freedom. . . . Despite the contention of some who would put their trust in a strong, centralized government in the nation's capital, Big Government sooner or later ceases to be either representative or responsible. It retains the appearance of a union of states and of popular representation, but abandons the substance."

Records of Governor Alfred E. Driscoll, New Jersey State Library, Bureau of Archives and History, Trenton, N.J.

Bryan, Brantz Mayer. "Alfred Eastlack Driscoll: Governor of New Jersey." Senior thesis, Princeton University, 1952.

Cutler, Robert G. "Charter Reviewed: The New Jersey Constitution, 1947–1957." Ph.D. dissertation, Princeton University, 1958.

Felzenberg, Alvin S. "The Impact of Gubernatorial Style on Policy Outcomes: An In Depth Study of Three New Jersey Governors." Ph.D. dissertation, Princeton University, 1978.

Wood, Robert. "The Metropolitan Governor." Ph.D. dissertation, Harvard University, 1950.

Alvin S. Felzenberg

ROBERT BAUMLE MEYNER (b. July 3, 1908), lawyer, governor of New Jersey, was born in Easton, Pennsylvania, the son of Gustave Herman and Mary Sophie (Baumle) Meyner. His parents, who were of German and Swiss ancestry, came from humble backgrounds: his father worked as a loom fixer and silk worker. When Robert was eight, his family moved to Phillipsburg, New Jersey. Except for a short stay at Paterson, his family remained in Phillipsburg. The need to earn a living occupied his youth, and he worked in various jobs as a newspaper boy, grocery clerk, garage mechanic, and foundry handyman. In 1926 Meyner graduated from Phillipsburg High School and entered Lafayette College in Easton, Pennsylvania, financing his education by working in the silk mills near Easton and Phillipsburg. He developed an early interest in politics in 1928, when he became president of the Young People's Al Smith for President Club at Lafayette.

From 1930 to 1933, he attended Columbia University Law School, and in 1934 he was admitted to the New Jersey bar. Working as a law clerk for the firm J. Emil Walscheid and Milton Rosenkranz in Union City and later in Jersey City, Meyner gained "a lot of experience but little money." Offered an opportunity to take over the practice of a deceased lawyer in Phillipsburg, Meyner returned to his native city in 1936. The next year he became a counsellor, and in 1940 he was admitted to practice before the United States Supreme Court. His practice centered on trial work. Early in his career he recognized the need for judicial integrity when he "suffered several traumatic experiences with judges." In Warren County he built a political base through his active role in the local, state and national bar associations—along with his work in civic and social organizations.

In 1941 Meyner first ran for political office but lost in the primary for the Warren County senate seat. After the start of World War II, he left for the military. On August 3 1943, he enlisted in the navy at the rank of lieutenant (j.g.). He used his legal training to defend sailors in court-martial trials, and later he became the commander of a gun crew on a merchant vessel. Discharged December 1945 as a lieutenant commander, he kept this rank in the naval reserve and returned to law and politics. In 1946 he ran for congressman against the powerful, and later infamous, J. Parnell Thomas, but the election went easily to Thomas. Meyner gained a political victory in 1947 when he defeated Republican Wayne Dumont, Jr., for the state senate seat in Warren County. From 1947 to 1951, Meyner gained political experience through work with legislative and party leaders and exerted his independence by criticizing the Republican administration for failing to clean up the corruption in Bergen County. Another expression of his strong will appeared when he cast the sole dissenting vote against the creation of the New Jersey Turnpike Authority, deprecating all such bodies because "they become grossly irresponsible to the will of the people." During his term as senator, Meyner became minority leader in 1950 and permanent chairman of the Democratic state convention. Despite party recognition, he experienced political defeat once again, when he lost his senate

seat to Dumont in a close race in 1951.

By 1953, Meyner seemed a has-been candidate. Few people thought that he would emerge as the Democratic choice for governor. Being from a rural county and having failed even to carry his home district, Meyner had an added political liability, his religion—he was an apostate from the Roman Catholic Church. Nevertheless, luck and hard work (two important reasons for his political success) reversed his fortune. Since 1949, New Jersey Democrats had been divided by a vacuum in state leadership. John V. Kenny had defeated the former state boss, Frank Hague, in his native Jersey City. A bloody political battle followed. Hague and his followers tried for the fourth time to regain power by supporting Elmer H. Wene, a flamboyant chicken farmer from South Jersey, in the 1953 Democratic gubernatorial primary. Kenny and other county leaders refused to accept Wene. In desperation, they turned to Robert Meyner. Offered a unique opportunity, the Warren County senator accepted and later commented, "I realized I had very little chance to win, but I knew it was the only chance I would ever have. I jumped at it."

Meyner's judgment proved correct. Winning only three out of New Jersey's twenty-one counties, he defeated Wene by only 1,683 votes, thanks in large measure to Hudson County's boss John V. Kenny and his 30,000 vote majority. In the general election Meyner faced a strong Republican opponent. The Republicans, who had held the governor's office for ten years, selected Paul L. Troast, a contractor who was chairman of the New Jersey Turnpike Authority. Meyner campaigned for strict law enforcement and again criticized the Republicans for making New Jersey "a mecca for syndicated gambling and a haven for the underworld." Meyner's campaign gained momentum when a prison scandal marred his opponent's reputation. Newspaper stories revealed that in 1951 Troast had written a letter to New York Governor Thomas E. Dewey asking commutation of the prison sentence of a convicted labor racketeer and extortionist, Joseph S. Fay. The famous "Fay Letter" became the turning point in the election. Meyner went on to victory with a 153,653-vote majority.

When elected governor, Meyner presented an imposing figure. Relatively young at forty-five he was almost six feet tall, and his gray curly hair and baritone voice made him physically a model governor. His political style was less glamorous. He was cautious, skeptical, and guarded in facing problems. Having boundless energy and an even temperament, he seemed well suited to govern a rapidly growing state. New Jersey was in the midst of a dynamic era, and Meyner's administration reflected this change.

A man of deep convictions, Meyner expressed an intense commitment to open government in his inaugural address of January 19, 1954: "I am a strong advocate of submitting important questions to the people on the ground that it makes for livelier, more responsive, and more responsible democracy." He followed this policy in March 1954, when he began a series of television-radio reports on the activities of the state administration. He courted the press by scheduling two news conferences a week, and he arranged a separate conference for editors of weeklies. In an attempt to gain bipartisan support for his legislative program, the governor held prelegislative conferences with both party leaders.

A major theme throughout Meyner's gubernatorial years was his pledge to "staff my administration with men and women who see government as a great challenge to imagination and enterprise." He often incurred the wrath of party leaders but remained determined to "get people into politics who aren't out to make a buck, who aren't out to take advantage of everything." Republicans and business and labor leaders provided advice and men to help fill four cabinet posts.

Adhering to his promise to clean house, Meyner in his first year as governor con-

centrated on exposing corruption in the Division of Employment Security. Harold G. Hoffman, a former governor (1935–1938), headed the division. When Meyner discovered inefficiencies, he sought the assistance of Prudential Insurance officials to accelerate the payment of unemployment insurance. After an initial inspection, Hoffman was suspended for improprieties. He died during the investigation and Meyner was accused of "killing him." But a letter Hoffman wrote to his daughter just before his death disclosed that he had used $300,000 in state funds to cover an embezzlement from the South Amboy Trust Co., of which he was president.

Meyner's first four years included more than exposing corruption and making qualified appointments. They saw the legalization of bingo and raffles, substantial increases in state aid to education, and the restructuring of Rutgers University to be "truly a state university." Teachers' salaries were also increased, as was aid to retarded and handicapped children. All fourteen state departments were reorganized to provide more efficient and closer communication with the public. Meyner centralized and mechanized motor vehicle registration and streamlined the budget bureau. Government costs were carefully regulated by vetoes of special-interest bills and investments of state funds in higher-interest-returning securities. Meyner presaged the women's liberation movement by appointing the first woman cabinet member in New Jersey. In appointing judges he carefully screened applicants and selected men of high stature. He showed conviction in supporting his appointees, as when he vigorously backed Joseph Weintraub's supervision of the Bistate Waterfront Commission.

On state finances, the governor preferred to follow rather than to lead the public. Faced with a Republican-dominated legislature, he refused to broach the problem of restructuring the state's tax system with an income or sales tax. Meyner relied on increases in excise taxes to finance a constantly rising state budget.

As the leader of his party, Meyner helped build the Democratic party throughout the state, and he made the party a twenty-one-county organization instead of the one-county, Hudson-dominated machine it had been for thirty years under Frank Hague. Although often called a "Democratic Eisenhower," Meyner spoke forcibly against McCarthyism and criticized the Wisconsin senator's activities as "a perversion of basic American principles." The energetic governor also used his office to defend court rulings on civil liberties and civil rights. Because of his capable administration and a nationally publicized romance, Meyner's popularity grew throughout his first term. In January 1957 he married Helen Day Stevenson, a distant cousin of Adlai Stevenson and the daughter of Eleanor B. and William E. Stevenson, the president of Oberlin College. Meyner's marriage, his ability as an orator, and his charming style made him the "Glamorous Governor of New Jersey." In 1957, Meyner ran for reelection against state Senator Malcolm S. Forbes. Despite Eisenhower's landslide victory the previous year, Meyner became the first governor to be reelected for a four-year term when he defeated Forbes by more than 200,000 votes and carried the Democrats to control of the assembly. Respected by both Democrats and Republicans, Meyner was at the pinnacle of his political career. Throughout his second term, he groomed himself for the possibility of national office by traveling, commenting on foreign policy, and criticizing Eisenhower; however, at home he continued to be a prudent administrator.

Meyner focused attention on the state's transportation problems. In dealing with rail and road problems, he relied on his highway commissioner, Dwight R. G. Palmer. Symbolic of the rubber and concrete era, Meyner spent $93 million a year for road-building. However, he did not ignore the rail services. A Rail Transpor-

tation Division was formed in the Highway Department to provide for rail improvements and consolidations. Rail subsidies were provided and, in 1959, a mass transit plan was proposed. Funds from the New Jersey Turnpike Authority were to be diverted to aid the deteriorating railroads, but opposition from Hudson County and rural areas defeated the proposal. Plans to have the Port of New York Authority take over the bankrupt Hudson and Manhattan Tubes were initiated. At the end of his administration Meyner advocated the construction of a jetport in Morris County, but he failed to convince the public. He constantly emphasized traffic safety, and New Jersey had one of the best safety records in the country.

Strong on conservation, Meyner started the reclamation of 15,000 acres of North Jersey's meadowland through the creation of the Meadowland Regional Development Agency. A "Green Acres" program attempted to regain land for recreational use. Educational expansion continued with increased construction and appropriations for higher education. Notable advances were also made in mental health, treatment of juvenile delinquents, care of the aged and consumer protection. The state's economy prospered with heavy investments in new industrial plants and the extensive growth of New Jersey's research facilities. Meyner continued to avoid a broad-base tax by using a corporate income tax.

Meyner's success as governor led him to the 1960 National Democratic Convention with the hope of achieving a national office or at least helping to determine the convention's choice. He joined Stuart Symington and Lyndon B. Johnson in an attempt to block the nomination of John F. Kennedy. But his luck and good timing ran out. Refusing to allow the New Jersey delegation to vote for Kennedy on the first ballot, Meyner lost the opportunity to make New Jersey the deciding state. Meyner had failed to emulate his idol, Woodrow Wilson and his political career began to decline.

Meyner spent his last years as governor

in recommending further improvements in transportation and education. When he concluded his term, he returned to law and private industry—accepting lucrative positions with banks and insurance companies and becoming the administrator of the cigarette industry's code on fair advertising. In 1969, he attempted to regain the governorship (having been constitutionally prohibited from running in 1961) and won the Democratic primary. But the charisma and appeal of the 1950s were gone. He lost in a one-sided race to William Cahill.

Meyner's stewardship of New Jersey left a legacy of efficiency and economy in government. Though not a social reformer or experimenter, he was certainly a good administrator. Perhaps he best expressed his philosophy of government and life in his first inaugural address: "Above all, we must ever be conscious that in government, as in life, nothing is ever permanently settled, nothing ever disposed of beyond the need for cautious study and action. It is a timeless process and an endless campaign against smug self-approval."

Records of Governor Robert B. Meyner, New Jersey State Library, Bureau of Archives and History, Trenton, N.J.

Felzenberg, Alvin S. "The Impact of Gubernatorial Style on Policy Outcomes: An In Depth Study of Three New Jersey Governors." Ph.D. dissertation, Princeton University, 1978.

William Lemmey

RICHARD JOSEPH HUGHES (b. August 10, 1909), lawyer, two-term governor, chief justice of the state supreme court, was born in Florence, Burlington County, to Richard Paul Hughes and Veronica (Gallagher) Hughes. His father, an ironworker and insurance broker, served as a state civil service commissioner, as principal keeper of Trenton State Prison, and as Burlington County Democratic chairman, and was otherwise active in politics and public affairs.

Richard J. Hughes graduated from Cathedral High School in Trenton, after which he studied at St. Charles College in Catonsville, Maryland, and at St. Joseph's College in Philadelphia. At one time he intended to become a Roman Catholic priest, but he turned to the study of law, receiving an LL.B. from New Jersey Law School in 1931. Admitted to the bar in 1932, he opened a law office in Trenton.

In 1937, after entering Democratic politics in Mercer County, he was elected statewide president of the Young Democrats and Democratic State Committee member from Mercer County. In 1938 he ran as a "Roosevelt Democrat" for Congress from the Fourth District. Though he lost decisively to Republican D. Lane Powers, he drew attention as a vigorous campaigner.

Appointed assistant United States attorney for New Jersey in December 1939, he prosecuted mail fraud, illegal tax withholding, and wartime subversion by members of the German-American Vocational League and similar groups. His careful preparations—and frequent convictions—enhanced his reputation and earned him a press accolade as "the nemesis of Nazis in New Jersey."

For Hughes the call of politics was irresistible. "I like politics," he said. "I think our politics for the next few years is going to be vitally important if we're going to keep our children out of another war." After he was elected Mercer County Democratic chairman in June 1945, he left his federal post and resumed private practice with Thorn Lord, who had been United States attorney over him. Lord and Hughes collaborated in politics as well as law, and under their leadership the Democrats won control of the Mercer County government in 1948.

On September 1, 1948, Acting Governor John M. Summerill, Jr., nominated Hughes to be judge of the Court of Common Pleas (which shortly thereafter was changed under the court reorganization to Mercer County Court). In February 1952, when William J. Brennan, Jr., was appointed to the state supreme court, Governor Alfred E. Driscoll named Hughes to replace him as superior court judge. Hughes was later designated assignment judge for Union County and eventually promoted to the appellate division of superior court.

His interest in juvenile problems and his reputation for being tough but fair and hard-working led Chief Justice Arthur T. Vanderbilt to appoint him head of a committee reviewing statutes that affected juvenile and domestic relations and probation services. The supreme court accepted that committee's recommendations, and as a result the state's juvenile and domestic relations courts were revised.

Several times Governor Robert B. Meyner considered Hughes for appointment to the state supreme court. Rather than rise further in the courts, however, Hughes resigned from the bench in November 1957 and resumed private law to support his family. (His first wife, the former Miriam McGrory, whom he had married in 1934, had died in 1950, leaving three sons and a daughter. In 1954 he had married Elizabeth [Sullivan] Murphy, a widow with three sons. The couple had a daughter and two sons.) In a lucrative private law practice Hughes represented the Association of New Jersey Railroads and the Public Service Electric & Gas Co. in legislative hearings and rate cases, and he defended polio vaccine manufacturers against antitrust charges.

With Governor Meyner's second term ending, state Democratic leaders divided over a successor. Hughes, backed by Lord, the Mercer County chairman, became a compromise choice, and the leaders from the other counties accepted him

in February 1961. His Republican opponent was James P. Mitchell, who had been secretary of labor under President Dwight D. Eisenhower. Since both candidates were Roman Catholics, New Jersey was assured of its first governor of that faith one year after John F. Kennedy was elected as the country's first Catholic president. Mitchell was better known, but Hughes was a better campaigner. Hughes's heartiness, wit, familiarity with state problems, criticism of Mitchell for refusing to debate, and tactful identification with Meyner's achievements generated considerable momentum, while Mitchell, handicapped by a broken leg, waged a lackluster campaign. On November 7, 1961, in a major upset, Hughes defeated Mitchell, 1,084,194 votes to 1,049,274. But the legislature remained split, the senate under Republican control and the general assembly under the Democrats.

Hughes's basic first-term problem was to expand state operations adequately to serve a rapidly growing population. He was constrained by the narrowness of his electoral mandate, by limited revenue due to lack of a broad-based tax, by county political organizations wary of gubernatorial power, and by a public uneducated to state needs. He stumped ceaselessly to build public support for the expansion of governmental operations and other policies he generally termed "Northern Democratic liberalism." By negotiating realistically he got Republican senate leaders to cooperate on compromise legislation, even though he was feuding with them over their "advise and consent" role on his nominations and vowing to destroy their "vicious" caucus.

His essential optimism helped him survive the voters' decisive rejection of his $750-million capital construction bond referendum in November 1963, for which he campaigned exhaustively and through which he hoped to defer the tax question and aid the state's economy. In that election the Democrats lost fourteen legislative seats; former Governor Meyner virtually declared his willingness to be the next Democratic gubernatorial candidate if Hughes chose not to run again, and the archcritical *Newark Evening News* called for Hughes's resignation. Rebounding, he proposed an income tax on February 3, 1964, to finance his record $590-million budget for 1964–65. His proposal stimulated debate but got nowhere.

In Hughes's first term he provided swift emergency relief to the seashore after a severe storm battered it in March 1962; suspended land sales in the Hackensack Meadows pending resolution of title claims; created the Commission to Study Meadowlands Development in May 1963, appointing Meyner as chairman; brought the Democratic National Convention for the first time to New Jersey (Atlantic City, August 1964); vetoed a bill requiring children in public schools to salute the flag and pledge allegiance in contravention to a United States Supreme Court ruling (June 1964); secured the takeover of the Hudson and Manhattan Railroad by the Port of New York Authority in return for approval of the construction of the World Trade Center; formed a citizens' committee, headed by Princeton University President Robert F. Goheen, to examine public higher education; and supported police behavior during civil disorders in Jersey City and Paterson, meanwhile urging social reforms to eliminate causes of discontent.

The character of the 1965 gubernatorial campaign shaped Hughes's second term. He expected sharp campaign debates on state priorities, based on his record and his charges of "legislative inaction." Instead, his Republican rival, state Senator Wayne Dumont, Jr., revived the flag salute controversy and vigorously belabored Hughes for not forcing Rutgers, the State University, to dismiss history professor Eugene D. Genovese, who had welcomed "the impending Viet Cong victory in Viet Nam" at a teach-in. Hughes upheld United States policy in Viet Nam and called Genovese "outrageously wrong," but nevertheless stoutly defended his right to speak. When Dumont refused to drop the issue and implied that

Hughes was tolerating treason, Hughes charged him with disregarding the Bill of Rights and instigating a process that would end in "book burning and concentration camps." The emotional dispute galvanized liberals and independents behind Hughes, who already had substantial labor support. He swept to victory on November 2, 1965, with 1,279,589 votes to Dumont's 915,996, a record plurality. Further, both legislative branches came under Democratic control for the first time since 1914.

Hughes now had a clear mandate, but he needed a major new source of revenue. He staked all on an income tax. He expected speedy legislative approval in the belief that many Democrats who owed their seats to his sweeping victory would vote along party lines. Consequently he neglected to court the Republicans energetically or to appeal to the wider public. However, he underestimated the Democratic legislators' fear of voter reprisal and overvalued the key Democratic county chairmen's reluctant commitments of support. With some Democrats defecting and Republicans solidly opposed, his income tax bill only narrowly passed the general assembly on March 17, 1966, and it never reached the floor of the senate, where it faced certain defeat. A chastened Hughes, "the most regular of Regular Democrats," never again relied solely on his party or its chiefs to back major legislation. Turning to a sales tax, he quickly reasserted leadership, secured bipartisan support, and enlisted a sizable public coalition that induced the legislature on April 26, 1966, to pass New Jersey's first permanent broad-based tax and finance an $875-million state budget.

Encouraged by this success, his administration released a torrent of bills for legislative action that altered the scope and structure of state government and its relationship to the people. But the Democratic tide ebbed in November 1967, when Republicans captured the legislature in sufficient strength to override gubernatorial vetoes. Hughes, therefore, in his final two years, made more compromises than he might have wished on measures affecting the large cities and increasing governmental services. During his eight years 2,174 laws were enacted, more than under any other governor except A. Harry Moore, who served nine years, and Alfred E. Driscoll, who served seven.

Some of the notable legislative and administrative actions in Hughes's second term involved the functions and organization of state government. The Department of Community Affairs became operative in March 1967, the State Commission of Investigation was created for a five-year period in January 1969, and the Division of Criminal Justice, the Office of State Public Defender, and the Office of Consumer Protection were set up in the Department of Law and Public Safety. The Department of Transportation replaced the State Highway Department in May 1966; it had an enlarged mission to upgrade rail and bus services. The Hackensack Meadowlands Commission was established in November 1968 to plan orderly development for a vast tract in the northeastern part of the state.

The state's role in education grew when the Department of Higher Education, separate from the existing Department of Education, was created in January 1967 with a chancellor and a state board. The county community college system was established in 1966, and construction was begun on new public medical schools at Newark and Piscataway between 1968 and 1970. Two new state colleges were approved, and fiscal autonomy was granted to the state colleges in 1969.

In finance, the Sales and Use Tax Act, with an initial levy of 3 percent, became effective in July 1966; banks got permission to expand across county lines, and voters approved a state lottery in a referendum in November 1969.

The public service roles of state governmental agencies and public authorities expanded enormously at this time. The Garden State Arts Center was constructed, despite a cost overrun from an estimated $1.6 million to over $6.5 million. Funding for the Public Broadcasting Authority was approved by referendum in November 1968, and the first state funds were allotted the New Jersey Symphony Orchestra in December 1969. In 1968 the Housing Finance Agency was set up within the Department of Community Affairs and a $12.5 million low-income housing assistance bond referendum was passed, and in May 1969 Hughes signed a bill that would eventually provide $1 million to tear down dilapidated structures in cities. Among Hughes's last measures was to sign into law in January 1970 an act allowing people to challenge alleged exclusionary zoning in communities they did not live in.

Two new bridges across the Delaware River in South Jersey were started in 1966, and a $640 million transportation bond referendum was approved by the voters in November 1968. The New Jersey Historical Commission was established in the Department of Education in 1966, and an Educational Opportunity Fund Act, providing support to college-bound disadvantaged youth, was enacted in 1968. In January 1969 the legislature appropriated $23 million as the state's share of county and municipal welfare costs. The Migrant Labor Act of December 1967 set higher living standards for seasonal farm workers, but an act providing unemployment benefits to striking workers, passed in April 1967, was repealed in February 1968. Purchasers of firearms were required to secure police identification cards (June 1966). These and similar measures that increased the dimensions of governmental authority and operations during Hughes's second term generally paralleled the greatly enlarged role of the federal government under President Lyndon B. Johnson's "Great Society" programs of the mid-1960s.

On July 14, 1967, Newark's Mayor Hugh J. Addonizio asked Hughes to dispatch state police and national guardsmen to end civil disorders in the black ghetto of the city. Hughes took personal charge of the law enforcement operations. He termed the disorders "plain and simple crime and not a civil rights protest" and asserted that "the line between the jungle and the law might as well be drawn here as any place in America." Hughes soon grasped the deeper socioeconomic causes of Newark's crisis. But his initial stance helped shape public opinion and perhaps encouraged excessively forceful police actions that injured innocent persons and prolonged the unrest. When violence erupted in Plainfield on July 16, Hughes allowed the state police to search for stolen weapons without warrants in a black neighborhood.

A commission of ten prominent citizens whom he named to analyze the disorders and recommend steps to prevent recurrence barely mentioned his role and actions in its report, issued in February 1968. Hughes hailed the report as "historic" but delayed implementing its recommendations because he was grappling with personal pessimism over urban problems and with the fear of voter backlash against his party. Members of the commission and of his cabinet increased the pressure for remedial action.

Further disorders followed the murder of Martin Luther King, Jr., on April 4, and he delivered a special legislative message on April 25 calling for a "moral recommitment" to the cities. He requested an initial $126.1 million to aid ghetto schools, improve law enforcement, and relieve local welfare burdens. The legislature appropriated $58.5 million, enough to start an urban aid program, and Hughes, consistent in his urban-oriented liberalism, voiced the conviction that the problems of New Jersey's cities were soluble.

Hughes was known nationally for stalwart support of the foreign policies of presidents John F. Kennedy and Lyndon B. Johnson. He once described the latter as "the master strategist of the century." He served on a presidential advisory committee on civil defense until 1967. He helped arrange Johnson's meeting with Soviet Premier Alexei Kosygin, June 23–25, 1967, at the state college in Glassboro. In August 1967, Johnson appointed Hughes to a panel to observe the South Vietnamese elections, which the governor judged to be open and fair. He did not break publicly with Johnson's policies until October 30, 1968, when he urged a bombing halt and a United States withdrawal from Viet Nam. In March 1968 he became chairman of the Democratic party's Equal Rights Committee.

At the party's Chicago convention in August, he headed the 82-vote New Jersey delegation, which endorsed Senator Hubert H. Humphrey's nomination for the presidency. Hughes served as chairman of the convention's Credentials Committee, which screened over one thousand delegate challenges. His firm handling of the challenges on the basis of nondiscrimination won overwhelming convention approval, but he lost his own rather low-keyed quest for the vice-presidential nomination to Senator Edmund Muskie. Hughes was "bitterly disappointed" by what he termed "the hate vote" which Governor George Wallace got in the presidential elections in New Jersey in November 1968, and he felt it facilitated Richard M. Nixon's capture of the state. After the Democratic defeat, Hughes urged the party to make internal reforms, press voter registration, and build "a coalition which includes labor and the blacks to correct such problems as urban ills." In Richard Nixon's first year in office, Hughes criticized the president for reducing urban assistance programs without seeking comparable cuts in funds for antiballistic missiles and the supersonic transport.

At the end of his governorship Hughes maintained that he had fulfilled his intentions of giving the state a sense of identity and destiny and aiding "the forgotten New Jerseyans." On January 16, 1970, he declared his family's net worth, which was $178,986; this unprecedented step exemplified the public disclosure he advocated for state officials.

He resumed private law practice, joining the Newark firm of Hughes, McElroy, Connell, Foley & Geiser, and becoming chairman of the American Bar Association's commission on improving prison facilities and rehabilitation procedures. He was named state Democratic national committeeman on February 27, 1970.

After state supreme court Chief Justice Pierre P. Garven died, Governor William T. Cahill nominated Hughes to replace him. Confirmed by the senate, Hughes was sworn on December 18, 1973, the first person in modern history to have been both governor and chief justice of New Jersey.

As chief justice he directed an increasingly activist court, which handed down pathbreaking decisions on zoning, legislative redistricting and thorough and efficient education. In 1979, when he reached the mandatory retirement age of 70, he went back to private legal practice.

Records of Governor Richard J. Hughes, New Jersey State Library, Bureau of Archives and History, Trenton, N.J.

Felzenberg, Alvin S. "The Impact of Gubernatorial Style on Policy Outcomes: An In Depth Study of Three New Jersey Governors." Ph.D. dissertation, Princeton University, 1978.

Leone, Richard C. "The Politics of Gubernatorial Leadership: Tax and Education Reform in New Jersey." Ph.D. dissertation, Princeton University, 1969.

Stanley B. Winters

WILLIAM THOMAS CAHILL (b. June 25, 1912) was born in Philadelphia. His parents, William and Rose (Golden) Cahill, moved to Camden in 1919. William, their only child, attended St. Mary's Grammar and Camden Catholic High schools. He graduated with a B.A. degree from Philadelphia's St. Joseph's College in 1933. While attending South Jersey (Rutgers)

Law School and receiving the LL.B. in 1937, he taught in the Camden public school system. Cahill served briefly as an FBI agent but, after passing the state bar in 1939, he entered the private practice of law in Camden. On February 1, 1941, he was married to a former high school classmate, Elizabeth Myrtetus. The couple would eventually have eight children, six girls and two boys.

At various times Cahill filled public offices typically held by politically oriented lawyers. He was Camden city prosecutor, 1944–45, and assistant county prosecutor, 1948–51. As a special deputy attorney general in 1951 he took part in a state investigation of organized crime and gambling in Bergen County. In 1951 Cahill also made his first try for elective public office, a successful campaign for state assemblyman. He served but one term, choosing a return to full-time law practice after the end of the 1953 legislative session. In 1958 he returned to the political wars, winning a congressional seat in a district drawn from Camden, Gloucester and Salem counties. He was reelected from this First District in 1960, 1962 and 1964 and, following reapportionment, from the Sixth District in 1966 and 1968. In the House of Representatives, Cahill was a member of the Judiciary Committee. He took particular interest in anticrime, civil rights and consumer affairs legislation, but he was also active in such areas as medical education, housing and immigration. Cahill developed an issue image much like that of United States Senator Clifford P. Case, one of moderate-to-liberal Republicanism. And, like Case, he generally enjoyed the support of organized labor.

Cahill's name was presented to the GOP's screening committee as a possible gubernatorial nominee in 1965, but he eventually withdrew it. He did not contest the nomination of state Senator Wayne Dumont, Jr. (Dumont, however, had to overcome a primary challenge by South Jersey Congressman Charles W. Sandman.) In 1969, Cahill, Sandman, and three other GOP hopefuls engaged in a free-swinging primary battle. Cahill was triumphant. He had received strong support from Bergen County party chairman Nelson Gross, who was riding the crest of his own victory as Richard M. Nixon's New Jersey strategist in 1968. During both primary and general election campaigns, Cahill projected a political personality as a blunt, forthright individual balanced by a quick smile and the traditional Irish sense of humor. Physically, in 1969, he was of medium build, five feet nine inches and 175 pounds, with gray hair and a ruddy complexion.

Cahill's Democratic opponent in the gubernatorial contest was former Governor Robert B. Meyner, who argued that he had the experience and sensitivity to meet the challenges ahead. It was "a matter of record," the Democratic nominee argued, that he had the capacity to manage the state's affairs prudently and effectively. For his part, Cahill characterized the Meyner administrations of the 1950s as "do-little," and he argued that Meyner himself was a passé politician who lacked the vision necessary to handle the increasing responsibilities of the governorship. Cahill endeavored to project the image of a dynamic, progressive statesman—"the" man to meet the needs of New Jersey.

There was more to the 1969 campaign than image projection; there were gut political questions as well. Could the Republicans sustain their party's momentum after the Nixon landslide? Would the hostility of Hudson County boss John V. Kenny and segments of organized labor deprive Meyner of the big-county vote usually considered essential for a Democratic victory? Did the voters want to give the GOP a chance at the State House after long years of Democratic control? Did they accept the Republican cry that it was "Sixteen Years Downhill. Time to Go Cahill"? The answers to these questions were apparently all in the affirmative, for on November 4, 1969, the Republicans achieved a classic landslide victory. Cahill swept twenty of twenty-one counties, and his party won impressive majorities in both houses of the state legislature—31 to 9 in the senate; 59 to 21 in the general assembly. Thus Cahill was in a position rare for a New Jersey governor—facing a friendly legislature—when he took over as the state's chief executive on January 20, 1970.

In his brief inaugural address, Governor Cahill pledged to root out corruption in government and refurbish the state's political image, badly tarnished by recurrent scandals involving organized crime and errant public officials. In setting a functional tone for his administration, Cahill implied that he would continue down the paths mapped out by the regimes of the 1960s. He placed particular emphasis on doing more—and better—in the fields of education, law enforcement and transportation, but he also promised action in such areas as housing and health care. These programs would require funding, and here the new governor faced his first crisis: a projected $268-million deficit for fiscal 1971. The outgoing Hughes administration had largely developed the budget for the new year, but it was Cahill's responsibility to introduce it and suggest how to achieve the income-outgo balance mandated by the state constitution. Cahill opted for a two-cent increase in the sales tax to bridge the budget gap, and the GOP-controlled legislature passed an authorizing statute on February 9.

The governor believed that this was a stopgap measure—that the state sorely needed tax and administrative reform to meet the needs of the 1970s adequately and efficiently. Accordingly, two study groups were authorized by executive order in the spring of 1970. The first was the Governor's Management Study Commission, headed by Prudential Insurance Company Vice-President William S. Field. The second, the New Jersey Tax Policy Committee, chaired by state Senator Harry L. Sears, included such blue-ribbon names as former governors Driscoll and Hughes. The management committee would report back that November; the tax committee did not issue its report until February 1972.

Meanwhile, the governor took advantage of Republican dominance to move a diversified program through the legislature in 1970–71. In the field of education, for example, Rutgers Medical School was merged with the New Jersey College of Medicine and Dentistry, a program of state aid to private and parochial schools was inaugurated and, in October of 1970, the so-called Bateman School Funding Act was passed. This law attempted to provide additional state funds for ratable-poor school districts and those with large numbers of disadvantaged students. Finally, in November 1971, the voters approved a $155-million bond issue for higher education facilities.

In the area of law enforcement, new legislation placed prosecutors in the six most populous counties on a full-time basis and created a Division of Criminal Justice to aid the attorney general in dealing with statewide crime and official corruption. In November 1970, the life of the temporary State Commission of Investigation, set up in 1968 to combat organized crime, was extended for five years. Cahill also promoted an ambitious drug control program that received statutory foundation in a Controlled Dangerous Substances law, as well as in new measures dealing with drug education and treatment.

The 1970–1971 legislators, active in the environmental field, passed a solid-waste management act promoting regional solutions to New Jersey's refuse problems, and a wetlands act giving the state controls over land use and pollution in estuaries and tidal areas. In November 1971, an $80-million "Green Acres" bond issue was approved, enabling New Jersey to continue its program of acquiring land for recreation and conservation. The Republican administration could also claim credit for a consumer protection law and a new program of financial aid to New Jersey's urban centers.

As indicated, Cahill's administrative study commission issued its report late in 1970. Reflecting a business management perspective, the report contained some seven hundred recommendations covering the state's seventeen principal departments, as well as sundry state and interstate agencies. One of its major aims was to reduce the governor's span of control by consolidating the functions of fifteen departments into four new "super-departments"—administration, planning and control, public services, and development. A reorganized attorney general's department would remain, but the secretary of state would be reduced to the role of the governor's political adviser, with scant administrative responsibility. A second key goal was to give the governor a centralized bloc of management controls —personnel, budgeting, purchasing, planning—over the state bureaucracy. The Civil Service Commission was to be abolished and many of its functions would be transferred to the proposed department of administration.

Such drastic executive branch changes would upset existing agency-clientele relationships, reduce the number of patronage positions available for political favorites, and decimate the civil service system. Small wonder, then, that the legislature rejected the commission's two central themes. Nonetheless, the Cahill administration carried out a number of its suggestions via executive order, administrative directive and, in a few cases, specific statutory authorization.

As William Cahill closed out the first half of his term, he had a generally impressive record. In addition to legislative and administrative accomplishments, it contained other "plus" items. Under his aegis a successful state lottery was begun, the New York football Giants were enticed into the sports complex being constructed in the Hackensack Meadows, riots in the Rahway prison and Yardville correctional center were dealt with in a firm, yet humane manner. On the negative side, New Jersey's cities showed few signs of revival, a chronic housing shortage continued, and the costs of proliferating welfare and education programs put inexorable pressure on the state budget. Two special messages from the governor failed to stimulate legislative action in the housing crisis. Finally the November 1971 elections curbed Republican legislative power. The GOP majority in the senate was reduced to 24-16, while the new assembly contained forty Democrats, thirty-nine Republicans, and one independent. The votes of four Hudson County Democrats enabled the GOP to secure the assembly speakership for 1972-73, but the party situation in the lower house was perilously close to stalemate.

The watershed year of the Cahill administration was 1972, the year it attempted basic fiscal reform, failed, and never really regained its momentum. As the year begun, events conspired to bring the state's fiscal problems into sharp focus. On January 19, Superior Court Judge Theodore Botter, in the landmark case *Robinson* v. *Cahill,* declared New Jersey's system of school finance unconstitutional and mandated that the legislature develop a new one. On February 14, Cahill presented the state with its first $2-billion budget, including a projected deficit of $126.8 million. On February 23, the prestigious Tax Policy Committee submitted its five-volume report and recommendations.

The committee's objective was a "balanced" tax structure for New Jersey, to be achieved by drastically reducing the role of the local property tax in New Jersey finance. The committee proposed that the state assume most of the responsibility for school support, that counties be relieved of such financial burdens as courts and welfare, and that a new, bloc-grant approach to urban aid be adopted. To fund this revolutionary shift in state-local responsibilities, the committee proposed a new statewide property tax of $1 per $100 of assessed valuation, a graduated income tax at rates ranging from 1.5 to 14 percent, and the elimination of various exemptions in the sales tax.

The governor said little about the report for the next few months, waiting to see what the public reaction would be.

This showed that New Jersey's traditional hostility towards the concept of an income tax was still very much alive. Cahill finally resolved to take the offensive, and on June 1 began a crusade in the press and on the podium to promote the basics of the committee program. Concurrently, GOP assembly leader Richard DeKorte prepared and introduced bills, and a special summer session of the legislature was convened. Despite the governor's salesmanship, the income-tax bill—the centerpiece of his fiscal reform package—was slaughtered in the assembly by a 52-23 vote on July 17, 1972.

The governor had other setbacks. During the summer, indictments were returned against Cahill's longtime friend and confidant, Secretary of State Paul J. Sherwin, and GOP fund raiser William C. Loughran, on bribery and extortion charges arising out of a highway construction contract. The two men were tried and convicted in October, tarnishing the administration's anticorruption image. The press also charged that the attorney general's office had tried to "cover up" the Sherwin affair. (This charge was later investigated and refuted by a special prosecutor.) In the November 1972 general elections the voters rejected a $650-million bond issue designed to update the state's highway and mass transit systems, as well as a proposed constitutional amendment that would have given the governor power to remove the secretary of state and attorney general at pleasure. (The 1947 constitution had specifically exempted these positions from the chief executive's broad removal power.)

Although the Cahill administration had clearly lost much of its initiative and at least some of its image, Richard M. Nixon's 1972 landslide victory in New Jersey led political seers to assert, as 1973 opened, that Cahill would again be the Republican standard-bearer, and that he would be almost impossible to beat in the upcoming gubernatorial contest. The governor himself presented an annual message to the legislature, on January 8, that was hardly a "farewell address" in tone and approach. Rather, Cahill spoke of unfinished business—in such areas as transportation, housing, urban aid and environmental protection—and of his dream of continuing to strive for "the achievement of greatness" by the state of New Jersey.

Cahill once more pointed to the need for tax reform but handed the legislature the mantle of responsibility in that area. That the lawmakers would, however, bestir themselves in an election year was a dubious proposition, as Cahill himself realized. Hence, his policy recommendations (except for a new, urban-oriented Safe and Clean Streets proposal) generally required little new financing, and he designed his fiscal 1974 budget to use existing revenue sources. Representing a $333.8-million increase from 1973's $2-billion budget, it showed how the costs of education, welfare, and other ongoing programs were continuing to escalate.

To no one's surprise, William Cahill announced on March 22, 1973, that he was a candidate for renomination. (Again to no one's surprise, Congressman Sandman entered the primary lists as well.) Cahill brushed aside the corruption issue: "I have enough confidence in the people of New Jersey that they know Bill Cahill is honest and that they know Bill Cahill has done his best to root out corruption in every area." But the issue did not die. On April 8, the press reported that state and federal agents were probing the activities of key administration and Republican figures. On April 19, indictments were returned against two GOP fund-raisers on bribery-conspiracy charges relating to the deposit of state funds in a politically favored bank. Then, in May there was a veritable parade of indictments involving various alleged irregularities, including aspects of the financing of Cahill's 1969 campaign. Among those indicted were former State Treasurer Joseph McCrane, Harry Sears, and Nelson Gross.

The simultaneous unraveling of the Watergate conspiracy added to the governor's woes. Press accounts embarrassing to incumbent President Nixon stood side by side with articles devastating to the cause of incumbent Governor Cahill. In the showdown vote on June 5, the governor carried only five counties, as Sandman secured the nomination in his third successive try. On the Democratic side, former Superior Court Judge Brendan T. Byrne, with strong organization support, easily won his party's nomination.

With politics taking center stage in the fall (all 120 legislative seats were at stake in 1973), Cahill conducted what was largely a holding operation to close out his gubernatorial term. He could, however, look back on another productive two years of policymaking, for the 1972–73 legislature added significant measures to the statute books. A modern optional charter law was passed for New Jersey counties, paralleling the Faulkner Act for municipalities; the Safe and Clean Neighborhoods Act was approved and funded; the state began a program of service grants to private colleges and universities; no-fault automobile insurance was introduced; a health-care facilities act was passed, as was legislation designed to cope with problem juveniles. The Coastal Area Facilities Review Act of 1973 (CAFRA) marked another major assumption of power by state government in the area of land-use control. On the other hand, Cahill failed in his efforts to obtain a general overhaul of New Jersey's planning and zoning laws. The legislature also refused to act on tax reform in 1973 despite a state supreme court decision on April 3, 1973, upholding the major thrust of the Botter ruling.

Following the November elections, the governor and his staff devoted most of their energies to budget preparation and to orienting the Byrne team to the responsibilities it would assume in January. William Cahill then returned to private life and the practice of law.

Records of Governor William T. Cahill, New Jersey State Library, Bureau of Archives and History, Trenton, N.J.

Felzenberg, Alvin S. "The Impact of Gubernatorial Style on Policy Outcomes: An In Depth Study of Three New Jersey Governors." Ph.D. dissertation, Princeton University, 1978.

Richard J. Connors

GENERAL BIBLIOGRAPHY

Books and Pamphlets

[Agnew, Daniel.] *Major Richard Howell of New Jersey.* [Philadelphia: n.p.,] 1876. Rutgers University Special Collections, New Brunswick, N.J.

Andrews, Charles M. *The Colonial Period of American History.* Vol. 3. New Haven: Yale University Press, 1934.

Applegate, John Stillwell. *Early Courts and Lawyers of Monmouth County. . . .* Freehold: [Monmouth County Bar Association,] 1911.

Baker, Ray Stannard. *Woodrow Wilson: Life and Letters.* 8 vols. Garden City, N.Y.: Doubleday, Page and Co., 1927–39.

Barnes, Viola F. *The Dominion of New England: A Study in British Colonial Policy.* New Haven: Yale University Press, 1923.

Bernard, Francis. *Select Letters on the Trade and Government of America. . . .* London: W. Bowyer and J. Nichols, 1774.

Bigelow, Samuel F., and Hagar, George J., eds. *The Biographical Cyclopedia of New Jersey. . . .* New York: National Americana Society, n.d.

The Biographical Encyclopedia of New Jersey in the Nineteenth Century. Philadelphia: Galaxy Publishing Co., 1877.

Bloodgood, Fred L. *The Quiet Hour.* Trenton: MacCrellish & Quigley, 1940.

Blum, John Morton. *Joe Tumulty and the Wilson Era.* Boston: Houghton Mifflin, 1951.

Breen, Timothy. *The Character of the Good Ruler: A Study of Puritan Political Ideas, 1630–1730.* New Haven: Yale University Press, 1970.

A Brief Sketch of the Life and Public Services of Theodore F. Randolph, Democratic Nominee for Governor of New Jersey. n.p.: Democratic Committee, 1868.

Cadman, John W. *The Corporation in New Jersey.* Cambridge, Mass.: Harvard University Press, 1949.

Calendar of State Papers, Colonial Series, America and West Indies, 1689–1720; Documents Relative to the Colonial History of the State of New York. Vols. 3–5.

Channing, Edward, and Coolidge, Archibald Cary, eds. *The Barrington-Bernard Correspondence. . . .* Cambridge, Mass.: Harvard University Press, 1912.

Connors, Richard J. *A Cycle of Power: The Career of Jersey City Mayor Frank Hague.* Metuchen, N.J.: Scarecrow Press, 1971.

_____. *The Process of Constitutional Revision in New Jersey, 1940–1947.* New York: National Municipal League, 1970.

Crystal, George. *This Republican Hoffman: The Life Story of Harold G. Hoffman, A Modern Fighter.* Hoboken, N.J.: n.p., 1934.

Cunningham, John T. *New Jersey: America's Main Road.* Garden City, N.Y.: Doubleday, 1966.

Cyclopedia of New Jersey Biography. . . . 6 vols. New York: The American Historical Society, 1923.

Dalton, Charles, ed. *English Army Lists and Commission Registers, 1661–1714.* Vol. 2. London: Eyre & Spottiswode, 1894.

————. *George the First's Army, 1714–1725.* Vol. 1. London: Eyre & Spottiswode, 1910.

Edge, Walter E. *A Jerseyman's Journal.* Princeton: Princeton University Press, 1948.

Ellis, Franklin. *History of Monmouth County. . . .* Philadelphia: R. T. Peck & Co., 1885.

Elmer, Lucius Q. C. *The Constitution and Government of the Province and State of New Jersey. . . .* In *Collections of the New Jersey Historical Society.* Vol. 7. Newark: Martin R. Dennis & Co., 1872.

Erdman, Charles R., Jr. *The New Jersey Constitution of 1776.* Princeton: Princeton University Press, 1929.

Fee, Walter R. *The Transition From Aristocracy to Democracy in New Jersey, 1789–1829.* Somerville, N.J.: Somerset Press, 1933.

Fisher, Edgar Jacob. *New Jersey as a Royal Province, 1738 to 1776.* New York: Columbia University, 1911.

Foster, John Y. *New Jersey and the Rebellion.* Newark: M. R. Dennis & Co., 1868.

Gerlach, Larry R. *Prologue to Independence: New Jersey in the Coming of the American Revolution.* New Brunswick: Rutgers University Press, 1975.

————. *William Franklin: New Jersey's Last Royal Governor.* Trenton: New Jersey Historical Commission, 1975.

Hall, Michael G. *Edward Randolph and the American Colonies, 1676–1703.* Chapel Hill: University of North Carolina Press, 1960.

Halsted, Oliver S. *Address upon the Character of the Late, the Honorable Isaac H. Williamson, Delivered before the Bar by Oliver S. Halsted.* Newark: A. Guest, 1844.

Hawke, David F. *The Colonial Experience.* Indianapolis: Bobbs-Merrill, 1966.

Higgins, Sophia. *The Bernards of Abington and Nether Winchendon: A Family History.* London: Longmans, Green, & Co., 1903.

Hirst, David W. *Woodrow Wilson, Reform Governor: A Documentary Narrative.* Princeton: D. Van Nostrand, 1965.

History of Morris County, New Jersey. . . . New York: Munsell, 1882.

Honeyman, A. Van Doren, ed. *History of Union County. . . .* Vols. 2, 3. New York: Lewis Historical Publishing Co., 1923.

————, ed. *Northwestern New Jersey: A History. . . .* Vols. 3, 4. New York: Lewis Historical Publishing Co., 1927.

Ingalsbe, Frederick W., comp. *Ingoldesby Genealogy.* Grand Rapids, Mich.: Press of U. G. Clarke, 1904.

Jennings, Samuel. *Truth Rescued from Forgery and Falsehood. . . .* Philadelphia: Reynier Janson, 1699.

Katz, Stanley. *Newcastle's New York: Anglo-American Politics, 1732–1753.* Cambridge, Mass.: Harvard University Press, 1968.

Kemmerer, Donald L. *Path to Freedom: The Struggle for Self-Government in Colonial New Jersey, 1703–1776.* Princeton: Princeton University Press, 1940.

Kerney, James. *The Political Education of Woodrow Wilson.* New York: Century, 1926.

Knapp, Charles M. *New Jersey Politics During the Period of the Civil War and Reconstruction.* Geneva, N.Y.: W. F. Humphrey, 1924.

Kull, Irving S., ed. *New Jersey: A History; Biographical and Genealogical Records.* Vol. 5. New York: The American Historical Society, 1930.

Lane, Wheaton J. *From Indian Trail to Iron Horse: Travel and Transportation in New Jersey, 1620–1860.* Princeton: Princeton University Press, 1939.

Leaming, Aaron, and Spicer, Jacob, eds. *The Grants, Concessions, and Original Constitutions of the Province of New*

Jersey. Philadelphia: William Bradford, 1758.

Lee, Francis Bazley. *Genealogical and Memorial History of the State of New Jersey.* 4 vols. New York: Lewis Historical Publishing Co., 1910.

――――. *History of New Jersey from the Most Remote Period to the Close of the 19th Century. . . .* Newark: Newark Book Publishing and Engraving Co., 1905.

――――, ed. *New Jersey as a Colony and as a State . . . : Biographical Volume.* Vol. 5. New York: Publishing Society of New Jersey, 1902.

[Leeds, Daniel.] *The Case Put and Decided. . . .* New York: W. Bradford, 1699.

Leiby, James R. *Charity and Correction in New Jersey: A History of State Welfare Institutions.* New Brunswick: Rutgers University Press, 1967.

The Letters to the Right Honourable the Earl of Hillsborough from Governor Bernard, General Gage, and the Honourable His Majesty's Council for the Province of Massachusetts-Bay. Boston: Edes and Gill, 1769.

Levine, Peter D. *The Behavior of State Legislative Parties in the Jacksonian Era: New Jersey, 1829–1844.* Rutherford, N.J.: Fairleigh Dickinson University Press, 1977.

Link, Arthur S. *Wilson.* 5 vols. Princeton: Princeton University Press, 1947–65.

Link, Arthur S., et al., eds. *The Papers of Woodrow Wilson.* 36 vols. to date. Princeton: Princeton University Press, 1966–.

Link, Eugene P. *Democratic-Republican Societies, 1790–1800.* New York: Columbia University Press, 1942.

Lockard, Duane. *The New Jersey Governor: A Study in Political Power.* Princeton: D. Van Nostrand, 1964.

Lott, John L., and Finch, James A., eds. *Official Opinions of the Attorneys-General of the United States.* Vol. 23. Washington: Government Printing Office, 1902.

McCarter, Robert H. *Memories of a Half Century at the New Jersey Bar.*

Camden: New Jersey State Bar Association, 1937.

McCormick, Richard P. *Experiment in Independence: New Jersey in the Critical Period, 1781–1798.* New Brunswick: Rutgers University Press, 1950.

――――. *The History of Voting in New Jersey. . . .* New Brunswick: Rutgers University Press, 1953.

――――. *New Jersey from Colony to State, 1609–1789.* Newark: The New Jersey Historical Society, 1981.

McKean, Dayton. *The Boss.* Boston: Houghton Mifflin, 1940.

McSeveney, Samuel T. *The Politics of Depression: Political Behavior in the Northeast, 1893–1896.* New York: Oxford University Press, 1972.

Moffat, William D., comp. *Addresses by John William Griggs.* n.p.: privately printed, 1930.

The Municipalities of Essex County. . . . Vols. 3, 4. New York: Lewis Historical Publishing Co., 1925.

Myers, William Starr. *George Brinton McClellan.* New York: Appleton-Century, 1934.

――――, ed. *The Story of New Jersey.* Vols. 4, 5. New York: Lewis Historical Publishing Co., 1945.

Nelson, William, ed. *The New Jersey Coast in Three Centuries.* 2 vols. New York: Lewis Publishing Co., 1902.

――――, ed. *Original Documents Relating to the Life and Administrations of William Burnet, Governor of New York and New Jersey, 1720–28.* Paterson: Press Printing and Publishing Co., 1897.

Nelson's Biographical Cyclopedia of New Jersey. 2 vols. New York: Eastern Historical Publishing Society, 1913.

Noble, Ransom E. *New Jersey Progressivism Before Wilson.* Princeton: Princeton University Press, 1946.

O'Connor, John E. *William Paterson: Lawyer and Statesman, 1745–1806.* New Brunswick: Rutgers University Press, 1979.

Ogden, Mary Depue, ed. *Memorial Cyclopedia of New Jersey.* 4 vols. Newark: Memorial History Co., 1915–1921.

Pasler, Rudolph J., and Margaret C. *The New Jersey Federalists.* Rutherford, N.J.: Fairleigh Dickinson University Press, 1975.

Personal and Political Sketch of Hon. Joel Parker. Freehold: Monmouth Democrat, 1871.

Pierce, Frank H., Jr. *The Governors of New Jersey.* Newark: Newark Evening News, [1952].

Pitney, Henry C., Jr., ed. *A History of Morris County, New Jersey, Embracing Upwards of Two Centuries, 1710–1913.* 2 vols. New York: Lewis Historical Publishing Co., 1914.

Platt, Hermann K., ed. *Charles Perrin Smith: New Jersey Political Reminiscences, 1828–1882.* New Brunswick: Rutgers University Press, 1965.

Pomfret, John E. *Colonial New Jersey: A History.* New York: Scribner's, 1973.

———. *The New Jersey Proprietors and Their Lands.* Princeton: D. Van Nostrand, 1964.

———. *The Province of East New Jersey, 1609–1702: The Rebellious Proprietary.* Princeton: Princeton University Press, 1962.

———. *The Province of West New Jersey, 1609–1702: A History of the Origins of an American Colony.* Princeton: Princeton University Press, 1956.

The Presidency. Sketch of the Democratic Candidate, Joel Parker. n.p., [1876].

Prince, Carl E. *New Jersey's Jeffersonian Republicans, 1789–1817.* Chapel Hill: University of North Carolina Press, 1967.

———. *William Livingston: New Jersey's First Governor.* Trenton: New Jersey Historical Commission, 1975.

Prince, Carl E., et al., eds. *The Papers of William Livingston.* 2 vols. to date. Trenton: New Jersey Historical Commission, 1979–.

Proceedings of the New Jersey Constitutional Convention of 1844. With an Introduction by John E. Bebout. Trenton: Federal Writers' Project, 1942.

Randolph, Theodore F. *Address of Governor Theodore F. Randolph of Morris to the Democratic State Convention, Assembled at Trenton, June 26, 1872.* Morristown: Louis C. Vogt, 1872.

———. *Letter of Governor Randolph of New Jersey, to Hon. Cortlandt Parker, Relating to Executive Prerogatives and Judicial Authority.* Trenton: Wm. T. Nicholson, 1871.

The Record of Leon Abbett . . . as Assemblyman, Senator and Governor. Jersey City: Heppenheimer, 1889.

Ricord, Frederick W. *Biographical Encyclopedia: Successful Men of New Jersey.* Vol. 1. New York: New Jersey Historical Publishing Co., 1896.

———, ed. *History of Union County, New Jersey.* Newark: East Jersey History Co., 1897.

Sackett, William E. *Modern Battles of Trenton. . . .* Vol. 1. Trenton: John L. Murphy, 1895.

———. *Modern Battles of Trenton. . . .* Vol. 2. New York: Neale Publishing Co., 1914.

Scannell's New Jersey's First Citizens. 6 vols. Paterson: J. J. Scannell, 1917–1927.

Schroth, Frank D. *The First Year, Being the Record of Accomplishment of George S. Silzer, Governor of New Jersey.* Trenton: MacCrellish & Quigley, 1924.

Sedgwick, Theodore, Jr. *A Memoir of the Life of William Livingston.* New York: Harper, 1833.

Shaw, Douglas V. *The Making of an Immigrant City: Ethnic and Cultural Conflict in Jersey City, New Jersey, 1850–1877.* New York: Arno Press, 1976.

Shaw, William H. *History of Essex and Hudson Counties, New Jersey.* Philadelphia: Everts and Peck, 1884.

Sheridan, Eugene R. *Lewis Morris, 1671–1746: A Study in Early American Politics.* Syracuse: Syracuse University Press, 1981.

Silzer, George S. *The Government of a State.* Newark: Soney & Sage Co., 1933.

Smith, William, Jr. *The History of the Province of New-York.* 2 vols. Edited by Michael Kammen. Cambridge,

Mass.: Harvard University Press, Belknap Press, 1972.

Snell, James P., et al. *History of Sussex and Warren Counties, New Jersey.* Philadelphia: Everts and Peck, 1881.

Sobel, Robert, and John Raimo, eds. *] iographical Directory of the Governor; of the United States, 1789–1978.* 4 vols. Westport, Conn.: Meckler Books, 1978.

Tanner, Edwin P. *The Province of New Jersey, 1664–1738.* New York: Columbia University Press, 1908.

Taylor, George Rogers. *The Great Tariff Debate, 1820–1830.* Boston: D. C. Heath, 1966.

Trueblood, D. Elton. *Robert Barclay.* New York: Macmillan, 1968.

Vance, Alanson A. *A Political Reminiscence.* Morristown, [1902].

Van Devander, Charles W. *The Big Bosses.* n.p.: Howell, Soskin Publishers, 1944.

Van Winkle, Daniel, ed. *History of the Municipalities of Hudson County . . . : Historical-Biographical.* Vol. 3. New York: Lewis Historical Publishing Co., 1924.

Venable, John D. *Out of the Shadow: The Story of Charles Edison.* East Orange, N.J.: Charles Edison Fund, 1978.

Westervelt, Frances A. *History of Bergen County . . . : Historical-Biographical.* Vol. 3. New York: Lewis Historical Publishing Co., 1923.

Whitehead, John. *The Judicial and Civil History of New Jersey.* [Boston]: Boston Historical Co., 1897.

Whitehead, William A. *Contributions to the Early History of Perth Amboy and the Adjoining Country . . .* New York: D. Appleton & Co., 1856.

———, ed. *The Papers of Lewis Morris.* In *Collections of The New Jersey Historical Society.* Vol. 4. New York: G. P. Putnam, 1852.

Who's Who in New Jersey. . . . Chicago: A. N. Marquis Co., 1939.

Williamson, Isaac H., and Wall, Garret P. *Opinion of I. H. Williamson esq. and Garret D. Wall, esq. in Relation to the Corporate Powers of the Trenton and New Brunswick Turnpike Company.*

Trenton: Joseph Justice, 1835.

Wilson, James Grant, ed. *The Memorial History of the City of New-York. . . .* 4 vols. New York: New York History Co., 1892–93.

Wright, William C. *The Secession Movement in the Middle Atlantic States.* Rutherford, N.J.: Fairleigh Dickinson University Press, 1973.

Articles

Alexander, Jack. "The Ungovernable Governor." *Saturday Evening Post* (January 23, 1943): p. 9.

Bernstein, David A. "William Livingston: The Role of the Executive in New Jersey's Revolutionary War." In *New Jersey in the American Revolution II,* edited by William C. Wright. Trenton: New Jersey Historical Commission, 1973.

Birkner, Michael J. "Peter Vroom and the Politics of Democracy." In *Jacksonian New Jersey,* edited by Paul A. Stellhorn. Trenton: New Jersey Historical Commission, 1979.

Brooks, Noah. "George T. Werts." *Harper's Weekly* 38 (March 3, 1894): 198.

Burritt, Richard D. "Another Edison Makes Some Discoveries." *New York Times Magazine* (October 12, 1941): pp. 16, 27.

Cody, Edward J. "The Growth of Toleration and Church-State Relations in New Jersey, 1689–1763: From Holy Men to Holy War." In *Economic and Social History of Colonial New Jersey,* edited by William C. Wright. Trenton: New Jersey Historical Commission, 1974.

[Colden, Cadwallader.] "Cadwallader Colden's *History of Governor William Cosby's Administration and of Lieutenant Governor George Clarke's Administration Through 1737."* The New-York Historical Society, *Collections* 68 (1935): 280–355.

Cook, Richard. "Lewis Morris—New Jer-

240 BIBLIOGRAPHY

sey's Colonial Poet-Governor." *Journal of the Rutgers University Library* 24 (1961): 100–113.

Dangerfield, George. "The Steamboat Case." In *Quarrels That Have Shaped the Constitution,* edited by John Garraty. New York: Harper & Row, 1964.

"The Direct Primary and the New Idea in New Jersey." *Outlook* 90 (September 12, 1908): 51–52.

Ellertsen, E. Peter. "Prosperity and Paper Money: The Loan Office Act of 1723." *New Jersey History* 85 (1967): 47–57.

Ershkowitz, Herbert. "Samuel L. Southard: A Case Study of Whig Leadership in the Age of Jackson." *New Jersey History* 88 (Spring 1970): 5–24.

Fennelly, Catherine. "William Franklin of New Jersey." *William and Mary Quarterly* 6 (1949): 361–82. Holdsworth, L.V. "The Problem of Edward Byllynge . . . His Connection with Cornwall." In *The Children of Light,* edited by H. H. Brinton. New York: Macmillan, 1938.

McGuire, Maureen. "Struggle over the Purse: Gov. Morris v. N.J. Assembly." *Proceedings of the New Jersey Historical Society* 82 (1964): 200–207.

Nadelhaft, J. R. "Politics and the Judicial Tenure Fight in Colonial New Jersey." *William and Mary Quarterly* 28 (January 1971): 46–63.

Namier, Lewis. "Charles Garth and His Connexions." *English Historical Review* 54 (July 1939): 443–70.

Nelson, William. "The Administration of William Burnet, 1720–28." In *The Memorial History of the City of New-York . . . ,* edited by James Grant Wilson. Vol. 2. New York: New York History Co., 1892. Nickalls, J. L. "The Problem of Edward Byllynge: His Writings . . . and Influence on the First Constitution of West Jersey." In *The Children of Light,* edited by H. H. Brinton. New York: Macmillan, 1938.

Nixon, John T. "The Circumstances Attending the Election of William Pennington . . . as Speaker of the Thirty-Sixth Congress." *Proceedings of the New Jersey Historical Society* 2 (1872): 207–20.

O'Connor, John E. "Legal Reform in the Early Republic: The New Jersey Experience." *American Journal of Legal History* 22 (April 1978): 95–117.

Ogden, Aaron. "Autobiography of Col. Aaron Ogden of Elizabethtown." *Proceedings of the New Jersey Historical Society* 12 (1892–1893): 15–31.

Pierce, Arthur D. "A Governor in Skirts." *Proceedings of the New Jersey Historical Society* 83 (1965): 1–9.

Pomfret, John E. "Edward Byllynge's Proposed Gift of Land to Indigent Friends." *Pennsylvania Magazine of History and Biography* 61 (1937): 88–92.

———. "The Problem of the West Jersey Concessions of 1676/77." *William and Mary Quarterly* 5 (1948): 95–105.

———. "Thomas Budd's 'True and Perfect Account' of Byllynge's Proprieties in West New Jersey." *William and Mary Quarterly* 5 (1948): 325–31.

Pumpelly, Josiah C. "Mahlon Dickerson, Industrial Pioneer and Old Time Patriot." *Proceedings of the New Jersey Historical Society* 11 (1891): 131–56.

Rubincam, Milton. "The Formative Years of Lord Cornbury, The First Royal Governor of New York and New Jersey." *New York Genealogical and Biographical Record* 81 (1904): 106–16.

Scanlon, James E. "English Intrigue and the Governorship of Robert Hunter." *New-York Historical Society Quarterly* 57 (1973): 199–211.

Scull, G. D. "Biographical Notice of Doctor Daniel Coxe, of London." *Pennsylvania Magazine of History and Biography* 7 (1883): 317–37.

Shipton, Clifford K. "Jonathan Belcher." In Shipton, Clifford K. *Sibley's Harvard Graduates.* Vol. 4. Cambridge, Mass.: Harvard University Press, 1933.

Sly, John F. "Walter Evans Edge, 1873–1956: A Tribute." *Proceedings of the New Jersey Historical Society* 79 (1961): 1–15.

Spencer, Charles Worthen. "The Cornbury Legend." *New York State Historical*

Association Proceedings 13 (1914): 309–20.

Steffens, Lincoln. "New Jersey: A Traitor State." *McClure's Magazine* 24 (April 1905): 649–64.

Stickle, Warren E. "Edward I. Edwards and the Urban Coalition of 1919." *New Jersey History* 90 (1972): 83–96.

Turner, Gordon B. "Lewis Morris and the Colonial Government Problem." *Proceedings of the New Jersey Historical Society* 67 (1949): 260–304.

Weart, Jacob. "Speaker William Pennington." *New Jersey Law Journal* 20 (July–August 1897): 230–39.

Whitehead, William A. "Biographical Sketch of William Franklin, Governor of New Jersey from 1763 to 1776." *Proceedings of the New Jersey Historical Society* 3 (1848): 137–59.

Yard, James S. "Joel Parker, 'The War Governor of New Jersey.' . . . " *Proceedings of the New Jersey Historical Society* 10 (1888–1889): 57–92.

Unpublished Studies

Beckwith, Robert R. "Mahlon Dickerson of New Jersey, 1770–1853." Ph.D. dissertation, Columbia University, 1964.

Birkner, Michael J. "Politics, Law and Enterprise in Jacksonian America: The Career of Samuel Lewis Southard." Ph.D. dissertation, University of Virginia, 1981.

Black, Frederick R. "The Last Lords Proprietors of West Jersey: The West Jersey Society, 1692–1702." Ph.D. dissertation, Rutgers University, 1964.

Bloom, Jeanne Gould. "Sir Edmund Andros." Ph.D. dissertation, Yale University, 1962.

Bryan, Brantz Mayer. "Alfred Eastlack Driscoll: Governor of New Jersey." Senior thesis, Princeton University, 1952.

Cutler, Robert G. "Charter Reviewed: The New Jersey Constitution, 1947–1957." Ph.D. dissertation, Princeton University, 1958.

Ershkowitz, Herbert. "New Jersey Politics During the Era of Andrew Jackson, 1820–1837." Ph.D. dissertation, New York University, 1965.

Fallaw, W. Robert. "The Rise of the Whig Party in New Jersey." Ph.D. dissertation, Princeton University, 1967.

Felzenberg, Alvin S. "The Impact of Gubernatorial Style on Policy Outcomes: An In Depth Study of Three New Jersey Governors." Ph.D. dissertation, Princeton University, 1978.

Herrmann, Frederick M. "Stress and Structure: Political Change in Antebellum New Jersey." Ph.D. dissertation, Rutgers University, 1976.

Hogarty, Richard A. "Leon Abbett of New Jersey: Precursor of the Modern Governor." Ph.D. dissertation, Princeton University, 1965.

Klein, Milton M. "The American Whig: William Livingston of New York." Ph.D. dissertation, Columbia University, 1954.

Latschar, John A. "East New Jersey, 1665–1682: Perils of a Proprietary Government." Ph.D. dissertation, Rutgers University, 1978.

Leone, Richard C. "The Politics of Gubernatorial Leadership: Tax and Education Reform in New Jersey." Ph.D. dissertation, Princeton University, 1969.

Levine, Peter D. "Party-in-the Legislature: New Jersey, 1829–1844." Ph.D. dissertation, Rutgers University, 1971.

McCreary, John R. "Ambition, Interest and Faction: Politics in New Jersey, 1702–1738." Ph.D. dissertation, University of Nebraska, 1971.

Mahoney, Joseph F. "New Jersey Politics After Wilson: Progressivism in Decline." Ph.D. dissertation, Columbia University, 1964.

Mariboe, William H. "The Life of William Franklin, 1730(31)–1813: *Pro Rege et Patria.*" Ph.D. dissertation, University of Pennsylvania, 1962.

Peterson, Kent A. "New Jersey Politics and National Policymaking, 1865–1868." Ph.D. dissertation, Princeton University, 1970.

Purvis, Thomas L. "The New Jersey Assembly, 1722–1776." Ph.D. dissertation, Johns Hopkins University, 1979.

Reynolds, John F. "Testing Democracy: Electoral Participation and Progressive Reform in New Jersey, 1888–1919." Ph.D. dissertation, Rutgers University, 1980.

Scanlon, James E. "A Life of Robert Hunter, 1666–1734." Ph.D. dissertation, University of Virginia, 1969.

Stellhorn, Paul A. "Depression and Decline: Newark, New Jersey, 1929–1941." Ph.D. dissertation, Rutgers University, 1981.

Stickle, Warren E. "New Jersey Democracy and the Urban Coalition: 1919–1932." Ph.D. dissertation, Georgetown University, 1971.

Strassburger, John R. "The Origins and Establishment of the Morris Family in the Society and Politics of New York and New Jersey, 1630-1746." Ph.D. dissertation, Princeton University, 1976.

Webb, Stephen Saunders. "Officers and Governors: The Role of the British Army in Imperial Politics and the Administration of the American Colonies, 1689–1722." Ph.D. dissertation, University of Wisconsin, 1965.

Wood, Robert. "The Metropolitan Governor." Ph.D. dissertation, Harvard University, 1950.

Manuscript and Records Collections

Records of Governor Leon Abbett, New Jersey State Library, Bureau of Archives and History, Trenton, N.J.

Alumni Biographical Collection, Seeley G. Mudd Library, Princeton University, Princeton, N.J.

Jonathan Belcher Letterbooks, Massachusetts Historical Society, Boston, Mass.

Jonathan Belcher Papers, The New Jersey Historical Society, Newark, N.J.

Biographical Collection, Rutgers University Special Collections, New Brunswick, N.J.

Joseph Bloomfield Letters, Rutgers University Special Collections, New Brunswick, N.J.

Records of Governor William T. Cahill, New Jersey State Library, Bureau of Archives and History, Trenton, N.J.

Cadwallader Colden Papers, The New-York Historical Society, New York, N.Y.

Mahlon Dickerson Diary, The New Jersey Historical Society, Newark, N.J.

Mahlon Dickerson Diary, Rutgers University Special Collections, New Brunswick, N.J.

Mahlon Dickerson Papers, The New Jersey Historical Society, Newark, N.J.

Philemon Dickerson Papers, The New Jersey Historical Society, Newark, N.J.

Records of Governor Alfred E. Driscoll, New Jersey State Library, Bureau of Archives and History, Trenton, N.J.

East Jersey Papers, The New Jersey Historical Society, Newark, N.J.

Walter E. Edge Papers, The New Jersey Historical Society, Newark, N.J.

Records of Governor Walter E. Edge, New Jersey State Library, Bureau of Archives and History, Trenton, N.J.

Records of Governor Charles Edison, New Jersey State Library, Bureau of Archives and History, Trenton, N.J.

Records of Governor Edward I. Edwards, New Jersey State Library, Bureau of Archives and History, Trenton, N.J.

Emmet Collection, New York Public Library, New York, N.Y.

Records of Governor James F. Fielder, New Jersey State Library, Bureau of Archives and History, Trenton, N.J.

Records of Governor John F. Fort, New Jersey State Library, Bureau of Archives and History, Trenton, N.J.

Gratz Collection, Historical Society of Pennsylvania, Philadelphia, Pa.

Records of Governor John W. Griggs, New Jersey State Library, Bureau of Archives and History, Trenton, N.J.

Records of Governor Harold G. Hoffman, New Jersey State Library, Bureau of Archives and History, Trenton, N.J.

Records of Governor Richard J. Hughes, New Jersey State Library, Bureau of Archives and History, Trenton, N.J.

Thomas Jefferson Papers, Library of Congress, Manuscript Division, Washington, D.C.

Records of Governor Morgan F. Larson, New Jersey State Library, Bureau of Archives and History, Trenton, N.J.

Livingston-Redmond Papers, Franklin D. Roosevelt Library, Hyde Park, N.Y.

Logan Family Papers, Historical Society of Pennsylvania, Philadelphia, Pa.

Records of Governor George C. Ludlow, New Jersey State Library, Bureau of Archives and History, Trenton, N.J.

Records of Governor George B. McClellan, New Jersey State Library, Bureau of Archives and History, Trenton, N.J.

Records of Governor Robert B. Meyner, New Jersey State Library, Bureau of Archives and History, Trenton, N.J.

Records of Governor A. Harry Moore, New Jersey State Library, Bureau of Archives and History, Trenton, N.J. Morris Family Papers, Rutgers University Special Collections, New Brunswick, N.J. Records of Governor Franklin Murphy, New Jersey State Library, Bureau of Archives and History, Trenton, N.J.

New Jersey Broadsides Collection, The New Jersey Historical Society, Newark, N.J.

New Jersey Letters, Rutgers University Special Collections, New Brunswick, N.J.

Charles Smith Olden Papers, Historical Society of Princeton, Princeton, N.J.

Ferdinand John Paris Papers, The New Jersey Historical Society, Newark, N.J.

William Paterson Papers, William Paterson College Special Collections, Wayne, N.J.

Charles A. Philhower Collection, Rutgers University Special Collections, New Brunswick, N.J.

Timothy Pickering Papers, Massachusetts Historical Society, Boston, Mass.

Rodman M. Price Papers, Huntington Library, San Marino, Cal.

Rodman M. Price Papers, Rutgers University Special Collections, New Brunswick, N.J.

Rodman M. Price Papers, University of California, Berkeley, Special Collections, Berkeley, Cal.

Rutherfurd Collection, The New-York Historical Society, New York, N.Y.

Ferdinand S. Schenck Papers, Rutgers University Special Collections, New Brunswick, N.J.

Records of Governor George S. Silzer, New Jersey State Library, Bureau of Archives and History, Trenton, N.J.

Smith Family Papers, Historical Society of Pennsylvania, Philadelphia, Pa.

Records of the Society for the Propagation of the Gospel in Foreign Parts, Series A, vols. 3 and 4, Library of Congress microfilm.

Samuel L. Southard Manuscripts, Library of Congress, Manuscript Division, Washington, D.C.

Samuel L. Southard Papers, Princeton University Special Collections, Princeton, N.J.

Records of Governor Edward C. Stokes, New Jersey State Library, Bureau of Archives and History, Trenton, N.J.

John W. Taylor Papers, The New-York Historical Society, New York, N.Y.

Joseph P. Tumulty Papers, Library of Congress, Manuscript Division, Washington, D.C.

Records of Governor Foster Voorhees, New Jersey State Library, Bureau of Archives and History, Trenton, N.J.

Peter D. Vroom Papers, Columbia University Library, New York, N.Y.

Peter D. Vroom Papers, The New Jersey Historical Society, Newark, N.J.

Peter D. Vroom Papers, Rutgers University Special Collections, New Brunswick, N.J.

Garret D. Wall Papers, Princeton University Special Collections, Princeton, N.J.

Garret D. Wall Papers, Rutgers University Special Collections, New Brunswick, N.J.

Marcus L. Ward Papers, The New Jersey Historical Society, Newark, N.J.

Marcus L. Ward Papers, Rutgers University Special Collections, New Brunswick, N.J.

Records of Governor George T. Werts, New Jersey State Library, Bureau of Archives and History, Trenton, N.J.

Anthony Walton White Papers, Rutgers University Special Collections, New Brunswick, N.J.

Isaac Williamson Papers, The New Jersey Historical Society, Newark, N.J.

Isaac Williamson Papers, New Jersey State Library, Bureau of Archives and History, Trenton, N.J.

Isaac Williamson Papers, Rutgers University Special Collections, New Brunswick, N.J.

Woodrow Wilson Collection, Princeton University Special Collections, Princeton, N.J.

Woodrow Wilson Papers, Library of Congress, Manuscript Division, Washington, D.C.

Records of Governor Woodrow Wilson, New Jersey State Library, Bureau of Archives and History, Trenton, N.J.

Oliver Wolcott Papers, Connecticut Historical Society, Hartford, Conn.

THE AUTHORS

MICHAEL C. BATINSKI, assistant professor of history at Southern Illinois University, is finishing a study of legislative behavior in New Jersey during the eighteenth century.

CLARK L. BECK, JR., assistant curator of Special Collections at Rutgers University, has been a regular contributor to the *Journal of the Rutgers University Libraries* since 1970. He was a coauthor of the exhibit catalogue *As We Saw Them: Westerners Interpret Japan, 1853–1912*, and is currently preparing a bibliography of the revolutionary war manuscript material at Rutgers.

ROBERT R. BECKWITH, professor of history at Montclair State College, is the author of *Mahlon Dickerson, Jacksonian Aristocrat* (1964).

MICHAEL J. BIRKNER, associate editor of *The Papers of Daniel Webster* (4 vols. to date; 1974–), is the author of several articles, including "Peter Vroom and the Politics of Democracy," in *Jacksonian New Jersey* (1979), and "Samuel L. Southard and the Origins of *Gibbons* v. *Ogden*," *Princeton University Library Chronicle* (1979).

FREDERICK R. BLACK, associate professor of history at the C. W. Post Center of Long Island University, has published articles in American colonial history, including "Provincial Taxation in Colonial New Jersey, 1704–1735," *New Jersey History* (1977), and "The Fate of the Con-

cessions," in *The West Jersey Concessions and Agreements of 1676/77: The Document, Its Background in English History, and Its Influence in the American Colonies* (1979).

EDWARD J. CODY, professor of history at Ramapo College, has published articles in religious history, including "The Growth of Toleration and Church-State Relations in New Jersey, 1689–1763: From Holy Men to Holy War," in *Economic and Social History of Colonial New Jersey* (1974). He is working on a textbook in American intellectual history.

RICHARD J. CONNORS, professor of government at Seton Hall University, is the author of *A Cycle of Power: The Career of Jersey City Mayor Frank Hague* (1971), *The Process of Constitutional Revision in New Jersey, 1940–47* (1970), and other monographs on government and politics.

SISTER SERAFINA D'ALESSIO teaches history at the Villa Victoria Academy, Trenton, New Jersey. A student of New Jersey politics in the nineteenth century, she did her graduate work at Catholic University.

PHILIP C. DAVIS, research supervisor at Needham, Harper and Steers Advertising Co., Chicago, Illinois, is the author of "Political Oligarchy, Egalitarianism and Continuity in New Jersey: 1840–1860," in *Jacksonian New Jersey* (1979), and a coauthor of "Party Competition and Mass Participation: The Case of the Democratizing Party System,

1824–1852," in *The History of American Electoral Behavior: Quantitative Studies* (1978).

HARRIS I. EFFROSS, research professor in the Bureau of Government Research at Rutgers University, is the author of *County Governing Bodies in New Jersey: Reorganization and Reform of Boards of Chosen Freeholders, 1798–1974* (1976), and many other works on New Jersey local government.

HERBERT ERSHKOWITZ, chairman of the Department of History at Temple University, is the author of many articles on Jacksonian politics, including "The Origins of the Whig and Democratic Parties in New Jersey, 1820–1837," in *Proceedings of the Second Annual Symposium of the New Jersey Historical Commission* (1971), and *Business Attitudes Towards American Foreign Policy, 1900–1917* (1967).

FRANK J. ESPOSITO dean of the Kean College School of Education, has lectured and published widely on the Lenni Lenape Indians of New Jersey. His publications include *Travelling New Jersey* (1978), and "New Jersey's Identity Crisis," in *The Outlook on New Jersey* (1979).

W. ROBERT FALLAW, professor of history at Washington College, is a specialist in nineteenth-century intellectual and political history.

ALVIN S. FELZENBERG received his Ph.D. in politics from Princeton University in 1978 with a dissertation titled "The Impact of Gubernatorial Style on Policy Outcomes," a study of the managerial styles of five New Jersey governors. He is a coauthor of *The Evolution of the Modern Presidency: A Bibliographical Survey* (1977).

LARRY R. GERLACH, professor of history at the University of Utah, has published many works on colonial and revolutionary New Jersey, including *Prologue to Independence: New Jersey in the American Revolution* (1976) and *New Jersey in the American Revolution, 1763–1783: A Documentary History* (1975). He is completing a biography of William Franklin.

FREDERICK M. HERRMANN, a member of the staff of the Division of Legislative Information and Research in the New Jersey Office of Legislative Services, is the author of "Anti-Masonry in New Jersey," in *New Jersey History* (1973), and "The Political Origins of the New Jersey State Insane Asylum, 1837–1860," in *Jacksonian New Jersey* (1979).

DAVID W. HIRST, senior research historian at Princeton University and senior associate editor of *The Papers of Woodrow Wilson* (36 vols. to date; 1966–), is the author of *Woodrow Wilson, Reform Governor: A Documentary Narrative* (1965).

RICHARD A. HOGARTY, professor of political science at the University of Massachusetts in Boston, was formerly staff director of the Governor's Special Task Force on Migrant Farm Labor in New Jersey and has been involved in charter reform efforts in the city of Boston. He is the author of *New Jersey Farmers And Migrant Housing Rules* (1966); The *Delaware River Drought Emergency* (1970); and *The Dilemma of Financial Disclosure in Massachusetts* (1978).

STANLEY NIDER KATZ, professor of history at Princeton University, has published many works in American colonial history, including *Newcastle's New York: Anglo-American Politics, 1732–1753* (1968), "The Politics of Law in Colonial America: Controversies Over Chancery Courts and Equity Law in the Eighteenth Century," *Perspectives in American History* (1971), and "Thomas Jefferson and the Right to Property in Revolutionary America," *Journal of Law and Economics* (1977).

EDWARD McM. LARRABEE, who has a Ph.D. in history from Columbia University, has taught anthropology at Hunter and John Jay colleges (CUNY). He has extensive experience at historical archeological sites, and is now a consultant in cultural resource research and management. His publications include "Recurrent Themes and Sequences in North American Culture Contact," *Transactions of the American Philosophical Society* (1976), which discusses the Brotherton experiment.

WILLIAM LEMMEY teaches history in Hicksville High School, New York. His publications include "The Last Hurrah Reconsidered," in Joel Schwartz and Daniel Prosser, eds., *Cities of the Garden State* (1977), and "Boss Kenny of Jersey City, 1949–1972," *New Jersey History* (1980).

ARTHUR S. LINK, George Henry Davis '86 Professor of American History at Princeton University, is the director and editor of *The Papers of Woodrow Wilson* (36 vols. to date; 1966–). Dr. Link is the author of the definitive biography of Wilson to 1917 (5 vols.; 1947–65) and many other works in twentieth-century American history.

JOSEPH F. MAHONEY, professor of history at Seton Hall University, is the author of many articles on New Jersey in the gilded age and the progressive era, including "The Impact of Industrialization on the New Jersey Legislature, 1870–1900: Some Preliminary Views," in *New Jersey Since 1860: New Findings and Interpretations* (1972).

JAMES KIRBY MARTIN, professor of history and chairman of the Department of History at the University of Houston, has published widely in colonial and revolutionary American history. His books include *Men in Rebellion: Higher Governmental Leaders and the Coming of the American Revolution* (1973), *The Human Dimensions of Nation Making: Essays on Colonial and Revolutionary America* (1976), and *In the Course of Human Events: An Interpretive Exploration of the American Revolution* (1979).

ROBERT C. MORRIS, assistant professor of history and head of Special Collections, Teachers College, Columbia University, is the author of *Reading, 'Riting and Reconstruction: The Education of Freedmen in the South, 1861–1870* (1981) and the editor of *Freedmen's Schools and Textbooks: Black Education in The South, 1861–1870* (6 vols., 1980).

RANSOM E. NOBLE, professor of history emeritus at Pratt Institute, is the author of *New Jersey Progressivism Before Wilson* (1946) and other publications on America since the Civil War.

JOHN E. O'CONNOR, associate professor of history at the New Jersey Institute of Technology, is the author of *William Paterson: Lawyer and Statesman, 1745–1806* (1979). He has also written articles on the colonial and early republican periods.

RUDOLPH J. PASLER, professor of history and political science at Salem Community College, is a coauthor of *The New Jersey Federalists* (1975).

FRANCES D. PINGEON teaches United States history at the Kent Place School in Summit, New Jersey. A doctoral candidate at Columbia University, she is the author of the pamphlet *Blacks in the Revolutionary Era* (1975) and several articles on slavery and blacks in New Jersey. She is a coauthor of *At Speedwell in the Nineteenth Century* (1981).

HERMANN K. PLATT teaches history at St. Peter's College. He is the editor of *Charles Perrin Smith: New Jersey Political Reminiscences, 1828–1882* (1965) and the author of several studies in New Jersey urban history, including "Jersey City and the United Railroad Companies, 1868: A Case Study of Municipal Weakness," *New Jersey History* (1973) and "The Jersey City Water-Rights Controversy, 1845–1850," *New Jersey History* (1976).

The late JOHN E. POMFRET, president of William and Mary College from 1941 to 1951, had a distinguished career as a teacher, scholar, and administrator. He was the author of many books and articles on colonial New Jersey, including *The Province of West New Jersey, 1609–1702:*

A History of the Origins of an American Colony (1956) and *The Province of East Jersey, 1609–1702: The Rebellious Proprietary* (1962). He died in November 1981.

CLEMENT ALEXANDER PRICE, associate professor of history at Rutgers University, Newark, is the author of "The Beleaguered City as Promised Land: Blacks in Newark, 1917–1947," in *Urban New Jersey Since 1870* (1975), and the editor of *Freedom Not Far Distant,* a documentary history of blacks in New Jersey (1980).

CARL E. PRINCE, professor of history at New York University and editor of *The Papers of William Livingston* (2 vols. to date; 1979–), is the author of *New Jersey's Jeffersonian-Republicans* (1967) and *The Federalists and the Origins of the U.S. Civil Service* (1977).

JEROME C. REDDY attended graduate school at Duke and Rutgers universities. He is a senior planner for the city of Plainfield, New Jersey.

DENNIS P. RYAN, coeditor of *The Papers of William Livingston* (2 vols. to date; 1979–), has written extensively on New Jersey in the American Revolution. His publications include "The Revolution in East Jersey: A Whig Profile," *New Jersey in the American Revolution II* (1973), and "Landholding, Opportunity, and Mobility in Revolutionary New Jersey," *William and Mary Quarterly* (1979).

VICTOR A. SAPIO, professor of history at Pensacola Junior College, is the author of *Pennsylvania and the War of 1812* (1970).

JAMES EDWARD SCANLON, professor of history at Randolph-Macon College, has published "British Intrigue and the Governorship of Robert Hunter," *New-York Historical Society Quarterly* (1973). His history of Randolph-Macon College is scheduled for publication in 1982.

JOEL SCHWARTZ, associate professor of history at Montclair State College, has pub-

lished widely in nineteenth-century New Jersey social and urban history. He is the author of "The Education Machine: The Struggle for Public School Systems in New Jersey Before the Civil War," in *Jacksonian New Jersey* (1979), and a coeditor of *Cities in the Garden State: Essays in the Urban and Suburban History of New Jersey* (1977).

HAROLD E. SELESKY, a doctoral candidate in history at Yale University, is the author of *A Guide to the Microfilm Edition of the Ezra Stiles Papers at Yale University* (1977) and "Patterns of Officeholding in the Connecticut General Assembly: 1725–1774," in G. J. Willauer, Jr., ed., *A Lyme Miscellany, 1776–1976* (1977).

EDWARD S. SHAPIRO, professor of history at Seton Hall University, is the author of over one hundred articles and reviews on American history, including "Jews," in *The New Jersey Ethnic Experience* (1977).

DOUGLAS V. SHAW, associate professor in the Department of Urban Studies at the University of Akron, has published several monographs on aspects of Jersey City since 1850, including *The Making of An Immigrant City: Ethnic and Cultural Conflict in Jersey City, New Jersey, 1850–1870* (1976).

EUGENE R. SHERIDAN, associate editor of *The Papers of Thomas Jefferson* (19 vols. to date; 1950–), is the author of "Daniel Coxe and the Restoration of Proprietary Government in East Jersey, 1690—a Letter," *New Jersey History* (1974) and *Lewis Morris 1671–1746: A Study in Early American Politics* (1981). He is now preparing a new edition of the papers of Lewis Morris.

DON C. SKEMER, editor of publications at The New Jersey Historical Society, is the author of *American History in Belgium and Luxembourg: A Bibliography* (1975) and of numerous articles in scholarly journals. He is the principal compiler of *Guide to Manuscript Collections of The New Jersey Historical Society* (1979).

PAUL A. STELLHORN, assistant director of the New Jersey Committee for the Humanities, is the author of "Boom, Bust and Boosterism: Attitudes, Residency and the Newark Chamber of Commerce, 1920–1941," in *Urban New Jersey Since 1870* (1975), a coeditor of the *Directory of New Jersey Newspapers, 1765–1970* (1976), and the editor of the papers of several New Jersey Historical Commission symposia. He is working on a history of Newark's business community in the 1920s and 1930s.

WARREN E. STICKLE, chief legislative assistant to Congressman Floyd J. Fithian of Indiana, is the author of several books and articles in post–Civil War American history, including "Ruralite and Farmer in Indiana: An Independent, Sporadic Voter and Country Bumpkin," *Agricultural History* (1974). He is a coeditor of *Bosses and Reformers: Urban Politics in America, 1880–1920* (1973).

JOHN STRASSBURGER, associate professor of history at Hiram College, received his Ph.D. from Princeton University.

EUGENE M. TOBIN, assistant professor of history at Hamilton College, has published many articles on New Jersey in the progressive era, including "Direct Action and Conscience: The 1913 Paterson Strike as Example of the Relationship Between Labor Radicals and Liberals," *Labor History* (1979). He is a coeditor of *The Age of Urban Reform: New Perspectives on the Progressive Era* (1977), and the author of *George L. Record and the Progressive Spirit* (1979).

STANLEY B. WINTERS, professor of history at the New Jersey Institute of Technology, edited *Newark, 1967–77: An Assessment* (1978). He is a coauthor of *From Riot to Recovery: Newark After Ten Years* (1979) and an associate editor of *Columns: Social Architecture* and *Studies in East European Social History*.

WILLIAM C. WRIGHT, head of the Bureau of Archives and History, New Jersey State Library, is the author of *The Secession Movement in the Middle Atlantic States* (1973), a coeditor of the *Directory of New Jersey Newspapers, 1765–1970* (1976), and the editor of the papers of several New Jersey Historical Commission symposia.

INDEX

A. Harry Moore School (Jersey City, N.J.), 199
Abbett, Leon, 141, 144, 146, 148, 149–54, 156, 157, 158, 162
Abolitionism, 127, 135
Adams, John, 85, 86
Adams, John Quincy, 97, 102, 108, 111
Addison, Joseph, 44
Addonizio, Hugh J., 226
Afro-Americans, 150; attitudes of governors toward, 103, 138, 152; civil rights legislation for, 152, 190, 217, 227; industrial education for, 172; suffrage for, 134. *See also* Slavery
Agriculture, 145, 199–200
Alexander, James, 46, 47, 49, 50, 54, 59–60, 61, 77
Alexander, William (Lord Stirling), 61, 69, 70, 75
Alien and Sedition Acts (United States, 1798), 92
Allentown, N.J., 126, 128
American Institute, 95
American party, 126, 128, 138, 150
American Peace Commission, 182
American Revolution, 57, 65, 71, 73, 74–75, 78–80, 84, 86, 91
American Whig, 78
Amherst, Jeffrey, 67
André, John, 75
Androboros (play), 45
Andros, Edmund, 16–17, 18–21, 28, 29, 31
Anglican Church, 21, 27, 29, 44, 45
Anne (queen of England), 36, 39, 42, 44
Anti-Jacksonians, 103, 106, 107, 108, 111. *See also* Jacksonians
Anti-Leislerian party, 38
Anti-Saloon League, 193, 197
Antill, Edward, 67
Apology for the True Christian Divinity, An, 24
Applejack Campaign, 191, 192
Arbuthnot, John, 44
Armstrong, John, 90
Associated Loyalists, 75
Atlantic City Daily Press, 186

Atlantic City, N.J., 183, 186, 225
Atlantic County, N.J., 109
Automobiles. *See* Highways: construction of; Motor-vehicle regulation

Baird, David, Jr., 199, 202, 203, 205, 215
Baltimore, Maryland, 95
Bank of the United States, 103
Bankruptcy Act (U.S.), 111
Banks, state, 90, 103. *See also* specific names of banking institutions
Barbados, 15, 18, 54
Barclay, David, 24, 25
Barclay, Robert, 24–27, 28, 31
Bartlet, Benjamin, 23
Basse, Jeremiah, 29, 32, 33–35, 40
Bateman School Funding Act (N.J., 1970), 230
Bayard, John, 82
Bedle, Joseph Dorsett, 141–43
Belcher, Jonathan, 58–62, 63
Bellomont, Richard (Lord Bellomont), 34
Benjamin Franklin Bridge, 188
Bergen County, N.J., 220, 226
Bergen Riot, 140
Berkeley, John (Lord Berkeley), 15, 16, 19, 44
Bernard, Francis, 62–65, 66
Bird, John T., 156
Bishops' Liquor Law (N.J.), 194
Bistate Waterfront Commission, 218, 221
Black, Charles C., 171
Blaine, James G., 175
Blair, James, 21
Blair, John Insley, 138
Blodgett, Rufus, 152, 156
Bloomfield, Joseph, 85–88, 92
Bloomfield, Moses, 86
Blue laws, 192
Board of General Proprietors of the Eastern Division of New Jersey: appointments by, 31, 32, 35, 70; authority of, 16, 36; litigation and, 59
Board of Loyalist Agents, 69
Board of Trade: appointments by, 32, 34, 42, 66; authority of, 33; conflicts with gov-

251